Exploring
Microeconomics

Fifth Canadian Edition

Robert L. Sexton
Pepperdine University

Peter N. Fortura
Algonquin College

Colin C. Kovacs
Algonquin College

Sarah Arliss, Contributor
Seneca College

NELSON

NELSON

Exploring Microeconomics, Fifth Canadian Edition

by Robert L. Sexton, Peter N. Fortura, and Colin C. Kovacs

VP, Product Solutions, K–20:
Claudine O'Donnell

Publisher, Digital and Print Content:
Katherine Baker-Ross

Marketing Manager:
Marcia Siekowski

Technical Reviewer:
Racquel Lindsay

Content Manager:
My Editor Inc.

Photo and Permissions Researcher:
Jessie Coffey

Senior Production Project Manager:
Imoinda Romain

Production Service:
SPi Global

Copy Editor:
June Trusty

Proofreader:
SPi Global

Indexer:
SPi Global

Design Director:
Ken Phipps

Higher Education Design PM:
Pamela Johnston

Cover Design:
Courtney Hellam

Cover Image:
Darryl Leniuk/Getty Images

Compositor:
SPi Global

Library and Archives Canada Cataloguing in Publication

Title: Exploring microeconomics / Robert L. Sexton, Pepperdine University, Peter N. Fortura, Algonquin College, Colin C. Kovacs, Algonquin College; Sarah Arliss, contributor, Seneca College.

Names: Sexton, Robert L., author. | Fortura, Peter, 1961– author. | Kovacs, Colin C., 1969– author. Arliss, Sarah author. | Sexton, Robert L., Exploring economics.

Description: Fifth Canadian edition. | Originally published as part of: Exploring economics. 1st Canadian edition. | Includes index.

Identifiers: Canadiana (print) 20190048824 | Canadiana (ebook) 20190048859 | ISBN 9780176877033 (softcover) | ISBN 9780176877170 (PDF)

Subjects: LCSH: Microeconomics—Textbooks. | LCGFT: Textbooks.

Classification: LCC HB172 .S49 2019 | DDC 338.5—dc23

ISBN-13: 978-0-17-687703-3
ISBN-10: 0-17-687703-7

To Cynthia, Laura, and Nicholas

P.N.F.

To Lindsay, Rowan, Seth, and Myles

C.C.K.

To Elizabeth, Katherine, and Tommy

R.L.S.

Brief Contents

Detailed Contents

About the Authors

Robert L. Sexton is Distinguished Professor of Economics at Pepperdine University. Professor Sexton has also been a Visiting Professor at the University of California at Los Angeles in the Anderson Graduate School of Management and the Department of Economics.

Professor Sexton's research ranges across many fields of economics: economics education, labour economics, environmental economics, law and economics, and economic history. He has written several books and has published numerous reference articles, many in top economic journals such as the *American Economic Review,* the *Southern Economic Journal,* the *Economics Letters,* the *Journal of Urban Economics,* and the *Journal of Economic Education.* Professor Sexton has also written more than 100 other articles that have appeared in books, magazines, and newspapers.

He received the Pepperdine Professor of the Year Award in 1991, the Harriet and Charles Luckman Teaching Fellow in 1994, the Tyles Professor of the Year in 1997, and the Howard A. White Award for Teaching Excellence in 2011.

Pepperdine University

Peter N. Fortura earned his undergraduate degree from Brock University, where he was awarded the Vice-Chancellor's Medal for academic achievement, and his Master of Arts from the University of Western Ontario in London, Ontario. He has taught economics at Algonquin College in Ottawa for over 20 years. Prior to that, he was an economist in the International Department of the Bank of Canada in Ottawa.

Professor Fortura has published articles on Canadian housing prices, Canada's automotive industry, and Canada's international competitiveness. As well, he is an author of the *Study Guide* to accompany *Principles of Microeconomics* by Mankiw, Kneebone, and McKenzie (Nelson Education, 7th edition), and co-author of the statistics textbook *Contemporary Business Statistics with Canadian Applications* (Pearson, 3rd edition).

He lives in Ottawa with his wife, Cynthia, and their children, Laura and Nicholas.

Peter Fortura

Colin C. Kovacs received his Master of Arts degree from Queen's University after completing his Bachelor of Arts degree at the University of Western Ontario. He has taught economics, statistics, and finance for nearly 25 years at both the DeVry College of Technology in Toronto and Algonquin College in Ottawa. His research papers have included *Determinants of Labour Force Participation Among Older Males in Canada* and *Minimum Wage—The Past and Future for Ontario.*

Professor Kovacs lives in Ottawa with his wife, Lindsay, and their children, Rowan, Seth, and Myles.

Algonquin College

Preface

Exploring Microeconomics, Fifth Canadian Edition, offers students a lively, back-to-the-basics approach designed to take the intimidation out of economics. With its short, self-contained learning units and its carefully chosen pedagogy, graphs, and photos, this text helps students master and retain the principles of economics. In addition, the current-events focus and modular format of presenting information makes *Exploring Microeconomics* a very student-accessible and user-friendly text. Driven by more than 70 years of combined experience teaching the economic principles course, the dedication and enthusiasm of Bob Sexton, Peter Fortura, and Colin Kovacs shine through in *Exploring Microeconomics.*

NEW TO THE FIFTH CANADIAN EDITION

Overall Highlights

As with previous editions of *Exploring Microeconomics,* attention has been paid to the structure and layout of each chapter to ensure that the material is presented in as clear and consistent a manner as possible. In addition, special attention has been given to the numerous examples and illustrations presented in each chapter to ensure that they are meaningful and relevant to today's student.

The end-of-chapter *For Your Review* questions and problems have been continued in this edition. *Blueprint Problems,* the review feature introduced in the previous edition, have been retained and have undergone revision to ensure they continue to provide relevant and meaningful insight into the methodologies surrounding key economic concepts. As in the previous edition, all *Blueprint Problems* are accompanied by full and annotated solutions.

Also returning in this fifth Canadian edition are the *Debate* and *Business Connection* features. Both have undergone revision and updating. While their content has been revised, the purpose of each remains the same—*Debate* features are designed to promote in-class discussion and self-exploration, and *Business Connection* features are designed to highlight the link between economic theory and business principles.

CHAPTER HIGHLIGHTS

Chapter 4: Bringing Supply and Demand Together

In this chapter, readers will find an expanded discussion of price controls in the Canadian economy. An investigation of Canadian dairy production and the pricing of dairy products in Canada provides the reader with a more in-depth understanding of this key topic and how it impacts the efficiency of market forces in Canada.

Chapter 7: Production and Costs

Greater insight has been added to the discussion of short-run production with the inclusion of average product as a means by which firm production can be evaluated and understood. The integration of average product into the existing total product and marginal product discussion will enhance the reader's understanding of how and why firm production behaves the way it does from an economic perspective. This integration is accomplished both in tabular form and graphically.

Chapter 9: Monopoly

Does price discrimination lead to higher profits for the price-discriminating monopolist? This important question is investigated as part of the newly expanded discussion of what price discrimination is and why it exists.

Chapter 11: Labour Markets and the Distribution of Income

With the federal governments' announcement of Opportunity for All—Canada's First Poverty Reduction Strategy, an official measure of poverty was defined for the first time in Canada's history: Canada's Official Poverty Line. Detailing the methodology, measure, coverage, and related statistics, the section on poverty has undergone complete revision to reflect these historic developments.

FEATURES OF THE BOOK

The Section-by-Section Approach

Exploring Microeconomics uses a section-by-section approach in which economic ideas and concepts are presented in short, self-contained units rather than in large blocks of text. Each chapter is composed of approximately six to eight bite-sized sections, typically presented in two to eight pages, that include all of the relevant graphs, tables, applications, boxes, photos, and definitions for the topic at hand. Our enthusiasm for and dedication to this approach stems from studying research on *learning theory*, which indicates that students retain information much better when it is broken down into short, intense, and exciting bursts of "digestible" information. Students prefer information divided into smaller, self-contained sections that are less overwhelming, more manageable, and easier to review before going on to new material. In short, students will be more successful in mastering and retaining economic principles using this approach, which is distinctly more compatible with modern communication styles.

But students aren't the only ones to benefit from this approach. The self-contained sections allow instructors greater flexibility in planning their courses. They can simply select or delete sections of the text as it fits their syllabus.

Highlighted Learning Tools

Key Questions   Each section begins with key questions designed to preview ideas and to pique students' interest in the material to come. These same questions are then used to structure the section material that follows, each question being prominently displayed as a section heading, with additional subheadings provided as needed. In addition to ensuring a clear instructional layout of each section and chapter, these key questions can also be used by students as a review resource. After reading the section material, if students are able to answer the key questions, they can go forward with confidence.

Section Checks   A *Section Check* appears at the end of each section and is designed to summarize the answers to the key questions posed at the beginning of the section. The summaries provided by the *Section Check* give students an opportunity to evaluate their understanding of major ideas before proceeding.

Debate Features   *Debate* features are designed to provide students with an opportunity to develop and express their opinions about a variety of economic issues. The "For" and "Against" arguments that accompany each debate topic make it easy to use these features to initiate in-class discussions. By engaging in informal debate regarding current economic policy, students will be able to link course content to current events as well as to their own personal lives. Questions have been added to encourage critical thinking.

Business Connection Features   *Business Connection* features are designed to help students see the link between economic theory and business fundamentals. They help students better understand the reasoning behind the empirical validity of economic theory, and they also aid in the grounding of abstract economic theory in more modern business principles. Accompanying each *Business Connection* feature are questions that can be used to either evaluate student understanding or initiate in-class discussion.

WHY DO WE NEED TO ABSTRACT?

How is economic theory like a GPS? Because of the complexity of human behaviour, economists must abstract to focus on the most important components of a particular problem. This is similar to how a GPS highlights the important information (and does not register many minor details) to help people get from here to there.

Economic theories cannot realistically include every event that has ever occurred. This is true for the same reason that a newspaper or history book does not include every world event that has ever happened. We must abstract. Without abstraction or simplification, the world is too complex to analyze.

Economic theories and models make some unrealistic assumptions. For example, we may assume there are only two countries in the world, producing two goods. Obviously, this is an abstraction from the real world. But if we can understand trade in a simplified world, it will help us understand trade in a more complex world. Similarly, sometimes economists make very strong assumptions, such as the assumption that all people seek self-betterment or all firms attempt to maximize profits. That is, economists use simplifying assumptions in their models to make the world more comprehendible. But only when we test our models using these assumptions can we find out if they are too simplified or too limiting.

How are economic theories and models like a road map? A road map of Canada may not include every creek, ridge, and valley between Vancouver and Halifax—indeed, such an all-inclusive map would be too complicated and confusing to be of much value. However, a GPS programmed to guide the traveller while referencing key details encountered along the way, such as highways and major attractions, will provide enough

Photos   *Exploring Microeconomics* contains a large number of colourful photos, which are an integral part of the book for both learning and motivation. The photos are carefully placed where they reinforce important concepts, and they are accompanied by captions designed to extend students' understanding of particular ideas.

For Your Review

Section 9.1

1. Which of the following could be considered a monopoly?
   a. Kate Hudson (an actress)
   b. BC Hydro
   c. the only doctor in a small town
   d. Ford Motor Company

2. Barriers to entry are important in the creation of monopolies because they keep competitors out of the industry. Although many types of barriers exist, historically, ownership of an essential resource, government patents and licences, and large entry costs have served as the primary barriers to entry. For each of the following cases, indicate which type of barrier created the monopoly.
   a. In the 1940s, the Aluminum Company of America owned all of the world's known bauxite deposits.
   b. A local cable TV company had the only government-issued licence to supply services in the area.
   c. The pharmaceutical company, MAXCO, invented and patented a new hair-growth drug.
   d. In the 1960s, Bell Canada provided long-distance telephone service by stringing millions of kilometres of copper wiring across Canada.

3. Evaluate the following statement regarding monopoly behaviour: "Since a monopoly firm is a *price maker*, it can charge whatever price it wants for whatever quantity it wants to sell."

4. Is it optimal for a monopolist to operate on the inelastic portion of the demand curve? Why or why not?

For Your Review   Provided at the end of each chapter, these problems allow students to test their understanding of chapter concepts. The *For Your Review* questions are organized into sections to match the corresponding sections in the text so that students and instructors can easily identify particular topics. To assist in the learning process, solutions to all odd-numbered questions are provided at the back of the book. With a variety of both problems and application-style questions to choose from, this section can also be used by instructors to assign homework questions directly from the text.

Blueprint Problem

Suppose the following table describes revenue and cost of production figures for the monopoly firm Carl's Calculators.

Output	Price	TVC	TFC	TC	AVC	AFC	ATC	MC
0	45	$0.00	$40.00	$40.00	—	—	—	—
1	40	$10.00	$40.00	$50.00	$10.00	$40.00	$50.00	$10.00
2	35	$16.00	$40.00	$56.00	$8.00	$20.00	$28.00	$6.00
3	30	$20.00	$40.00	$60.00	$6.67	$13.33	$20.00	$4.00
4	25	$29.00	$40.00	$69.00	$7.25	$10.00	$17.25	$9.00
5	20	$44.00	$40.00	$84.00	$8.80	$8.00	$16.80	$15.00
6	15	$68.00	$40.00	$108.00	$11.00	$6.67	$17.67	$22.00
7	10	$104.00	$40.00	$144.00	$14.86	$5.71	$20.57	$38.00

   a. Determine Carl's profit-maximizing output using the total approach.
   b. Determine Carl's profit-maximizing output using the marginal approach. Use the four-step method and describe each step.

Blueprint Problems   Integrated into the end-of-chapter *For Your Review* sections, these fully annotated problems and their solutions are intended to provide additional insight into key economic topics and issues. Intentionally designed to mirror the accompanying *For Your Review* problems, each *Blueprint Problem* allows students to "walk through" a completed solution, seeing the essential steps necessary to successfully complete a key economic question.

Chapter in Review Cards Located at the back of the textbook, these detachable *Chapter in Review* cards are designed to give students a summary overview of key chapter concepts at a glance. Each *Chapter in Review* card contains the following information:

- **Chapter Summary:** A point-form summary response to the section's key questions, highlighting the most important concepts of each section, is provided.
- **Key Terms:** A list of key terms allows students to test their mastery of new concepts. Both the definition and page number are included so that students can easily find a key term in a chapter.
- **Key Exhibits/Graphs:** Given the importance and explanatory ability of exhibits and graphical representations in economics, a list of key figures is provided for each chapter.
- **Key Equations:** A list of key equations enables students to quickly refer to important formulas.

INSTRUCTORS

The **Nelson Education Teaching Advantage (NETA)** program delivers research-based instructor's resources that promote student engagement and higher-order thinking to enable the success of Canadian students and educators. Be sure to visit Nelson Education's **Inspired Instruction** website at www.nelson.com/inspired to find out more about NETA. Don't miss the testimonials of instructors who have used NETA supplements and watched student engagement increase!

The following instructor's resources have been created for *Exploring Microeconomics*, Fifth Canadian Edition. Access these ultimate tools for customizing lectures and presentations at www.nelson.com/instructor.

Instructor's Solutions Manual: Answers to all *For Your Review* questions in the textbook are provided in this manual, separated from the Instructor's Manual for easier reference. Students can access only the odd-numbered solutions in the Answer Key at the back of the book. The solutions were prepared by the text co-author, Colin Kovacs, and independently checked for accuracy by Racquel Lindsay, University of Toronto.

NETA Test Bank: This resource was prepared by Russell Turner, Fleming College. It includes over 1550 multiple-choice questions written according to NETA guidelines for effective construction and development of higher-order questions. Also included are more than 300 true/false and approximately 100 essay-type questions.

The NETA Test Bank is available in a new, cloud-based platform. **Nelson Testing Powered by Cognero®** is a secure online testing system that allows you to author, edit, and manage test bank content from any place you have Internet access. No special installations or downloads are needed, and the desktop-inspired interface, with its drop-down menus and familiar, intuitive tools, allows you to create and manage tests with ease. You can create multiple test versions in an instant, and import or export content into other systems. Tests can be delivered from your learning management system, your classroom, or wherever you want. Nelson Testing Powered by Cognero for *Exploring Microeconomics*

can also be accessed through htp://www.nelson.com/login and http://login.cengage .com. Printable versions of the Test Bank in Word and PDF versions are available with the instructor's resources for the textbook.

NETA PowerPoint: Microsoft® PowerPoint® lecture slides for every chapter have been adapted by Ifeanyichukwu Uzoka of Sheridan College. We offer two separate collections. The Basic PowerPoint collection contains an average of 40 slides per chapter. This collection is a basic outline of the chapter and contains key figures, tables, and photographs from the fifth Canadian edition of *Exploring Microeconomics*. The Expanded PowerPoint collection includes an average of 65 slides per chapter and provides a more complete overview of the chapter. NETA principles of clear design and engaging content have been incorporated throughout, making it simple for instructors to customize the deck for their courses.

Image Library: This resource consists of digital copies of figures, short tables, and photographs used in the book. Instructors may use these images to customize the NETA PowerPoint or create their own PowerPoint presentations.

Instructor's Manual: The *Instructor's Manual* to accompany *Exploring Microeconomics,* Fifth Canadian Edition, has been prepared by Phil Ghayad and Michel Mayer of Dawson College. This manual is organized according to the textbook chapters and includes teaching tips and active learning exercises. (Answers to all *For Your Review* exercises in the text are now provided in the separate Instructor's Solutions Manual supplement described earlier.).

DayOne: Day One—Prof InClass is a PowerPoint presentation that instructors can customize to orient students to the class and their textbook at the beginning of the course.

Aplia + MindTap

MindTap is the digital platform that propels students from memorization to mastery, helping to challenge them, build their confidence, and empower them to be unstoppable. **Aplia**™ is an application in the MindTap platform that has proven to significantly improve outcomes and elevate thinking by increasing student effort and engagement. Aplia makes it easy to assign frequent online homework assignments and assessments, ensuring students master important concepts. Developed by teachers, Aplia assignments connect concepts to the real world and focus on the unique course challenges faced by students. The MindTap content for *Exploring Microeconomics*, Fifth Canadian Edition, was updated and revised by Jason Dean of Sheridan College. The Aplia problems for *Exploring Microeconomics*, Fifth Canadian Edition, were updated and revised by Hanika Bhojwani-Chen of Centennial College.

The challenging and interactive activities within Aplia guide students through assignments, moving them from basic knowledge and understanding to application and practice. Look for the Aplia logo in the MindTap app dock to explore all that Aplia has to offer. With Aplia, instructors can do the following:

- easily set their course with pre-built, flexible homework assignments;
- author questions (single choice, multiple choice, true/false, essay and numeric entry);
- create custom assignments and populate them with self-authored—and Aplia-authored—questions; and
- inspire students to learn from their mistakes and reward them for effort with the Grade It Now feature that enables three attempts at different versions of a question.

The MindTap content for *Exploring Microeconomics*, Fifth Canadian Edition, was updated and revised by James Dean at Sheridan College.

STUDENT ANCILLARIES

Aplia + MindTap

Stay organized and efficient with MindTap—a single destination with all your course materials and study tools you need to succeed. Leverage the latest learning technology to stay on track with your learning. For this generation of digital natives, guidance is key to student confidence and engagement. MindTap makes learning a more constant part of your life, motivating you to take a more active role in learning and course preparedness.

- Personalized content in an easy-to-use interface helps you achieve better grades.
- The new MindTap Mobile App allows for learning anytime, anywhere with flashcards, quizzes and notifications.
- The MindTap Reader lets you highlight and take notes online, right within the pages, and easily reference them later.
- ReadSpeaker will read the text to you.

Aplia guides you through assignments, moving from basic knowledge and understanding to application and practice. These challenging and interactive activities are designed to reinforce important concepts. With Aplia, you can do the following:

- learn from mistakes and reinforce your learning with Grade It Now, which provides three attempts at a question;
- get immediate step-by-step feedback; and
- gain understanding through real-world application of concepts.

Acknowledgments

Producing the fifth Canadian edition of *Exploring Microeconomics* has truly been a team effort. We would like to thank the editorial, production, and marketing teams at Nelson Education for their hard work and effort. First, our appreciation goes to Claudine O'Donnell, Vice President, Product Solutions, who has provided the vision and leadership for the Canadian editions of the text.

We would like to thank Katherine Baker-Ross, publisher at Nelson, for her continuing support. Thank you to Katherine Goodes, Content Manager, for her helpful advice and constant encouragement. Thanks also to Imoinda Romain, Senior Production Project Manager; June Trusty, Copy Editor; Marcia Siekowski, Marketing Manager; and all the marketing and sales representatives at Nelson Education Ltd. Special thanks are extended to Sarah Arliss at Seneca College for providing the engaging and insightful *Business Connection* and *Debate* boxes.

We are grateful to our families for their patience and encouragement.

Finally, we would like to acknowledge the reviewers of the Canadian editions, past and present, for their comments and feedback:

Vick Barylak, *Sheridan College*
Aurelia Best, *Centennial College*
Jim Butko, *Niagara College*
Darren Chapman, *Fanshawe College*
Bruno Fullone, *George Brown College*
Jeffrey Dzikowicz, *Red River College*
James Hnatchuk, *Champlain Regional College*
Geraldine Joosse, *Lethbridge College*
Susan Kamp, *University of Alberta*
Michael Leonard, *Kwantlen Polytechnic University*
Nargess Kayhani, *Mount Saint Vincent University*
Margaret Rose Olfert, *University of Saskatchewan*
Jay Perry, *Niagara College*
John Pirrie, *St. Lawrence College*
Geoffrey Prince, *Centennial College*
Sheila J. Ross, *Southern Alberta Institute of Technology*
Judith Skuce, *Georgian College*
Norm Smith, *Georgian College*
Martha Spence, *Confederation College*
Lucia Vojtassak, *Trent University*
Carl Weston, *Mohawk College*

Their thoughtful suggestions were very important to us in providing input and useful examples for the fifth Canadian edition of this book.

P.N.F.
C.C.K.

1

The Role and Method of Economics

section 1.1

Economics: A Brief Introduction

- What is economics?
- Why study economics?
- What distinguishes macroeconomics from microeconomics?

WHAT IS ECONOMICS?

Some individuals think economics involves the study of the stock market and corporate finance, and it does—in part. Others think that economics is concerned with the wise use of money and other matters of personal finance, and it is—in part. Still others think that economics involves forecasting or predicting what business conditions will be like in the future, and again, it does—in part.

Growing Wants and Scarce Resources

Precisely defined, **economics** is the study of the allocation of our limited resources to satisfy our unlimited wants. **Resources** are inputs—such as land, human effort and skills, and machines and factories—used to produce goods and services. The problem is that our wants exceed our limited resources, a fact that we call *scarcity*. Scarcity forces us to make choices on how to best use our limited resources. This is **the economic problem**: Scarcity forces us to choose, and choices are costly because we must give up other opportunities that we value. This economizing problem is evident in every aspect of our lives. Choosing between a trip to the gym or the coffee shop, or between finishing an assignment or chatting online, can be understood more easily when one has a good handle on the "economic way of thinking."

economics
the study of the allocation of our limited resources to satisfy our unlimited wants

resources
inputs used to produce goods and services

the economic problem
Scarcity forces us to choose, and choices are costly because we must give up other opportunities that we value.

Articles related to economics— either directly or indirectly— are common in the news media. News headlines might trumpet: Gasoline Prices Soar; Stocks Rise; Stocks Fall; Prime Minister Vows to Increase National Defence Spending; Health-Care Costs Continue to Rise.

Economics Is All Around Us

Although many things that we desire in life are considered to be "noneconomic," economics concerns anything that is considered worthwhile to some human being. For instance, love, sexual activity, and religion have value for most people. Even these have an economic dimension. Consider love and sex, for example. One product of love—the institution of the family—is an important economic decision-making unit. Also, sexual activity results in the birth of children, one of the most important "goods" that many humans want. Economic forces have played a central role in the evolution of the family unit, from the traditional "nuclear family" (Dad, Mom, and two kids) to dual-income families, to dual-income no-kids (DINKs) families. Concerns for spiritual matters have likewise received economists' scrutiny, as they have led to the development of institutions such as churches, mosques, and temples that provide religious and spiritual services. These services are goods that many people want.

Even time has an economic dimension. In fact, perhaps the most precious single resource is time. We all have the same limited amount of time per day, and how we divide our time between work and leisure (including perhaps study, sleep, exercise, etc.) is a distinctly economic matter. If we choose more work, we must sacrifice leisure. If we choose to study, we must sacrifice time with friends, or time spent sleeping or watching TV. Virtually everything we decide to do, then, has an economic dimension.

Living in a world of scarcity involves trade-offs. As you are reading this text, you are giving up other things you value, such as shopping, spending time on Facebook, text messaging with friends, going to the movies, sleeping, or working out. When we know what the trade-offs are, we can make better choices from the options all around us, every day.

WHY STUDY ECONOMICS?

Among the many good reasons to study economics, perhaps the best reason is that so many of the things of concern in the world around us are at least partly economic in character. A quick look at media headlines reveals the vast range of problems that are related to economics—global warming, health care, education, and social assistance. The study of economics improves your understanding of these concerns. A student of economics becomes aware that, at a basic level, much of economic life involves choosing among alternative possible courses of action—making choices between our conflicting wants and desires in a world of scarcity. Economics provides some clues as to how to intelligently evaluate these options and determine the most appropriate choices in given situations. But economists learn quickly that there are seldom easy, clear-cut solutions to the problems we face: The easy problems were solved long ago!

Many students take introductory postsecondary economics courses because these are part of the core curriculum requirements. But why do the committees that establish these requirements include economics? In part, economics helps develop a disciplined method of thinking about problems as opposed to simply memorizing solutions. The problem-solving tools you will develop by studying economics will prove valuable to you in both your personal and professional life, regardless of your career choice. In short, the study of economics provides a systematic, disciplined way of thinking.

Using This Stuff

The basic tools of economics are valuable to people in all walks of life and in all career paths. Journalists benefit from economics because the problem-solving perspective it teaches trains them to ask intelligent questions whose answers will better inform their readers. Engineers, architects, and contractors usually have alternative ways to build. Architects learn to combine technical expertise and artistry with the limitations imposed by finite resources. That is, they learn how to evaluate their options from an economic perspective. Business owners face similar problems, because costs are a constraint in both creating and marketing a new product. Will the added cost of developing a new and improved product be outweighed by the added sales revenues that are expected to result? Economists can, however, pose these questions and provide criteria that business owners can use in evaluating the appropriateness of one design as compared to another. The point is that the economic way of thinking causes those in many types of fields to ask the right kind of questions.

WHAT DISTINGUISHES MACROECONOMICS FROM MICROECONOMICS?

Like psychology, sociology, anthropology, and political science, economics is considered a social science. Economics, like the other social sciences, is concerned with reaching generalizations about human behaviour. Economics is the study of people. It is the social science that studies the choices people make in a world of limited resources.

Economics and the other social sciences often complement one another. For example, a political scientist might examine the process that led to the adoption of a certain tax policy, whereas an economist might analyze the impact of that tax policy. Or, whereas a psychologist may try to figure out what makes the criminal mind work, an economist might study the factors causing a change in the crime rate. Social scientists, then, may be studying the same issue but from different perspectives.

Conventionally, we distinguish two main branches of economics: macroeconomics and microeconomics. **Macroeconomics** is the study of the **aggregate** or total economy; it looks at economic problems as they influence the whole of society. Topics covered in macroeconomics include discussions of inflation, unemployment, business cycles, and economic growth. **Microeconomics** is the study of the smaller units within the economy. Topics include the decision-making behaviour of firms and households and their interaction in markets for particular goods or services. Microeconomic topics also include discussions of health care, agricultural subsidies, the price of everyday items such as running shoes, the distribution of income, and the impact of labour unions on wages. To put it simply, microeconomics looks at the trees whereas macroeconomics looks at the forest.

macroeconomics
the study of the aggregate economy, including the topics of inflation, unemployment, and economic growth

aggregate
the total amount—such as the aggregate level of output

microeconomics
the study of the smaller units within the economy, including the topics of household and firm behaviour and how they interact in the marketplace

SECTION CHECK

- Economics is the study of the allocation of our limited resources to satisfy our unlimited wants.
- Economics is a problem-solving social science that teaches you how to ask intelligent questions.
- Macroeconomics deals with the aggregate, or total, economy, while microeconomics focuses on smaller units within the economy.

Economic Theory

- What are economic theories?
- Why do we need to abstract?
- What is a hypothesis?
- What is the *ceteris paribus* assumption?
- Why are observations and predictions harder in the social sciences?
- What distinguishes between correlation and causation?
- What are positive analysis and normative analysis?

WHAT ARE ECONOMIC THEORIES?

theory
an established explanation that accounts for known facts or phenomena

A **theory** is an established explanation that accounts for known facts or phenomena. Specifically, economic theories are statements or propositions about patterns of human behaviour that are expected to take place under certain circumstances. These theories help us to sort out and understand the complexities of economic behaviour. We expect a good theory to explain and predict well. A good economic theory, then, should help us to better understand and, ideally, predict human economic behaviour.

WHY DO WE NEED TO ABSTRACT?

How is economic theory like a GPS? Because of the complexity of human behaviour, economists must abstract to focus on the most important components of a particular problem. This is similar to how a GPS highlights the important information (and does not register many minor details) to help people get from here to there.

Economic theories cannot realistically include every event that has ever occurred. This is true for the same reason that a newspaper or history book does not include every world event that has ever happened. We must abstract. Without abstraction or simplification, the world is too complex to analyze.

Economic theories and models make some unrealistic assumptions. For example, we may assume there are only two countries in the world, producing two goods. Obviously, this is an abstraction from the real world. But if we can understand trade in a simplified world, it will help us understand trade in a more complex world. Similarly, sometimes economists make very strong assumptions, such as the assumption that all people seek self-betterment or all firms attempt to maximize profits. That is, economists use simplifying assumptions in their models to make the world more comprehendible. But only when we test our models using these assumptions can we find out if they are too simplified or too limiting.

How are economic theories and models like a road map? A road map of Canada may not include every creek, ridge, and valley between Vancouver and Halifax—indeed, such an all-inclusive map would be too complicated and confusing to be of much value. However, a GPS programmed to guide the traveller while referencing key details encountered along the way, such as highways and major attractions, will provide enough information to travel by car from Vancouver to Halifax. Likewise, an economic theory provides a broad view, not a detailed examination, of human economic behaviour.

WHAT IS A HYPOTHESIS?

The beginning of any theory is a **hypothesis**, a testable proposition that makes some type of prediction about behaviour in response to certain changes in conditions. In economic theory, a hypothesis is a testable prediction about how people will behave or react to a change in economic circumstances. For example, if the price of iPads increased, we might hypothesize that fewer iPads would be sold, or if the price of iPads fell, we might hypothesize that more iPads would be sold. Once a hypothesis is stated, it is tested by comparing what it predicts will happen to what actually happens.

hypothesis
a testable proposition

Using Empirical Analysis

To see whether a hypothesis is valid, we must engage in an **empirical analysis**. That is, we must examine the data to see whether the hypothesis fits well with the facts. If the hypothesis is consistent with real-world observations, it is accepted; if it does not fit well with the facts, it is "back to the drawing board."

    Determining whether a hypothesis is acceptable is more difficult in economics than it is in the natural or physical sciences. Chemists, for example, can observe chemical reactions under laboratory conditions. They can alter the environment to meet the assumptions of the hypothesis and can readily manipulate the variables (chemicals, temperatures, and so on) crucial to the proposed relationship. Such controlled experimentation is seldom possible in economics. The laboratory of economists is usually the real world. Unlike a chemistry lab, economists cannot easily control all the other variables that might influence human behaviour.

empirical analysis
the examination of data to see whether the hypothesis fits well with the facts

From Hypothesis to Theory

After gathering their data, economic researchers must then evaluate the results to determine whether the hypothesis is supported or refuted. If supported, the hypothesis can then be tentatively accepted as an economic theory.

    Economic theories are always on probation. A hypothesis is constantly being tested against empirical findings. Do the observed findings support the prediction? When a hypothesis survives a number of tests, it is accepted until it no longer predicts well.

WHAT IS THE *CETERIS PARIBUS* ASSUMPTION?

Virtually all economic theories share a condition usually expressed by use of the Latin expression ***ceteris paribus***. This roughly means "let everything else be equal" or "holding everything else constant." In trying to assess the effect of one variable on another, we must isolate their relationship from other events that might also influence the situation that the theory tries to explain or predict. To make this clearer, we will illustrate this concept with a couple of examples.

ceteris paribus
holding everything else constant

    Suppose you develop your own theory describing the relationship between studying and exam performance: If I study harder, I will perform better on the test. That sounds logical, right? Holding other things constant (*ceteris paribus*), this is likely to be true. However, what if you studied harder but inadvertently overslept the day of the exam? What if you were so sleepy during the test that you could not think clearly? Or what if you studied the wrong material? Although it may look as if additional studying did not improve your performance, the real problem may lie in the impact of other variables, such as sleep deficiency or how you studied.

WHY ARE OBSERVATIONS AND PREDICTIONS HARDER IN THE SOCIAL SCIENCES?

Working from observations, scientists try to make generalizations that will enable them to predict certain events. However, observation and prediction are more difficult in the social sciences than in physical sciences such as chemistry, physics, and astronomy. Why? The major reason for the difference is that the social scientists, including economists, are concerned with *human* behaviour. And human behaviour is more variable and often less readily predictable than the behaviour of experiments observed in a laboratory. However, by looking at the actions of a large group of people, economists can still make many reliable predictions about human behaviour.

Economists Predict on a Group Level

Economists' predictions usually refer to the collective behaviour of large groups rather than to that of specific individuals. Why is this? Looking at the behaviours of a large group allows economists to discern general patterns of actions. For example, consider what would happen if the price of air travel from Canada to Europe was drastically reduced, say from $1500 to $500, because of the invention of a more fuel-efficient jet. What type of predictions could we make about the effect of this price reduction on the buying habits of typical consumers?

Individual Behaviour

Let's look first at the responses of individuals. As a result of the price drop, some people will greatly increase their intercontinental travel, enjoying theatre weekends in London or week-long trips to France to indulge in French food. Some people, however, are terribly afraid to fly, and a price reduction will not influence their behaviour in the slightest. Others might detest Europe and, despite the lowered airfares, prefer to spend a few days in Vancouver instead. A few people might respond to the airfare reduction very negatively: At the lower fare, they might make fewer trips to Europe, because they might believe (rightly or wrongly) that the price drop would be accompanied by a reduction in the quality of service, greater crowding, or reduced safety. In short, we cannot predict with any level of certainty how a given individual will respond to this airfare reduction.

Group Behaviour

Group behaviour is often more predictable than individual behaviour. When the weather gets colder, more firewood is sold. Some individuals may not buy firewood (e.g., if they don't have a fireplace in their home), but we can predict with great accuracy that a group of individuals will establish a pattern of buying more firewood. Similarly, while we cannot say what each individual will do, within a group of persons, we can predict with great accuracy that more flights to Europe from Toronto will be sold at lower prices, holding other things such as income and preferences constant. We cannot predict exactly how many more airline tickets will be sold at $500 than at $1500, but we can predict the direction of the impact and approximate the extent of the impact. By observing the relationship between the price of goods and services and the quantities people purchase in different places and during different time periods, it is possible to make some reliable generalizations about how much people will react to changes in the prices of goods and services. Economists use this larger picture of the group for most of their theoretical analysis.

WHAT DISTINGUISHES BETWEEN CORRELATION AND CAUSATION?

Without a theory of causation, no scientist could sort out and understand the enormous complexity of the real world. But one must always be careful not to confuse correlation with causation. In other words, the fact that two events usually occur together (**correlation**) does not necessarily mean that one caused the other to occur (**causation**). For example, say a groundhog awakes after a long winter of hibernation, climbs out of his hole, sees his shadow, and then six weeks of bad weather ensue. Did the groundhog cause the bad weather? It is highly unlikely.

Steve Estvanik/Shutterstock.com

Perhaps the causality may run in the opposite direction. Although a rooster may always crow before the sun rises, it does not cause the sunrise; rather, the early light from the sunrise causes the rooster to crow.

The Positive Correlation between Ice Cream Sales and Crime

Did you know that when ice cream sales rise, so do crime rates? What do you think causes the two events to occur together? Some might think that a sugar "high" caused by the ice cream causes the higher crime rate. Excess sugar in a snack was actually used in court testimony in a murder case—the so-called "Twinkie defence." However, it is more likely that crime peaks in the summer because of weather, more people on vacation (leaving their homes vacant), teenagers out of school, and so on. It just happens that ice cream sales also peak in those months because of weather. The lesson: One must always be careful not to confuse correlation with causation and to be clear on the direction of the causation.

The Fallacy of Composition

One must also be careful with problems associated with aggregation (summing up all the parts), particularly the **fallacy of composition**. This fallacy states that even if something is true for an individual, it is not necessarily true for many individuals as a group. For example, say you are at a concert and you decide to stand up to get a better view of the stage. This works as long as no one else stands up. But what would happen if everyone stood up at the same time? Then, standing up would not let you see better. Hence, what may be true for an individual does not always hold true in the aggregate. The same can be said of arriving to class early to get a better parking place—what if everyone arrived early? Or studying harder to get a better grade in a class that is graded on a curve—what if everyone studied harder? All of these are examples of the fallacy of composition.

WHAT ARE POSITIVE ANALYSIS AND NORMATIVE ANALYSIS?
Positive Analysis

Most economists view themselves as scientists seeking the truth about the way people behave. They make speculations about economic behaviour, and then (ideally) they try to assess the validity of those predictions based on human experience. Their work emphasizes how people *do* behave, rather than how people *should* behave. In the role of scientist, an economist tries to observe, objectively, patterns of behaviour without

People tend to drive slower when the roads are covered with ice. In addition, more traffic accidents occur when the roads are icy. So, does driving slower cause the number of accidents to rise? No, it is the icy roads that lead to both lower speeds and more accidents.

correlation
two events that usually occur together

causation
when one event causes another event to occur

fallacy of composition
Even if something is true for an individual, it is not necessarily true for a group.

positive analysis
an objective, value-free approach, utilizing the scientific method

reference to the appropriateness or inappropriateness of that behaviour. This objective, value-free approach, utilizing the scientific method, is called **positive analysis**. In positive analysis, we want to know the impact of variable A on variable B. We want to be able to test a hypothesis. For example, the following is a positive statement: If rent controls are imposed, vacancy rates will fall. This statement is testable. A positive statement does not have to be a true statement, but it does have to be a testable statement.

However, keep in mind that it is doubtful that even the most objective scientist can be totally value-free in his or her analysis. An economist may well emphasize data or evidence that supports his hypothesis, putting less weight on other evidence that might be contradictory. This, alas, is human nature. But a good economist/scientist strives to be as fair and objective as possible in evaluating evidence and in stating conclusions based on the evidence.

Normative Analysis

normative analysis
a subjective, biased approach

Like everyone, economists have opinions and make value judgments. When economists, or anyone else for that matter, express opinions about some economic policy or statement, they are indicating in part how they believe things should be, not just facts as to the way things are. **Normative analysis** is a subjective, biased approach, where one expresses opinions about the desirability of various actions. Normative statements involve judgments about what should be or what ought to happen. For example, one could judge that incomes should be more equally distributed. If there is a change in tax policy that makes incomes more equal, there will be positive economic questions that can be investigated, such as how work behaviour will change. But we cannot say, as scientists, that such a policy is good or bad; rather, we can point to what will likely happen if the policy is adopted.

Positive vs. Normative Statements

The distinction between positive and normative analysis is important. It is one thing to say that everyone should have universal health care, a normative statement, and quite another to say that universal health care would lead to greater worker productivity, a testable positive statement. It is important to distinguish between positive and normative analysis because many controversies in economics revolve around policy considerations that contain both. When economists start talking about how the economy should work rather than how it does work, they have entered the normative world of the policymaker. Anytime you see the word *should*, be aware that you are in the realm of normative economics. Positive statements are about *what is*, normative statements are about what *ought to* or *should be*. In short, positive statements are attempts to *describe* what happens and why it happens, while normative statements are attempts to *prescribe* what should be done. But sometimes the two are intertwined.

Why Economists Disagree

Although economists differ frequently on economic policy questions, there is probably less disagreement than the media would have you believe. Disagreement is common in most disciplines: Tech-savvy consumers cannot agree which operating system is superior—Windows or Mac; historians can be at odds over the interpretation of historical events; psychologists disagree on proper ways to rear children; and nutritionists debate the merits of large doses of vitamin C.

The majority of disagreements in economics stem from normative issues, as differences in values or policy beliefs result in conflict. For example, a policy might increase efficiency at the expense of fairness or equity, or it might help a current generation at the expense of a future generation. Because policy decisions involve trade-offs, they will always involve the potential for conflict.

Freedom vs. Fairness

Some economists are concerned about individual freedom and liberty, thinking that any encroachment on individual decision making is, other things equal, bad. People with this philosophic bent are inclined to be skeptical of any increased government involvement in the economy.

On the other hand, some economists are concerned with what they consider an unequal, "unfair," or unfortunate distribution of income, wealth, or power, and view governmental intervention as desirable in righting injustices that they believe exist in a market economy. To these persons, the threat to individual liberty alone is not sufficiently great to reject governmental intervention in the face of perceived economic injustice.

The Validity of an Economic Theory

Aside from philosophic differences, there is a second reason why economists may differ on any given policy question. Specifically, they may disagree as to the validity of a given economic theory for the policy in question. Suppose two economists have identical philosophical views that have led them to the same conclusion: To end injustice and hardship, unemployment should be reduced. To reach the objective, the first economist believes the government should lower taxes and increase spending, whereas the second economist believes increasing the amount of money in public hands by various banking policies will achieve the same results with fewer undesirable consequences. The two economists differ because the empirical evidence for economic theories about the cause of unemployment appears to conflict. Some evidence suggests government taxation and spending policies are effective in reducing unemployment, whereas other evidence suggests that the prime cause of unnecessary unemployment lies with faulty monetary policy. Still other evidence is consistent with the view that, over long periods, neither approach mentioned here is of much value in reducing unemployment, and that unemployment will be part of our existence no matter what macroeconomic policies we follow.

Although you may not believe it after reading the previous discussion, economists don't always disagree. In fact, according to a survey among members of the American Economic Association, most economists agree on a wide range of issues, including rent control, import tariffs, export restrictions, the use of wage and price controls to curb inflation, and the minimum wage.

SECTION CHECK

- ■ Economic theories are statements used to explain and predict patterns of human behaviour.
- ■ Economic theories, through abstraction, provide a broad view of human economic behaviour.
- ■ A hypothesis makes a prediction about human behaviour and is then tested.
- ■ In order to isolate the effects of one variable on another, we use the *ceteris paribus* assumption.
- ■ With its focus on human behaviour, which is more variable and less predictable, observation and prediction are more difficult in the social sciences.
- ■ The fact that two events are related does not mean that one caused the other to occur.
- ■ Positive analysis is objective and value-free, while normative analysis involves value judgments and opinions about the desirability of various actions.

Scarcity

- What is scarcity?
- What are goods and services?

Most of economics is knowing certain principles really well and knowing when and how to apply them. In the following sections, some important tools are presented that will help you understand the economic way of thinking. These few basic ideas will repeatedly occur throughout the text. If you develop a good understanding of these principles and master the problem-solving skills inherent in them, they will serve you well for the rest of your life.

WHAT IS SCARCITY?

scarcity
the situation that exists when human wants exceed available resources

As we have already mentioned, economics is concerned primarily with **scarcity**—the situation that exists when human wants exceed available resources. We may want more "essential" items like food, clothing, schooling, and health care. We may want many other items like vacations, cars, computers, and concert tickets. We may want more friendship, love, knowledge, and so on. We also may have many goals—perhaps an A in this class, a university education, and a great job. Unfortunately, people are not able to fulfill all of their wants—material desires and nonmaterial desires. And as long as human wants exceed available resources, scarcity will exist.

Scarcity and Resources

The scarce resources used in the production of goods and services can be grouped into four categories: labour, land, capital, and entrepreneurship.

labour
the physical and mental effort used by people in the production of goods and services

Labour is the total of both physical and mental effort used by people in the production of goods and services.

land
the natural resources used in the production of goods and services

Land includes the "gifts of nature" or the natural resources used in the production of goods and services. Trees, animals, water, minerals, and so on are all considered to be "land" for our purposes, along with the physical space normally thought of as land.

capital
the equipment and structures used to produce goods and services

Capital is the equipment and structures used to produce goods and services. Office buildings, tools, machines, and factories are all considered capital goods. When we invest in factories, machines, research and development, or education, we increase the potential to create more goods and services in the future. Capital also includes **human capital**, the productive knowledge and skills people receive from education and on-the-job training.

human capital
the productive knowledge and skill people receive from education and on-the-job training

Entrepreneurship is the process of combining labour, land, and capital together to produce goods and services. Entrepreneurs make the tough and risky decisions about what and how to produce goods and services. Entrepreneurs are always looking for new ways to improve production techniques or to create new products. They are lured by the chance to make a profit. It is this opportunity to make a profit that leads entrepreneurs to take risks.

entrepreneurship
the process of combining labour, land, and capital together to produce goods and services

However, entrepreneurs are not necessarily a John Molson (Molson Brewery), a Wallace McCain (frozen food empire), or a William or Alfred Billes (Canadian Tire). In some sense, we are all entrepreneurs when we try new products or when we find better ways to manage our households or our study time. Rather than money, then, our profits might take the form of greater enjoyment, additional time for recreation, or better grades.

WHAT ARE GOODS AND SERVICES?

Goods are those items that we value or desire. Goods tend to be tangible—objects that can be seen, held, heard, tasted, or smelled. **Services** are intangible acts for which people are willing to pay, such as legal services, medical services, and dental care. Services are intangible because they are less overtly visible, but they are certainly no less valuable than goods. All goods and services, whether tangible or intangible, are produced from scarce resources and can be subjected to economic analysis. If there are not enough goods and services for all of us, we will have to compete for those scarce goods and services. That is, scarcity ultimately leads to competition for the available goods and services, a subject we will return to often in the text.

goods
items we value or desire

services
intangible acts that people want

Bads

In contrast to goods, **bads** are those items that we do not desire or want. For most people, garbage, pollution, weeds, and crime are bads. People tend to eliminate or minimize bads, so they will often pay to have bads, like garbage, removed. The elimination of the bad—garbage removal, for example—is a good.

bads
items that we do not desire or want

Business *CONNECTION*

ECONOMICS IN BOTH BUSINESS AND LIFE

Why are business students required to study economics, and why so early in their chosen programs? The simple answer is that economics is really the game of life and that studying it can help students in business and other disciplines learn and appreciate how to better manage both their professional careers and their private households. Economics is, at its foundation, learning how decisions are made—whether the decisions are for consumers and firms or for households and governments. In making these decisions, we analyze (1) choices, benefits, and costs; (2) the way our decisions affect individual wants and needs; and (3) the way individual decisions affect people in general (consumers and society).

In today's economy, there is less emphasis on content (as it changes so quickly and is readily available online) and more emphasis on learning how to learn. In this respect, studying economics helps students to learn critical thinking skills. Students must also disengage from their phones and learn communication skills—these are the major skills that employers will be looking for. So, learning economics is not only for and about business, it is also a medium we can use to hone our thinking and communication skills—skills we'll use for the rest of our lives. It can be an important, high-impact course for everybody.

From a purely business point of view, profit is the ultimate goal, yet maximizing profits is just one of a number of strategies that a firm may follow. Others include focusing on growth, revenue generation, cash flow, cost reduction, product/service differentiation, product/service elimination, and vertical or horizontal integration. Each of these strategies will have a different effect on the decisions of price and quantity over short, medium, or longer terms. All of these strategies seek to answer the three basic economic questions: (1) What to produce? (2) How to produce it? and (3) For whom? Finding the answers requires a knowledge of the basics of economics decision making.

Students should also recognize that there is only one constant, that time and circumstances change. What worked months or years ago may not work today or in the future, and what's good for individuals is not necessarily good for everyone and vice versa. Individuals and firms need to appreciate these changes, and economics and economic thinking teach us how to recognize and respect our changing environment so that we can make the changes that will be best for our particular goal(s).

Historically, business was all about maximizing profit for the benefit of shareholders. But this world is changing because of three significant realities that our parents never dealt with: (1) globalization, (2) environmental limitations to growth, and (3) automation and artificial intelligence (AI). Profits will still be required to keep firms in business, but all stakeholders—including firms, consumers, and governments—may no longer expect profits to be the main goal. In fact, AI and automation may force firms and governments to actually pay people *not* to work—and that will require a complete redefinition of many of the macroeconomic foundations we've relied on for centuries. Many firms now see themselves as socially responsible and emphasize other factors, such as the sustainability of the business and using the firm as a vehicle for employment and for achieving

(continued)

a higher standard of living for all. How those goals are achieved require economic decisions.

No matter what choice you make in terms of what you do in your career, where you work, what you produce, where you live, what you do in your leisure time, or even where you spend your time, economics will play a role in your decisions. So now you can appreciate why economics is not restricted to business, but rather why we see it as a major player in the game of life.

1. What do you think is the single most important thing you'll learn from studying economics that will assist you in your business/working career?

2. From an economic perspective, what do you think differentiates entrepreneurs from others working in business?

3. Do you think entrepreneurs are born, or do you think anyone can learn to be an entrepreneur? What are your reasons for your opinion?

Everyone Faces Scarcity

We all face scarcity because we cannot have all of the goods and services that we desire. However, because we all have different wants and desires, scarcity affects everyone differently. For example, a child in a developing country may face a scarcity of food and clean drinking water, whereas a rich person may face a scarcity of garage space for his growing antique car collection. Likewise, a harried middle-class working mother may find time for exercise particularly scarce, whereas a pharmaceutical company may be concerned with the scarcity of the natural resources it uses in its production process. Although its effects vary, no one can escape scarcity.

SECTION CHECK

- Scarcity exists when our wants exceed the available resources of land, labour, capital, and entrepreneurship.
- Goods and services are things that we value.

section 1.4 Opportunity Cost

- Why do we have to make choices?
- What do we give up when we have to choose?
- Why are "free" lunches not free?

WHY DO WE HAVE TO MAKE CHOICES?

We may want nice homes, two luxury cars in every garage, wholesome and good-tasting food, personal trainers, and therapists, all enjoyed in a pristine environment with zero pollution. If we had unlimited resources, and thus an ability to produce all of the goods and services anyone wanted, we would not have to choose among those desires. If we did not have to make meaningful economic choices, the study of economics would not be necessary. The essence of economics is to understand fully the implications that scarcity has for wise decision making. This suggests another way to define economics: *Economics is the study of the choices we make among our many wants and desires.*

WHAT DO WE GIVE UP WHEN WE HAVE TO CHOOSE?

We are all faced with scarcity and, as a consequence, we must make choices. Because none of us can afford to buy everything we want, each time we do decide to buy one good or service, we reduce our ability to buy other things we would also like to have. If you buy a new car this year, you may not be able to afford your next best choice—the vacation you've been planning. You must choose. The cost of the car to you is the value of the vacation that must be forgone. The highest or best forgone opportunity resulting from a decision is called the **opportunity cost**. For example, time spent running costs time that could have been spent doing something else that is valuable—perhaps spending time with friends or studying for an upcoming exam. Another way to put this is that "to choose is to lose" or "an opportunity cost is an opportunity lost." To get more of anything that is desirable, you must accept less of something else that you also value.

opportunity cost
the highest or best forgone opportunity resulting from a decision

One of the reasons why vehicle drivers talk so much on their cellphones is that they have little else to do with their time while driving—a low opportunity cost. However, drivers should not use cellphones while driving because this is a distraction; by not giving full attention to their driving, they are giving up safety. Trade-offs are everywhere. This particular trade-off is why many jurisdictions have made the use of a cellphone while driving illegal.

Bill Gates, Tiger Woods, and Mark Zuckerberg all quit university or college to pursue their dreams. Tiger Woods dropped out of Stanford to join the PGA golf tour. Bill Gates dropped out of Harvard to start a software company. Mark Zuckerberg also dropped out of Harvard to continue working on his social networking site Facebook. Staying in school would have cost each of them millions of dollars. We cannot say it would have been the wrong decision to stay in school, but it would have been costly. For each of them, the opportunity cost of staying in school was high.

Drivers who talk on their cellphones or put on make-up while driving are attempting to make better use of their time while in the vehicle. However, the distractions these activities cause can result in a tragic trade-off.

Money Prices and Costs

If you go to the store to buy groceries, you have to pay for the items you buy. This amount is called the *money price*. It is an opportunity cost, because you could have used the money to purchase other goods and services. However, additional opportunity costs include the nonprice costs incurred to acquire the groceries—time spent getting to the grocery store, finding a parking space, actually shopping, and waiting in the checkout line. The nonprice costs are measured by assessing the sacrifice involved—the value you place on what you would have done with the time if you had not gone shopping. So the cost of grocery shopping is the price paid for the goods plus the nonprice costs incurred.

Minerva Studio/iStock/Thinkstock

Remember that many costs do not involve money but are still costs. Should I major in accounting or human resources? Should I go to college or university? Should I get an MBA now or work and wait a few years to go back to school?

Policymakers are unavoidably faced with opportunity costs too. Consider airline safety. Both money costs and time costs affect airline safety. New airline safety devices cost money (luggage inspection devices, fuel tank safeguards, new radar equipment, and so on), and time costs are quite relevant with the new safety checks. Time waiting in line costs time that could be spent doing something that is valuable. New airline safety requirements could also actually cost lives. If the new safety equipment costs are passed on in the form of higher airline ticket prices, people may choose to travel by car, which is far more dangerous per kilometre than air travel is. Opportunity costs are everywhere! And the real cost of anything is what you have to give up to get it.

The Opportunity Cost of Going to School or Having a Child

The average person often does not correctly consider opportunity costs when thinking about costs. For example, the opportunity cost of going to school is not just the direct expense of tuition and books; of course, those expenses do involve an opportunity cost, because the money used for books and tuition could be used for other things that you value. But what about the nonmoney costs? That is, going to school also includes the opportunity cost of your time. Specifically, the time spent going to school is time that could have been spent on a job earning, say, $30 000 a year. And how often do people consider the opportunity cost of raising a child to the age of 18? There are the direct costs: food, visits to the dentist, clothes, piano lessons, and so on. But there are also additional costs incurred in rearing a child. Consider the cost if one parent chooses to give up his or her job to stay at home: Then, the time spent in child-rearing is time that could have been used making money and pursuing a career.

WHY ARE "FREE" LUNCHES NOT FREE?

The expression *there's no such thing as a free lunch* clarifies the relationship between scarcity and opportunity cost. Suppose the school cafeteria is offering "free" lunches today. Although the lunch is free to you, is it really free from society's perspective? The answer is no, because some of society's scarce resources will have been used in the preparation of the lunch. The issue is whether the resources that went into creating that lunch could have been used to produce something else of value. Clearly, the scarce resources that went into the production of the lunch, such as the labour and materials (food-service workers, lettuce, meat, plows, tractors, fertilizer, and so forth) could have been used in other ways. They had an opportunity cost, and thus were not free. Whenever you hear the word "free"—free libraries, free admission, and so on—an alarm should go off in your head. Very few things are free in the sense that they use none of society's scarce resources. So what does a free lunch really mean? It is, technically speaking, a "subsidized" lunch—a lunch using society's scarce resources, but one for which you personally do not have to pay.

SECTION CHECK

- Scarcity means we all have to make choices.
- When we are forced to choose, we give up the next highest-valued alternative.
- Because the production of any good uses up some of society's resources, there is no such thing as a free lunch.

Marginal Thinking

- What do we mean by *marginal thinking*?
- What is the rule of rational choice?

WHAT DO WE MEAN BY *MARGINAL THINKING*?

Most choices involve how *much* of something to do, rather than whether or not to do something. It is not *whether* you eat, but *how much* you eat. Hopefully, the question is not *whether* to study this semester but instead *how much* to study this semester. For example, "If I studied a little more, I might be able to improve my grade," or "If I had a little better concentration when I was studying, I could improve my grade." This is what economists call **marginal thinking** because the focus is on the additional, or incremental, choices. Marginal choices involve the effects of adding to or subtracting from the current situation. In short, it is the small (or large) incremental changes to a plan of action.

Always watch out for the difference between average and marginal costs. Suppose the cost to an airline of flying 250 passengers from Edmonton to Montreal was $100 000. The average cost per seat would be $400 (the total cost divided by the number of seats—$100 000/250). If ten people are on standby and willing to pay $300 for a seat on the flight, should the airline sell them a ticket? Yes! The unoccupied seats earn nothing for the airline. The airline pays the $400 average cost per seat regardless of whether or not someone is sitting in the seat. What the airline needs to focus on are the additional (marginal) costs of a few extra passengers. The marginal costs are minimal—slight wear and tear on the airplane, handling some extra baggage, and ten extra in-flight meals. In this case, thinking at the margin can increase total profits, even if it means selling at less-than-average cost of production.

Auctions are another good example of marginal thinking. Prices are bid up marginally as the auctioneer calls out one price after another. When a bidder views the new price (the marginal cost) to be greater than the value she places on the good (the marginal benefit), she withdraws from further bidding.

marginal thinking
focusing on the additional, or incremental, choices

WHAT IS THE RULE OF RATIONAL CHOICE?

In trying to make themselves better off, individuals will pursue an activity if the expected marginal benefits are greater than the expected marginal costs—this is the **rule of rational choice**. The term *expected* is used with marginal benefits and costs because the world is uncertain in many important respects, so the actual result of changing behaviour may not always make people better off—but on average it will. However, as a matter of rationality, people are assumed to engage only in behaviour that they think ahead of time will make them better off. That is, individuals will pursue an activity only if the expected marginal benefits are greater than the expected marginal costs, or $E(MB) > E(MC)$. This fairly unrestrictive and realistic view of individuals seeking self-betterment can be used to analyze a variety of social phenomena.

Suppose that you have to get up for an 8 A.M. class but have been up very late. When the alarm goes off at 7 A.M., you are weighing the marginal benefits and marginal costs of an extra 15 minutes of sleep. If you perceive the marginal benefits of

rule of rational choice
Individuals will pursue an activity if the expected marginal benefits are greater than the expected marginal costs.

15 minutes of sleep to be greater than the marginal costs of those extra minutes, you may choose to hit the snooze button. Or perhaps you may decide to blow off class completely. But it's unlikely you will choose that action if it is the day of the final exam, because it is now likely that the **net benefits**—the difference between the expected marginal benefits and expected marginal costs—of skipping class have changed. When people have opportunities to better themselves, they usually take them. And they will continue to seek those opportunities as long as they expect a net benefit from doing so.

net benefits

the difference between the expected marginal benefits and expected marginal costs

The rule of rational choice is simply the rule of being sensible, and most economists believe that individuals act *as if* they are sensible and apply the rule of rational choice to their daily lives. It is a rule that can help us understand our decision to study, walk, shop, exercise, clean house, cook, and perform just about every other action. It is also a rule that we will continue to use throughout the text because whether we are consumers, producers, or policymakers, we all must compare the expected marginal benefits and the expected marginal costs to determine the best level to consume, produce, or develop policies.

To help illustrate the concepts of marginal thinking and rational choice, consider the number of cakes a small neighbourhood bakery in suburban Vancouver can produce daily. The bakery employs three people. After performing a business analysis, we are able to determine the following daily production schedule: one employee, 25 cakes; two employees, 45 cakes; three employees, 60 cakes. What each employee can individually (or incrementally) produce represents that person's marginal benefit (*MB*)—these values are determined in the following table.

What would you be willing to give up to eliminate the rush-hour congestion you face? Think of the number of hours drivers waste each year sitting in traffic in Canada's largest cities. It costs the Canadian economy hundreds of millions of dollars a year in lost wages and wasted fuel.

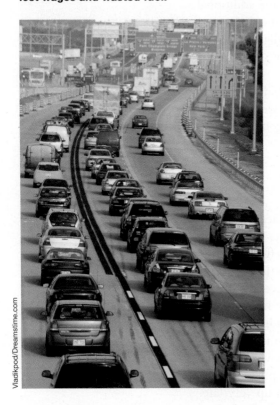

Vladikpod/Dreamstime.com

Employees	Total Production	Marginal Benefit (*MB*)
0	0	
		25
1	25	
		20
2	45	
		15
3	60	

How the bakery pays its employees provides us with another illustration of marginal thinking. If each employee is paid $55 a day, this is the individual (or incremental) cost of each employee—interpreted as the marginal cost (*MC*) of each worker.

We can now use these two illustrations of marginal thinking to help determine whether the bakery has the right number of employees. If a cake sells for $3, the daily *MB* of each employee would be as follows: first employee $75 (25 cakes × $3); second employee $60 (20 cakes × $3); third employee $45 (15 cakes × $3). Based on this information, the first employee represents $20 of positive net benefit [$75(*MB*) − $55(*MC*) = $20 net benefit]; the second employee represents $5 of positive net benefit [$60(*MB*) − $55(*MC*) = $5 net benefit]; while the third employee represents $10 of negative net benefit [$45(*MB*) − $55(*MC*) = −$10 net benefit]. The rule of rational choice would indicate that the bakery should hire the first two employees, but not the third employee.

Zero Pollution Would Be Too Costly

Let's use the concept of marginal thinking to evaluate pollution levels. We all know the benefits of a cleaner environment, but what would we have to give up—that is, what marginal costs would we have to incur—in order to achieve zero pollution? A lot! You could not drive a car, fly in a plane, or even ride a bike, especially if everybody else was riding bikes too (because congestion is a form of pollution). How would you get to school or work, or go to the movies or the grocery store? Everyone would have to grow their own food because transporting, storing, and producing food uses

DEBATE

SHOULD EVERY NEW POLITICIAN HAVE TO BE EDUCATED IN ECONOMIC THEORY BEFORE BEING ALLOWED TO SIT AS A LAWMAKER OR POLICYMAKER?

Economics is about making decisions; for microeconomics, it's primarily about how individuals and firms make decisions, and for macroeconomics, it's about how decisions are made based on how the possible outcome looks from a wider perspective and how it might affect society as a whole.

For many years, almost any individual could stand for office in our democracies—the person just needed to put his or her name forward. However, as our society has become more complex and regulated (by both government and corporate policies), it is no longer sufficient that a layperson can understand the outcomes, effects, and costs well enough to make a good "gut" decision. Perhaps it's time that any elected politician should possess at least a basic understanding of micro- and macroeconomic theory. People who had taken such courses in postsecondary study would be free to sit immediately after election. Those who hadn't taken such courses would be required to do so before they could construct and vote on the bills that affect their constituents.

For:

As many of society's problems and conflict originate as an economic problem (scarcity of something, an allocation issue, a choice between alternatives with both benefits and costs to each), it makes sense that those who make decisions for a society have an open and objective mind that can understand and appreciate the gravity of such decisions, both in the short and long term, and especially the impact on those that it affects. They need to understand that not all costs can be quantified, especially those that put values over monetary benchmarks. Economically well-schooled politicians would understand that there are not only explicit costs in making decisions, but implicit as well—and that the choice of not doing something has itself a cost associated with it.

A politician who appreciates the lens of an economist would appreciate the complexities of decisions where

what's good for the individual is not necessarily good for the masses, and what's good for the masses may not be good for individuals, where decisions are based not solely on one's intellect, but on knowledge as well. Surely, we should expect that those who make decisions for society should bring a higher level of thinking to the process, not just a "gut" instinct.

Against:

Politics is a process in which many individuals from diverse backgrounds can come together and develop and debate different policies, regardless of their formal education. Requiring some form of formal education (even just some economics courses) should not be the case for someone who wants to represent a society. Countless individuals have served their country well without ever having finished high school, let alone having acquired a postsecondary education.

What if an otherwise well-qualified individual failed to get even a passing grade in an economics course? Should that mark the end of that person's political aspirations, or should the voters pass judgment on his or her qualifications?

1. How could a requirement for basic economic understanding be constructed so that it doesn't serve as a barrier to those who might be challenged in passing such a course but could still serve our society?

2. If you don't believe in your elected representatives having a basic understanding of economics, do you think there should be some form of competence that they need before making laws? What might that look like?

3. Having a requirement of completing a theoretical course stinks of elitism, and sets a standard that only those who can understand some complex theory can serve as community leaders. Does this not then marginalize those on the lower socioeconomic scale?

machinery and equipment that pollutes. And even growing your own food would be a problem because many plants emit natural pollutants. We could go on and on. The point is *not* that we shouldn't be concerned about the environment; rather, we have to weigh the expected marginal benefits of a cleaner environment against the expected marginal costs of a cleaner environment. This is not to say the environment should not be cleaner, only that zero pollution levels would be far too costly in terms of what we would have to give up.

Optimal (Best) Levels of Safety

Just as we can have optimal (or best) levels of pollution that are greater than zero, it is also true for crime and safety. Take crime. What would it cost society to have zero crime? It would be prohibitively costly to divert a tremendous amount of our valuable resources toward the total elimination of crime. In fact, it would be impossible to eliminate crime totally. But it would also be costly to reduce crime significantly. Since lower crime rates are costly, society must decide how much it is willing to give up: The additional resources for crime prevention can come only from limited resources, which could be used to produce something else possibly valued even more.

The same is true for safer products. Nobody wants defective tires on their cars, or cars that are unsafe and roll over at low speeds. However, there are optimal amounts of safety that are greater than zero too. The issue is not safe versus unsafe products but rather *how much* safety consumers want. It is not risk versus no risk but rather *how much* risk are we willing to take? Additional safety can come only at higher costs. To make all products perfectly safe would be impossible, so we must weigh the benefits and costs of safer products. In fact, according to one U.S. study by Sam Peltzman, a University of Chicago economist, additional safety features in cars (mandatory safety belts, padded dashboards) in the late 1960s may have had little impact on highway fatalities. Peltzman found that making cars safer led to more reckless driving and more accidents. Although the safety regulations did result in fewer deaths per automobile accident, the total number of deaths remained unchanged because there were more accidents.

Reckless driving has benefits—getting somewhere more quickly—but it also has costs—possibly causing an accident or even a fatality. Rational people will compare the marginal benefits and marginal costs of safer driving and make the choices that they believe will get them to their destination safely. We would expect that even thrill-seekers would slow down if there were higher fines and/or increased law enforcement. It would change the benefit–cost equation for reckless driving (as would bad brakes, bald tires, and poor visibility). On the other hand, compulsory seat belts and air bags might cause motorists to drive more recklessly.

SECTION CHECK

- Economists are usually interested in the effects of additional, or marginal, changes in a given situation.
- The rule of rational choice states that individuals will pursue an activity if they expect the marginal benefits to be greater than the marginal costs, or $E(MB) > E(MC)$.

Incentives Matter

- Can we predict how people will respond to changes in incentives?
- What are positive and negative incentives?

CAN WE PREDICT HOW PEOPLE WILL RESPOND TO CHANGES IN INCENTIVES?

In acting rationally, people are responding to incentives. That is, they are reacting to the changes in expected marginal benefits and expected marginal costs. In fact, much of human behaviour can be explained and predicted as a response to incentives. Consider the economic view of crime. Why do criminals engage in their "occupation"? Presumably because the "job," even with its risks, is preferred to alternative forms of employment. For criminals, the benefits of their actions are higher and/or the opportunity costs of them are lower than is the case for noncriminals. In some cases, criminals cannot get a legitimate job at a wage they would find acceptable, so the cost of crime in terms of other income forgone may be quite low. At other times, the likelihood of being caught is small, so the expected cost is negligible. Also, for some, the moral cost of a crime is low, whereas for others it is high. The benefits, in terms of wealth gained, are clear. If the expected gains or benefits from committing a crime outweigh the expected costs, the activity is pursued.

For most policy purposes, the primary concern is not what causes the level of crime to be what it is but, rather, what causes the level of crime to change. Changes in the crime rate can be largely explained in terms of such a benefit–cost framework. If the benefits of crime rise, say, in the form of larger real "hauls," and/or if the costs fall due to a reduced likelihood of being caught or of being imprisoned if caught, then economists would expect the amount of crime to rise. Likewise, economists would expect the crime rate to fall in response to increased police enforcement, stiffer punishments, or an increase in the employment rate. Whether this analysis tells the complete story is debatable, but use of the economic framework in thinking about the problem provides valuable insight.

WHAT ARE POSITIVE AND NEGATIVE INCENTIVES?

Almost all of economics can be reduced to incentive [$E(MB)$ versus $E(MC)$] stories, where consumers and producers are driven by incentives that affect expected costs or benefits. Prices, wages, profits, taxes, and subsidies are all examples of economic incentives. Incentives can be classified into two types: positive and negative. **Positive incentives** are those that either increase benefits or reduce costs and thus result in an increased level of the related activity or behaviour. **Negative incentives**, on the other hand, either reduce benefits or increase costs, resulting in a decreased level of the related activity or behaviour. For example, a tax on cars that emit lots of pollution (an increase in costs) would be a negative incentive that would lead to a reduction in emitted pollution. On the other hand, a subsidy (the opposite of a tax) for hybrid cars—part electric, part internal combustion—would be a positive incentive

positive incentives
incentives that either reduce costs or increase benefits, resulting in an increase in the activity or behaviour

negative incentives
incentives that either increase costs or reduce benefits, resulting in a decrease in the activity or behaviour

A subsidy for hybrid electric vehicles (HEVs) would be a positive incentive that would encourage greater production and consumption of these vehicles. A wide variety of incentives are offered by governments to encourage the expanded use of alternative-fuel vehicles.

WENN Ltd/Alamy Stock Photo

that would encourage greater production and consumption of hybrid cars. Human behaviour is influenced in predictable ways by such changes in economic incentives, and economists use this information to predict what will happen when the benefits and costs of any choice are changed. In short, economists study the incentives and consequences of particular actions.

Because most people seek opportunities that make them better off, we can predict what will happen when incentives are changed. If salaries increase for engineers and decrease for MBAs, we would predict fewer people would go to a business graduate school and more would go into engineering. A permanent change to a much higher price of gasoline would lead us to expect fewer gas guzzlers on the highway. People who work on commission tend to work harder. If the price of downtown parking increased, we would predict that commuters would look for alternative methods to get to work that would save money.

If households were taxed to conserve water, economists would expect people to use less water—and substantially less water than if they were simply asked to conserve water. Some people are charitable and some people are stingy, but if you change the tax code to give even greater deductions for charitable contributions, we can predict that more people will be charitable, even some of those who are stingy. Incentives matter.

SECTION CHECK

- People respond to incentives in predictable ways.
- A positive incentive decreases costs or increases benefits, thus encouraging consumption or production, while a negative incentive increases costs or reduces benefits, thus discouraging consumption or production.

Specialization and Trade

- Why do people specialize?
- How do specialization and trade lead to greater wealth and prosperity?

WHY DO PEOPLE SPECIALIZE?

As you look around, you can see that people specialize in what they produce. They tend to dedicate their resources to one primary activity, whether it be child-rearing, driving a bus, or making bagels. Why is this? The answer, short and simple, is opportunity costs. By concentrating on the production of one, or a few, goods or services, individuals are **specializing**. This allows them to make the best use of (and thus gain the most benefit from) their limited resources. A person, a region, or a country can gain by specializing in the production of the good or service in which they have a comparative advantage. That is, if they can produce a good or service at a lower opportunity cost than others, we say that they have a **comparative advantage** in the production of that good or service.

> **specializing**
> *concentrating on the production of one, or a few, goods or services*

> **comparative advantage**
> *occurs when a person or a country can produce a good or service at a lower opportunity cost than others can*

For example, should a lawyer who types 100 words per minute hire an administrative assistant to type her legal documents if the assistant can type only 50 words per minute? The answer to this question depends on the particular comparative advantages of the lawyer and the administrative assistant. Consider a job that would take the lawyer five hours and the administrative assistant ten hours to complete. If the lawyer makes $100 an hour, and the administrative assistant earns $15 an hour, who has the comparative advantage?

If the lawyer types her own documents, it will cost $500 ($100 per hour × 5 hours). If she has the administrative assistant type her documents, it will cost $150 ($15 per hour × 10 hours). Clearly, then, the lawyer should hire the administrative assistant to type her documents because the administrative assistant has the comparative advantage (lower opportunity cost) in this case, despite being half as good in absolute terms.

We All Specialize

We all specialize to some extent and rely on others to produce most of the goods and services we want. The work that we choose to do reflects our specialization. For example, we may specialize in selling or fixing automobiles. The wages from that work can then be used to buy goods from a farmer who has chosen to specialize in the production of food. Likewise, the farmer can use the money earned from selling his produce to get his tractor fixed by someone who specializes in that activity.

Specialization is evident not only among individuals but among regions and countries as well. In fact, the story of the economic development of Canada involves specialization. Within Canada, the prairies with their wheat, the Maritime provinces of eastern Canada with their fishing fleets, and Alberta with its oil and gas are all examples of regional specialization.

The Advantages of Specialization

In a small business, employees may perform a wide variety of tasks—from hiring to word processing to marketing. As the size of the company increases, each employee can perform a more specialized job, with a consequent increase in output per worker.

The primary advantages of specialization are that employees acquire greater skill from repetition, they avoid wasted time in shifting from one task to another, and they do the types of work for which they are best suited. Specialization also promotes the use of specialized equipment for specialized tasks.

The advantages of specialization are seen throughout the workplace. For example, in larger firms, specialists conduct personnel relations and accounting is in the hands of full-time accountants; such jobs are too critical in large firms to be done by someone with half a dozen other tasks to perform. The owner of a small retail store selects the location for the store primarily through guesswork, placing it where she believes sales will be high or where an empty, low-rent building is available. In contrast, larger chains have store sites selected by experts who have experience in analyzing the factors that make different locations relatively more desirable, like traffic patterns, income levels, demographics, and so on.

HOW DO SPECIALIZATION AND TRADE LEAD TO GREATER WEALTH AND PROSPERITY?

Trade, or voluntary exchange, directly increases wealth by making both parties better off (or they wouldn't trade). It is the prospect of wealth-increasing exchange that leads to productive specialization. That is, trade increases wealth by allowing a person, a region, or a nation to specialize in those products that it produces at a lower opportunity cost and to trade for those products that others produce at a lower opportunity cost. That is, we trade with others because it frees up time and resources to do other things that we do better. For example, say Canada is better at producing wheat than Brazil, and Brazil is better at producing coffee than Canada. Canada and Brazil would each benefit if Canada produces wheat and trades some of it to Brazil for coffee. Coffee growers in Canada could grow coffee in expensive greenhouses, but it would result in higher coffee costs and prices, while leaving fewer resources available for employment in more productive jobs, such as wheat production. This is true for individuals, too. Imagine Tom had 10 kilograms of tea and Katherine had 10 kilograms of coffee. However, Tom preferred coffee to tea and Katherine preferred tea to coffee. So if Tom traded his tea to Katherine for her coffee, both parties would be better off. Trade simply reallocates existing goods, and voluntary exchange increases wealth by making both parties better off, or they would not agree to trade.

In short, if we divide the tasks and produce what we do *relatively* best and trade for the rest, we will be better off than if we were self-sufficient—that is, without trade. Imagine life without trade, where you were completely self-sufficient—growing your own food, making your own clothes, working on your own car, building your own house. Do you think you would be better off?

SECTION CHECK

- Specialization is important for individuals, businesses, regions, and nations. It allows them to make the best use of their limited resources.
- Specialization and trade increase wealth by allowing a person, a business, a region, or a nation to specialize in those products that it produces at a lower opportunity cost and to trade for those products that others produce at a lower opportunity cost.

The Three Economic Questions Every Society Faces

- What is to be produced?
- How are the goods and services to be produced?
- Who will get the goods and services?

Collectively, our wants far outstrip what can be produced from nature's scarce resources. So how should we allocate those scarce resources? Some methods of resource allocation might seem bad and counterproductive, like the "survival of the fittest" competition that exists in the jungle. Physical violence has been used since the beginning of time, as people, regions, and countries attack one another to gain control over resources. One might argue that governments should allocate scarce resources on the basis of equal shares or according to need. However, this approach poses problems because of diverse individual preferences, the problem of ascertaining needs, and the negative work and investment incentives involved. In reality, society is made up of many approaches to resource allocation. For now, we will focus on one form of allocating goods and services found in most countries—the market system.

Because of scarcity, certain economic questions must be answered, regardless of the level of affluence of the society or its political structure. We will consider three fundamental questions that inevitably must be faced: (1) What is to be produced? (2) How are the goods and services to be produced? (3) Who will get the goods and services? These questions are unavoidable in a world of scarcity.

WHAT IS TO BE PRODUCED?

How do individuals control production decisions in market-oriented economies? Questions arise such as "Should we produce lots of cars and just a few school buildings, or relatively few cars and more school buildings?" The answer to this and other such questions is called **consumer sovereignty**—how consumers vote on economic affairs with their dollars (or pounds or yen) in a market economy. Consumer sovereignty explains how individual consumers in market economies determine what is to be produced. High-definition televisions, digital cameras, cellphones, digital video recorders (DVRs), iPods, and tablets, for example, became part of our lives because consumers "voted" hundreds of dollars apiece on these goods. As they bought more plasma TVs, consumers "voted" fewer dollars for tube TVs. Similarly, CDs gave way to downloadable music as consumers voted for these items with their dollars. As consumers vote for more fuel-efficient cars and healthier foods, firms that want to remain profitable must listen and respond.

consumer sovereignty
Consumers vote on economic affairs with their dollars in a market economy.

How Different Types of Economic Systems Answer the Question "What Is to Be Produced?"

Economies are organized in different ways to answer the question of what is to be produced. The dispute over the best way to answer this question has inflamed passions for centuries. Should central planning boards make the decisions, as in China and North Korea? In **command economies**, the government uses central planning

command economy
The government uses central planning to coordinate most economic activities.

to coordinate most economic activities. Under this type of regime, decisions about how many tractors or automobiles to produce are largely determined by a government official or a committee associated with the central planning organization. That same group decides on the number and size of school buildings, refrigerators, shoes, and so on. Other countries—including Canada, the United States, much of Europe, and, increasingly, Asia and elsewhere—have largely adopted a decentralized decision-making process in which literally millions of individual producers and consumers of goods and services determine what and how many will be produced. An economy that allocates goods and services through the private decisions of consumers, input suppliers, and firms is often referred to as a **market economy**. Actually, no nation has a pure market economy. Most countries, including Canada, are said to have a **mixed economy**. In such economies, the government and the private sector together determine the allocation of resources.

market economy
Goods and services are allocated based on the private decisions of consumers, input suppliers, and firms.

mixed economy
Government and the private sector together determine the allocation of resources.

HOW ARE THE GOODS AND SERVICES TO BE PRODUCED?

Because of scarcity, all economies, regardless of their political structure, must decide how to produce the goods and services that they want. Goods and services can generally be produced in several ways. For example, a ditch can be dug by many workers using their hands, by a few workers with shovels, or by one person with a backhoe. Someone must decide which method is most appropriate. The larger the quantity of the good and the more elaborate the form of capital, the more labour that is saved and is thus made available for other uses. (Remember, goods like shovels and large earth-moving machines used to produce goods and services are called *capital*.) From this example, you might be tempted to conclude that it is desirable to use the biggest, most elaborate form of capital. But would you really want to plant your spring flowers with huge earth-moving machinery? That is, the most capital-intensive method of production might not always be the best. The best method is the least-cost method.

The Best Form of Production

The best or optimal form of production will usually vary from one economy to the next. For example, earth-moving machinery is used to dig large ditches in Canada, the United States, and Europe, whereas in developing countries, such as India, China, or Pakistan, shovels are often used. Similarly, a person in Canada might use a power lawn mower to cut the grass, whereas in a developing country, a hand mower might be used or grass might not be cut at all. Why do these "optimal" forms of production vary so drastically? Compared to capital, labour is relatively cheap and plentiful in developing countries but relatively scarce and expensive in Canada. In contrast, capital (machines and tools, mainly) is comparatively plentiful and cheap in Canada but scarcer and more costly in developing countries. That is, in developing countries, production tends to be more **labour-intensive**, using a large amount of labour. In Canada, production tends to be more **capital-intensive**, using a large amount of capital. Each nation tends to use the production processes that conserve its relatively scarce (and thus relatively more expensive) resources and use more of its relatively abundant resources.

labour-intensive
production that uses a large amount of labour

capital-intensive
production that uses a large amount of capital

WHO WILL GET THE GOODS AND SERVICES?

In every society, some mechanism must exist to determine how goods and services are to be distributed among the population. Who gets what? Why are some people able to consume or use far more goods and services than others? This question of distribution is so important that wars and revolutions have been fought over it. Both the French and Russian revolutions were concerned fundamentally with the distribution of goods and services. Even in societies where political questions are usually settled peacefully, the question of the distribution of income is an issue that always arouses strong emotional responses. As we will see, in a market economy with private ownership and control of the means of production, the amount of goods and services one is able to obtain depends on one's income, which in turn depends on the quantity and quality of the scarce resources that the individual controls. For example, Connor McDavid makes a lot of money because he has unique and marketable skills as a hockey player.

To say that this may or may not be "fair" is an opinion at the centre of the *efficiency* versus *equity* dilemma in economics. As an economy, do you focus on getting the most you can from your scarce resources (efficiency) or should the emphasis be on equally distributing the benefits of those resources to all (equity)? Some economists believe that individual freedom and choice are central to economic well-being. When limitations are placed on these individual freedoms, these economists believe that economic efficiency will suffer. On the other hand, some economists are concerned with the economic inequalities and unfairness created by production and distribution. For example, to these economists, government intervention is a valuable tool in making society more equitable. Regardless of which side of the debate is chosen, one truth is certain: Decisions regarding the three economic questions raised in this section play a central role in shaping the efficiency and equity of an economy.

Photo by Jeff Vinnick/NHLI via Getty Images

Connor McDavid gets paid a lot of money because he controls a scarce resource: his talent and name recognition. As we will see in later chapters, people's talents and other goods and services in limited supply relative to demand will command high prices.

SECTION CHECK

- Every economy has to decide what to produce. In a market economy, millions of buyers and sellers determine what and how much to produce, while in a command economy, the government coordinates economic activity. In a mixed economy, the government and the private sector determine the allocation of resources.
- The best form of production is the one that conserves the relatively scarce (more costly) resources and uses more of the abundant (less costly) resources. When capital is relatively scarce and labour is plentiful, production tends to be labour-intensive. When capital is relatively abundant and labour is relatively scarce, production tends to be capital-intensive.
- In a market economy, the amount of goods and services one is able to obtain depends on one's income. The amount of one's income depends on the quantity and the quality of the scarce resources that the individual controls.

For Your Review

Section 1.1

1. Write your own definition of *economics*. What are the main elements of the definition?

2. Would the following topics be covered in microeconomics or macroeconomics?
   a. the effects of an increase in the supply of lumber on the home-building industry
   b. changes in the national unemployment rate
   c. the effect of interest rates on the machine-tool industry
   d. the effect of interest rates on the demand for investment goods
   e. the way a firm maximizes profits

Section 1.2

3. Are the following statements normative or positive, or do they contain both normative and positive statements?
   a. A higher income tax rate would generate increased tax revenues. Those extra revenues should be used to give more government aid to the poor.
   b. The study of physics is more valuable than the study of sociology, but both should be studied by all postsecondary students.
   c. An increase in the price of wheat will decrease the amount of wheat purchased. However, it will increase the amount of wheat supplied to the market.
   d. A decrease in the price of butter will increase the amount of butter purchased, but that would be bad because it would increase Canadians' cholesterol levels.
   e. The birth rate is reduced as economies urbanize, but that also leads to an increased average age of developing countries' populations.

4. Which of the following economic statements are positive and which are normative?
   a. A tax increase will increase unemployment.
   b. The government should reduce funding for social assistance programs.
   c. Tariffs on imported wine will lead to higher prices for domestic wine.
   d. A decrease in the capital gains tax rate will increase investment.
   e. Goods purchased on the Internet should be subject to provincial sales taxes.
   f. A reduction in interest rates will cause inflation.

5. Do any of the following statements involve fallacies? If so, which ones do they involve?
   a. Because sitting in the back of classrooms is correlated with getting lower grades in the class, students should always sit closer to the front of the classroom.
   b. Historically, the stock market rises in years the NFC team wins the Super Bowl and falls when the AFC wins the Super Bowl. I am rooting for the NFC team to win for the sake of my investment portfolio.

   c. When a hockey team spends more to get better players, it is more successful, which proves that all the teams should spend more to get better players.

   d. Gasoline prices were higher last year than in 1970, yet people purchased more gas, which contradicts the law of demand.

   e. An increase in the amount of money I have will make me better off, but an increase in the supply of money in the economy will not make Canadians as a group better off.

6. Why are observation and prediction more difficult in economics than in chemistry?

7. Why do economists look at group behaviour rather than individual behaviour?

Section 1.3

8. Explain the difference between poverty and scarcity.

9. The automotive revolution after World War II reduced the time involved for travel and shipping goods. This innovation allowed the Canadian economy to produce more goods and services since it freed resources involved in transportation for other uses. The transportation revolution also increased wants. Identify two ways in which vehicle manufacturers evoked new wants.

10. Which of the following goods are scarce?

   a. garbage

   b. salt water in the ocean

   c. clothes

   d. clean air in a big city

   e. dirty air in a big city

   f. public libraries

Section 1.4

11. The price of a one-way bus trip from Toronto to Ottawa is $150. Sarah, a school-teacher, pays the same price in February (during the school year) as in July (during her vacation), so the cost is the same in February as in July. Do you agree?

12. You work as a tutor at your school, making $15 per hour. Yesterday, you decided to cancel your two-hour tutoring appointment in order to meet friends for a coffee. The coffee cost you $3.50. What was the opportunity cost of this decision in dollars?

13. List the opportunity costs of the following:

   a. going to college or university

   b. missing a lecture

   c. withdrawing and spending $100 from your savings account, which earns 5 percent interest annually

   d. going snowboarding on the weekend before final examinations

14. Why does inaction have consequences?

15. In most countries, the birth rate has fallen as incomes and the economic opportunities for women have increased. Use economics to explain this pattern.

Blueprint Problem

Assume that the total cost to Steve of producing additional sets of headphones at his factory is represented by the following schedule: 1 pair, $9; 2 pairs, $21; 3 pairs, $35; 4 pairs, $53; 5 pairs, $75 (for simplicity, assume all costs are variable, there are no fixed costs).

    a. Calculate the marginal cost (*MC*) of each pair of headphones.

    b. Suppose Steve sells each pair of headphones for $16. How many pairs of headphones will he make if his decision is based on rational choice?

Blueprint Solution

Number of Headphones Produced	Total Production Cost
0	$0
1	9
2	21
3	35
4	53
5	75

This problem is better understood if it is presented in a table.

Notice that if Steve decides not to make any headphones, his total cost is zero. This is due to the assumption that all of Steve's costs are variable and none are fixed.

a.

Number of Headphones Produced	Total Production Cost	Marginal Production Cost of Each Pair of Headphones
0	$0	
1	9	$9
2	21	12
3	35	14
4	53	18
5	75	22

To determine the marginal production cost of each pair of headphones, calculate the incremental cost resulting from the production of each additional pair of headphones. The third column displays the marginal cost (*MC*) of each pair of headphones.

b.

Number of Headphones Produced	MC	MB	Net Benefit	Production Decision
1	$9	$16	$7	Produce
2	12	16	4	Produce
3	14	16	2	Produce
4	18	16	−2	Do not produce
5	22	16	−6	Do not produce

This question involves using the rule of rational choice. The determination of the marginal benefit (*MB*) is based on the assumption that Steve sells all of his pairs of headphones at the same price of $16.

Steve will make only those pairs of headphones that generate positive net benefit for his business, that is $E(MB) > E(MC)$. The determination of net benefit provides the rationale for the production decision.

Section 1.5

16. Assume the total benefits to Mark from trips to a local amusement park during the year are given by the following schedule: 1 trip, $60; 2 trips, $115; 3 trips, $165; 4 trips, $200; 5 trips, $225; 6 or more trips, $240.

   a. What is Mark's marginal benefit of the third trip? The fifth trip?

   b. If the admission price to the amusement park was $45 per day, how many times would Mark be willing and able to go in a year? What if the price was $20 per day? Explain.

   c. If the amusement park offered a year-long pass for $200 rather than a per-day admission price, would Mark be willing to buy one? If so, how many times would he go? Explain.

17. Assume the total cost of producing widgets was $4200 for 42 units; $4257 for 43 units; $4332 for 44 units; and $4420 for 45 units.

   a. What is the marginal cost of producing the 43rd unit? The 45th unit?

   b. If the widget producer could sell at $60 per unit—however many he could produce—how many would he choose to produce? If he could sell at $80 per unit—however many he could produce—how many would he choose to produce? Explain.

18. Imagine that you are trying to decide whether to cross a street without using the designated crosswalk at the traffic signal. What are the expected marginal benefits of crossing? What are the expected marginal costs? How would the following conditions change your benefit–cost equation?

    a. The street was busy.

    b. The street was empty and it was 3:00 A.M.

    c. You were in a huge hurry.

    d. There was a police officer 10 metres away.

    e. The closest crosswalk was 1 kilometre away.

    f. The closest crosswalk was 5 metres away.

19. Which of the following activities require marginal thinking, and why?

    a. studying

    b. eating

    c. driving

    d. shopping

    e. getting ready for a night out

20. Explain why following the rule of rational choice makes a person better off.

Section 1.6

21. Which of the following are positive incentives? Negative incentives? Why?

    a. a fine for not cleaning up after your dog defecates in the park

    b. a trip to Hawaii paid for by your parents or significant other for earning an A in your economics course

    c. a higher tax on cigarettes and alcohol

    d. a subsidy for installing solar panels on your house

22. The penalty for drug trafficking in Singapore is death. Do you think there would be more drug traffickers in Singapore if the mandatory sentence was five years, with parole for good behaviour?

23. Under China's former family planning law (commonly referred to as its one-child policy), those who followed the policy were offered rewards, loans, and other forms of social assistance, depending on socioeconomic status. People who did not comply with the policy were subject to penalties such as fines and confiscation of personal property. Excess children could also be subject to educational and health sanctions. What behaviour was the Chinese government attempting to promote with these types of incentives? Identify which aspects of the law were negative incentives and which were positive incentives.

Section 1.7

24. Throughout history, many countries have chosen the path of autarky, choosing to not trade with other countries. Explain why this path would make a country poorer.

25. Farmer Fran can grow soybeans and corn. She can grow 1500 kilograms of soybeans or 3000 kilograms of corn on a hectare of her land for the same cost. The price of soybeans is $1.50 per kilogram and the price of corn is $0.60 per kilogram. Show the benefits to Fran of specialization. What should she specialize in?

26. Which region has a comparative advantage in the following goods?
    a. wheat: Colombia or Canada
    b. coffee: Colombia or Canada
    c. lumber: Alberta or British Columbia
    d. oil: Alberta or British Columbia

27. a. Why is it important that the country or region with the lower opportunity cost produce the good?
    b. How would you use the concept of comparative advantage to argue for reducing restrictions on trade between countries?

Section 1.8

28. What are the three basic economic questions? How are decisions made differently in a market economy than in command economies?

29. Adam was a university graduate with a double major in economics and art. A few years ago, Adam decided that he wanted to pursue a vocation that utilized both of his talents. In response, he shut himself up in his studio and created a watercolour collection, "Graphs of Famous Recessions." With high hopes, Adam put his collection on display for buyers. After several years of displaying his econ art, however, the only one interested in the collection was his eight-year-old sister, who wanted the picture frames for her room. Recognizing that Adam was having trouble pursuing his chosen occupation, Adam's friend Karl told him that the market had failed. What do you think? Is Karl right?

Appendix

GRAPHS ARE AN IMPORTANT ECONOMIC TOOL

Sometimes the use of visual aids, such as graphs, greatly enhances our understanding of a theory. It is much the same as finding your way to a friend's house with the aid of a map rather than with detailed verbal or written instructions. Graphs are important tools for economists. They allow us to understand better the workings of the economy. To economists, a graph can be worth a thousand words. This text will use graphs throughout to enhance the understanding of important economic relationships. This appendix provides a guide on how to read and create your own graphs.

The most useful graph for our purposes is one that merely connects a vertical line (the **Y-axis**) with a horizontal line (the **X-axis**), as seen in Exhibit 1. The intersection of the two lines occurs at the origin, which is where the value of both variables is equal to zero. In Exhibit 1, the graph has four quadrants or "boxes." In this textbook we will be primarily concerned with the shaded box in the upper right-hand corner. This portion of the graph deals exclusively with positive numbers. Always keep in mind that moving to the right on the horizontal axis and up along the vertical axis each lead to higher values.

Y-axis
the vertical axis on a graph

X-axis
the horizontal axis on a graph

pie chart
a circle divided into proportionate slices that represent various quantities that add up to 100 percent

bar graph
represents data using vertical bars rising from the horizontal axis

time-series graph
shows changes in the value of a variable over time

USING GRAPHS AND CHARTS

Exhibit 2 presents three common types of graphs. A **pie chart** is a circle divided into proportionate slices that represent various quantities that add up to 100 percent. The pie chart in Exhibit 2(a) shows what college students earn. That is, each slice in the pie chart represents the percentage of college students in a particular earnings category.

A **bar graph** represents data using vertical bars rising from the horizontal axis. Exhibit 2(b) is a bar graph that shows the sales of wireless phone service by province for a new company that has just entered the Canadian market. The height of the line represents sales in millions of dollars. Bar graphs are used to show a comparison of the sizes of quantities of similar items.

Exhibit 2(c) is a **time-series graph**. This type of graph shows changes in the value of a variable over time. This is a visual tool that allows us to observe important trends over a certain time period. In Exhibit 2(c) we see a graph that shows trends in the stock price of the company Fly-by-Chance for the period January to December. The horizontal axis shows us the passage of time, and the vertical axis shows us the stock price in dollars per share.

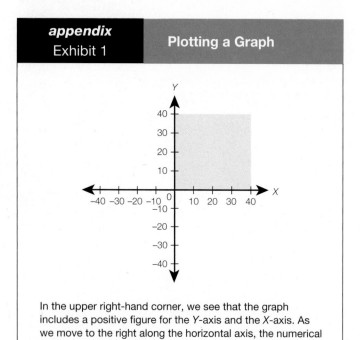

appendix Exhibit 1	Plotting a Graph

In the upper right-hand corner, we see that the graph includes a positive figure for the Y-axis and the X-axis. As we move to the right along the horizontal axis, the numerical values increase. As we move up along the vertical axis, the numerical values increase.

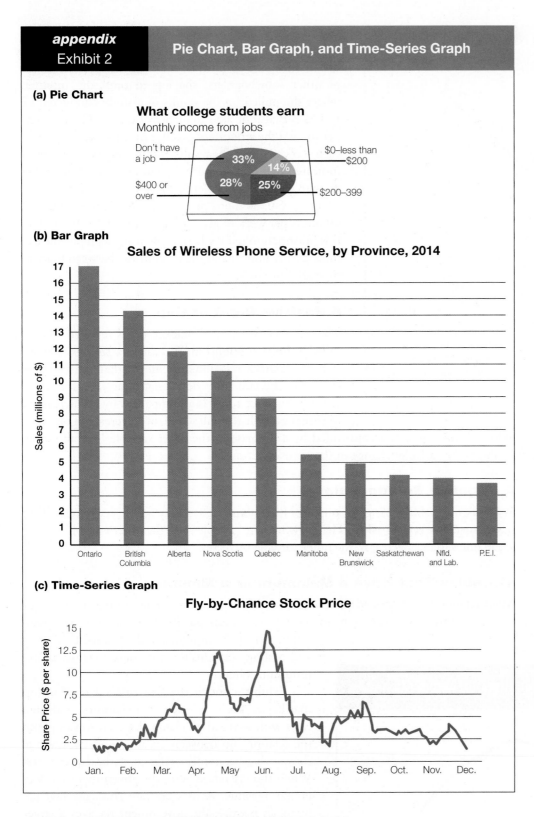

appendix
Exhibit 2
Pie Chart, Bar Graph, and Time-Series Graph

(a) Pie Chart

What college students earn

Monthly income from jobs

Don't have a job — 33%

14% — $0–less than $200

$400 or over — 28%

25%

$200–399

(b) Bar Graph

Sales of Wireless Phone Service, by Province, 2014

Sales (millions of $)

Ontario, British Columbia, Alberta, Nova Scotia, Quebec, Manitoba, New Brunswick, Saskatchewan, Nfld. and Lab., P.E.I.

(c) Time-Series Graph

Fly-by-Chance Stock Price

Share Price ($ per share)

Jan. Feb. Mar. Apr. May Jun. Jul. Aug. Sep. Oct. Nov. Dec.

USING GRAPHS TO SHOW THE RELATIONSHIP BETWEEN TWO VARIABLES

Although the graphs and chart in Exhibit 2 are important, they do not allow us to show the relationship between two variables (a **variable** is something that is measured by a number, such as your height). To more closely examine the structure and functions of graphs, let us consider the story of Katherine, an avid snowboarder who has aspirations of

variable

something that is measured by a number, such as your height

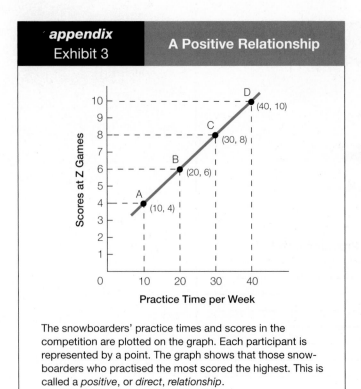

appendix Exhibit 3 — A Positive Relationship

The snowboarders' practice times and scores in the competition are plotted on the graph. Each participant is represented by a point. The graph shows that those snowboarders who practised the most scored the highest. This is called a *positive*, or *direct*, *relationship*.

positive relationship
when two variables change in the same direction

negative relationship
when two variables change in opposite directions

winning the Z Games next year. To get there, however, she will have to put in many hours of practice. But how many hours? In search of information about the practice habits of other snowboarders, she logged onto the Internet, where she pulled up the results of a study conducted by ESPM 3 that indicated the score of each Z Games competitor and the amount of practice time per week spent by each snowboarder. The results of this study (see Exhibit 3) indicated that snowboarders had to practise 10 hours per week to receive a score of 4.0, 20 hours per week to receive a score of 6.0, 30 hours per week to get a score of 8.0, and 40 hours per week to get a perfect score of 10. What does this information tell Katherine? By using a graph, she can more clearly understand the relationship between practice time and overall score.

A Positive Relationship

The study on scores and practice times revealed what is called a direct relationship, also called a *positive relationship*. A **positive relationship** means that the variables change in the same direction. That is, an increase in one variable (practice time) is accompanied by an increase in the other variable (overall score), or a decrease in one variable (practice time) is accompanied by a decrease in the other variable (overall score). In short, the variables change in the same direction.

A Negative Relationship

When two variables change in opposite directions, we say they are inversely related, or have a **negative relationship**. That is, when one variable rises, the other variable falls, or when one variable decreases, the other variable increases.

Variables That Have a Maximum or a Minimum

Many relationships described in economic models have maximum or minimum values. For example, firms are always looking to make the maximum possible profits; one way they can achieve this is by minimizing their costs. Exhibits 4 and 5 show relationships that have maximum and minimum values.

Exhibit 4 shows the first case—a relationship that begins positive, reaches a maximum, and then ends with a negative relationship. This example of the relationship between tax rates and tax revenue shows what economists refer to as the *Laffer curve*. When the tax rate is zero, the government receives no tax revenue. As the tax rate rises, tax revenue increases because the government receives a larger percentage of people's incomes. In the exhibit, a tax rate of 50 percent generates the maximum tax revenue of $15 million. As the tax rate continues to rise, it may be the case that the incentive to earn more income begins to decline, causing tax revenue to fall. If the tax rate was increased to 100 percent,

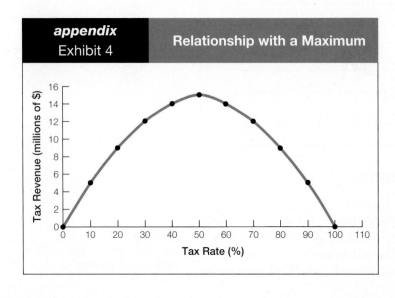

appendix Exhibit 4 — Relationship with a Maximum

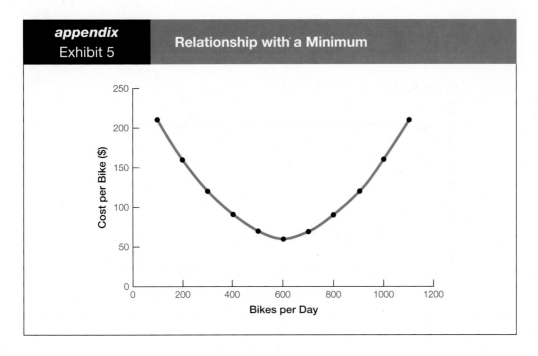

appendix
Exhibit 5

Relationship with a Minimum

there would be no incentive to earn income because it would all be taxed away; as a result, no tax revenue would be generated.

Exhibit 5 illustrates the opposite case—a relationship that begins negative, reaches a minimum, and then returns positive. Most economic costs are seen as following this relationship. As a bicycle manufacturer increases its output, per bike costs of production begin to fall, perhaps as workers develop special skills and the benefits of teamwork emerge. At a level of 600 bikes per day, the cost per bike is minimized at $60 per bike. However, as production is increased beyond 600 bikes per day, the cost per bike begins to rise, perhaps as the bike factory is forced to operate beyond its efficient capacity.

Variables That Are Not Related

There are still other situations in economics in which the change in one variable has no impact on the value of another variable. Exhibit 6 provides a graphical depiction of a curious relationship—a student's grade in economics and the lunar cycle. Since a

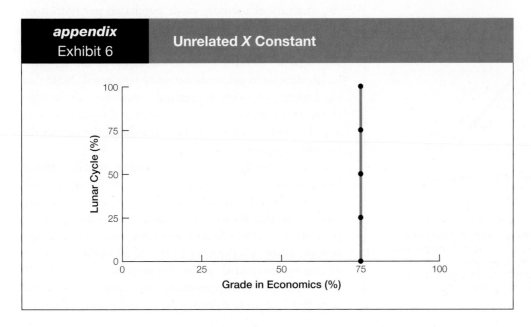

appendix
Exhibit 6

Unrelated X Constant

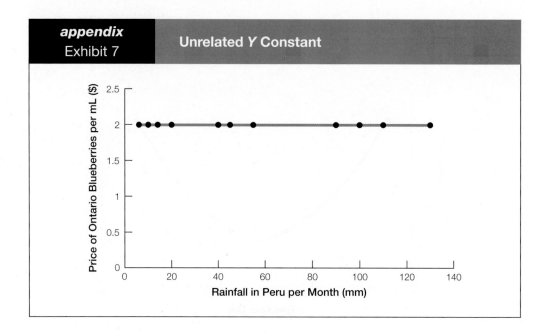

appendix
Exhibit 7

Unrelated Y Constant

student's grade in economics is not affected by the lunar cycle, no relationship exists. If a student grade of 75 percent is plotted on the horizontal axis, with the lunar cycle plotted on the vertical axis, the curve is vertical.

Exhibit 7 illustrates another curious relationship—the price of blueberries grown in Ontario and the average rainfall in Peru. Since the price of blueberries grown in Ontario, plotted on the vertical axis, does not vary with the monthly rainfall in Peru, plotted on the horizontal axis, the curve is horizontal.

THE GRAPH OF A DEMAND CURVE

One of the most important graphs in all of economics is the demand curve. In Exhibit 8, we see Emily's individual demand curve for digital camera memory cards. It shows the price of memory cards on the vertical axis and the quantity of memory cards purchased per month on the horizontal axis. Every point in the space shown represents a price and quantity combination. The downward-sloping line, labelled *Demand curve*, shows the different combinations of price and quantity purchased. Note that the higher you go on the vertical (price) axis, the smaller the quantity purchased on the horizontal (quantity) axis, and the lower the price on the vertical axis, the greater the quantity purchased.

In Exhibit 8, we see that moving up the vertical price axis from the origin, the price of memory cards increases from $5 to $25 in increments of $5. Moving out along the horizontal quantity axis, the quantity purchased increases from zero to five memory cards per month. Point A represents a price of $25 and a quantity of one memory card, point B represents a price of $20 and a quantity of two memory cards, point C, $15 and a quantity of three memory cards, and so on. When we

appendix
Exhibit 8

A Negative Relationship

The downward slope of the curve means that price and quantity purchased are inversely, or negatively, related: when one increases, the other decreases. That is, moving down along the demand curve from point A to point E, we see that as price falls, the quantity purchased increases. Moving up along the demand curve from point E to point A, we see that as the price increases, the quantity purchased falls.

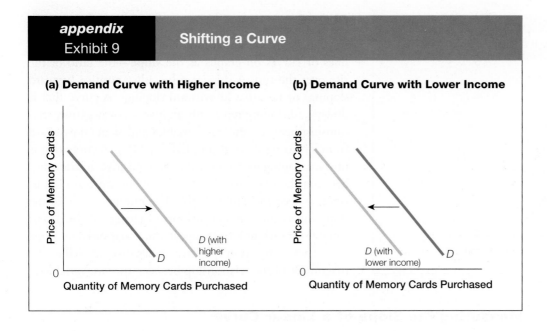

appendix
Exhibit 9

Shifting a Curve

(a) Demand Curve with Higher Income

Price of Memory Cards

D

D (with higher income)

0

Quantity of Memory Cards Purchased

(b) Demand Curve with Lower Income

Price of Memory Cards

D (with lower income)

D

0

Quantity of Memory Cards Purchased

connect all the points, we have what economists call a *curve*. As you can see, curves are sometimes drawn as straight lines for ease of illustration. Moving down along the curve, we see that as the price falls, a greater quantity is demanded; moving up the curve to higher prices, a smaller quantity is demanded. That is, when memory cards become less expensive, Emily buys more memory cards. When memory cards become more expensive, Emily buys fewer memory cards, perhaps choosing to go to the movies or download some music instead.

USING GRAPHS TO SHOW THE RELATIONSHIP AMONG THREE VARIABLES

Although only two variables are shown on the axes, graphs can be used to show the relationship among three variables. For example, say we add a third variable—income—to our earlier example. Our three variables are now income, price, and quantity purchased. If Emily's income rises, say she gets a raise at work, she is now able and willing to buy more memory cards than before at each possible price. As a result, the whole demand curve shifts outward (rightward) compared to the old curve. That is, she uses some of her additional income to buy more memory cards. This is seen in the graph in Exhibit 9(a). On the other hand, if her income falls, say she quits her job to go back to school, she now has less income to buy memory cards. This causes the whole demand curve to shift inward (leftward) compared to the old curve. This is seen in the graph in Exhibit 9(b).

The Difference between a Movement along and a Shift in the Curve

It is important to remember the difference between a movement between one point and another along a curve and a shift in the whole curve. A change in one of the variables on the graph, like price or quantity purchased, will cause a movement along the curve, say from point A to point B, as shown in Exhibit 10. A change in one of the variables not shown (held constant in order to show only the relationship between price and quantity), like income in our example, will cause the whole curve to shift. The change from D_0 to D_1 in Exhibit 10 shows such a shift.

appendix
Exhibit 10

Shifts vs. Movements

Price of Memory Cards

A

B

D_0 D_1

0

Quantity of Memory Cards Purchased

SLOPE

In economics, we sometimes refer to the steepness of the lines or curves on graphs as the **slope**—the ratio of the rise over the run. A slope can be either positive (upward sloping) or negative (downward sloping). A curve that is downward sloping represents an inverse, or negative, relationship between the two variables and slants downward from left to right, as seen in Exhibit 11(a). A curve that is upward sloping represents a direct, or positive, relationship between the two variables and slants upward from left to right, as seen in Exhibit 11(b). The numeric value of the slope shows the number of units of change of the *Y*-axis variable for each unit of change in the *X*-axis variable. Slope provides the direction (positive or negative) as well as the magnitude of the relationship between the two variables.

slope

the ratio of rise (change in the Y variable) over the run (change in the X variable)

Measuring the Slope of a Linear Curve

A straight-line curve is called a *linear curve*. The slope of a linear curve between two points measures the relative rates of change of two variables. Specifically, the slope of a linear curve can be defined as the ratio of the change in the *Y* value to the change in the *X* value. The slope can also be expressed as the ratio of the rise to the run, where the rise is the change in the *Y* variable (along the vertical axis) and the run is the change in the *X* variable (along the horizontal axis).

In Exhibit 12, we show two linear curves, one with a positive slope and one with a negative slope. In Exhibit 12(a), the slope of the positively sloped linear curve from point A to point B is 1/2, because the rise is 1 (from 2 to 3) and the run is 2 (from 1 to 3). In Exhibit 12(b), the negatively sloped linear curve has a slope of −4, a rise of −8 (a fall

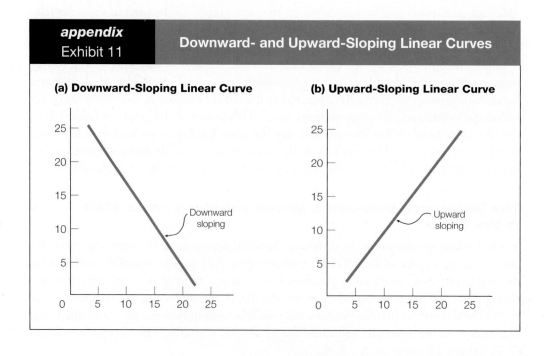

appendix
Exhibit 11

Downward- and Upward-Sloping Linear Curves

(a) Downward-Sloping Linear Curve

25

20

15

Downward sloping

10

5

0   5   10   15   20   25

(b) Upward-Sloping Linear Curve

25

20

15

Upward sloping

10

5

0   5   10   15   20   25

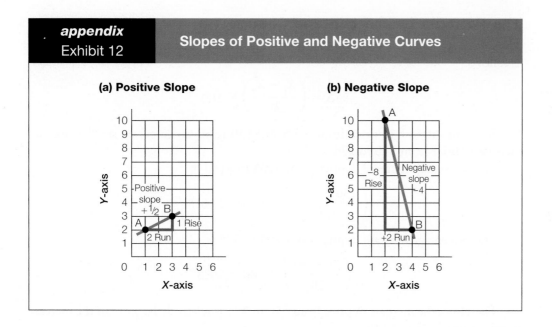

(a) Positive Slope

(b) Negative Slope

of 8 from 10 to 2), and a run of 2 (from 2 to 4), which gives us a slope of -4 ($-8/2$). Note the appropriate signs on the slopes: The negatively sloped line carries a minus sign and the positively sloped line, a plus sign.

Finding the Slope of a Nonlinear Curve

In Exhibit 13, we show the slope of a nonlinear curve. A nonlinear curve is a line that actually curves. Here the slope varies from point to point along the curve. However, we can find the slope of this curve at any given point by drawing a straight-line tangent to that point on the curve. A tangency is when a straight line just touches the curve without actually crossing it. At point A, we see that the positively sloped line that is tangent to the curve has a slope of 1—the line rises one unit and runs one unit. At point B, the line is horizontal, so it has zero slope. At point C, we see a slope of -2 because the negatively sloped line has a rise of -2 units (a fall of two units) for every one unit run.

Remember, many students have problems with economics simply because they fail to understand graphs, so make sure that you understand this material before going on to Chapter 2.

Percentage Change

In economics, the determination of the percentage change in a quantity is a common calculation. The advantage of calculating percentage change (as opposed to simple absolute change) is that percentage change provides a more accurate measure of the magnitude of the change. For example, is an increase in price from $105 to $130 relatively larger or smaller than an increase in price from $50 to $75? In both cases, the difference (absolute increase) is the same at $25, but what about the relative (percentage) change?

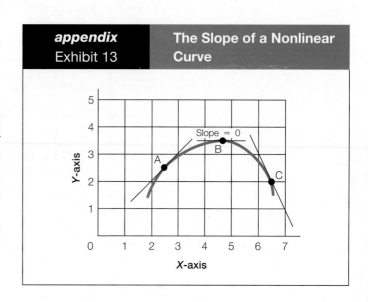

The Formula for Percentage Change

The percentage change in a value that is originally x_0 and changes to x_1 can be expressed as follows:

$$\%\Delta = \left(\frac{X_1 - X_0}{X_0}\right) \times 100$$

So, is an increase in price from \$105 to \$130 relatively larger or smaller than an increase in price from \$50 to \$75?

The percentage increase in price from \$105 to \$130 is

$$\left(\frac{130 - 105}{105}\right) \times 100 = 23.81\%$$

The percentage increase in price from \$50 to \$75 is

$$\left(\frac{75 - 50}{50}\right) \times 100 = 50\%$$

Therefore, the increase in price from \$50 to \$75 is relatively larger than the increase in price from \$105 to \$130.

For Your Review   (Chapter 1 Appendix)

1. What are the coordinates of the points of the following graph?

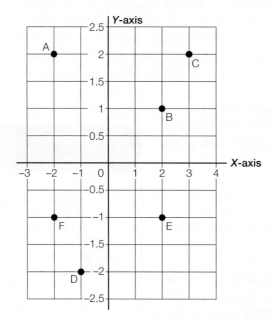

2. Refer to the following pie chart, which shows the percentage of sales by vehicle type in 2018.

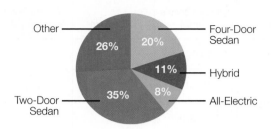

a. What percentage of the cars sold in 2018 were all-electric vehicles?
b. What percentage of the cars sold in 2018 were four-door sedans?
c. What was the most popular vehicle type for 2018 based on sales?
d. What was the least popular vehicle type for 2018 based on sales?

3. Refer to the following bar graph, which shows the number of boys and girls participating in campus recreational leagues in each of four semesters.

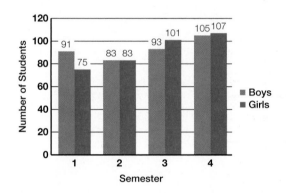

a. In which semesters were more boys than girls registered in campus recreational leagues?
b. In which semesters were more girls than boys registered in campus recreational leagues?
c. In which semesters did the same number of girls and boys register in campus recreational leagues?
d. Looking at all four semesters, what was the total number of boys registered in campus recreational leagues?

4. Plot the relationships described in the following tables on separate graphs (plot the variables in the left-hand columns on the horizontal axis and the variables in the right-hand columns on the vertical axis).

Graph 1		Graph 2		Graph 3	
Temperature (°C)	Ice Cream Sales (cones)	Year	Value of Tom's Car ($)	Shoe size	Grade Point Average (GPA)
20	30	2018	14 000	8	3.5
22	50	2017	15 000	9	3.5
24	70	2016	16 000	10	3.5
26	90	2015	17 000	11	3.5
28	110	2014	18 000	12	3.5

How would you describe the resulting graphs: upward sloping, downward sloping, or unrelated?

5. Refer to the following graph.

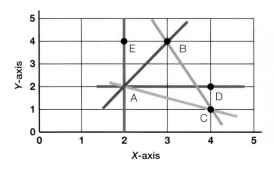

Calculate the slope between the following sets of points.

a. A to B

b. B to C

c. A to C

d. E to A

e. A to D

6. Calculate the percentage change in each of the following scenarios.

a. The temperature increases from 12°C to 18°C.

b. The price of a laptop computer falls from $800 to $760.

c. The Consumer Price Index (CPI) increases from 105.3 to 106.1.

d. The number of emergency calls to campus security decreased from 912 last semester to 862 this semester.

The Production Possibilities Curve

- What is a production possibilities curve?
- What is efficiency?
- How is opportunity cost measured?
- What is the law of increasing opportunity costs?

WHAT IS A PRODUCTION POSSIBILITIES CURVE?

The economic concepts of scarcity, choice, and trade-offs can be shown with a simple graph called a *production possibilities curve*. The **production possibilities curve** represents the potential total output combinations of any two goods for an economy, given the inputs and technology available to the economy. That is, it illustrates an economy's potential for allocating its limited resources in producing various combinations of goods in a given time period.

production possibilities curve

the potential total output combinations of any two goods for an economy, given the inputs and technology available

Because you have only so many hours a week to study, studying more for economics and less for accounting might hurt your grade in accounting, *ceteris paribus*. Life is full of trade-offs.

A Straight-Line Production Possibilities Curve—Grades in Economics and Accounting

What would the production possibilities curve look like if you were "producing" grades in two of your classes—say, economics and accounting? In Exhibit 1, we draw a hypothetical production possibilities curve for your expected grade in economics on the vertical axis and your expected grade in accounting on the horizontal axis. Assume, because of a part-time restaurant job, you choose to study ten hours a week and that you like both courses and are equally adept at studying for both courses.

We see in Exhibit 1 that the production possibilities curve is a straight line. For example, if all ten hours are spent studying economics, the expected grade in economics is 85 percent (an A) and the expected grade in accounting is 45 percent (an F). Moving down the

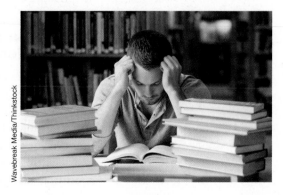

Wavebreak Media/Thinkstock

section 2.1
Exhibit 1

Production Possibilities Curve: "Producing" Grades in Economics and Accounting

The production possibilities curve highlights the concept of trade-offs. Assuming you choose to study a total of ten hours a week, moving down the production possibilities curve shows that if you use your time to study accounting instead of economics you can raise your expected grade in accounting but only at the expense of lowering your expected grade in economics. With a straight-line production possibilities curve, the opportunity costs are constant.

production possibilities curve, we see that as you spend more of your time studying accounting and less on economics, you can raise your expected grade in accounting but only at the expense of lowering your expected grade in economics. Specifically, moving down along the straight-line production possibilities curve, the trade-off is one letter-grade lower in economics for one higher letter-grade in accounting. That is, with a straight-line production possibilities curve, the opportunity costs are constant.

The trade-offs between expected grades in economics and accounting are the result of holding study time constant (ten hours per week) and all other factors that could increase your ability to learn, such as software study packages.

Of course, if you increased your study time it would be possible to expect higher grades in both courses. But that would be on a new production possibilities curve; along this production possibilities curve we are assuming that technology and the number of study hours are given. In the next section, the coverage is expanded to cover the more realistic case of a bowed production possibilities curve.

Production Alternatives on the Bowed Production Possibilities Curve

To more clearly illustrate the production possibilities curve, imagine an economy that produces just two goods: food and shelter. The fact that we have many goods in the real world makes actual decision making more complicated, but it does not alter the basic principles being illustrated. Each point on the production possibilities curve shown in Exhibit 2 represents the potential amounts of food and shelter that can be produced in a given time period, given the quantity and quality of resources available in the economy for production.

Note in Exhibit 2 that if we devoted all of our resources to making units of shelter, we could produce 10 units of shelter, but no food (point A). If, on the other hand, we chose to devote all of our resources to food, we could produce 80 units of food, but no shelter (point E).

In reality, nations would rarely opt for production possibility A or E, preferring instead to produce a mixture of goods. For example, the economy in question might produce 9 units of shelter and 20 units of food (point B), or perhaps 7 units of shelter and 40 units of food (point C). Still other combinations along the curve, such as point D, are possible.

Production Alternatives Off the Production Possibilities Curve

The economy cannot operate at point N (not attainable) during the given time period because there are presently not enough resources to produce that level of output. However, it is possible the economy can operate inside the production possibilities curve, at point I (inefficient). If the economy is operating at point I, or at any other point inside the production possibilities curve, it is not at full capacity and is operating inefficiently. In short, the economy is not using all of its scarce resources efficiently; as a result, actual output is less than potential output.

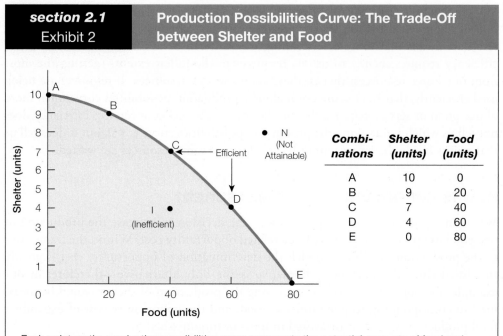

section 2.1 Exhibit 2	Production Possibilities Curve: The Trade-Off between Shelter and Food

Combi- nations	Shelter (units)	Food (units)
A	10	0
B	9	20
C	7	40
D	4	60
E	0	80

Each point on the production possibilities curve represents the potential amounts of food and shelter that can be produced in a given time period, given the quantity and quality of resources available in the economy to use for production. All the points on the production possibility curve are efficient. Any points in the shaded area, like point I, are inefficient. Any point outside the production possibilities curve, like point N, is not attainable at the present time.

WHAT IS EFFICIENCY?

Most modern economies have resources that are idle, at least for some period of time—like during periods of high unemployment. If those resources were not idle, people would have more scarce goods and services available for their use. Unemployed resources create a serious problem. For example, consider an unemployed construction worker who is unable to find work at a "reasonable" wage, or those unemployed in depressed times when factories are already operating below capacity. Clearly, the resources of these individuals are not being used efficiently.

The fact that factories can operate below capacity suggests that it is not just labour resources that should be most effectively used. Rather, all resources entering into production must be used effectively. However, for several reasons, social concern focuses on labour. First, labour costs are the largest share of production costs. Also, unemployed or underemployed labourers (whose resources are not being used to their full potential) may have mouths to feed at home, whereas an unemployed machine does not (although the owner of the unemployed machine may).

Inefficiency and Efficiency

Suppose for some reason there is widespread unemployment or resources are not being put to their best use. The economy would then be operating at a point, such as I, inside the production possibilities curve where the economy is operating inefficiently. At point I, 4 units of shelter and 40 units of food are being produced. By putting unemployed resources to work or by putting already employed resources to better use, we could expand the output of shelter by 3 units (moving to point C) without giving up any units of food. Alternatively, we could boost food output by 20 units (moving to point D) without reducing shelter output. We could even get more of both food and shelter moving to a point on the curve between C and D. Increasing or improving the utilization of resources, then, can lead to greater output of all goods. An efficient use of our resources means that more of everything we want can be available for our use. Thus, efficiency requires society to use its resources to the fullest extent—getting the most from our scarce resources; that is, there are no wasted resources. If resources are being used efficiently, that is, at some point along a production possibilities curve, then more of one good or service requires the sacrifice of another good or service. Efficiency does not tell us which point along the production possibilities curve is *best*, but it does tell us that points inside the curve cannot be best because some resources are wasted.

HOW IS OPPORTUNITY COST MEASURED?

When an economy is operating efficiently, the decision to increase the production of one good or service will carry with it a related opportunity cost. Within the framework of the production possibility model, the determination of opportunity cost is greatly simplified since the next best alternative is the only alternative—therefore, in our example, the opportunity cost of increasing the production of shelter would be measured in corresponding forgone units of food, and the opportunity cost of expanding food production would be measured in units of forgone shelter.

Note in Exhibit 2 that if the economy is currently operating at point D (producing 4 units of shelter and 60 units of food), the decision to increase the amount of shelter it produces to 7 units will have an opportunity cost of 20 units of food—as this is the amount of food that the economy must give up to gain the additional units of shelter. In the diagram, this gain of shelter and related opportunity cost would involve the movement along the production possibilities curve from point D to point C.

WHAT IS THE LAW OF INCREASING OPPORTUNITY COSTS?

Note that in Exhibits 2 and 3, the production possibilities curve is not a straight line like that in Exhibit 1. It is concave from below (i.e., bowed outward from the origin). Looking at the figures, you can see that at very low food output, an increase in the amount of food produced will lead to only a small reduction in the units of shelter produced. For example, increasing food output from 0 to 20 (moving from point A to point B on the curve) requires the use of resources capable of producing 1 unit of shelter. This means that for the first 20 units of food, 1 unit of shelter must be given up. When food output is higher, however, more units of shelter must be given up when switching additional resources from the production of shelter to food. Moving from point D to point E, for example, an increase in food output of 20 (from 60 to 80) reduces the production of shelter from 4 to 0. At this point, then, the cost of those 20 additional units of food is 4 units of shelter, considerably more than the 1 unit of shelter required in the earlier scenario. This difference shows us that opportunity costs have not remained constant, but have risen, as more units of food and fewer units of shelter are produced.

The **law of increasing opportunity cost** refers to the concept that, as more of one item is produced by an economy, the opportunity cost of additional units of that product rises. It is this increasing opportunity cost, then, that is represented by the bowed production possibilities curve.

The Reason for the Law of Increasing Opportunity Cost

The basic reason for the law of increasing opportunity cost is that some resources and skills cannot be easily adapted from their current uses to alternative uses. For example, at low levels of food output, additional increases in food output can be obtained easily

law of increasing opportunity cost
As more of one item is produced by an economy, the opportunity cost of additional units of that product rises.

section 2.1
Exhibit 3

Increasing Opportunity Cost and the Production Possibilities Curve

The production possibilities curve also illustrates the opportunity cost of producing more of a given product. For example, if we were to increase food output from 40 units to 60 units (moving from point C to point D), we must produce 3 fewer units of shelter. The opportunity cost of those 20 additional units of food is the 3 units of shelter we must forgo. We can see that moving down the curve from A to E, each additional 20 units of food costs society more and more shelter—the law of increasing opportunity cost.

by switching relatively low-skilled carpenters from making shelter to producing food. However, to get even more food output, workers who are less well suited or appropriate for producing food (i.e., they are better adapted to making shelter) must be released from shelter making in order to increase food output. For example, a skilled carpenter may be an expert at making shelter but a very bad farmer, because he lacks the training and skills necessary in that occupation. So, using the skilled carpenter to farm results in a relatively greater opportunity cost than using the poor carpenter to farm. Hence, the production of additional units of food becomes increasingly costly as progressively even lower-skilled farmers (but good carpenters) convert to farming.

In short, resources tend to be specialized. As a result, we lose some of their productivity when we transfer those resources from producing what they are relatively good at to producing something they are relatively bad at.

Business *CONNECTION*

WHAT CAN THE PPC OFFER MANAGERS?

The production possibilities curve (PPC) can be extremely helpful to entrepreneurs, especially those in small and medium-sized businesses. The curve represents the potential total output combinations of any two goods for an economy, given the inputs and technology available to the economy. It's not so much that managers will construct their own PPCs, but rather that using the model can help their thinking. The PPC demonstrates a number of economic concepts: growth, choice, opportunity cost, law of diminishing returns, marginal benefits, and inflationary pressures. It can be used in a broad context (e.g., when thinking about investing in consumer goods versus capital

goods) or in a narrow perspective (e.g., when deciding on whether a plant should produce Smooth Joy bars versus Chewy Delight bars).

In general terms, the marketing side of the business is responsible for revenue (as opposed to the operations side, which is responsible for expenses). If managers of the firm feel that demand is growing, they may decide to increase the production of their plant. In terms of the PPC, the firm could presently be operating at three different levels: (1) significantly below capacity, or the PPC curve's boundary, (2) slightly below capacity, or (3) at capacity. If the firm is operating significantly below capacity, it can comfortably

(continued)

increase production without any concern about rising costs of production—it may actually lower average unit prices as it increases production. As the plant approaches full production, it will experience increased costs—for example, managers might have to pay overtime to employees. At capacity, there is no way to increase production without investing in expanding capacity, which can mean investing in capital (equipment) and/or plant size (land).

The PPC also helps the managers to visualize what the level of production should be. Producing at capacity does not allow the plant to look for new accounts, because the increased production increases the company's costs, but producing at levels slightly below capacity allows for a company to increase production both in the short and long term without major cost increases. If the occasional increase turns out to be more permanent, then managers look to expand the business.

It is vital that the marketing and operations side of the business be in sync—the last thing the firm needs is new business if it is at capacity, because that means higher costs and the pressures of meeting delivery times. This situation illustrates one reason why some young businesses fail by growing too fast they think all growth is good. In fact, however, only managed growth is good, because taking on more than the firm can deal with can lead it into failure.

The PPC can be helpful to both the marketing and operations sides when they are making decisions on the firm's product mix. For example, the firm can produce product A or product B. On the PPC, this is demonstrated by moving along the curve toward one axis or another. If demand dictates that more of product A should be made, the plant has to decide whether to make less of product B in order to make more of product A (opportunity cost). But what do managers do when demand for product B remains high and demand for product A increases significantly?

Here, the firm has to decide if it wants to expand. If it can't expand, then the decision could be to meet the increase in demand for product A and decrease production of product B, or the firm could actually increase the price of product A and leave existing production levels where they are. You'll see why this is when you learn about supply and demand in the next few chapters.

Finally, managers should be aware that as they near the plant's capacity, they have to spend considerably more for just a little bit of return. It's the same concept for you as a student—you have to spend a lot more time to move your grade up from 95 percent to 98 percent than you do to raise your grade from 50 to 60 percent. For managers, this means higher costs, and even though they could reach near capacity, would they really want to from a profitability perspective? This demonstrates the mindset of why operation managers might decide to operate at levels slightly below capacity.

Keeping the concepts of the PPC model in mind while making both marketing and operations decisions will be of great benefit to managers. This is more strategic thinking than tactical thinking—areas that successful managers have to be good at all of the time.

1. There are a number of reasons why a firm shouldn't be producing at its capacity. Can you think of some other reasons not discussed here? In each case, in your opinion, why should the firm be operating at less than capacity?

2. It is true that one of the main reasons new firms fail is that they grow too fast. Thinking of the PPC, what are other risks or reasons that could lead to business failure?

3. Why do you think costs increase for a firm the closer it gets to operating at capacity?

SECTION CHECK

- The production possibilities curve represents the potential total output combinations of two goods available to a society, given its resources and existing technology.
- Efficiency requires society to use its resources to the fullest extent—no wasted resources. If the economy is operating within the production possibilities curve, the economy is operating inefficiently.
- The cost of altering production within the production possibilities curve framework, at efficiency, is measured in forgone units of the sole alternative.
- A bowed production possibilities curve means that the opportunity costs of producing additional units of a good rise as society produces more of that good (the law of increasing opportunity costs).

Economic Growth and the Production Possibilities Curve

- How do we show economic growth on the production possibilities curve?
- How can we summarize the production possibilities curve?

HOW DO WE SHOW ECONOMIC GROWTH ON THE PRODUCTION POSSIBILITIES CURVE?

How have some nations been able to rapidly expand their output of goods and services over time, whereas others have been unable to increase their standards of living at all?

The economy can grow only with qualitative or quantitative changes in the factors of production—land, labour, capital, and entrepreneurship. Advancement in technology, improvements in labour productivity, or new sources of natural resources (such as previously undiscovered oil) could all lead to outward shifts of the production possibilities curve.

This idea can be clearly illustrated by using the production possibilities curve (Exhibit 1). In terms of the production possibilities curve, economic growth means an outward shift in the possible combinations of goods and services produced. With growth comes the possibility to have more of both goods than were previously available. Suppose we were producing at point C (7 units of shelter, 40 units of food) on our original production possibilities curve. Additional resources and/or new methods of using them (technological progress) can lead to new production possibilities, creating the potential for more of all goods (or more of some with no less of others). These increases would shift the production possibilities curve outward. For example, if the government introduces programs that make it easier for workers to get an education and relevant workplace expertise (called *human capital*), such as training workers to make shelter, this increases the productivity of these workers. As a result, they will produce more units of shelter. This means, ultimately, that fewer resources will be used to make shelter, freeing them to be used for farming—resulting in more units of food. Notice that at point F (future) on the new curve, it is possible to produce 9 units of shelter and 70 units of food, more of both goods than was previously produced, at point C. Alternatively, as evidenced by land degradation and depletion of natural resources, resources can be lost over time. This has a negative impact on production, shifting the production possibilities curve inward.

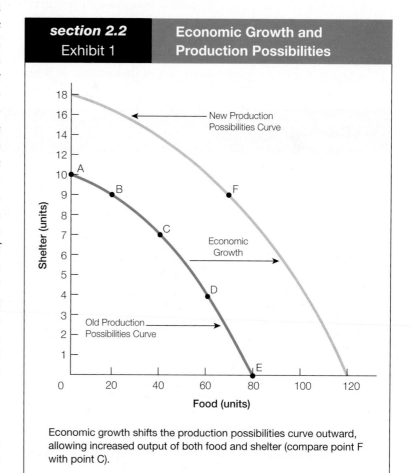

| *section 2.2*
Exhibit 1 | **Economic Growth and Production Possibilities** |

Economic growth shifts the production possibilities curve outward, allowing increased output of both food and shelter (compare point F with point C).

Growth Doesn't Eliminate Scarcity

With all of this discussion of growth, it is important to remember that growth, or increases in a society's output, does not make scarcity disappear. Even when output has grown more rapidly than the population so that people are made better off, they still face trade-offs: At any point along the production possibilities curve, in order to get more of one thing, you must give up something else. There are no free lunches on the production possibilities curve.

Capital Goods vs. Consumption Goods

Economies that choose to invest more of their resources for the future will grow faster than those that don't. To generate economic growth, a society must produce fewer consumer goods—like pizza, digital cameras, cellphones, cars, and so on—in the present and produce more capital goods. The society that devotes a larger share of its productive capacity to capital goods (machines, factories, tools, and education), rather than consumption goods (computer games, cups of coffee, and vacations), will experience greater economic growth. It must sacrifice some present consumption of consumer goods and services in order to experience growth in the future. Why? Investing in capital goods, like computers and other new technological equipment, as well as upgrading skills and knowledge, expands the ability to produce in the future. It shifts the economy's production possibilities outward, increasing the future production capacity of the economy. That is, the economy that invests more now (consumes less now) will be able to produce, and therefore consume, more in the future. In Exhibit 2, we see that Economy A invests more in capital goods than Economy B. Consequently, Economy A's production possibilities curve shifts out farther than Economy B's over time.

To better understand the significance of these two production alternatives, it may help to apply the distinction to the Canadian economy. Which type of economy is Canada, Economy A or Economy B? In Canada, consumption expenditure is nearly three times that of investment. As a result, the Canadian economy is best represented by the

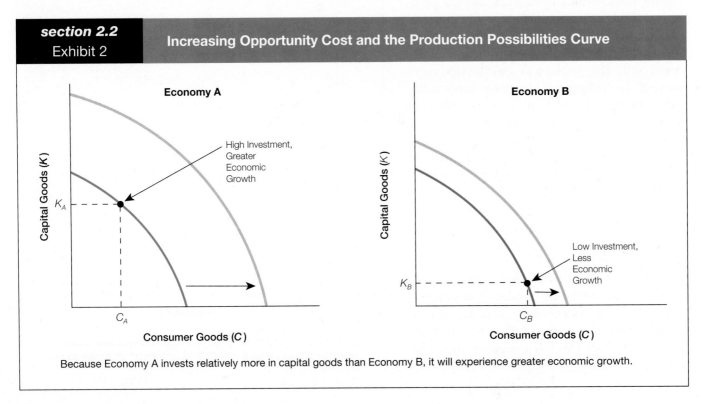

| *section 2.2* Exhibit 2 | **Increasing Opportunity Cost and the Production Possibilities Curve** |

Because Economy A invests relatively more in capital goods than Economy B, it will experience greater economic growth.

Economy B illustration. By comparison, China's gross savings amount is more than double that of Canada's. Clearly then, China is best represented by the Economy A illustration.

POM POM/Shutterstock.com

The Effects of a Technological Change on the Production Possibilities Curve

In Exhibit 3, we see that a technological advance does not have to impact all sectors of the economy equally: There is a technological advance in food production but not in housing production. The technological advance in agriculture causes the production possibilities curve to extend out farther on the horizontal axis, which measures food production. We can move to any point on the new production possibilities curve. For example, the move from point A on the original curve to point B on the new curve would result in 150 more units of food (500 – 350) and the same amount of housing—200 units. Or, we could move from point A to point C, which would allow us to produce more units of both food and housing. How do we produce more housing, when the technological advance occurred in agriculture? The answer is that the technological advance in agriculture allows us to produce more from a given quantity of resources. That is, it allows us to shift some resources out of agriculture into housing. This is actually an ongoing story in Canadian economic history. In colonial days, almost all of the Canadian population made a living in agriculture. Today, it is less than 3 percent.

From the analogue type to touch-screen devices, technological progress has had a dramatic impact on the cellphone industry. At first, cellphones had only one purpose—to allow a person to call someone else while on the move. Today, smartphones can send and receive emails, text message, store music and images, take and send pictures, and even provide television and the Internet.

HOW CAN WE SUMMARIZE THE PRODUCTION POSSIBILITIES CURVE?

The production possibilities curve shown in Exhibit 4 illustrates the choices faced by an economy that makes military goods and consumer goods. How are the economic concepts of scarcity, choice, opportunity costs, efficiency, and economic growth illustrated in this production possibilities curve framework? In Exhibit 4, we can show scarcity because resource combinations outside the initial production possibilities curve, like point D, are unattainable without economic growth. If the economy is operating efficiently, we are somewhere on that production possibilities curve, like point B or point C. However, if the economy is operating

| *section 2.2* Exhibit 3 | The Effects of Change on the Production Possibilities Curve |

A move from point A to point C will lead to more housing and food. A move from point A to point B will lead to more food and the same level of housing.

section 2.2
Exhibit 4

Production Possibilities Curve

Point A, inside the initial production possibilities curve, represents inefficiency. Points B and C, on the curve, are efficient points and represent two possible output combinations. Point D can be attained only with economic growth, illustrated by the outward shift in the production possibilities curve.

inefficiently, we are operating inside that production possibilities curve, like point A. We can also see in this graph that to get more military goods you must give up consumer goods—that is, there is an opportunity cost. Finally, we see that over time, with economic growth, the whole production possibilities curve can shift outward, making point D now attainable.

DEBATE

COSTS AND BENEFITS: SHOULD HIGHER EDUCATION BE FULLY SUBSIDIZED FOR THE CONSUMER/STUDENT?

One of the most pressing issues facing students lately is their ability to pay higher tuition fees for college or university courses. There are many reasons why higher education is good for individuals and for society at large, so many students and politicians (because students vote!) are attempting to make education more accessible without raising tuition fees. In fact, many are advocating for the elimination of tuition fees completely.

While there are some compelling reasons to eliminate tuition costs, there are also some very solid reasons not to eliminate them. Which side of the debate are you on? Sometimes you should be careful what you wish for—it might come true!

For:

As the cost of education has increased significantly over the last decades, students are having to shoulder a higher percentage of the costs of their education, thus making a higher education less accessible for many. And many of those attending college or university face acquiring a significant amount of debt to pay for their tuition fees. The elimination of these fees altogether would provide access to individuals who want a higher education without the acquisition of a heavy debt load. This is especially true for those who come from families that have

lower income levels. Paying for tuition is generally the largest barrier to attaining a higher education.

Some countries already pick up the full cost of higher education because they recognize that the benefits of educating individuals are more than offset by the benefits that society gains from their education. In all societies, higher levels of education lead to more productivity for the nation and higher rates of income for successful graduates. Also, people with more education usually draw less from social services and social safety nets provided by the state, so not only are the costs of providing those services lower, but so too are the administrative costs to the system as a whole.

Against:

As you have already realized from reading this textbook, there is no "free lunch." For everything there is a cost—perhaps not to you directly, but somewhere there is a cost that must be paid. In the case of higher education, it is recognized that the major benefit of education accrues to the individual gaining it; therefore, the individual should be paying the lion's share of the cost of that education. However, we've seen that there are social benefits to achieving an education. As a result, society has agreed to pay the greater share, leaving the individual student to pay a lesser, but still significant, share.

Some students argue that they will pay for their education through the taxes they will pay throughout life. This is true, but if one's taxes were to reflect the amount of cost for the education one gets, should those that don't have an education get a tax rebate for the portion of their taxes that go to general education for the population? And what about those who have many kids—should their taxes be increased to pay for their kids' education?

What about students who receive an education in Canada, and then move to another country far away? Canada has paid for their education but receive very little or no future benefit from that investment. The same argument can be made for immigrants who have recently arrived and therefore have not paid into the system but gain immediate benefits, such as free tuition. Should that be the case, or should individuals have to reside in Canada for a set time period before becoming eligible for a free college or university education?

A common belief is that when there is no personal payment for a good or service, individuals value that good or service less than if they had paid for it. With free tuition, for example, there would be less incentive for students to do well in courses or even to finish their education.

As a professor, I would have no qualms about subsidizing students who are serious about gaining an education, but if a student failed my course *for lack of effort or not showing up*, I think that student should pay the international student rate (which is 100 percent of the cost of the course) to take it again. If the student legitimately failed the course because they had difficulty in understanding the content but attended the majority of classes and did all the assignments/tests, then I would have no problem subsidizing them to take the course again.

1. There are multiple compelling arguments for governments to fully subsidize education. Can you provide other reasons not mentioned here that might convince a politician to support tuition-free education?

2. Since an education is a major benefit for the individual gaining it, shouldn't the individual pay at least a majority of the cost of that education?

3. How would you structure a tuition-free program for students that is fair and equitable to both students and the taxpayer? Do you agree with the professor's suggestion of a middle ground? What improvements would you make?

SECTION CHECK

- Economic growth is represented by an outward shift of the production possibilities curve, indicating an increase in the possibility of producing more of all goods. Despite this, scarcity inevitably remains a fact of life.
- The production possibilities model is an effective way of illustrating the economic concepts of scarcity, choice, opportunity costs, efficiency, and economic growth.

section

2.3

Market Prices Coordinate Economic Activity

- What is a market?
- What are the roles of buyers and sellers in a market?
- How does a market system allocate scarce resources?
- What is a market failure?

WHAT IS A MARKET?

Although we usually think of a market as a place where some sort of exchange occurs, a market is not really a place at all. A **market** is the process of buyers and sellers exchanging goods and services. This means that supermarkets, the Toronto Stock Exchange, drugstores, roadside stands, garage sales, Internet stores, and restaurants are all markets.

market
the process of buyers and sellers exchanging goods and services

Every market is different. That is, the conditions under which the exchange between buyers and sellers takes place can vary. These differences make it difficult to precisely define a market. After all, an incredible variety of exchange arrangements exists in the real world—organized securities markets, wholesale auction markets, foreign exchange markets, real estate markets, labour markets, and so forth.

Goods being priced and traded in various ways at various locations by various kinds of buyers and sellers further compound the problem of defining a market. For some goods, such as housing, markets are numerous but limited to a geographic area. Homes in Niagara Falls, Ontario, for example (about 130 kilometres from downtown Toronto), do not compete directly with homes in Toronto. Why? Because people who work in Toronto will generally look for homes within commuting distance. Even within cities, there are separate markets for homes, differentiated by amenities such as bigger houses, newer houses, larger lots, and better schools.

In a similar manner, markets are numerous but geographically limited for a good such as cement. Because transportation costs are so high relative to the selling price, the good is not shipped any substantial distance and buyers are usually in contact only with local producers. Price and output are thus determined in a number of small markets. In other markets, like those for gold or automobiles, markets are global. The important point is not what a market looks like, but what it does—it facilitates trade.

WHAT ARE THE ROLES OF BUYERS AND SELLERS IN A MARKET?

The roles of buyers and sellers in markets are important. The buyers, as a group, determine the demand-side of the market. Buyers include the consumers who purchase the goods and services and the firms that buy inputs—labour, capital, and raw materials. Sellers, as a group, determine the supply side of the market. Sellers include the firms that produce and sell goods and services, and the resource owners who sell their inputs to firms—workers who "sell" their labour and resource owners who sell raw materials and capital. It is the interaction of buyers and sellers that determines market prices and output—through the forces of supply and demand.

In Chapter 3, we focus on how supply and demand work in a competitive market—one in which there are a number of buyers and sellers. Because most markets contain a large degree of competitiveness, the lessons of supply and demand can be applied to many different types of problems.

The supply and demand model is particularly useful in markets like agriculture, finance, labour, construction, services, wholesale, and retail. In short, a model is only as good as it explains and predicts. The model of supply and demand is very good at predicting changes in prices and quantities in many markets, large and small.

HOW DOES A MARKET SYSTEM ALLOCATE SCARCE RESOURCES?

efficiency

getting the most from society's scarce resources

In a world of scarcity, competition is inescapable, and one method of allocating resources among competing uses is the market system. The market system provides a way for millions of producers and consumers to allocate scarce resources. For the most part, markets are efficient. To an economist, **efficiency** is achieved when the economy gets the most out of its scarce resources. In short, efficiency makes the economic pie as large as possible.

Buyers and sellers indicate their wants through their action and inaction in the marketplace, and it is this collective "voice" that determines how resources are allocated. But how is this information communicated? Market prices serve as the language of the market system. By understanding what these market prices mean, you can get a better understanding of the vital function that the market system performs.

Markets may not always conform to your desired tastes and preferences. You may think that markets produce too many fast foods, face-lifts, and Justin Bieber albums. Some markets are illegal—the market for cocaine, the market for stolen body parts, and the market for child pornography. Markets do not come with a moral compass; they simply provide what buyers are willing and able to pay for and what sellers are willing and able to produce.

Market Prices Provide Important Information

Market prices communicate important information to both buyers and sellers. These prices communicate information about the relative availability of products to buyers, and they provide sellers with critical information about the relative value that consumers place on those products. In effect, market prices provide a way for both buyers and sellers to communicate about the relative value of resources. This communication results in a shifting of resources from those uses that are less valued to those that are more valued. We will see how this works beginning in Chapter 3.

The basis of a market economy is the voluntary exchange and the price system that guide people's choices and produce solutions to the questions of what goods to produce and how to produce and distribute them. Take something as simple as the production of a pencil. Where did the wood come from? Perhaps British Columbia or Quebec. The graphite may have come from the mines in northern Ontario, and the rubber may be from Malaysia. The paint, the glue, the metal piece that holds the eraser—who knows? The point is that market forces coordinated this activity among literally thousands of people, some of whom live in different countries and speak different languages. The market system brought these people together to make a pencil that sells for $1.50 for 20 of them. It all happened because the market system provided the incentive for people to pursue activities that benefit others. This same process produces millions of goods and services around the world, from automobiles and computers to pencils and paper clips. The same is true of the iPod and iPhone.

In countries that do not rely on the market system, there is no clear communication between buyers and sellers. In the former Soviet Union, where quality was virtually nonexistent, there were shortages of quality goods and surpluses of low-quality goods. For example, there were thousands of tractors without spare parts and millions of pairs of shoes that were left on shelves because the sizes did not match those of the population.

Property Rights and the Legal System

In a market economy, private individuals and firms own most of the resources. For example, when consumers buy houses, cars, or pizzas, they have purchased the right to use these goods in ways they, not someone else, see fit. These rights are called *property rights*. Property rights are the rules of our economic game. If well defined, property rights give individuals the incentive to maintain, improve, and conserve their property to preserve or increase its value.

The market system can work only if the government enforces the rules. That is, one of the key functions of the government is to provide a legal framework that protects and enforces property rights and contracts. Markets, like baseball games, need umpires. It is the government that plays this role when it defines and protects the rights of people and their property through the legal system and police protection. That is, by providing rules and regulations, government can make markets work more efficiently. Private enforce-

Apple employees have learned how to combine almost 500 generic parts to make something of much greater value. The whole is greater than the sum of the parts. There is not one person at Apple or in the world who could put together an iPhone all alone. It takes many people, making many parts, living all over the world.

Tanjala Gica/Shutterstock.com

ment is possible, but as economic life becomes more complex, political institutions have become the major instrument for defining and enforcing property rights.

The government defines and protects property rights through the legal system and public policy. The legal system ensures the rights of private ownership, the enforcement of contracts, and the legal status for businesses. The legal system serves as the referee, imposing penalties on violators of our legal rules. Property rights also include intellectual property—the property rights that an owner receives through patents, copyrights, and trademarks. These rights give the owner long-term protection that encourages individuals to write books, music, and software programs and to invent new products. In short, well-defined property rights encourage investment, innovation, exchange, conservation, and economic growth.

WHAT IS A MARKET FAILURE?

market failure
when the economy fails to allocate resources efficiently on its own

The market mechanism is a simple but effective and efficient general means of allocating resources among alternative uses. When the economy fails to allocate resources efficiently on its own, however, it is known as **market failure**. For example, a steel mill might put soot and other forms of "crud" into the air as a by-product of making steel. When it does this, it imposes costs on others not connected with using or producing steel from the steel mill. The soot may require homeowners to paint their homes more often, entailing a cost. And studies show that respiratory diseases are greater in areas with more severe air pollution, imposing costs and often shortening life itself. In addition, the steel mill might discharge chemicals into a stream, thus killing wildlife and spoiling recreational activities for the local population. In this case, the steel factory emits too much pollution but does not bear the cost of its polluting actions. In other words, by transferring the pollution costs onto society, the firm has lowered its costs of production and is now producing more than the ideal output. This is inefficient because it is an overallocation of resources.

Markets can also produce too little of a good—research, for example. The government might decide to subsidize promising scientific research that may benefit many people, such as cancer research.

Whether the market economy has produced too little (underallocation) or too much (overallocation), the government can improve society's well-being by intervening.

In addition, we cannot depend on the market economy to always communicate accurately. Some firms may have market power to distort prices in their favour. For example, the only regional cement company in the area has the ability to charge a higher price and provide a lower-quality product than if the company was in a highly competitive market. In this case, the lack of competition can lead to higher prices and reduced product quality. And without adequate information, unscrupulous producers may be able to misrepresent their products to the disadvantage of unwary consumers.

The Market Distribution of Income

Sometimes a painful trade-off exists between how much an economy can produce efficiently and how that output is distributed—the degree of equality. There is no guarantee that the market economy will provide everyone with adequate amounts of food, shelter, and transportation. That is, not only does the market determine what goods are going to be produced and in what quantities, but it also determines the distribution of output among members of society.

As with other aspects of government intervention, the degree-of-equity argument can generate some sharp disagreements. What is "fair" for one person may seem highly "unfair" to someone else. Although one person may find it terribly unfair for some individuals to earn many times the amount earned by other individuals who work equally hard, another person may find it highly unfair to ask one group, the relatively rich, to pay a much higher proportion of their income in taxes than another group.

Government policymakers make decisions recognizing that there is a trade-off between efficiency (creating a bigger pie) and equality (dividing that pie). Some policies, like a progressive income tax system, Employment Insurance, and welfare programs, are aimed at redistributing the pie. While these programs aim to achieve a more equal distribution of income, they also may distort incentives for others to work hard and produce more goods and services. But that does not mean the poor should be ignored because helping them distorts incentives. We just need to recognize that there are trade-offs.

Government Does Not Always Have the Solution

Just because the government could improve the distribution of income situation does not mean it will. After all, the political process has its own set of problems, such as special interests, short-sightedness, and imperfect information. For example, government may reduce competition through tariffs and quotas, or it may impose inefficient regulations that restrict entry. Consequently, government, like markets, has shortcomings and imperfections; the cost of government policies can exceed the benefits. Citizens failing to understand the difference between actual and ideal government performance will find it difficult to decide the appropriate role for government.

SECTION CHECK

- Markets consist of buyers and sellers exchanging goods and services with one another.
- Buyers determine the demand-side of the market and sellers determine the supply-side of the market.
- Through voluntary exchange and the price system, the market system provides a way for producers and consumers to allocate scarce resources.
- A market failure occurs when an economy fails to allocate resources efficiently on its own.

section

2.4

The Circular Flow Model

- What are product markets?
- What are factor markets?
- What is the goods and services flow?
- What is the income flow?
- What is the circular flow model?

How do we explain how millions of people in an economy interact when it comes to buying, selling, producing, working, hiring, and so on? A continuous flow of goods and services is bought and sold between the producers of goods and services (which we call *firms*) and the buyers of goods and services (which we call *households*). A continuous flow of income also moves from firms to households, as firms buy inputs to produce the goods and services they sell. In our simple economy, these exchanges take place in product markets and factor markets.

WHAT ARE PRODUCT MARKETS?

product markets
the markets for consumer goods and services

Product markets are the markets for consumer goods and services. In the product market, households are buyers and firms are sellers. Households buy the goods and services that firms produce and sell.

WHAT ARE FACTOR MARKETS?

factor (input) markets
the market in which households sell the use of their inputs (capital, land, labour, and entrepreneurship) to firms

Factor, or **input**, **markets** are the markets where households sell the use of their inputs (capital, land, labour, and entrepreneurship) to firms. In the factor markets, households are the sellers and the firms are the buyers.

WHAT IS THE GOODS AND SERVICES FLOW?

goods and services flow
the continuous flow of inputs and outputs in an economy

The **goods and services flow** represents the continuous flow of inputs and outputs in an economy. Households make inputs available to producers through the factor markets. These inputs are then turned into outputs which are then bought by households.

WHAT IS THE INCOME FLOW?

income flow
the continuous flow of income and expenditure in an economy

The **income flow** represents the continuous flow of income and expenditure in an economy. Households receive money payments from firms as compensation for the labour, land, capital, and entrepreneurship needed to produce goods and services. These payments take the form of wages (salaries), rent, interest payments, and profits, respectively. The payments from households to firms are for the purchase of goods and services.

WHAT IS THE CIRCULAR FLOW MODEL?

circular flow model of income and output
an illustration of the continuous flow of goods, services, inputs, and payments between firms and households

The simple **circular flow model of income and output** is an illustration of the continuous flow of goods, services, inputs, and payments between firms and households. A simple depiction of the model is presented in Exhibit 1. In the top half of the exhibit, product markets, households purchase goods and services that firms have produced. In the lower half of the exhibit, factor (or input) markets, households sell the inputs that firms use to produce goods and services. The income flow (going clockwise in Exhibit 1) describes how households receive income—money income—and use that income to buy goods and services—consumption spending. The goods and services flow (going counterclockwise in Exhibit 1) details how households supply inputs—capital, land, labour, and entrepreneurship—to firms that use them in the production of outputs—goods and services.

Let's take a simple example to see how the circular flow model works. Suppose a teacher's supply of labour generates personal income in the form of wages (the factor market), which she can use to buy automobiles, vacations, food, and other goods (the product market). Suppose she buys an automobile (product market); the automobile dealer now has revenue to pay for his inputs (factor market)—wages to workers, purchase of new cars to replenish his inventory, rent for his building, and so on. So we see that in the simple circular flow model, income flows from firms to households (factor markets) and spending flows from households to firms (product markets). The simple circular flow model shows how households and firms interact in product markets and in factor markets and how product markets and factor markets are interrelated.

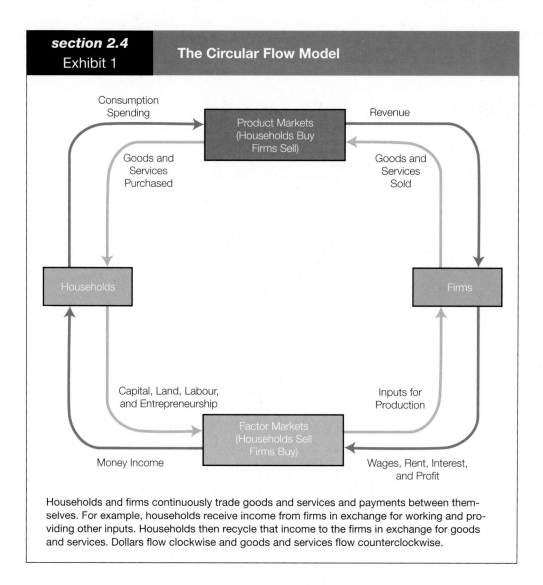

section 2.4
Exhibit 1

The Circular Flow Model

Consumption Spending

Product Markets (Households Buy Firms Sell)

Revenue

Goods and Services Purchased

Goods and Services Sold

Households

Firms

Capital, Land, Labour, and Entrepreneurship

Inputs for Production

Factor Markets (Households Sell Firms Buy)

Money Income

Wages, Rent, Interest, and Profit

Households and firms continuously trade goods and services and payments between themselves. For example, households receive income from firms in exchange for working and providing other inputs. Households then recycle that income to the firms in exchange for goods and services. Dollars flow clockwise and goods and services flow counterclockwise.

The circular flow model can become much more complex but here it is presented merely to introduce the major markets and players in the economy. For example, the model can be extended to show the role of government, the financial sector, and foreign markets. Our simple model also does not show how firms and households send some of their income to the government for taxes or how households save some of their income for savings. Households are not the only buyers in the economy—firms, government, and foreigners buy some of the goods and services.

SECTION CHECK

- In the product market, households are buyers and firms are sellers.
- In the factor markets, households are the sellers and firms are the buyers.
- The goods and services flow represents the continuous flow of inputs and outputs in an economy.
- The income flow represents the continuous flow of income and expenditure in an economy.
- The circular flow model illustrates the flow of goods, services, and payments among firms and households.

For Your Review

Section 2.1

1. Assume that the production possibilities for Alberta are the following combinations of kegs of beer and sides of beef.

Beer (kegs)	Beef (sides)
55	0
54	1
52	2
49	3
45	4
40	5
34	6
27	7
19	8
10	9
0	10

   a. Construct the production possibilities frontier for beer and beef on the grid below.

b. Given the information above, what is the opportunity cost of the 55th keg of beer in Alberta? Of the 6th side of beef? Of the 9th side of beef?

c. Suppose Alberta is currently producing 4 sides of beef and 45 kegs of beer. What is the opportunity cost of 5 more sides of beef in Alberta?

d. Would the combination of 40 kegs of beer and 4 sides of beef be efficient? Why or why not?

e. Is the combination of 9 kegs of beer and 10 sides of beef possible for Alberta? Why or why not?

Blueprint Problem

Assume that an economy is characterized by the following production possibilities.

Bread (loaves)	Computers (units)
75	0
70	1
60	2
45	3
25	4
0	5

a. Construct the production possibilities curve (PPC) for this economy.

b. Does this economy's production possibilities curve exhibit the law of increasing opportunity cost? Provide sufficient proof.

c. Suppose that a new technique for baking loaves of bread is invented and the production of bread doubles, while computer production remains unchanged. Illustrate this outcome using the PPC model.

Blueprint Solution

a.

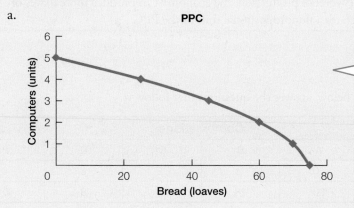

When plotting the PPC, place each product on a separate axis. Since both bread and computers are dependent variables—dependent on resources—they can be plotted on either axis.

b.

Bread (loaves)		Computers (units)	
Total Production	Marginal Production	Total Production	Marginal Production
75		0	
70	5 loaves of bread	1	1st computer
60	10 loaves of bread	2	2nd computer
45	15 loaves of bread	3	3rd computer
25	20 loaves of bread	4	4th computer
0	25 loaves of bread	5	5th computer

By calculating the marginal changes in both production schedules, we are able to answer this question. Notice that the opportunity cost of computer production—the amount of bread production that is forgone as computer production is increased—is increasing. Therefore, the law of increasing opportunity cost is proven.

c.

Notice that the number of computers this economy can produce remains unchanged. However, at every level of production, the economy can produce more loaves of bread. This generates a nonproportional shift of the PPC.

2. Using the table below, answer the questions that follow it.

Combinations					
	A	B	C	D	E
Pizza	0	1	2	3	4
Robots	20	18	14	8	0

a. What are the assumptions for a given production possibilities curve?

b. What is the opportunity cost of one pizza when moving from point B to point C? When moving from point D to point E?

c. Do these combinations demonstrate constant or increasing opportunity costs?

3. Imagine that you are the sole inhabitant of a small island that produces only two goods: cattle and wheat. About a quarter of the land is not fertile enough for growing wheat, so cattle graze on it. What would happen if you tried to produce more and more wheat, extending your planting even to the less fertile soil?

Sections 2.1 and 2.2

4. How would the following events be shown using a production possibilities curve for shelter and food?

   a. The economy is experiencing double-digit unemployment.

   b. Economic growth is increasing at over 5 percent per year.

   c. Society decides it wants less shelter and more food.

   d. Society decides it wants more shelter and less food.

5. Suppose the following production possibility table represents the province of Quebec.

	A	B	C	D	E	F
Cheese	45	42	36	27	15	0
Tractors	0	10	20	30	40	50

   a. Construct the production possibilities frontier (PPF) for cheese and tractors.

   b. Does this production possibilities frontier illustrate the law of increasing opportunity cost? Explain.

   c. Suppose a technological advance increases the efficiency of cheese production, leaving tractor production unaffected. What impact would this have on the PPF for the province of Quebec?

   d. Suppose tractors represent *capital goods* and cheese represents *consumption goods*. If the province of Quebec altered its production from combination B to combination E, what impact could this have on the future economic growth of the province?

6. Given the following production possibilities curve, answer the questions that follow it.

   a. Does this production possibilities curve show increasing opportunity costs? Explain.

   b. What is the opportunity cost of moving from point I to point D? Explain.

   c. What is the opportunity cost of moving from point C to point B?

   d. Which of points A–E is the most efficient? Explain.

e. Which of the identified production alternatives is currently impossible for this economy to achieve? What must happen in order for this production alternative to become attainable?

f. Which of the identified production alternatives is currently attainable but inefficient? What must happen in order for this production alternative to become efficient?

Section 2.2

7. Economy A produces more capital goods and fewer consumer goods than Economy B. Which economy will grow more rapidly? Draw two production possibilities curves, one for Economy A and one for Economy B. Demonstrate graphically how one economy can grow more rapidly than the other.

8. A politician running for prime minister of Canada promises to build new schools and new prisons if elected, without sacrificing any other goods and services. Using the production possibilities curve between schools and prisons, explain under what conditions the politician would be able to keep her promise.

9. Why one nation experiences economic growth and another does not is a question that has intrigued economists since Adam Smith wrote *An Inquiry into the Nature and Causes of the Wealth of Nations* in 1776. Explain why each of the following would limit economic growth.

a. The politically connected elite secure a large share of a country's output and put the proceeds into foreign banks.

b. The national philosophy is "Live for the moment and forget about tomorrow."

c. The government closes all of the schools so more people will be available for work.

d. The country fears military invasion and spends half of its income on military goods.

10. How does education add to a nation's capital stock?

Section 2.3

11. Evaluate the validity of the following statement: "Canadians spend millions of dollars every year shopping online, buying everything from investment products to children's toys. However, due to the virtual nature of these transactions (buyers and sellers do not actually meet in person), these exchanges do not occur in what economists would consider markets."

12. What role do buyers and sellers have in a market?

13. Prices communicate information about the relative value of resources. Which of the following would cause the relative value and, hence, the price, of potatoes to rise?

a. A fungus infestation wipes out half of the Prince Edward Island potato crop.

b. The price of potato chips rises.

c. Scientists find that eating potato chips makes you better-looking.

d. The prices of wheat, rice, and other potato substitutes fall dramatically.

14. People communicate with each other in the market through the effect their decisions to buy or sell have on prices. Indicate how each of the following would affect prices by putting a check mark in the appropriate space.

a. People who see an energetic and lovable Jack Russell terrier in a popular TV series want Jack Russell terriers as pets. The price of Jack Russell terriers ____ rises ____ falls.

b. Retirees flock to Tampa, Florida, to live. The price of housing in Tampa ___ rises ___ falls.

c. Weather-related crop failures in Colombia and Costa Rica reduce coffee supplies. The price of coffee ___ rises ___ falls.

d. Wheat fields in Alberta are replaced with oil rigs. The price of wheat ___ rises ___ falls.

e. More and more students graduate from Canadian medical schools. The income of Canadian doctors ___ rises ___ falls.

15. Is the market for laptop computers local, national, or global?

Section 2.4

16. Identify where the appropriate entries go in the circular flow diagram below.

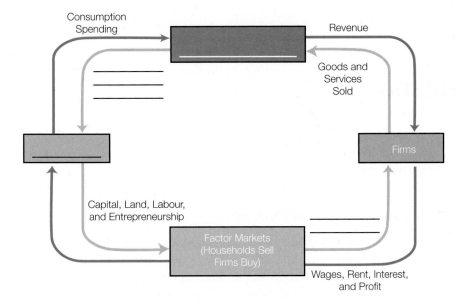

17. Identify whether each of the following transactions takes place in the factor market or the product market.

a. Billy buys a sofa from Home Time Furniture for his new home.

b. Home Time Furniture pays its manager her weekly salary.

c. The manager buys dinner at Billy's Café.

d. After he pays all of his employees their wages and pays his other bills, the owner of Billy's Café takes his profit.

18. Consider the following scenario.

Claire works as a rental agent for Hanson Car Rentals, earning $800 a week. She has set up an automatic $40 withdrawal each week to pay for her gym membership at Fit for Life. Fit for Life pays Markus $70 to teach a weekly kickbox-cardio class. Next week, Markus plans to spend $200 on a rental car from Hanson to visit his aunt in Winnipeg.

a. Which of the events in this scenario occur in the factor market?

b. Which of the events in this scenario occur in the product market?

section

3.1

Demand

- What is the law of demand?
- What is an individual demand schedule and curve?
- What is a market demand curve?

WHAT IS THE LAW OF DEMAND?

demand

the quantity of a good or service that consumers are both willing and able to purchase over a period of time at various prices

Economists use the term **demand** to describe the quantity of a good or service that consumers are both willing and able to purchase over a given period of time at various prices. Simply desiring something is not enough for consumer behaviour to be considered demand. For example, although I may desire my own private island in the Bahamas, since I do not possess the financial ability to buy one, my quantity demanded is zero. Similarly, although I may have the income to buy a new expensive Armani suit, since I have no desire to do so, again my quantity demanded is zero.

law of demand

the quantity of a good or service demanded varies inversely (negatively) with its price, ceteris paribus

Sometimes, observed behaviour is so pervasive it is considered to be a law—like the law of demand. According to the **law of demand**, the quantity of a good or service demanded varies inversely (negatively) with its price, *ceteris paribus*. More directly, the law of demand says that, other things being equal, when the price (P) of a good or service falls, the quantity demanded (Q_D) increases, and conversely, if the price of a good or service rises, the quantity demanded decreases.

$$P\uparrow \Rightarrow Q_D\downarrow \text{ or } P\downarrow \Rightarrow Q_D\uparrow$$

The Negative Relationship between Price and Quantity Demanded

The law of demand describes a negative (inverse) relationship between price and quantity demanded. When price goes up, the quantity demanded goes down, and vice versa. But why is this so? One reason for the negative relationship is what economists call *diminishing marginal utility*—the concept that in a given time period, an individual will receive less satisfaction from each successive unit of a good consumed. For example, a second ice cream cone will yield less satisfaction than the first, a third will yield less satisfaction than the second, and so on. It follows from diminishing marginal utility that if people derive decreasing amounts of satisfaction from successive units, consumers will buy additional units only if the price is reduced.

Other reasons for this inverse relationship are the substitution and income effects. According to the **substitution effect**, at higher prices, buyers increasingly substitute other goods for the good that now has a higher relative price. For example, if the price of orange juice increases, some consumers may substitute other juices for orange juice, such as apple or tomato juice, or perhaps water, milk, or coffee. According to the **income effect**, higher prices make the buyer feel poorer, causing a lowering of quantity demanded (since they cannot buy the same quantity of goods as they did when prices were lower). For example, when the price of pizza rises, this results in a decrease in the purchasing power of the consumer's income, which will usually lead to the consumer buying less pizza.

substitution effect
At higher prices, buyers increasingly substitute other goods for the good that now has a higher relative price.

income effect
At higher prices, buyers feel poorer, causing a lowering of quantity demanded.

WHAT IS AN INDIVIDUAL DEMAND SCHEDULE AND CURVE?

The **individual demand schedule** is a table that shows the relationship between the price of the good and the quantity demanded. For example, suppose Elizabeth enjoys eating apples. How many kilograms of apples would Elizabeth be willing and able to buy at various prices during the year? At a price of $3 a kilogram, Elizabeth buys 15 kilograms of apples over the course of a year. If the price is higher, at $4 per kilogram, she might buy only 10 kilograms; if it is lower, say $1 per kilogram, she might buy 25 kilograms of apples during the year. Elizabeth's demand for apples for the year is summarized in the demand schedule in Exhibit 1. Elizabeth might not be consciously aware of the amounts that she would purchase at prices other than the prevailing one, but that does not alter the fact that she has a schedule in the sense that she would have bought various other amounts had other prices prevailed. It must be emphasized that the schedule is a list of alternative possibilities. At any one time, only one of the prices will prevail, so a certain quantity will be purchased.

individual demand schedule
a table that shows the relationship between price and quantity demanded

An Individual Demand Curve

An **individual demand curve** is a graphical representation that shows the inverse relationship between price and quantity demanded. By plotting the different prices and corresponding quantities demanded in Elizabeth's demand schedule in Exhibit 1 and then connecting them, we can create an individual demand curve for Elizabeth (Exhibit 2). From the curve, we can see that when the price is higher, the quantity demanded is lower, and when the price is lower, the quantity demanded is higher. The demand curve shows how the quantity demanded of the good changes as its price varies.

individual demand curve
a graphical representation that shows the inverse relationship between price and quantity demanded

section 3.1 Exhibit 1	Elizabeth's Demand Schedule for Apples

Price (per kilogram)	Quantity Demanded (kilograms per year)
$5	5
4	10
3	15
2	20
1	25

WHAT IS A MARKET DEMAND CURVE?

Although we introduced this concept in terms of the individual, economists usually speak of the demand curve in terms of large groups of people—a whole nation, a community, or a trading area. As you know,

Elizabeth's Demand Curve for Apples

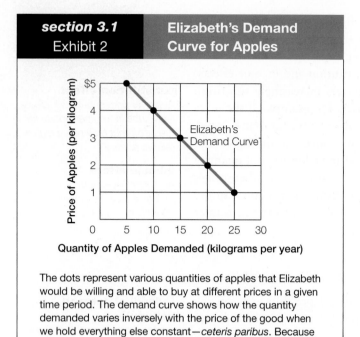

The dots represent various quantities of apples that Elizabeth would be willing and able to buy at different prices in a given time period. The demand curve shows how the quantity demanded varies inversely with the price of the good when we hold everything else constant—*ceteris paribus*. Because of this inverse relationship between price and quantity demanded, the demand curve is downward sloping.

market demand curve

the horizontal summation of individual demand curves

every single individual has his or her demand curve for every product. The horizontal summation of individual demand curves is called the **market demand curve**.

Suppose the consumer group comprises Homer, Marge, and the rest of their small community, Springfield, and that the product is still apples. The effect of price on the quantity of apples demanded by Marge, Homer, and the rest of Springfield is given in the demand schedule and demand curves shown in Exhibit 3. At $4 per kilogram, Homer would be willing and able to buy 20 kilograms of apples per year, Marge would be willing and able to buy 10 kilograms, and the rest of Springfield would be willing and able to buy 2970 kilograms. At $3 per kilogram, Homer would be willing and able to buy 25 kilograms of apples per year, Marge would be willing and able to buy 15 kilograms, and the rest of Springfield would be willing and able to buy 4960 kilograms. The market demand curve is simply the (horizontal) sum of the quantities Homer, Marge, and the rest of Springfield demand at each price. That is, at $4, the quantity demanded in the market would be 3000 kilograms of apples (20 + 10 + 2970 = 3000), and at $3, the quantity demanded in the market would be 5000 kilograms of apples (25 + 15 + 4960 = 5000).

In Exhibit 4, we offer a more complete set of prices and quantities from the market demand for apples during the year. Remember, the market demand curve shows the amounts that all the buyers in the market would be willing and able to buy at various prices. For example, if the price of apples is $2 per kilogram, consumers in the market would collectively be willing and able to buy 8000 kilograms per year. At $1 per kilogram, the amount demanded would be 12 000 kilograms per year.

The market demand curve is the negative (inverse) relationship between price and the total quantity demanded, while holding constant all other factors that affect how much consumers are able and willing to pay, *ceteris paribus*. For the most part, we are interested in how the market works, so we will primarily use the market demand curves.

Every Boxing Day, eager consumers line up at the break of dawn in front of retailers that are advertising deep discounts and two-for-one deals. Although they didn't want to buy the televisions, game consoles, clothing, and computers at the regular asking prices, many clearly want these goods at a lower price—the law of demand.

section 3.1
Exhibit 3

Creating a Market Demand Curve

a. Creating a Market Demand Schedule for Apples

Quantity Demanded (kilograms per year)

Price (per kilogram)	Homer	+	Marge	+	Rest of Springfield	=	Market Demand
$4	20	+	10	+	2970	=	3000
$3	25	+	15	+	4960	=	5000

b. Creating a Market Demand Curve for Apples

section 3.1
Exhibit 4

A Market Demand Curve

a. Market Demand Schedule for Apples

Price (per kilogram)	Total Quantity Demanded (kilograms per year)
$5	1000
4	3000
3	5000
2	8000
1	12 000

b. Market Demand Curve for Apples

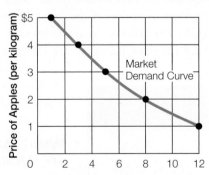

The market demand curve shows the amounts that all buyers in the market would be willing to buy at various prices. If the price of apples is $2 per kilogram, consumers in the market would collectively be willing to buy 8000 kilograms per year. At $1 per kilogram, the amount demanded would be 12 000 kilograms per year.

section

3.2

Shifts in the Demand Curve

- What is the difference between a change in demand and a change in quantity demanded?
- What are the determinants of demand?
- Can we review the distinction between changes in demand and changes in quantity demanded?

WHAT IS THE DIFFERENCE BETWEEN A CHANGE IN DEMAND AND A CHANGE IN QUANTITY DEMANDED?

change in quantity demanded

a change in a good's price leads to a change in quantity demanded, a move along a given demand curve

change in demand

a change in a determinant of demand leads to a change in demand, a shift of the entire demand curve

Understanding the relationship between price and quantity demanded is so important that economists make a clear distinction between it and the various other factors that can influence consumer behaviour. A change in a good's price is said to lead to a **change in quantity demanded**. That is, it "moves you along" a given demand curve. The demand curve is drawn under the assumption that all other things are held constant, except the price of the good. However, economists know that price is not the only thing that affects the quantity of a good that people buy. The other factors that influence the demand curve are called *determinants of demand* and a change in these other factors *shifts the entire demand curve*. These determinants of demand are called *demand shifters* and they lead to a **change in demand**.

WHAT ARE THE DETERMINANTS OF DEMAND?

An increase in demand shifts the demand curve to the right; a decrease in demand shifts the demand curve to the left, as seen in Exhibit 1. Changes in demand such as these are the result of demand shifters. Some of the possible demand shifters are the prices of related goods, income, number of buyers, tastes, and expectations. We will now look more closely at each of these variables.

The Prices of Related Goods

In deciding how much of a good or service to buy, consumers are influenced by the price of that good or

section 3.2
Exhibit 1

Demand Shifts

An increase in demand shifts the demand curve to the right. A decrease in demand shifts the demand curve to the left.

service, a relationship summarized in the law of demand. However, consumers are also influenced by the prices of *related* goods and services—substitutes and complements.

Substitutes   Substitutes are generally goods for which one could be used in place of the other. To many, substitutes would include butter and margarine, domestic and foreign cars, movie tickets and on-demand TV programs, jackets and sweaters, Petro Canada and Shell gasoline, and Nikes and Adidas.

Suppose you go into a store to buy a couple of six packs of Coca-Cola and you see that Pepsi is on sale for half its usual price. Is it possible that you might decide to buy Pepsi instead of Coca-Cola? Economists argue that this is the case, and empirical tests have confirmed that people are responsive to both the price of the good in question and the prices of related goods. In this example, Pepsi and Coca-Cola are said to be substitutes. Two goods are **substitutes** if an increase (a decrease) in the price of one good causes an increase (a decrease) in the demand for another good, a direct (or positive) relationship. In Exhibit 2(a), we see that as the price of Coca-Cola increased—a movement up along your demand curve for it—you increased your demand for Pepsi, resulting in a shift in the demand for Pepsi (Exhibit 2[b]).

substitute
An increase (a decrease) in the price of one good causes an increase (a decrease) in the demand for another good.

Complements   Complements are goods that "go together," often consumed and used simultaneously, such as skis and bindings, peanut butter and jam, hot dogs and buns, digital music players and downloadable music, and printers and ink cartridges. If an increase (a decrease) in the price of one good causes a decrease (an increase) in the demand of another good (an inverse or negative relationship), the two goods are called **complements**. For example, in Exhibit 3(a), we see that as the price of computers increases, the quantity demanded of computers falls (a movement in demand). And with fewer computers being purchased, we would expect people to decrease their demand (a leftward shift) for printers (Exhibit 3[b]).

complement
An increase (a decrease) in the price of one good causes a decrease (an increase) in the demand of another good.

Income

Economists have observed that generally the consumption of goods and services is positively related to the income available to consumers. Empirical studies support the notion that as individuals receive more income, they tend to increase their purchases

section 3.2
Exhibit 2

Substitute Goods

a. Market for Coca-Cola   b. Market for Pepsi

section 3.2
Exhibit 3

Complementary Goods

a. Market for Computers

b. Market for Printers

of most goods and services. Other things held equal, rising income usually leads to an increase in the demand for goods (a rightward shift of the demand curve), and decreasing income usually leads to a decrease in the demand for goods (a leftward shift of the demand curve).

Normal and Inferior Goods

If when income increases, the demand for a good increases and decreases when income decreases, the good is called a **normal good**. Most goods are normal goods. Consumers will typically buy more cellphones, clothes, pizzas, and trips to the movies as their incomes rise. However, if when income increases, the demand for a good decreases and increases when income decreases, the good is called an **inferior good**. For example, for most people inferior goods might include inexpensive cuts of meat, used cars, gently used clothing, and macaroni and cheese. The term *inferior* in this sense does not refer to the quality of the good in question but shows that when income changes, demand changes in the opposite direction (inversely).

Consider how an increase in income can affect the market for automobiles and the market for public transit. Automobiles are generally considered a normal good, so a rise in income will increase the demand for automobiles (Exhibit 4[a]). However, the demand for public transit may fall, as higher incomes allow consumers to buy automobiles. The demand for public transit would then be an inferior good (Exhibit 4[b]).

normal good

If income increases, the demand for a good increases; if income decreases, the demand for a good decreases.

inferior good

If income increases, the demand for a good decreases; if income decreases, the demand for a good increases.

section 3.2
Exhibit 4

Normal and Inferior Goods

a. Normal Goods

b. Inferior Goods

For example, if people's incomes rise and they increase their demand for movie tickets, we say that movie tickets are a normal good. But if people's incomes fall and they increase their demand for bus rides, we say bus rides are an inferior good. Whether goods are normal or inferior, the point here is that income influences demand—usually positively, but sometimes negatively.

Number of Buyers

The demand for a good or service will vary with the size of the potential consumer population. The demand for wheat, for example, rises as population increases because the added population wants to consume wheat products, like bread or cereal. Marketing experts, who closely follow the patterns of consumer behaviour with regard to a particular good or service, are usually vitally concerned with the "demographics" of the product—the vital statistics of the potential consumer population, including size, income, and age characteristics. For example, market researchers for baby-food companies keep a close watch on the birth rate.

Tastes

The demand for a good or service may increase or decrease suddenly with changes in fashions or fads. Taste changes may be triggered by advertising or promotion, by a news story, by the behaviour of some popular public figure, and so on. Taste changes are particularly noticeable in apparel. Skirt lengths, coat lapels, shoe styles, and tie widths change frequently.

Changes in preferences naturally lead to shifts in demand. Much of the predictive power of economic theory, however, stems from the assumption that tastes are relatively stable, at least over a substantial period of time. Tastes *do* change, though. A person may grow tired of one type of recreation or food and try another type. Changes in occupation, number of dependants, state of health, and age also tend to alter preferences. The birth of a baby may cause a family to spend less on recreation and more on food and clothing. Illness increases the demand for medicine and lessens purchases of other goods. A cold winter increases the demand for natural gas. Changes in customs and traditions also affect preferences, and the development of new products draws consumer preferences away from other goods. Digital music files have replaced compact discs, just as flat-screen TVs have replaced traditional tube TVs. A change in information can also impact consumers' demand. For example, an outbreak of *Escherichia coli* or new information about a defective and/or dangerous product, such as a baby crib, can reduce demand.

Expectations

Sometimes the demand for a good or service in a given period will increase or decrease because consumers expect the good to change in price or availability at some future date. If people expect the future price to be higher, they will purchase more of the good now before the price increase—an increase in the demand today. If people expect the future price to be lower, they will purchase less of the good now and wait for the price decrease—a decrease in the demand today. For example, if you expect the price of computers to fall soon, you may be less willing to buy one today. Or you might buy next year's Halloween decorations on November 1 during a post-Halloween sale. That is, expectations of higher prices in the future could increase your demand now.

Body piercing and tattoos have risen in popularity in recent years. As the preference for these types of personal expression increases, the demand for these services is shifted to the right. According to the Pew Research Center, 32 percent of 18- to 29-year-olds acknowledged having at least one tattoo.

Brenda Carson/Shutterstock.com

A change in consumers' expectations about their future incomes can also shift the demand curve. For example, if you expect to earn additional income next month, you may be more willing to dip into your current savings to buy something this month. If you expect your income to fall in the future, you may choose to save more today and reduce your demand for some goods.

CAN WE REVIEW THE DISTINCTION BETWEEN CHANGES IN DEMAND AND CHANGES IN QUANTITY DEMANDED?

Economists put particular emphasis on the impact on consumer behaviour of a change in the price of a good. We are interested in distinguishing between consumer behaviour related to the price of a good itself (movement *along* a demand curve) from behaviour related to other factors changing (shifts of the demand curve).

As indicated earlier, if the price of a good changes, we say that this leads to a *"change in quantity demanded."* In Exhibit 5, the movement from A to B is called an *increase in quantity demanded,* and the movement from B to A is called a *decrease in quantity demanded.* Economists use the phrase "increase in quantity demanded" or "decrease in quantity demanded" to describe movements along a given demand curve. If one of the other factors (determinants) influencing consumer behaviour changes, we say there is a *change in demand.* In Exhibit 5, the change from A to C is called an *increase in demand,* and the change from C to A is called a *decrease in demand.* The phrase "increase in demand" or "decrease in demand" is reserved for a shift in the whole curve. So if an individual buys more CDs because the price fell, we say there was an increase in quantity demanded. However, if she buys more CDs even at the current price, say $10, we say there is an increase in demand. The effects of some of the other determinants that cause a change in demand (shifters) are reviewed in Exhibit 6.

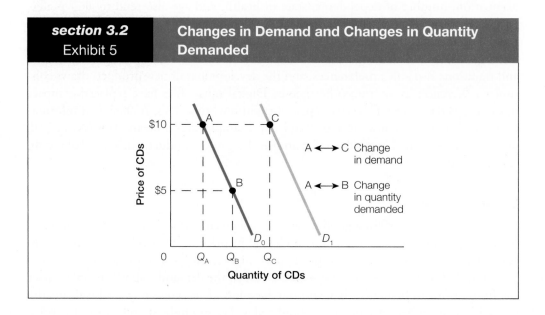

section 3.2
Exhibit 5

Changes in Demand and Changes in Quantity Demanded

section 3.2
Exhibit 6

Possible Demand Shifters

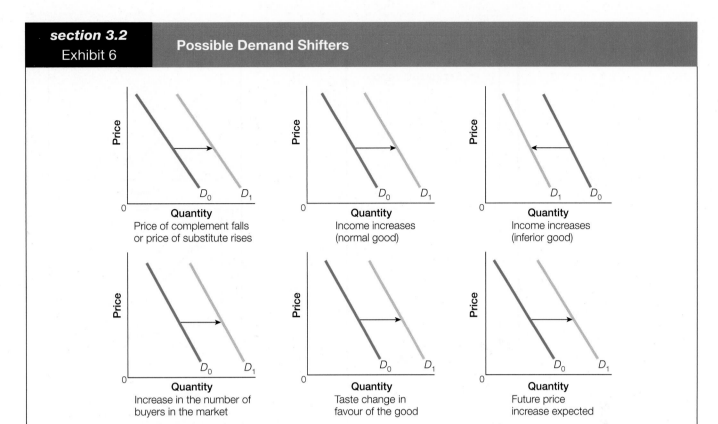

Price of complement falls
or price of substitute rises

Income increases
(normal good)

Income increases
(inferior good)

Increase in the number of
buyers in the market

Taste change in
favour of the good

Future price
increase expected

SECTION CHECK

- A change in the quantity demanded describes a movement along a given demand curve in response to a change in the price of the good. A change in demand shifts the entire demand curve in response to a change in some determinant of demand.
- Some possible determinants of demand (demand shifters) are the prices of related goods, income, number of buyers, tastes, and expectations.

Change in Variable and Change in Demand

Variable	Change in Variable	Change in Demand
1. Price of a complement good	↑	

(continued)

Variable	Change in Variable	Change in Demand
2. Price of a substitute good	↑	
3. Income (normal good)	↑	
4. Income (inferior good)	↑	
5. Number of buyers	↑	
6. Tastes and preferences	↑	
7. Expected future price	↑	

Supply

- What is the law of supply?
- What is an individual supply curve?
- What is a market supply curve?

WHAT IS THE LAW OF SUPPLY?

In a market, the answer to the fundamental question "What do we produce, and in what quantities?" depends on the interaction of both buyers and sellers. Demand is only half the story. The term **supply** refers to the quantity of a good or service that producers are both willing and able to make available for sale. It is an equally important factor that must be weighed by decision makers in all societies. As with demand, the price of the good is an important factor. And just as with demand, factors other than the price of the good are also important to suppliers, such as the cost of inputs or advances in technology. Although behaviour will vary among individual suppliers, economists expect, other things being equal, that the quantity supplied will vary directly with the price of the good, a relationship called the **law of supply**. According to the law of supply, the higher the price of the good (P), the greater the quantity supplied (Q_S), and the lower the price of the good, the smaller the quantity supplied, *ceteris paribus*.

$$P\uparrow \Rightarrow Q_S\uparrow \text{ or } P\downarrow \Rightarrow Q_S\downarrow$$

The relationship described by the law of supply is a direct, or positive, relationship, because the variables move in the same direction.

A Positive Relationship between Price and Quantity Supplied

Firms supplying goods and services want to increase their profits, and the higher the price per unit, the greater the profitability generated by supplying more of that good. For example, if you were an apple grower, wouldn't you much rather be paid $5 a kilogram than $1 a kilogram, *ceteris paribus*?

There is another reason that supply curves are upward sloping. In Chapter 2, the law of increasing opportunity costs demonstrated that when we hold technology and input prices constant, producing additional units of a good will require increased opportunity costs. That is, when we produce something, we use the most efficient resources first (those with the lowest opportunity cost) and then draw on less efficient resources (those with a higher opportunity cost) as more of the good is produced. Because costs per unit rise as more are produced, sellers must receive a higher price to increase the quantity supplied, *ceteris paribus*.

In order to get more oil, drillers must sometimes drill deeper or go into unexplored areas, and they still may come up with a dry hole. If it costs more to increase oil production, then oil prices would have to rise in order for producers to increase their output.

supply
the quantity of a good or service that producers are both willing and able to make available for sale

law of supply
The higher (lower) the price of the good, the greater (smaller) the quantity supplied, ceteris paribus.

WHAT IS AN INDIVIDUAL SUPPLY CURVE?

To illustrate the concept of an individual supply curve, consider the amount of apples that an individual supplier, John Macintosh, is willing and able to supply in one year. The law of supply can be illustrated, like the law of demand, by a table or a graph. John's supply schedule for apples is shown in Exhibit 1(a). The price–quantity supplied combinations were then plotted and joined to create the individual supply curve

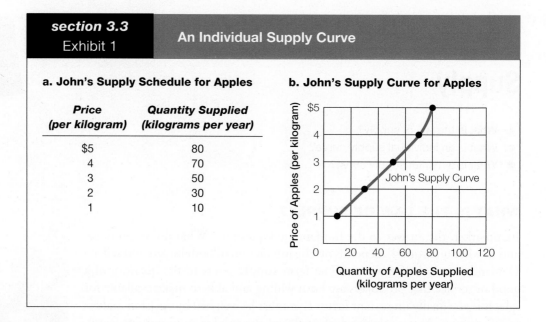

section 3.3
Exhibit 1
An Individual Supply Curve

a. John's Supply Schedule for Apples

Price (per kilogram)	Quantity Supplied (kilograms per year)
$5	80
4	70
3	50
2	30
1	10

b. John's Supply Curve for Apples

individual supply curve
a graphical representation that shows the positive relationship between price and quantity supplied

shown in Exhibit 1(b). The resulting **individual supply curve** is a graphical representation that shows the positive relationship between the price and the quantity supplied. Note that the individual supply curve is upward sloping as you move from left to right. At higher prices, it will be more attractive to increase production. Existing firms, or growers, will produce more at higher prices than at lower prices.

WHAT IS A MARKET SUPPLY CURVE?

market supply curve
the horizontal summation of individual supply curves

The **market supply curve** can be thought of as the horizontal summation of individual supply curves. The market supply schedule, which reflects the total quantity supplied at each price by all of the apple producers, is shown in Exhibit 2(a). Exhibit 2(b) illustrates the resulting market supply curve for this group of apple producers.

section 3.3
Exhibit 2
A Market Supply Curve

a. Market Supply Schedule for Apples

Quantity Supplied (kilograms per year)

Price	John	+	Other Producers	=	Market Supply
$5	80	+	7920	=	8000
4	70	+	6930	=	7000
3	50	+	4950	=	5000
2	30	+	2970	=	3000
1	10	+	990	=	1000

b. Market Supply Curve for Apples

The dots on this graph indicate different quantities of apples that producers would be willing and able to supply at various prices. The line connecting those combinations is the market supply curve.

section 3.4

Shifts in the Supply Curve

- What is the difference between a change in supply and a change in quantity supplied?
- What are the determinants of supply?
- Can we review the distinction between a change in supply and a change in quantity supplied?

WHAT IS THE DIFFERENCE BETWEEN A CHANGE IN SUPPLY AND A CHANGE IN QUANTITY SUPPLIED?

Changes in the price of a good lead to changes in quantity supplied by suppliers, just as changes in the price of a good lead to changes in quantity demanded by buyers. Similarly, a change in supply, whether an increase or a decrease, will occur for reasons other than changes in the price of the product itself, just as changes in demand are due to factors (determinants) other than the price of the good. In other words, a change in the price of the good in question is shown as a movement along a given supply curve, leading to a change in quantity supplied. A change in any other factor that can affect supplier behaviour (input prices, the prices of related products, expectations, number of suppliers, technology, regulation, taxes and subsidies, and weather) results in *a shift in the entire supply curve,* leading to a change in supply.

WHAT ARE THE DETERMINANTS OF SUPPLY?

An increase in supply shifts the supply curve to the right; a decrease in supply shifts the supply curve to the left, as seen in Exhibit 1. We will now look at some of the possible determinants of supply—factors that determine the position of the supply curve—in greater depth.

Input Prices

Suppliers are strongly influenced by the costs of inputs used in the production process, such as steel used for

section 3.4
Exhibit 1   **Supply Shifts**

An increase in supply shifts the supply curve to the right.
A decrease in supply shifts the supply curve to the left.

automobiles and microchips used in computers. For example, higher labour, materials, energy, or other input costs increase the costs of production, causing the supply curve to shift to the left at each and every price. If input prices fall, this will lower the costs of production, causing the supply curve to shift to the right—more will be supplied at each and every price.

The Prices of Related Products

Consider a car manufacturer that produces both electric and natural gas models of its vehicles. If the price of the natural gas vehicles falls, producers will reduce their quantity supplied, as seen in Exhibit 2(a). What effect would this lower price of the natural gas vehicles have on the manufacturer's decision to produce electric models of their cars? Easy question—it would increase the supply of the electric models because electric and natural gas models of car are *substitutes in production* because both goods can be produced using the same resources. You would want to produce relatively fewer of the model that had fallen in price (natural gas) and relatively more of the now more attractive other model (electric).

This example demonstrates why the price of related products is important as a supply shifter as well as a demand shifter. Producers tend to substitute the production of more profitable products for that of less profitable products. This is desirable from society's perspective as well because more profitable products tend to be those considered more valuable by society, whereas less profitable products are usually considered less valuable. Hence, the lower price in the natural gas vehicle market has caused an increase in supply (a rightward shift) in the electric vehicle market, as seen in Exhibit 2(b).

Alternatively, if the price of natural gas vehicles, a substitute in production, increases, then that model becomes more profitable. This leads to an increase in the quantity supplied of natural gas vehicles. Consequently, manufacturers will shift their resources out of the relatively lower priced models (electric); the result is a decrease in supply of electric vehicles.

section 3.4 Exhibit 2   Substitutions in Production

a. Market for Natural Gas Vehicles

Price of Natural Gas Vehicles (vertical axis); Quantity of Natural Gas Vehicles Supplied (horizontal axis)

b. Market for Electric Vehicles

Price of Electric Vehicles (vertical axis); Quantity of Electric Vehicles (horizontal axis)

If plant and equipment can be used to produce either natural gas or electric vehicles, a decrease in the price of natural gas vehicles (a movement along the supply curve) may cause some automobile manufacturers to shift out of the production of natural gas vehicles and into the production of electric vehicles—shifting the electric vehicle supply curve to the right.

Other examples of substitutes in production include farmers who have to decide between producing wheat or corn, or construction companies that have to choose between building single-family houses or commercial buildings.

Some goods are *complements in production.* Producing one good does not prevent the production of the other, but actually enables production of the other. For example, asphalt (which is used in road construction and roof shingles) is a marketable by-product obtained from the process of refining crude oil. Refined crude oil itself has a wide variety of applications, such as gasoline, jet fuel, diesel fuel, and home heating oil. Suppose the price of refined crude oil, say gasoline, rises and as a result, refineries increase the quantity supplied of gasoline, moving up the supply curve for gasoline, as seen in Exhibit 3(a). When refineries produce more gasoline, they automatically produce more asphalt. Thus, when the price of gasoline increases, the supply of the related good, asphalt, shifts to the right, as seen in Exhibit 3(b). Suppose the price of gasoline falls, and as a result, the quantity supplied of gasoline falls; this leads to a decrease (a leftward shift) in the supply of asphalt.

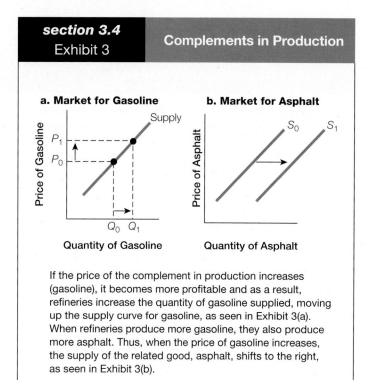

section 3.4
Exhibit 3   **Complements in Production**

a. Market for Gasoline   **b. Market for Asphalt**

If the price of the complement in production increases (gasoline), it becomes more profitable and as a result, refineries increase the quantity of gasoline supplied, moving up the supply curve for gasoline, as seen in Exhibit 3(a). When refineries produce more gasoline, they also produce more asphalt. Thus, when the price of gasoline increases, the supply of the related good, asphalt, shifts to the right, as seen in Exhibit 3(b).

Other examples of complements in production where goods are produced simultaneously from the same resource include a lumber mill that produces lumber and sawdust and a dairy that produces skim milk and cream.

Expectations

Another factor shifting supply is suppliers' expectations. If producers expect a higher price in the future, they will supply less now than they otherwise would have, preferring to wait and sell when their goods will be more valuable. Similarly, if producers expect now that the price will be lower later, they will supply more now. For example, oil refiners will often store some of their spring supply of gasoline to sell it in the summer because gasoline prices typically peak in summer. In addition, some of the heating oil for the fall is stored for sale in the winter when heating oil prices peak.

Number of Suppliers

We are normally interested in market demands and supplies (because together they determine prices and quantities) rather than in the behaviour of individual consumers and firms. As we discussed earlier, the supply curves of individual suppliers can be summed horizontally to create a market supply curve. An increase in the number of suppliers leads to an increase in supply, denoted by a rightward shift in the supply curve. For example, think of the number of smartphones that have entered the market over the last ten years, shifting the supply curve of smartphones to the right. An exodus of suppliers has the opposite impact, a decrease in supply, which is indicated by a leftward shift in the supply curve.

Business *CONNECTION*

USING DEMAND AND SUPPLY

Just as economics is the game of life, so demand and supply are the game of business. Students sometimes ask whether firms construct their own demand and supply curves, and if so, how. In reality, few firms actually do such analysis and those that do are usually larger firms that have the resources. Most of our economy is built on small and medium-sized enterprises (SMEs) and they simply don't have the time, money, or know-how to build such elaborate models. That triggers another question: Why do we have to learn this anyway if it's not used? The fact is that entrepreneurs and managers use their knowledge of demand and supply every day to make business decisions, even though you won't see evidence of the graphs on their desks.

These decision makers have learned the basics of demand and supply and they know instinctively how certain stimuli will affect their firm. They spend hours trying to understand where their firm's strengths, weaknesses, opportunities, or threats (SWOT) lie, as well as considering how they will respond. Threats generally shift the demand curves leftward, whereas positive responses are opportunities that may shift the curves rightward. A firm building on its strengths will shift demand (and supply) rightward, and ignoring the weaknesses will likely bring leftward shifts of the curves. The process relies less on having to literally illustrate the movements of the curves than it does on understanding that they will move. Managing both internal and external change is what business is all about. Let's investigate a bit more.

Managers constantly face the realities of external changes, and if you've taken basic business courses you will likely be thinking now about political, economic, social, and technological (PEST) factors analysis. A PEST analysis looks at the external issues that entrepreneurs cannot change. All of the PEST factors affect demand for a company's products and how it responds in supplying the product. Managers ignore these factors at their peril.

Once confronted with the external environment, managers do respond. They may want to increase revenues, increasing quantity (Q) or perhaps they leave Q as is and increase prices (P). Remember that an increase in price will result in a decrease in quantity demanded. Perhaps the

managers need to seek new markets, or compete against substitutions—here they are shifting the demand curve. How do they do that? Remember that managers can't change the PEST factors, they can only use that information. What they can change are the 4Ps (price, product, place, and promotion). Managers can, and do, change Ps to try to meet or change the market demand, shifting the demand curve rightward if they want to grow the market, or shifting it leftward if they are contracting (which they sometimes do).

Once the demand curve has shifted, it's the operations side of the business that responds to meeting the new realities by shifting the supply curve. If the firm doesn't respond and leaves the supply curve static, and the demand has shifted rightward, then it will have produced its own shortage and consumers may turn to competitors to buy the goods they want—which means lost sales, or opportunity costs, to the firm. If on the other hand, the firm ramps up production beyond what consumers want, the firm will have produced its own surplus, which will require lowering prices later or having to accept sunk costs if the firm has to scrap the product. Either way, those are losses to the firm.

Clearly a dance between the theory and the practical application of economics goes on in every firm every day. You don't necessarily have to see evidence of theory to know that it's working—you just have to look at what's happening within the firm daily to see the practical application of demand and supply at work.

1. Which do you think occurs first in the economy: businesses responding to changes in demand or consumers responding to changes in the supply of goods and services? What do you think would happen if the opposite occurred?

2. In your opinion, has the rise of e-commerce and online purchasing increased growth in the economy? In what other ways has e-commerce affected the economy?

3. There is a plethora of "dollar stores" that purchase the oversupply of many manufacturers and sell it at a discount. Do you think this is efficient for the economy? Thinking broadly, do you think consumers and businesses benefit or not? Explain.

Technology

Technological change can lower the firm's costs of production through productivity advances. These changes allow the firm to spend less on inputs and produce the same level of output. Human creativity works to find new ways to produce goods and services using fewer or less costly inputs of labour, natural resources, or capital. In recent years, despite generally rising prices, the prices of electronic equipment such as computers, cellphones, and flat-screen TVs have fallen dramatically. At any given price this year, suppliers are willing to provide many more (of a given quality of) computers than in previous years simply because technology has dramatically reduced the cost of providing them. Graphically, the increase in supply is indicated by a shift to the right in the supply curve.

Regulation

Supply may also change because of changes in the legal and regulatory environment in which firms operate. Government regulations can influence the costs of production to the firm, leading to cost-induced supply changes similar to those just discussed. For example, if new safety or anti-pollution requirements increase labour and capital costs, the increased cost will result, other things equal, in a decrease in supply, shifting the supply curve to the left, or up. An increase in a government-imposed minimum wage may have a similar effect by raising labour costs and decreasing supply in markets that employ many low-wage workers. However, deregulation—the process by which governments reduce or outright eliminate restrictions on individuals or businesses— can shift the supply curve to the right.

Taxes and Subsidies

Certain types of taxes can also increase the costs of production borne by the supplier, causing the supply curve to shift to the left at each price. The opposite of a tax (a subsidy) can lower the firm's costs and shift the supply curve to the right. For example, the government sometimes provides farmers with subsidies to encourage the production of certain agricultural products.

Weather

In addition, weather can certainly affect the supply of certain commodities, particularly agricultural products and transportation services. A drought or freezing temperatures will almost certainly cause the supply curves for many crops to shift to the

DEBATE

IS IT ETHICAL TO GROW CORN FOR FUEL?

For:
Over the past decade, the market has adjusted to rising gas prices by blending ethanol into gasoline. The widespread use of corn-based ethanol has been a boon for farmers, who are free to choose which markets to participate in. Most farmers will choose to grow the crop that provides the greatest return on their investment and at present, corn is an extremely lucrative crop.

Note, though, that as there is a rise in the number of hectares devoted to corn, there is a drop in the number of hectares devoted to wheat and soy crops, which increases the price of wheat and soy crops and benefits the farmers who grow those crops.

This is the market in action and there is nothing unethical about it. Surely you can defend the farmers' decisions.

Against:
In the long term, growing crops for fuel rather than for food will mean higher prices for food around the world and that will hurt the poorest people the most. This is unethical because the market, rather than an act of nature, is causing famine—the poor simply can't afford food.

Clearly, the benefits flow to those who can afford fuel, so the poor get relatively little marginal benefit and those who cannot afford the higher costs of basic food staples now pay a much higher marginal cost than they otherwise would.

Those who believe the market should consider ethical issues along with prices would likely support a less efficient market. Just because farmers can supply a crop for an alternative use, should they?

Questions:
1. Why has the price of gas at the pumps risen—because of increased consumption (more people driving) or because of an increasing scarcity in the supply of crude oil?
2. Should we promote growing corn for our transportation needs?
3. Is there a conflict between the wider society's needs and the individual farmer's needs?

section 3.4
Exhibit 4

Change in Supply vs. Change in Quantity Supplied

A ←→ B Change in quantity supplied

B ←→ C Change in supply

left, whereas exceptionally good weather can shift a supply curve to the right. For example, during the summer of 2015, record-breaking temperatures and extremely low rainfalls across western Canada caused chaos for farmers as they grappled with the worst drought in more than a decade. Several counties in Alberta were forced to declare states of agricultural emergency, while the Saskatchewan government loosened crop insurance rules to aid impacted farmers.

CAN WE REVIEW THE DISTINCTION BETWEEN A CHANGE IN SUPPLY AND A CHANGE IN QUANTITY SUPPLIED?

If the price of a good changes, we say this leads to a *change in the quantity supplied.* For example, in Exhibit 4, if the price of wheat rises from P_0 to P_1, the market for wheat experiences a movement from A to B. If one of the other factors influences sellers' behaviour, we say this leads to a *change in supply.* For example, if production costs fall because of a wage decrease or lower fuel costs, other things remaining constant, we would expect an increase in supply—that is, a rightward shift in the supply curve as illustrated by the change from B to C in Exhibit 4. Alternatively, if some variable, like lower input prices, causes the costs of production to fall, the supply curve will shift to the right. Exhibit 5 illustrates the effect of some of the determinants that cause shifts in the supply curve.

section 3.4
Exhibit 5

Possible Supply Shifts

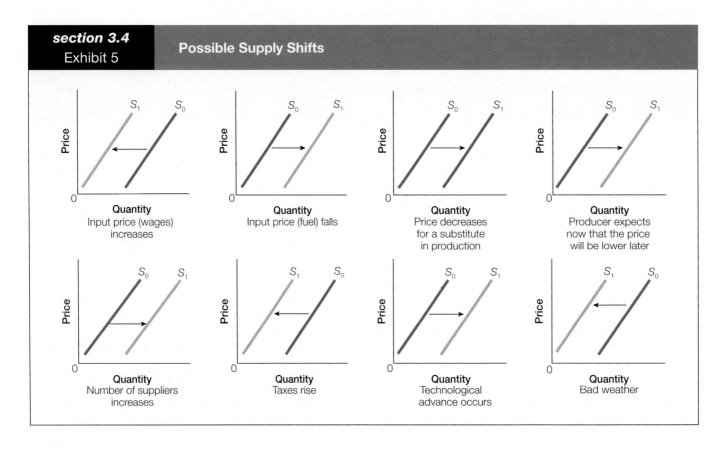

SECTION CHECK

- A movement along a given supply curve is caused by a change in the price of the good in question. As we move along the supply curve, we say there is a change in the quantity supplied. A shift of the entire supply curve is called a *change in supply*.
- Input prices, the prices of related products, expectations, the number of suppliers, technology, regulation, taxes and subsidies, and weather can all lead to changes in supply (shifts in supply).

Change in Variable and Change in Supply

Variable	Change in Variable	Change in Supply
1. Input prices	↑	
2. Price of substitute in production	↑	
3. Price of complement in production	↑	
4. Expected future price	↑	

(continued)

Variable	Change in Variable	Change in Supply
5. Number of suppliers	↑	
6. Government regulation	↑	
7. Taxes	↑	
8. Subsidies	↑	
9. Technology	↑	

For Your Review

Section 3.1

1. Assume the following demand schedule information:

Ben		Boris		Bilal	
P	**Q_D**	**P**	**Q_D**	**P**	**Q_D**
$5	1	$5	2	$5	3
4	2	4	4	4	6
3	3	3	6	3	9
2	4	2	8	2	12
1	5	1	10	1	15

a. Complete the market demand schedule if Ben and Bilal are the only demanders, and graph the market demand curve.

P	**Q_D**
$5	
4	
3	
2	
1	

b. Complete the market demand schedule if Boris joins Ben and Bilal in the market, and graph the market demand curve.

P	**Q_D**
$5	
4	
3	
2	
1	

c. Complete the market demand schedule if Ben now leaves the market and only Boris and Bilal remain, and graph the market demand curve.

P	Q_D
$5	
4	
3	
2	
1	

2. What is the difference between an individual demand curve and a market demand curve?

3. The following table shows Hillary's demand schedule for Cherry Blossom lotion. Graph Hillary's demand curve.

Price (dollars per mL)	Quantity Demanded (mL per week)
15	5
12	10
9	15
6	20
3	25

4. The following table shows Cherry Blossom lotion demand schedules for Hillary's friends, Marita and Jacquie. If Hillary, Marita, and Jacquie constitute the whole market for Cherry Blossom lotion, complete the market demand schedule and graph the market demand curve.

Price (dollars per mL)	Quantity Demanded (mL per week)			
	Hillary	Marita	Jacquie	Market
15	5	0	15	_____
12	10	5	20	_____
9	15	10	25	_____
6	20	15	30	_____
3	25	20	35	_____

Section 3.2

5. What would be the effects of each of the following on the demand for hamburger in Swift Current, Saskatchewan. In each case, identify the responsible determinant of demand.

   a. The price of chicken falls.

   b. The price of hamburger buns doubles.

   c. Scientists find that eating hamburger prolongs life.

   d. The population of Swift Current doubles.

6. What would be the effect of each of the following on the demand for Chevrolets in Canada? In each case, identify the responsible determinant of demand.

   a. The price of Fords plummets.

   b. Consumers believe that the price of Chevrolets will rise next year.

   c. The incomes of Canadians rise.

   d. The price of gasoline falls dramatically.

7. The following graph shows three market demand curves for cantaloupe. Starting at point A, which point represents

   a. an increase in quantity demanded?

   b. an increase in demand?

   c. a decrease in demand?

   d. a decrease in quantity demanded?

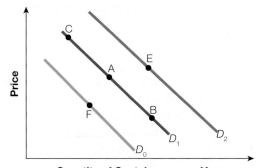

8. Using the demand curve, show the effect of the following events on the market for beef.

   a. Consumer income increases.

   b. The price of beef increases.

   c. An outbreak of mad cow disease occurs.

   d. The price of chicken (a substitute) increases.

   e. The price of barbecue grills (a complement) increases.

9. Draw the demand curves for the following goods. If the price of the first good listed rises, what will happen to the demand for the second good, and why?

   a. hamburgers and ketchup

   b. Coca-Cola and Pepsi

   c. iPhones and iPhone cases

   d. golf clubs and golf balls

   e. skateboards and razor scooters

10. If plane travel is a normal good and bus travel is an inferior good to plane travel, how will each respond to an increase in people's incomes?

11. Using the graph below, answer the following questions:

    a. What is the shift from D_0 to D_1 called?

    b. What is the movement from B to A called?

    c. What is the movement from A to B called?

    d. What is the shift from D_1 to D_0 called?

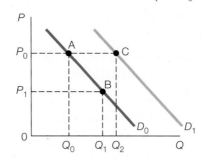

12. Show and describe what would happen to the market demand curve for a good in each of the following cases:

    a. an increase in the price of a substitute and a decrease in the price of a complement

    b. a decrease in the price of a substitute and an increase in the price of a complement

    c. an increase in the number of buyers and an increase in income, for a normal good

    d. a decrease in the number of buyers and an increase in income, for an inferior good

    e. a decrease in expected future prices and a shift in tastes away from the good

Section 3.3

13. Felix is a wheat farmer who has two fields he can use to grow wheat. The first field is right next to his house and the topsoil is rich and thick. The second field is 16 kilometres away in the mountains and the soil is rocky. At current wheat prices, Felix produces only from the field next to his house because the market price for wheat is just high enough to cover his costs of production, including a reasonable profit. What would have to happen to the market price of wheat for Felix to have the incentive to produce from the second field?

14. The following table shows the supply schedule for Rolling Rock Oil Co. Plot Rolling Rock's supply curve on a graph.

Price (dollars per barrel)	Quantity Demanded (barrels per month)
5	10 000
10	15 000
15	20 000
20	25 000
25	30 000

15. The following table shows the supply schedules for Rolling Rock and two other petroleum companies, Armadillo Oil and Pecos Petroleum. Assuming these three companies make up the entire supply side of the oil market, complete the market supply schedule and draw the market supply curve on a graph.

Quantity Supplied (barrels per month)				
Price (dollars per barrel)	Rolling Rock	Armadillo	Pecos	Market
5	10 000	8000	2000	_____
10	15 000	10 000	5000	_____
15	20 000	12 000	8000	_____
20	25 000	14 000	11 000	_____
25	30 000	16 000	14 000	_____

16. Assume the following supply schedule information.

Sacha		Steve		Sean	
P	Q_s	P	Q_s	P	Q_s
$5	10	$5	15	$5	5
4	8	4	12	4	4
3	6	3	9	3	3
2	4	2	6	2	2
1	2	1	3	1	1

a. Complete the market supply schedule if Sacha and Steve are the only suppliers, and graph the market supply curve.

P	Q_s
$5	
4	
3	
2	
1	

b. Complete the market supply schedule if Sean joins Sacha and Steve in the market, and graph the market supply curve.

P	Q_s
$5	
4	
3	
2	
1	

c. Complete the market supply schedule if Sacha now leaves the market and only Steve and Sean remain, and graph the market supply curve.

P	Q_s
$5	
4	
3	
2	
1	

Section 3.4

17. Using the graph below, answer the following questions:

 a. What is the shift from S_0 to S_1 called?

 b. What is the movement from A to B called?

 c. What is the movement from B to A called?

 d. What is the shift from S_1 to S_0 called?

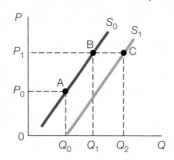

18. Show and describe what would happen to the market supply curve for a good in each of the following cases.

 a. an increase in the number of suppliers and an increase in subsidies

 b. a decrease in the number of suppliers and an increase in taxes

 c. an increase in input prices and increasing costs of regulation

 d. producers expect now that the price will be lower later

19. Many farmers in western Canada have the choice between growing fields of wheat or growing fields of corn, due to the nearly identical resources required to cultivate each crop. If the price of corn increased, what would be the effect on

 a. the supply of corn?

 b. the supply of wheat?

20. What would be the effect of each of the following on the supply of ketchup in Canada? In each case, identify the responsible determinant of supply.

 a. Tomato prices skyrocket (ketchup is made from tomatoes).

 b. Parliament places a 26 percent tax on ketchup production.

 c. Entrepreneurs invent a new, faster tomato crusher to make ketchup.

21. What would be the effects of each of the following on the supply of coffee worldwide? In each case, identify the responsible determinant of supply.

 a. Freezing temperatures wipe out half of Brazil's coffee crop.

 b. The wages of coffee workers in Latin America rise as unionization efforts succeed.

    c. Indonesia offers big subsidies to its coffee producers.

    d. Genetic engineering produces a super coffee bean that grows faster and needs less care.

    e. Coffee suppliers expect prices to be higher in the future.

22. What would be the effect of each of the following on the supply of automobiles in Canada? In each case, identify the responsible determinant of supply.

    a. North American automobile makers are successful in negotiating wage reductions with their unionized workforce.

    b. Automobile manufacturers in India and China begin to sell their vehicles in Canada.

    c. The Canadian government decides to implement a specific tax on automobiles (the tax is to be paid by the automobile producers).

    d. Technological innovation in computer design and robotic assembly dramatically increase the efficiency of manufacturing automobiles in Canada.

23. The following graph shows three market supply curves for cantaloupe. Compared to point A, which point represents

    a. an increase in quantity supplied?

    b. an increase in supply?

    c. a decrease in quantity supplied?

    d. a decrease in supply?

24. Molasses is a marketable by-product of sugar refining. That is, the more product that sugar refineries produce, the more molasses they generate. Molasses itself is used as an additive in livestock feed as well as the principal ingredient in the distillation of rum. If the price of sugar increased, what would be the effect on

    a. the supply of sugar?

    b. the supply of molasses?

25. If a guitar manufacturer increased its wages in order to keep its workers, what would happen to the supply of guitars as a result?

Sections 3.2 and 3.4

26. Show the impact of each of the following events on the oil market.

    [**Note:** The 15 countries that comprise the Organization of the Petroleum Exporting Countries (OPEC) exert considerable control of the world market for oil.]

    a. OPEC becomes more effective in limiting the supply of oil.

    b. OPEC becomes less effective in limiting the supply of oil.

    c. The price for natural gas (a substitute for heating oil) rises.

    d. New oil discoveries occur in Alberta.

    e. Electric and hybrid cars become subsidized and their prices fall.

Market Equilibrium Price and Quantity

- What are the equilibrium price and the equilibrium quantity?
- What is a shortage and what is a surplus?

In the last chapter, we learned about demand and supply separately. We now bring the market supply and market demand together.

WHAT ARE THE EQUILIBRIUM PRICE AND THE EQUILIBRIUM QUANTITY?

market equilibrium
the point at which the market supply and the market demand curves intersect

equilibrium price
the price at the intersection of the market supply and demand curves; at this price, the quantity demanded equals the quantity supplied

equilibrium quantity
the quantity at the intersection of the market supply and demand curves; at this quantity, the quantity demanded equals the quantity supplied

The **market equilibrium** is found at the point at which the market supply and the market demand curves intersect. It is at market equilibrium that two important values are determined: equilibrium price and equilibrium quantity. The **equilibrium price** is the price at the intersection of the market supply and demand curves. At this price, the quantity demanded equals the quantity supplied; that is, the amount that buyers are willing and able to buy is exactly equal to the amount that sellers are willing and able to produce. The **equilibrium quantity** is the quantity at the intersection of the market supply and demand curves. At this quantity, the quantity demanded equals the quantity supplied.

The equilibrium market solution is best understood with the help of a simple graph. Let's return to the apple example we used in our earlier discussions of supply and demand in Chapter 3. Exhibit 1 combines the market demand curve for apples with the market supply curve. At $3 per kilogram, buyers are willing to buy 5000 kilograms of apples and sellers are willing to supply 5000 kilograms of apples. Neither may be "happy" about the price, because the buyers would like a lower price and the sellers would like a higher price. But both buyers and sellers are able to carry out their purchase and sales plans at that $3 price. However, at any other price, either suppliers or demanders would be unable to trade as much as they would like.

A Hypothetical Market Supply and Demand Schedule for Apples

Price	Quantity Supplied	Quantity Demanded	Difference	State of Market
$5	8000 kg	1000 kg	7000 kg	Surplus
4	7000	3000	4000	Surplus
3	5000	5000	0	Equilibrium
2	3000	8000	−5000	Shortage
1	1000	12 000	−11 000	Shortage

The equilibrium is $3 per kilogram and 5000 kilograms of apples, where quantity demanded and quantity supplied are equal. At higher prices, quantity supplied exceeds quantity demanded, resulting in a surplus. Below $3, quantity demanded exceeds quantity supplied, leading to a shortage.

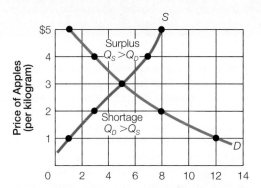

WHAT IS A SHORTAGE AND WHAT IS A SURPLUS?

What happens when the market price is not equal to the equilibrium price? As you can see in Exhibit 1, at $4 per kilogram, the quantity of apples demanded would be 3000 kilograms, but the quantity supplied would be 7000 kilograms. At that price, a **surplus** would exist, where quantity supplied exceeded quantity demanded. That is, at this price, growers would be willing to sell more apples than demanders would be willing to buy. To cut growing inventories, frustrated suppliers would cut their price and cut back on production. And as price falls, consumers buy more, ultimately eliminating the unsold surplus and returning the market to the equilibrium.

What would happen if the price of apples was cut to $1 per kilogram? The yearly quantity demanded of 12 000 kilograms would be greater than the 1000 kilograms that producers would be willing to supply at that low price. So, at $1 per kilogram, a **shortage** would exist, where quantity demanded exceeded quantity supplied. Because of the apple shortage, frustrated buyers would be forced to compete for the existing supply, bidding up the price. The rising price would have two effects: (1) Producers would be willing to increase the quantity supplied; and (2) the higher price would decrease the quantity demanded. Together, these two effects would ultimately eliminate the shortage, returning the market to the equilibrium.

surplus
where quantity supplied exceeds quantity demanded

shortage
where quantity demanded exceeds quantity supplied

An NHL playoff game is a high-demand, limited-supply sporting event. With a number of tickets going to corporate sponsors and individuals affiliated with the two teams playing in the game, in addition to the heightened interest because the home team has made the playoffs, the quantity demanded far exceeds the quantity supplied at the face value of the tickets. Consequently, some fans are willing to pay much more for these tickets from scalpers who buy the tickets at face value and try to resell them at a higher price.

DEBATE

WHERE THERE'S A MARKET, SHOULD PEOPLE BE ALLOWED TO TRADE FREELY, WITHOUT STATE LIMITATIONS OR INTERVENTION?

For:

Just as all humans are said to have a price, so every *thing* has its price. That applies equally to ice cream, school uniforms, bagels, drugs, weapons, sexual favours, and human organs. Trading a product at a price acceptable to at least one buyer satisfies both the consumer and the producer, and so ensures that the market trades at the most efficient level—regardless of legal or moral issues.

Both the demand side and the supply side should be free to establish their own trade criteria. After all, trade means satisfying the needs and wants of both the demanders and the suppliers, and if both parties agree, who is the state or society to interfere in the transactions?

Anyone who advocates for the superiority of a free market system should have no difficulty with moral or ethical issues, because what matters is the superiority of the market, not its particulars. Drug users and sellers should make their own decisions about their actions, for example. The same should be true for weapons and those who sell their bodies.

There are also a number of individuals in dire economic situations, especially those in underdeveloped countries, who could benefit from selling one of their kidneys. Don't all markets trade at the most efficient levels, so that people should be allowed to trade freely?

Against:

Not everything has its price. In exploring demand and supply, we find that goods or services trade at levels where both the consumer and the supplier are mutually satisfied at an agreed-on price. But not all markets trade at the most efficient levels, and in fact, some markets are unethical or illegal. Some products and services should simply not be offered or sold in a civilized society.

While individual choice and need generally take precedence in an open market, we still need to have limitations for the public good. Some people can't make informed decisions—those who are underage, for example, or those who lack the necessary intellectual ability. Even if individuals have the capacity to make informed decisions, do they always have enough information to do so? For example, do individuals in developing countries appreciate the long-term risks associated with donating a kidney, or is the lure of available money unduly influencing their decisions?

There are also cases where the public good overrides the individual's benefit, such as in the selling of automatic assault weapons. At some point, individual freedom gives way to society's best interests and safety.

Surely society has seen the harm that can come from lack of intervention when these trades take place in the open market, making state limitations and intervention necessary. In fact, aren't there situations where the state should intervene proactively?

Questions:

1. Since individuals are allowed to donate organs (such as kidneys), why can't they sell their organs to someone who is willing to pay?
2. What practical, moral, or ethical issues might there be in relation to selling an organ?
3. Who should decide what is practical, moral, or ethical in such a case?

Producers independently decide how much they are going to produce and at what price, and consumers will show up at websites, garage sales, restaurants, and stores to buy those goods and services. Sometimes there might be too much supplied, while at other times there might not be enough. But over time, these mistakes will be corrected by the process of adjustment in supply and demand. So whether the price starts off too high or too low, the activities of the many buyers and sellers will move the market toward equilibrium. Once equilibrium is reached, buyers and sellers are satisfied in their ability to buy and sell at that price, and there is no longer any pressure on prices. How quickly do markets adjust to equilibrium? It depends on the type of market. But in most competitive markets, shortages and surpluses tend to be temporary.

SECTION CHECK

- The intersection of the supply and demand curves shows the equilibrium price and equilibrium quantity in a market.
- A surplus is where quantity supplied exceeds quantity demanded. A shortage is where quantity demanded exceeds quantity supplied.

Changes in Equilibrium Price and Quantity

- What happens to equilibrium price and equilibrium quantity when the demand curve shifts?
- What happens to equilibrium price and equilibrium quantity when the supply curve shifts?
- What happens when both supply and demand shift in the same time period?

When one of the many determinants of demand or supply (input prices, prices of related products, number of suppliers, expectations, technology, and so on) changes, the demand and supply curves will shift, leading to changes in the equilibrium price and equilibrium quantity. To accomplish an objective and ultimately accurate analysis of a change in demand and supply, it is important that the theoretical concepts first developed in Chapter 3 are correctly applied. One way you can ensure that your demand–supply analysis of a given event is complete is by asking yourself the following three questions:

1. Which side of the market is being affected by the event in question, demand or supply?
2. Is the event in question a "shift" or a "movement"?
3. Is the event in question having an expansionary or contractionary impact on the market?

We first consider a change in demand.

WHAT HAPPENS TO EQUILIBRIUM PRICE AND EQUILIBRIUM QUANTITY WHEN THE DEMAND CURVE SHIFTS?

A shift in the demand curve—caused by a change in the price of a related good (a substitute or a complement), income, the number of buyers, tastes, or expectations—results in a change in both equilibrium price and equilibrium quantity. But how and why does this happen? This result can be best explained through the presentation of a brief case.

The energy drink market in Canada has experienced dramatic growth. In both 2011 and 2012, sales growth for this sector of the beverage market exceeded 20 percent. The industry leader, Red Bull, with a 42 percent share of the energy drink market, sold an impressive $2.9 billion worth of product in 2012—a 28 percent improvement over the previous year's sales.

With names like Rockstar and Monster, these beverages appeal to and are aggressively marketed to the urban fast-paced consumer. How can the record growth in this market segment best be explained? The following are the answers to those three important questions:

1. The case describes how consumer behaviour (fuelled by advertising and lifestyle demands) is impacting market growth; therefore, the event is demand-side.

Getty Images

section 4.2
Exhibit 1

Growth in the Energy Drink Market

The demand for energy drinks has increased significantly. These increases in demand, coupled with a fixed supply, mean a higher price and a greater quantity.

2. The case makes no reference to the price of energy drinks changing; therefore, the event will be illustrated as a shift.
3. The case details how the aggressive and targeted advertising of energy drink manufacturers has resonated with busy, time-constrained consumers; therefore, the event is expansionary.

In conclusion, due to the fast-rising demand for energy drinks, this market segment has experienced rapid growth. As shown in Exhibit 1, the rightward shift of the demand curve results in an increase in both equilibrium price and equilibrium quantity.

Let's look at a second case of how changing demand can impact equilibrium price and equilibrium quantity. In 2008 to 2009, measured economic activity in the Canadian economy declined by nearly $20 billion (producing what economists refer to as a *recession*). In response to this recession, while median after-tax family income remained virtually unchanged (for example a family of two or more people consistently received around $65 500), many Canadian families experienced a decline in income due to job loss or reduction in hours worked.

Over this same time period, according to data compiled by the Conference Board of Canada, limited-service restaurants (such as McDonald's and Subway) surpassed full-service restaurants (such as The Keg and Earls) in terms of their overall percentage of sales. From these observations, what conclusions can be drawn about these two segments of the restaurant market? Again, let's answer this using our three questions:

1. The case describes how consumers, in response to a decline in their income, make adjustments to the types of restaurants they visit; therefore, the event is demand-side.
2. The case focuses on the impact of consumer income on demand; therefore, the event will be illustrated as a shift.
3. The case reveals that as consumers' incomes declined due to recession pressures, the demand for full-service restaurants declined, while the demand for limited-service restaurants increased; therefore, depending on the particular market segment, the event is either expansionary or contractionary.

section 4.2
Exhibit 2

Decline in Consumer Income

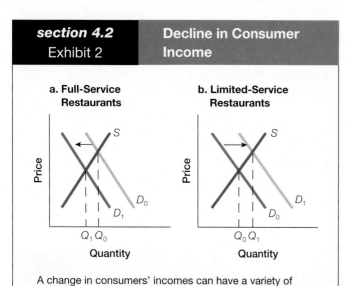

A change in consumers' incomes can have a variety of effects on demand, depending on the type of good or service. In the case of full-service restaurants, 2008 to 2009 declines in family incomes resulted in lower demand, whereas for limited-service restaurants, that same decline in income produced an increase in demand.

In conclusion, the case seems to indicate that full-service restaurants fit the definition of a normal good, and limited-service restaurants fit the definition of an inferior good. As shown in Exhibit 2, the restaurant market exhibited two distinct responses. In the full-service segment (a), demand declined, shifting the demand curve leftward, causing equilibrium price and quantity to decline. However, in the limited-service segment (b), demand increased, shifting the demand curve rightward, causing equilibrium price and quantity to increase.

WHAT HAPPENS TO EQUILIBRIUM PRICE AND EQUILIBRIUM QUANTITY WHEN THE SUPPLY CURVE SHIFTS?

Like a shift in demand, a shift in the supply curve also influences both equilibrium price and equilibrium quantity, assuming that demand for the product has not changed. Let's look at another case. Between 2000 and 2013, the price of flat-screen TVs declined dramatically. Industry data reveal that in 2000, a 20-inch flat-screen TV would have cost around $1200, whereas by 2013, that same 20-inch TV cost less than $100. Furthermore, an investigation into the technology of manufacturing flat-screen displays reveals that, since 2000, the machines necessary for producing the displays have increased in capacity by 800 percent. Translation: Bigger machines, cheaper TVs. How can this technological development explain the dramatic reduction in the price of flat-screen TVs?

1. The case describes how a technological innovation in production is impacting the ability of electronic manufacturers to produce their product; therefore, the event is supply-side.
2. The case highlights the impact of technology on production; therefore, the event will be illustrated as a shift.
3. The case indicates that as production technology has improved, the ability of manufacturers to make more product available has also increased; therefore, the event is expansionary.

In conclusion, as shown in Exhibit 3, the lower cost of producing flat-screen TVs—and the subsequent increase in profitability—shifts the supply curve to the right. This increase in supply lowers equilibrium price and increases equilibrium quantity.

Let's look at a second case of how equilibrium price and quantity can be impacted by a change in supply. Tequila, originally associated with Mexican ranchers and cowboys and increasingly the choice of mainstream North American consumers, is an alcoholic beverage produced from the agave plant. With its production carefully regulated and limited to five Mexican states, the 2007 failure of the agave crop had a devastating impact on the industry. The price of a bottle of tequila increased 50 to 60 percent in Canada, translating into about a $10 jump in price at the liquor store. How can demand supply analysis explain the significantly higher price of tequila?

1. The case details how the availability of inputs in a market is a factor in determining market price; therefore the event is supply-side.
2. The case's focus on production inputs as the independent variable means the event will be illustrated as a shift.
3. The case draws a relationship between the failure of the agave crop and the higher price of tequila worldwide (results for Canada provided specifically). As a result, the event is contractionary.

section 4.2 Exhibit 3 | **Advances in Production Technology**

Advances in the technology of producing flat-screen displays enable manufacturers to produce flat-screen TVs more efficiently and therefore more profitably. This increase in profit encourages more supply, shifting the supply curve rightward. Equilibrium price decreases and equilibrium quantity increase as a result.

section 4.2
Exhibit 4

Loss of a Critical Input

Tequila is produced by extracting the juice from the agave plant. Therefore, failure of the agave crop shifts the supply curve for tequila leftward, leading to a higher equilibrium price and lower equilibrium quantity, *ceteris paribus*.

Therefore, the supply of tequila shifts leftward due to the failure of the agave crop, without which tequila cannot be produced. As shown in Exhibit 4, this decline in supply results in the predicted increase in equilibrium price and decrease in equilibrium quantity.

WHAT HAPPENS WHEN BOTH SUPPLY AND DEMAND SHIFT IN THE SAME TIME PERIOD?

We have discussed that as part of the continual adjustment process that occurs in the marketplace, supply and demand can each shift in response to many different factors, with the market then adjusting toward the new equilibrium. We have, so far, considered what happens when just one such change occurs at a time. In these cases, we learned that the results of these adjustments in supply and demand on the equilibrium price and quantity are predictable. However, both supply and demand very often will shift in the same time period. Can we predict what will happen to equilibrium prices and equilibrium quantities in these situations?

As you will see, when supply and demand move at the same time, we can predict the change in one variable (price or quantity), but we are unable to predict the direction of the effect on the other variable with any certainty. This change in the second variable, then, is said to be indeterminate because it cannot be determined without additional information about the size of the relative shifts in supply and demand. This concept will become clearer to you as we work through the following example.

An Increase in Supply and a Decrease in Demand

When considering this scenario, it might help you to break it down into its individual parts. As you learned in the last section, an increase in supply (a rightward shift in the supply curve) results in a decrease in the equilibrium price and an increase in the equilibrium quantity. A decrease in demand (a leftward movement of the demand curve), on the other hand, results in a decrease in both the equilibrium price and the equilibrium quantity. These shifts are shown in Exhibit 5(a). Taken together, then, these changes will clearly result in a decrease in the equilibrium price because both the increase in supply and the decrease in demand work to push this price down. This drop in equilibrium price (from P_0 to P_1) is shown in the movement from E_0 to E_1.

The effect of these changes on equilibrium price is clear, but how does the equilibrium quantity change? The impact on equilibrium quantity is indeterminate because the increase in supply increases the equilibrium quantity and the decrease in demand decreases it. In this scenario, the change in the equilibrium quantity will vary depending on the relative changes in supply and demand. If, as shown in Exhibit 5(a), the decrease in demand is greater than the increase in supply, the equilibrium quantity will decrease. If, however, as shown in Exhibit 5(b), the increase in supply is greater than the decrease in demand, the equilibrium quantity will increase.

section 4.2
Exhibit 5

section 4.2
Exhibit 5 | **Shifts in Supply and Demand**

**a. A Little Increase in Supply and a
Big Decrease in Demand**

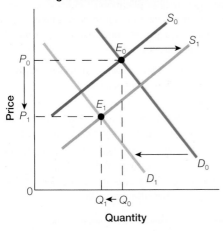

**b. A Big Increase in Supply and a
Little Decrease in Demand**

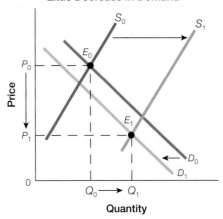

If the decrease in demand (leftward shift) is greater than the increase in supply (rightward shift), the equilibrium price and equilibrium quantity will fall.

If the increase in supply (rightward shift) is greater than the decrease in demand (leftward shift), the equilibrium price will fall and the equilibrium quantity will rise.

Business *CONNECTION*

EQUILIBRIUM DETERMINES PRICE

Beyond knowing and understanding the equilibrium price and quantity of products in their industry, businesspeople often try to understand what will happen to prices if there is a change in the market. When asked to explain why prices are at a certain level, they quickly reply that present price levels are simply a reflection of market demand and supply. Strictly speaking, they are correct. In the absence of a detailed analysis, which most small and medium-sized enterprises cannot afford, most of these managers or owners might not realize why this is the case. A basic four-step economic analysis would show them what impact a market change might have on their revenues.

In the four-step analysis, the entrepreneur simply responds to a change in the environment by asking these four questions:

1. Which curve is affected? (Is it a demand or supply issue?)
2. Is price the issue, or is it something else? (If it's price, it's a movement *along* the curve; if it's something else, it's a *shift* of the curve. Numerous factors can shift demand and supply—work at finding which factor is affecting the change.)
3. Is the change an increase or a decrease?

4. How much change is involved? (Is the change small or large?)

Managers—and students—can use this scenario with any business problem. The following example illustrates how the analysis plays out. (You're encouraged to walk yourself through any problem to see how useful the analysis steps can be. Read a business article on the Internet for problem ideas. If you can complete the analysis, you're thinking like a manager!)

Scenario: An Apple ad campaign for its new iPhone was successful. At the same time, Apple announced that it's moving some of its iPhone manufacturing back to North America because it can use cheaper automated processes.

Let's deal with each situation separately, using the four-step analysis: (1) Is the ad campaign a demand or supply issue? Clearly, it's a demand issue, so it will affect the demand curve. (2) Is the issue price or something else? It's something else, so it will *shift* the demand curve—what causes the shift is a change in tastes or preferences, which is one of the factors that shift demand. (3) A positive or negative change?

(continued)

The ad campaign is successful, so it will shift the demand curve rightward. (4) How much? Here, you will need to draw a simple demand and supply model, shift the demand curve rightward a little, and then draw a second curve, shifting it rightward a lot.

Now analyze the second issue: (1) Is it a demand or supply issue? It's a supply issue. (2) Is it price, or something else? Something else—in this case, it's a decrease in input (capital) prices. (3) Which direction? Lower input costs will shift the supply curve rightward—Apple can make more units for the same price as before! (4) Finally, by how much? Again, you have to go to your model drawing and shift the supply curve rightward, first a little and then a lot. From the final diagram, you will see that equilibrium quantity will always be more than it was before the changes, but price is indeterminate. To see what happens to price, you look at the intersections of small (or large) changes in demand and large (or small) changes in supply. Depending on your confidence in which curve will shift more or less

to the other side, your answer to a price change will come from there.

To answer these questions, companies often create powerful econometric models to simulate different economic scenarios, often referred to as "what-if" scenarios. This simple yet elegant practical application of economic theory is extremely useful to business managers in forecasting new equilibrium quantities and prices, and even a company's future revenues and profits over time.

1. What tools do you think businesses can use to establish their own demand and supply issues?

2. What role do time and time lags have on a business that is attempting to establish its own market equilibrium? What items would you think would be affected by time lags?

3. In what ways do large businesses have advantages over smaller businesses in establishing their own level of equilibrium? Give some specific examples of how these advantages would affect equilibrium.

The Combinations of Supply and Demand Shifts

The eight possible changes in demand and/or supply are presented in Exhibit 6, along with the resulting changes in equilibrium quantity and equilibrium price. Although you could memorize the impact of the various possible changes in demand and supply, it would be more worthwhile to draw a graph, as shown in Exhibit 7, whenever a situation of changing demand and/or supply arises. Remember that an increase in either demand or supply means a rightward shift in the curve, whereas a decrease in either demand or supply means a leftward shift. Also, when both demand and supply change, one of the two equilibrium values—price or quantity—will change in an indeterminate manner (can increase, decrease, or stay the same) depending on the size of the change in demand relative to the change in supply.

section 4.2 Exhibit 6	The Effect of Changing Demand and/or Supply		
If Demand	**and Supply**	**Then Equilibrium Quantity**	**and Equilibrium Price**
1. Increases	Stays unchanged	Increases	Increases
2. Decreases	Stays unchanged	Decreases	Decreases
3. Stays unchanged	Increases	Increases	Decreases
4. Stays unchanged	Decreases	Decreases	Increases
5. Increases	Increases	Increases	Indeterminate*
6. Decreases	Decreases	Decreases	Indeterminate*
7. Increases	Decreases	Indeterminate*	Increases
8. Decreases	Increases	Indeterminate*	Decreases

*May increase, decrease, or remain the same, depending on the size of the change in demand relative to the change in supply.

section 4.2
Exhibit 7
The Combinations of Supply and Demand Shifts

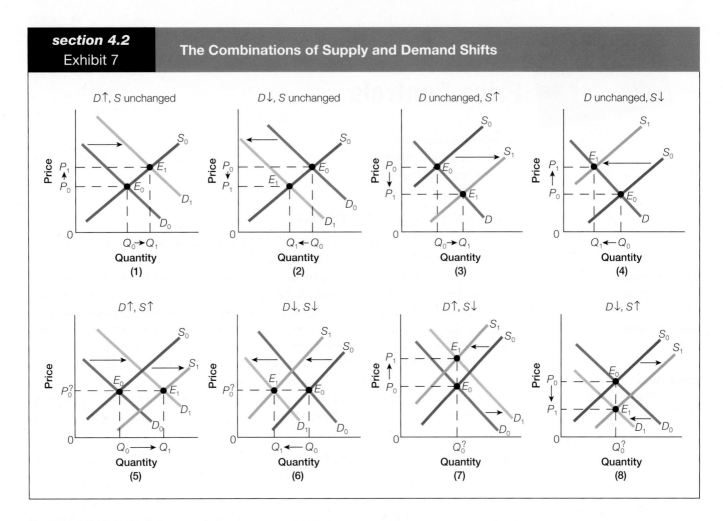

SECTION CHECK

- Changes in demand will cause a change in the equilibrium price and quantity, *ceteris paribus.*
- Changes in supply will cause a change in the equilibrium price and quantity, *ceteris paribus.*
- When there are simultaneous shifts in both supply and demand curves, either the equilibrium price or the equilibrium quantity will be indeterminate without more information.

Price Controls

- What are price controls?
- What are price ceilings?
- What are price floors?

WHAT ARE PRICE CONTROLS?

price controls
government-mandated minimum and maximum prices

price ceiling
a legally established maximum price

price floor
a legally established minimum price

Although nonequilibrium prices can occur naturally, reflecting uncertainty, they seldom last for long. Governments, however, may impose nonequilibrium prices for significant time periods. **Price controls** are government-mandated minimum and maximum prices that sometimes force prices above or below what they would be in equilibrium. The motivations for price controls vary with the market under consideration. For example, a **price ceiling**—a legally established maximum price—is often set for goods deemed important to low-income households, like housing. Or a **price floor**—a legally established minimum price—may be set on wages because wages are the primary source of income for most people.

Price controls are not always implemented by the federal government. Provincial governments can and do impose local price controls. One fairly well-known example of regional price controls is rent controls, which limit how much landlords can charge for rental housing.

WHAT ARE PRICE CEILINGS?

Rent controls have been imposed in Prince Edward Island, Quebec, Ontario, Manitoba, and British Columbia. Although the rules may vary, generally the price (or rent) of an apartment remains fixed over the tenure of an occupant, except for allowable annual increases tied to the cost of living or some other price index. When an occupant moves out, the owners can usually, but not always, raise the rent to a near-market level for the next occupant. The controlled rents for existing occupants, however, are generally well below market rental rates.

Results of Rent Controls

Rent controls distort market signals and lead to shortages. In addition, they often do not even help the intended recipients—low-income households. Most people living in rent-controlled apartments have a good deal, one that they would lose by moving as their family circumstances or income change. Tenants thus are reluctant to give up their governmentally granted right to a below-market-rent apartment. In addition, because the rents received by landlords are constrained and below market levels, the rate of return (roughly, the profit) on housing investments falls compared to that on other forms of real estate not subject to rent controls, like office rents or mortgage payments on condominiums. Hence, the incentive to construct new housing is reduced. Where rent controls are truly effective, there is generally little new construction going on, resulting in a shortage of apartments that persists and grows over time.

Also, when landlords are limited in what rent they can charge, there is little incentive to improve or upgrade apartments, such as by putting in new kitchen appliances or new carpeting. In fact, there is some incentive to avoid routine maintenance, thereby lowering the cost of apartment ownership to a figure approximating the controlled rental price, although the quality of the housing stock will deteriorate over time.

In extreme cases, the repercussions of rent controls can be life-threatening. For example, when four floors of his building caved in, killing three of his neighbours, Uttamchand K. Soiatwala, owner of a successful textile business, refused to leave his two-bedroom, rent-controlled apartment in Mumbai, India. The city then cut off his electricity and water and threatened to arrest his wife, but he still wouldn't leave. In all, 58 tenants refused to leave a rent-controlled apartment building that was considered too dangerous by city officials. Why did these residents take this risk? Cheap rent— $8.50 a month. There is tremendous tension in the market for Mumbai rent-controlled properties between landlords who can't afford to keep up their properties and tenants who will go to extraordinary lengths and even risk their lives to keep their units.

Another impact of rent control is that it promotes housing discrimination. Where rent controls do not exist, a prejudiced landlord might willingly rent to someone he believes is undesirable simply because the undesirable family is the only one willing to pay the requested rent (and the landlord is not willing to lower the rent substantially to get a desirable family, since this could translate into the loss of thousands of dollars in income). With rent controls, many families are likely to want to rent the controlled apartment, some desirable and some undesirable as seen by the landlord, simply because the rent is at a below-equilibrium price. The landlord can indulge in his "taste" for discrimination without any additional financial loss beyond that required by the controls.

Consequently, he will be more likely to choose to rent to a desirable family, perhaps a family without children or pets, rather than an undesirable one, perhaps one with a lower income and so a greater risk of nonpayment.

Exhibit 1 shows the impact of rent control. If the price ceiling is set below the market price, the quantity demanded will increase to Q_D from Q^* and the quantity supplied will fall to Q_S from Q^*. The rent control policy will therefore create a shortage, the difference between Q_D and Q_S.

section 4.3
Exhibit 1   **Rent Controls**

The impact of a price ceiling (a rent control law) set below the equilibrium price is a shortage.

WHAT ARE PRICE FLOORS?

The argument for minimum-wage legislation is simple: Existing wages for workers in some types of labour markets do not allow for a very high standard of living, and a set minimum wage allows those workers to live better than before. Provincial and territorial government legislation makes it illegal to pay most workers an amount below the current legislated minimum wage.

Let us examine graphically the impact of a minimum-wage law on low-skilled workers. In Exhibit 2, suppose the government sets the minimum wage, W_{MIN}, above the market equilibrium wage, W_E. In Exhibit 2, we see that the price floor is binding; that is, there is a surplus of low-skilled workers at W_{MIN} because the quantity of labour supplied is greater than the quantity of labour demanded. The reason for the surplus of low-skilled workers (unemployment) at W_{MIN} is that more people are willing to work than employers are willing and able to hire.

Notice that not everyone loses as a result of a minimum-wage law. Those workers who continue to hold jobs now have higher incomes (those workers between 0 and Q_D in Exhibit 2). However, many low-skilled workers suffer as a result of minimum-wage legislation—they either lose their jobs or are unable to get them in the first place (those between Q_D and Q_S in Exhibit 2). Although studies disagree somewhat on the precise magnitudes, they largely agree that minimum-wage laws do create some unemployment, and that the unemployment is concentrated among teenagers—the least-experienced and least-skilled members of the labour force.

Exhibit 3 shows the provincial minimum-wage rates (including the date on which they became effective) and the 2017 provincial unemployment rates (for both the youth segment of the population and the overall population) from across Canada.

If the minimum wage was raised to $30 an hour, one group that could experience a rise in unemployment would be teenagers.

section 4.3
Exhibit 2

section 4.3
Exhibit 2

The Unemployment Effects of a Minimum Wage on Low-Skilled Workers

The impact of a price floor (a minimum wage) set above the equilibrium price is a surplus—in this case, a surplus of low-skilled workers.

The data in Exhibit 3 reveal two interesting facts regarding minimum-wage rates and youth unemployment: (1) Youth unemployment varies considerably, even between provinces that have similar minimum-wage levels, and (2) in all jurisdictions that impose a minimum wage on their labour market, youth unemployment exceeds the rate of unemployment in the overall population.

It is this second conclusion that economists point to when they suggest that effective minimum-wage levels produce unemployment—especially in marginal segments of the labour market, such as the youth segment. Can the entire difference between the overall rate of unemployment and youth unemployment be attributed to the existence of minimum-wage legislation? Clearly not, but we must acknowledge it is a contributing factor.

section 4.3
Exhibit 3

Provincial Minimum Wages and Unemployment Rates

Province	Minimum Wage ($/hr.)	Effective Date	Unemployment Rate (%) (2017)	
			15–24 Years	15 Years and Over
British Columbia	11.35	Sep. 15, 2017	8.6	5.1
Alberta	13.60	Oct. 1, 2017	13.2	7.8
Saskatchewan	10.96	Oct. 1, 2017	11.8	6.3
Manitoba	11.15	Oct. 1, 2017	11.7	5.4
Ontario	14.00	Jan. 1, 2018	12.3	6.0
Quebec	11.25	May 1, 2017	10.3	6.1
New Brunswick	11.25	Apr. 1, 2018	13.5	8.1
Nova Scotia	11.00	Apr. 1, 2018	16.8	8.4
PEI	11.55	Apr. 1, 2018	13.2	9.8
Newfoundland and Labrador	11.00	Oct. 1, 2017	17.6	14.8
Canada			11.6	6.3

SOURCES: Minimum-wage rates, Canada: http://srv116.services.gc.ca/dimt-wid/sm-mw/rpt1.aspx; unemployment rates: Statistics Canada, Table 282-0086, *Labour Force Survey* estimates (LFS), supplementary unemployment rates by sex and age group, annual (percentage) (2).

Most Canadian workers are not affected by the minimum-wage law because in the market for their skills, they earn wages that exceed the minimum wage. For example, minimum-wage legislation will not affect the unemployment rate for accountants. In Exhibit 4, we see the labour market for skilled and experienced workers. In this market the minimum wage (the price floor) is not binding because these workers are earning wages that far exceed the minimum wage—W_E is much higher than W_{MIN}.

The above analysis does not "prove" minimum-wage laws are "bad" and should be abolished. To begin with, there is the empirical question of how much unemployment is caused by minimum-wage legislation. Secondly, some might believe that the cost of unemployment resulting from a minimum-wage law is a reasonable price to pay for assuring that those with jobs get a "decent" wage. The analysis does point out, however, that there is a cost to having minimum-wage legislation, and the burden of this falls not only on low-skilled workers and employers but also on consumers of products made more costly by the minimum-wage law.

Canadian Dairy Production: Another Example of a Price Floor

Another example of price floors can be found by looking at the price controls that have been imposed on dairy products produced in Canada since the 1970s. While initially implemented to ensure a fair return for farmers and greater price stability for processors and consumers, these price controls have ultimately resulted in milk prices being nearly 50 percent higher in Canada than in the United States and cheese prices being almost 25 percent higher. To understand how this discrepancy in price has happened, we need to understand the role that price controls play in the dairy industry.

The price farmers receive for raw milk is set by the Canadian Dairy Commission, a Crown corporation composed mainly of dairy farmers. This "farm gate" price is not based on what the market is willing to pay, but on the costs of production, market conditions, and what is determined to be a fair profit for producers.

Processors take the raw milk and turn it into fluid milk, yogurt, and other dairy products. The price these processors sell the finished product to retailers for is subject to a second price control. Referred to as a "floor price," processors cannot sell their dairy products for less than a minimum wholesale price. And the controls don't end there. At the final stage, retailers have a minimum price they must charge for milk. The floor price plus the retailer's expenses and margins is what consumers end up paying for a litre of milk in Canada.

section 4.3 Exhibit 4	**The Unemployment Effects of Minimum-Wage Legislation on Skilled Workers**

There is no impact of a price floor on the market for skilled and experienced workers. In this market, the price floor (the minimum wage) is not binding.

unintended consequences

the secondary effects of an action that may occur after the initial effects

Unintended Consequences

When markets are altered for policy reasons, it is wise to remember that actions do not always have the results that were initially intended—**unintended consequences** or secondary effects may occur after the initial effects of actions. As economists, we must always look for the secondary effects of an action that may occur, along with the initial effects. For example, the government is often well intentioned when it adopts price controls to help low-skilled workers or tenants in search of affordable housing; however, such policies can also cause unintended consequences, which may completely undermine the intended effects. For example, rent controls may have an immediate effect of lowering rents, but secondary effects may well include very low vacancy rates, discrimination against low-income and large families, and deterioration of the quality of rental units. Similarly, a sizable increase in the minimum-wage rate may help many low-skilled workers or apprentices, but will result in higher unemployment and/or a reduction in fringe benefits, such as vacations and discounts to employees. Society has to make tough decisions, and if the government subsidizes some program or group of people in one area, then something must always be given up somewhere else. The "law of scarcity" cannot be repealed!

SECTION CHECK

- Price controls involve government mandates to keep prices above or below the market-determined equilibrium price.
- Price ceilings are government-imposed maximum prices. When price ceilings are set below the equilibrium price, shortages will result.
- Price floors are government-imposed minimum prices. When price floors are set above the equilibrium price, surpluses will result.

For Your Review

Section 4.1

1. If a price is above the equilibrium price, explain the forces that bring the market back to the equilibrium price and quantity. If a price is below the equilibrium price, explain the forces that bring the market back to the equilibrium price and quantity.

2. The following table shows the hypothetical monthly demand and supply schedules for bottles of maple syrup in Winnipeg.

Price	Quantity Demanded (bottles)	Quantity Supplied (bottles)
$6	700	100
7	600	200
8	500	300
9	400	400
10	300	500

a. What is the equilibrium price of a bottle of maple syrup in Winnipeg?

b. At a price of $7 per bottle, is there equilibrium, a surplus, or a shortage? If it is a surplus or shortage, how large is it?

c. At a price of $10, is there equilibrium, a surplus, or a shortage? If it is a surplus or shortage, how large is it?

3. The market for tablet computers is represented by the following demand and supply schedules.

Price ($)	Quantity Demanded (millions of units)	Quantity Supplied (millions of units)
100	8.2	4.7
200	7.6	5.0
300	7.1	5.2
400	6.3	6.3
500	5.9	6.9
600	5.1	7.3
700	4.1	8.1

a. What is the equilibrium price and quantity of tablet computers?

b. Over what range of price would the tablet computer market exhibit a shortage of computers? How would the market self-regulate a solution to this disequilibrium situation?

c. Over what range of price would the tablet computer market exhibit a surplus of computers? How would the market self-regulate a solution to this disequilibrium situation?

Sections 4.1 and 4.2

4. Assume the following information for the demand and supply schedules for coffee.

Price ($)	Quantity Demanded (thousands of kg)	Quantity Supplied (thousands of kg)
6	3	9
5	4	7
4	5	5
3	6	3
2	7	1

a. Graph the corresponding demand and supply curves and identify the equilibrium price and quantity of coffee?

b. At the price of $6, would there be a shortage or a surplus and how large would it be?

c. At the price of $3, would there be a shortage or a surplus and how large would it be?

d. If the demand for coffee decreased by 3000 kg at every price, would there be a shortage or a surplus and how much would it be at the price of $4?

e. Using the original amounts of supply and demand, if the supply for coffee increased by 6000 kg at every price, would there be a shortage or a surplus and how much would it be at the price of $2?

5. Assume the following information for the demand and supply schedules for Good Z.

Price per Unit	Quantity Demanded	Quantity Supplied
$10	10	55
9	20	50
8	30	45
7	40	40
6	50	35
5	60	30
4	70	25
3	80	20
2	90	15
1	100	10

a. Draw the corresponding supply and demand curves.

b. What is the equilibrium price per unit and quantity traded?

c. If the price was $9, would there be a shortage or a surplus? How large?

d. If the price was $3, would there be a shortage or a surplus? How large?

e. If the demand for Z increased by 15 units at every price, what would be the new equilibrium price and quantity traded?

f. Given the original demand for Z, if the supply of Z was increased by 15 units at every price, what would be the new equilibrium price and quantity traded?

6. The market for baseball tickets at your school's stadium, which seats 2000, is the following:

Price per Unit	Quantity Demanded	Quantity Supplied
$2	4000	2000
4	2000	2000
6	1000	2000
8	500	2000

a. What is the equilibrium price?

b. What is unusual about the supply curve?

c. At what prices would a shortage occur?

d. At what prices would a surplus occur?

e. Suppose that the addition of new students (all big baseball fans) next year will add 1000 to the quantity demanded at each price. What will this increase do to next year's demand curve? What will be the new equilibrium price?

Section 4.2

Blueprint Problem

Using supply and demand curves, show the effect of the following events on the market for gasoline in North America:

a. world economic growth resulting in rising consumer incomes

b. hostilities in the Middle East and domestic refinery problems

Blueprint Solution

a.

Market for Gasoline

Step 2: Event Analysis

Answer the three questions detailed in the chapter:

1. Consumer incomes are a demand-side variable.

2. Consumer incomes are a shift variable (that is, a nonprice determinant of demand).

3. If consumer incomes increase and gasoline is assumed to be a normal good, then the event is expansionary.

Step 1: The Initial Equilibrium

Using comparative statistics to determine the impact of each event requires starting the analysis from an initial equilibrium— point A.

Step 3: New Equilibrium

Once the event analysis has been completed, re-establish the market back into equilibrium— point B. Compare the "new" and "initial" equilibriums.

As a result of world economic growth and rising consumer incomes, the gasoline market will experience an increase in demand, causing both the equilibrium price and the quantity of gasoline to rise.

b.

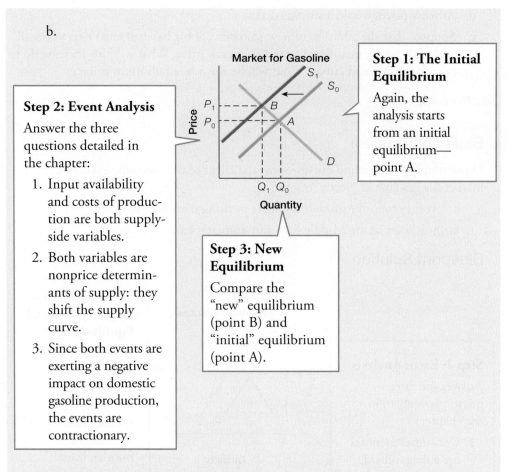

Step 1: The Initial Equilibrium

Again, the analysis starts from an initial equilibrium—point A.

Step 2: Event Analysis

Answer the three questions detailed in the chapter:

1. Input availability and costs of production are both supply-side variables.

2. Both variables are nonprice determinants of supply: they shift the supply curve.

3. Since both events are exerting a negative impact on domestic gasoline production, the events are contractionary.

Step 3: New Equilibrium

Compare the "new" equilibrium (point B) and "initial" equilibrium (point A).

The continued hostilities in the Middle East, where the majority of the globe's crude oil is produced, coupled with domestic refinery problems, will cause the North American market for gasoline to experience a decrease in supply, causing equilibrium price to increase and equilibrium quantity to decline.

7. Does an increase in supply create a shortage or a surplus at the original price?

8. Using supply and demand curves, show the effect of each of the following events on the market for wheat.

   a. A major wheat-producing area in Saskatchewan suffers a drought.

   b. The price of corn decreases (assume that many farmers can grow either corn or wheat).

   c. The Prairie provinces have great weather.

   d. The price of fertilizer declines.

   e. More individuals start growing wheat.

9. Beginning from an initial equilibrium, draw the effects of the following changes in terms of the relevant supply and demand curves.

   a. an increase in the price of hot dogs on the hamburger market

   b. a decrease in the number of taxi companies in Halifax on cab trips

   c. the effect of El Niño rainstorms destroying the strawberry crops in Ontario

10. Use supply and demand curves to show the following:
    a. simultaneous increases in supply and demand, with a large increase in supply and a small increase in demand
    b. simultaneous increases in supply and demand, with a small increase in supply and a large increase in demand
    c. simultaneous decreases in supply and demand, with a large decrease in supply and a small decrease in demand
    d. simultaneous decreases in supply and demand, with a small decrease in supply and a large decrease in demand

11. Why do 10 A.M. classes fill up before 8 A.M. classes during class registration? Use supply and demand curves to help explain your answers.

12. What would happen to the equilibrium price and equilibrium quantity in the following cases?
    a. an increase in income for a normal good and a decrease in the price of an input
    b. a technological advance and a decrease in the number of buyers
    c. an increase in the price of a substitute and an increase in the number of suppliers
    d. producers' expectations that prices will soon fall and a reduction in consumer tastes for the good

13. In Canada, why is fresh fruit (apples, strawberries, peaches) less expensive in the summer than in the winter? Use supply and demand curves to help explain your answer.

14. If both buyers and sellers of grapes expect grape prices to rise in the near future, what will happen to grape prices and sales today?

Section 4.3

15. Refer to the following supply and demand curve diagram.

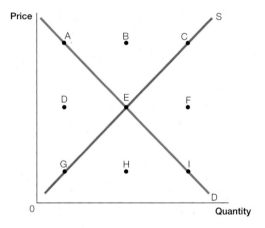

    a. Starting from an initial equilibrium at E, what shift or shifts in supply and/ or demand could move the equilibrium price and quantity to each of points A through I?
    b. Starting from an initial equilibrium at E, what would happen if both a decrease in the price of a substitute in production and an increase in income occurred, if it is a normal good?
    c. Starting from an initial equilibrium at E, what would happen if both an increase in the price of an input and an advance in technology occurred?

    d. If a price floor is imposed above the equilibrium price, which of A through I would tend to be the quantity supplied, and which would tend to be the quantity demanded? Which would be the new quantity exchanged?

    e. If a price ceiling is imposed below the equilibrium price, which of A through I would tend to be the quantity supplied, and which would tend to be the quantity demanded? Which would be the new quantity exchanged?

16. Draw a supply and demand curve diagram with a price floor above the equilibrium price, and indicate the quantity supplied and quantity demanded at that price and the resulting surplus.

    a. What happens to the quantity supplied, the quantity demanded, and the surplus if the price floor is raised? If it is lowered?

    b. What happens to the quantity supplied, the quantity demanded, and the surplus if, for a given price floor, the demand curve shifts to the right?

    c. What happens to the quantity supplied, the quantity demanded, and the surplus if, for a given price floor, the supply curve shifts to the right?

17. Draw a supply and demand curve diagram with a price ceiling below the equilibrium price, and indicate the quantity supplied and quantity demanded at that price, and the resulting shortage.

    a. What happens to the quantity supplied, the quantity demanded, and the shortage if the price ceiling is raised? If it is lowered?

    b. What happens to the quantity supplied, the quantity demanded, and the shortage if, for a given price ceiling, the demand curve shifts to the right?

    c. What happens to the quantity supplied, the quantity demanded, and the shortage if, for a given price ceiling, the supply curve shifts to the right?

18. Why do price floors and price ceilings both reduce the quantity of goods traded in those markets?

19. What would be the impact of a price floor set above the equilibrium price for dairy products? Below the equilibrium price?

20. Giving in to pressure from voters who claim that local theatre owners are gouging their customers with ticket prices as high as $10 per movie, the city council of a local municipality imposes a price ceiling of $2 on all movies. What effect is this likely to have on the market for movies in this particular city? What will happen to the quantity of tickets demanded? What will happen to the quantity supplied? Who gains? Who loses?

Price Elasticity of Demand

- What is price elasticity of demand?
- How do we measure consumers' responses to price changes?
- How do we use the "midpoint method" in calculating price elasticities of demand?
- What determines the price elasticity of demand?

If the local sports team increases the price it charges for game tickets, what impact will that have on tickets sales? From our earlier discussion about the law of demand, we know that at a higher price, the quantity demanded for game tickets will be lower, but will ticket sales fall by a little or a lot? That is, from the law of demand, we know the direction of the relationship between price and quantity demanded (it is inverse), but what we do not know is the *magnitude* of the relationship. To answer this question, we need to take a more in-depth look into the relationship between price and quantity demanded—we need to learn about the concept of *elasticity*.

Some of the results in this chapter may surprise you. A devastating drought in western Canada that destroyed much of this year's wheat crop would leave some wheat farmers better off. Ideal weather that led to a bountiful crop of wheat everywhere would leave some wheat farmers worse off. As you will soon find out, these issues hinge importantly on the tools of *elasticity*.

In this chapter, we also see the importance of *elasticity* in determining how the burden of a tax is allocated between buyers and sellers. If a tax is levied on the seller, will the seller pay all of the taxes? If the tax is levied on the buyer, who pays the larger share of taxes? We will see that *elasticity* is critical in the determination of tax burden. Elasticities will also help us to more fully understand many policy issues—from illegal drugs to luxury taxes. For example, if the federal government were to impose a large tax on pharmaceuticals, what do you think would happen to pharmaceutical sales? What would happen to employment in the pharmaceutical industry?

WHAT IS PRICE ELASTICITY OF DEMAND?

**price elasticity of
demand**

*a measure of the responsive-
ness of quantity demanded to a
change in price*

In learning and applying the law of demand, we have established the basic fact that quantity demanded changes inversely with changes in price, *ceteris paribus*. But how much does quantity demanded change? The extent to which a change in price impacts quantity demanded may vary considerably from product to product and over the various price ranges for the same product. The **price elasticity of demand** measures the responsiveness of quantity demanded to a change in price. More specifically, price elasticity is defined as the percentage change in quantity demanded divided by the percentage change in price:

$$\text{Price elasticity of demand } (E_D) = \frac{\text{Percentage change in quantity demanded}}{\text{Percentage change in price}}$$

Note that, following the law of demand, there is an inverse relationship between price and quantity demanded. For this reason, price elasticity of demand is, in theory, always negative. In practice, however, this quantity is always expressed in absolute value terms, as a nonnegative number, for simplicity.

HOW DO WE MEASURE CONSUMERS' RESPONSES TO PRICE CHANGES?

It is important to understand the basic intuition behind elasticities. This can be best understood by initially focusing on the percentage changes in quantity demanded and price.

Think of elasticity as an elastic rubber band. If the quantity demanded is very responsive to even a small change in price, we call it *elastic*. On the other hand, if even a huge change in price results in only a small change in quantity demanded, then the demand is said to be *inelastic*. For example, if a 10 percent increase in the price leads to a 50 percent reduction in the quantity demanded, we say that demand is *elastic* because the quantity demanded is very sensitive to the price change.

$$E_D = \frac{\%\Delta Q_D}{\%\Delta P} = \frac{50\%}{10\%} = 5$$

Demand is elastic in this case because a 10 percent change in price led to a larger (50 percent) change in quantity demanded.

Alternatively, if a 10 percent increase in the price leads to a 1 percent reduction in quantity demanded, we say that demand is *inelastic* because the quantity demanded did not respond much to the price reduction.

$$E_D = \frac{\%\Delta Q_D}{\%\Delta P} = \frac{1\%}{10\%} = 0.10$$

Demand is inelastic in this case because a 10 percent change in price led to a smaller (1 percent) change in quantity demanded.

The Ranges of the Price Elasticity of Demand

Economists refer to a variety of demand curves based on the magnitude of their elasticity. A demand curve or a portion of a demand curve can be elastic, or inelastic, or unit elastic. A demand curve is

Elastic $(E_D > 1)$ if Percentage change in Q_D > Percentage change in P

Inelastic $(E_D < 1)$ if Percentage change in Q_D < Percentage change in P

Unit elastic $(E_D = 1)$ if Percentage change in Q_D = Percentage change in P

Elastic Demand Segments

An **elastic demand segment** is a portion of the demand curve where the percentage change in quantity demanded is greater than the percentage change in price ($E_D > 1$). In this case, a given percentage increase in price, say 2 percent, leads to a larger percentage change in quantity demanded, say 20 percent, as seen in Exhibit 1(a). If the curve was perfectly elastic, a small percentage increase in price would cause the quantity demanded to fall dramatically to zero. For example, say there were two side-by-side roadside fruit stands selling the same quality of apples. If one stand had lower prices, then the higher-priced fruit stand would soon be selling no apples. In Exhibit 1(b), a perfectly elastic demand curve (horizontal) is illustrated. Economists define the elasticity of demand in this case as infinity, because the quantity demanded is infinitely responsive to even a very small percentage change in price.

© David Wei/Alamy Stock Photo

If bus fares increase, will ridership fall a little or a lot? It all depends on the price elasticity of demand. If the price elasticity of demand is elastic, a \$0.50 price increase will lead to a relatively large reduction in bus travel as riders find viable substitutes. If the price elasticity of demand is inelastic, a \$0.50 price increase will lead to a relatively small reduction in bus ridership as riders are not able to find good alternatives to bus transportation.

Inelastic Demand Segments

An **inelastic demand segment** is a portion of the demand curve where the percentage change in quantity demanded is less than the percentage change in price ($E_D < 1$). In this case, a given percentage (e.g., 10 percent) change in price is accompanied with a smaller (e.g., 5 percent) reduction in quantity demanded, as seen in Exhibit 2(a). If the demand curve is perfectly inelastic, the quantity demanded is the same regardless of the price, as illustrated in Exhibit 2(b).

Unit Elastic Demand Segments

Goods for which E_D equals one ($E_D = 1$), that is, where the percentage change in quantity demanded is equal to the percentage change in price, are said to have **unit elastic demand**. In this case, the percentage change in quantity demanded is the same as the percentage change in price that caused it. For example, as illustrated in Exhibit 3, a 10 percent increase in price will lead to a 10 percent reduction in quantity demanded.

elastic demand segment
a portion of the demand curve where the percentage change of quantity demanded is greater than the percentage change in price ($E_D > 1$)

inelastic demand segment
a portion of the demand curve where the percentage change of quantity demanded is less than the percentage change in price ($E_D < 1$)

unit elastic demand
demand with a price elasticity of 1; the percentage change in quantity demanded is equal to the percentage change in price

section 5.1 Exhibit 1	Elastic Demand

a. Elastic Demand ($E_D > 1$)

$$E_D = \frac{\%\Delta Q_D}{\%\Delta P} = \frac{0.20}{0.02} = 10$$

P_1
P_0 ↑ 2%ΔP

Price

D

20%ΔQ_D

0 Q_1 Q_0

Quantity

A small percentage change in price leads to a larger percentage change in quantity demanded.

b. Perfectly Elastic Demand ($E_D = \infty$)

P_1
P_0 ↑ΔP

Price

D

ΔQ_D

0 Q_1 Q_0

Quantity

A small percentage change in price will change quantity demanded by an infinite amount.

section 5.1
Exhibit 2

Inelastic Demand

a. Inelastic Demand ($E_D < 1$)

$$E_D = \frac{\%\Delta Q_D}{\%\Delta P} = \frac{0.05}{0.10} = 0.5$$

A change in price leads to a smaller percentage change in quantity demanded.

b. Perfectly Inelastic Demand ($E_D = 0$)

The quantity demanded does not change regardless of the percentage change in price.

section 5.1
Exhibit 3

Unit Elastic Demand

$$E_D = \frac{\%\Delta Q_D}{\%\Delta P} = \frac{0.10}{0.10} = 1$$

The percentage change in quantity demanded is the same as the percentage change in price that caused it ($E_D = 1$).

HOW DO WE USE THE "MIDPOINT METHOD" IN CALCULATING PRICE ELASTICITIES OF DEMAND?

Now that we have looked at the basic theory of elasticities by focusing on the percentage changes in quantity demanded and price, suppose we wanted to perform the same calculation using points from a demand curve. What we would soon realize is that the direction of the calculation has an impact on our answer! To help understand this potential problem, consider the following example:

Point	Price	Quantity
A	$2	100
B	$4	40

When going from point A to point B, the percentage increase in price is 100 percent $\left[\left(\dfrac{\$4-\$2}{\$2}\right) \times 100\right]$ and the percentage decline in quantity is 60 percent $\left[\left(\dfrac{40-100}{100}\right) \times 100\right]$, giving us a price elasticity of demand coefficient of 0.6 (60/100). However, when we go from point B to point A, the percentage decrease in price is 50 percent, and the percentage increase in quantity is 150 percent, giving us a price elasticity of demand coefficient of 3 (150/50).

The reason for the different answers in the above case is due to the traditional method for calculating percentage. According to the traditional approach, the change in the given values is divided by the initial value in determining percentage change. However, since this initial value can be different depending on whether you are starting from point A or from point B, you can, and often do, get different answers. To solve this problem, a technique known as the *midpoint method* is used in place of the traditional approach. The midpoint method uses a midpoint (or average) of the initial and final values in calculating percentage change, as opposed to an initial value. And since this midpoint value is the same regardless of the direction of the calculation, we always get the same answer. Consider the same example again, now using the midpoint method.

Point	Price	Quantity
A	$2	100
B	$4	40
Midpoint	$3	70

According to the midpoint method, when going from point A to point B, the percentage increase in price is 67 percent $\left[\left(\dfrac{\$4 - \$2}{\left(\dfrac{\$4 + \$2}{2} \right)} \right) \times 100 \right]$ and the percentage decline in quantity is 86 percent $\left[\left(\dfrac{40 - 100}{\left(\dfrac{40 + 100}{2} \right)} \right) \times 100 \right]$, giving us a price elasticity of demand coefficient of 1.3 (86/67). Conveniently, when we go from point B to point A, the percentage decrease in price is 67 percent $\left[\left(\dfrac{\$2 - \$4}{\left(\dfrac{\$2 + \$4}{2} \right)} \right) \times 100 \right]$ and the percentage increase in quantity is 86 percent $\left[\left(\dfrac{100 - 40}{\left(\dfrac{100 + 40}{2} \right)} \right) \times 100 \right]$, giving us a price elasticity of demand coefficient of 1.3 (86/67). Problem solved!

Price elasticity of demand between two points, (Q_A, P_A) and (Q_B, P_B), can then be expressed in terms of the midpoint method with the following formula:

$$E_D = \frac{\%\Delta Q_D}{\%\Delta P} = \frac{\dfrac{Q_A - Q_B}{\left(\dfrac{Q_A + Q_B}{2} \right)}}{\dfrac{P_A - P_B}{\left(\dfrac{P_A + P_B}{2} \right)}}$$

WHAT DETERMINES THE PRICE ELASTICITY OF DEMAND?

As you have learned, the elasticity of demand for a specific good refers to movements along its demand curve as its price changes. A lower price will increase quantity demanded, and a higher price will reduce quantity demanded. But what factors will influence the magnitude of the change in quantity demanded in response to a price change? That is, what will make the demand curve relatively more elastic (where Q_D is responsive to price changes), and what will make the demand curve relatively less elastic (where Q_D is less responsive to price changes)?

For the most part, the price elasticity of demand depends on the following factors: (1) the availability of close substitutes, (2) the proportion of income spent on the good, and (3) the amount of time that has elapsed since the price change.

Availability of Close Substitutes

Goods *with* close substitutes tend to have more elastic demands. Why? Because if the price of such a good increases, consumers can easily switch to other, now relatively lower-priced substitutes. There are many examples, such as butter and margarine, one brand of root beer as opposed to another, or different brands of gasoline, where the ease of substitution will make demand quite elastic for most individuals. Goods *without* close substitutes, such as insulin for diabetics, cigarettes for chain smokers, or heroin for addicts, tend to have inelastic demands.

The degree of substitutability may also depend on whether the good is a necessity or a luxury. Goods that are necessities, like food, cannot be easily substituted for and thus tend to have lower elasticities than luxury items, like jewellery.

Narrowly Defined Goods

When the demand for a good is broadly defined, it tends to be less elastic than when it is narrowly defined. For example, the elasticity of demand for food, a very broad category, tends to be inelastic because there are very few substitutes for food. But for a certain type of food, like pizza, a narrowly defined good, it is much easier to find a substitute— perhaps tacos, burgers, or French fries. That is, the demand for a particular type of food is more elastic because there are more and better substitutes than for food as an entire category.

Proportion of Income Spent on the Good

The smaller the proportion of income spent on a good, the lower its elasticity of demand. If the amount spent on a good relative to income is small, then the impact of a change in its price on one's budget will also be small. As a result, consumers will respond less to price changes for these goods than for similar percentage changes in large-ticket items, where a price change could have a potentially large impact on the consumer's budget. For example, a 50 percent increase in the price of salt will have a much smaller impact on consumers' behaviour than a similar percentage increase in the price of a new automobile. Similarly, a 50 percent increase in the cost of university tuition will have a greater impact on students' (and sometimes parents') budgets than a 50 percent increase in beer prices.

Time

For many goods, the more time that people have to adapt to a new price change, the greater the elasticity of demand. Immediately after a price change, consumers may be unable to locate very good alternatives or easily change their consumption patterns. But the more time that passes, the more time consumers have to find or develop suitable substitutes and to plan and implement changes in their patterns of consumption. For example, drivers may not respond immediately to an increase in gas prices, perhaps believing it to be temporary. However, if the price persists over a longer period, we would expect people to drive less, buy more fuel-efficient cars, move closer to work, carpool, take the bus, or even bike to work. Hence, for many goods, especially nondurable goods (goods that do *not* last a long time), the short-run demand curve is generally less elastic than the long-run demand curve, as illustrated by Exhibit 4.

section 5.1
Exhibit 4

Short-Run and Long-Run Demand Curves

For many goods, like gasoline, price is much more elastic in the long run than the short run because buyers take time to change their consumption patterns. In the short run, the increase in price from P_0 to P_1 has only a small effect on the quantity demanded for gasoline. In the long run, the effect of the price increase will be much larger.

Estimated Price Elasticities of Demand

Because of shifts in supply and demand curves, researchers have a difficult task when trying to estimate empirically the price elasticity of demand for a particular good or service. Despite this difficulty, Exhibit 5 presents some estimates for the price elasticity of demand for certain goods. As you would expect, certain goods like air travel, gasoline, and legal services are all relatively price inelastic in the short run because buyers have fewer substitutes. On the other hand, air travel in the long run is much more sensitive to price (elastic) because the available substitutes are much more plentiful. Exhibit 5 shows that the long-run price elasticity of demand for air travel is 2.4, which means that a 1 percent increase in price will lead to a 2.4 percent reduction in quantity demanded. Notice, in each case where the data is available, the estimates of the long-run price elasticities of demand are greater than the short-run price elasticities of demand. In short, the price elasticity of demand is greater when the price change persists over a longer time period.

section 5.1 Exhibit 5	**Price Elasticities of Demand for Selected Goods**	
Good	**Short Run**	**Long Run**
Salt	–	0.1
Air travel	0.1	2.4
Gasoline	0.2	0.7
Jewellery and watches	0.4	0.7
Legal services	0.4	–
Alcohol	0.9	3.6
Movies	0.9	3.7
China, glassware	1.5	2.6
Automobiles	1.9	2.2
Chevrolets	–	4.0

SOURCES: Adapted from Robert Archibald and Robert Gillingham, "An Analysis of the Short-Run Consumer Demand for Gasoline Using Household Survey Data," *Review of Economics and Statistics 62* (November 1980), pp. 622–628; Hendrik S. Houthakker and Lester D. Taylor, *Consumer Demand in the United States: Analyses and Projections* (Cambridge, MA: Harvard University Press, 1970), pp. 56–149; and Richard Voith, "The Long-Run of Demand for Consumer Rail Transportation," *Journal of Urban Economics 30* (November 1991), pp. 360–371.

SECTION CHECK

- Price elasticity of demand measures the percentage change in quantity demanded divided by the percentage change in price.
- If the demand for a good is price elastic in the relevant range, quantity demanded is very responsive to a price change. If the demand for a good is relatively price inelastic, quantity demanded is not very responsive to a price change.
- The "midpoint method" for calculating percentage change involves using the average of the changing values, thereby eliminating the direction bias found in the traditional approach.
- The price elasticity of demand depends on (1) the availability of close substitutes, (2) the proportion of income spent on the good, and (3) the amount of time that buyers have to respond to a price change.

Total Revenue and Price Elasticity of Demand

● How does the price elasticity of demand impact total revenue?
● How does price elasticity of demand change along a linear demand curve?

HOW DOES THE PRICE ELASTICITY OF DEMAND IMPACT TOTAL REVENUE?

The price elasticity of demand for a good also has implications for total revenue. Total revenue (TR) is simply the price of the good (P) times the quantity of the good sold (Q): $TR = P \times Q$. In Exhibit 1, we see that when the demand is price elastic ($E_D > 1$), total revenues will rise as the price declines because the percentage increase in the quantity demanded is greater than the percentage reduction in price. For example, if the price of a good is cut in half (say from $10 to $5) and the quantity demanded more than doubles (say from 40 to 100), total revenue will rise from $400 ($10 × 40 = $400) to $500 ($5 × 100 = $500). Equivalently, if the price rises from $5 to $10 and the quantity demanded falls from 100 to 40 units, then total revenue falls from $500 to $400. As this example illustrates, if the demand curve is relatively elastic, total revenue varies inversely with a price change.

You can see from the following what happens to total revenue when demand is price elastic. (Note: The sizes of the price and quantity arrows represent the sizes of the percentage changes.)

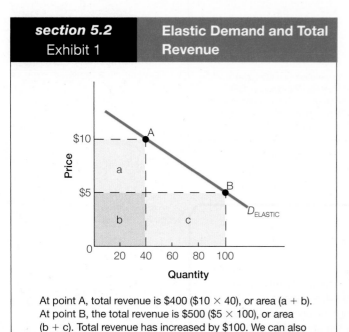

section 5.2	Elastic Demand and Total
Exhibit 1	Revenue

At point A, total revenue is $400 ($10 × 40), or area (a + b). At point B, the total revenue is $500 ($5 × 100), or area (b + c). Total revenue has increased by $100. We can also see in the graph that total revenue has increased because the area (b + c) is greater than area (a + b), or c > a.

When Demand Is Price Elastic

$$\downarrow TR = \uparrow P \times Q \downarrow$$

or

$$\uparrow TR = \downarrow P \times Q \uparrow$$

On the other hand, if demand for a good is relatively inelastic ($E_D < 1$), the total revenue will be lower at lower prices than at higher prices because a given price reduction will be accompanied by a proportionately smaller increase in quantity demanded. For example, as seen in Exhibit 2, if the price of a good is cut, say from $10 to $5, and the quantity demanded less than doubles—say it increases from 30 to 40—total revenue will fall from $300 ($10 × 30 = $300) to $200 ($5 × 40 = $200). Equivalently, if the price increases from $5 to $10 and the quantity demanded falls from 40 to 30, total revenue will increase from $200 to $300. To summarize, then, if the demand curve is inelastic, total revenue will vary directly with a price change.

When Demand Is Price Inelastic

$$\uparrow TR = \overset{\uparrow}{P} \times \overset{\downarrow}{Q}$$

or

$$\downarrow TR = \overset{\downarrow}{P} \times \overset{\uparrow}{Q}$$

In this case, the net effect on total revenue is reversed but easy to see. (Again, the sizes of the price and quantity arrows represent the sizes of the percentage changes.)

An example will help us appreciate the relationship we have just established between price elasticity of demand and total revenue. Is a poor wheat harvest bad for all farmers? Is a great wheat harvest good for all farmers? The answers to these questions may seem obvious at first, but elasticity will reveal to us some interesting solutions.

As shown in Exhibit 3(a), if demand for wheat is inelastic, a reduction in supply without a simultaneous reduction in demand will result in a higher price for wheat and a rise in total revenues for farmers. The increase in price will cause farmers to lose the revenue indicated by area c; however, they will gain the area indicated by area a. The net result will be an overall increase in revenue equal to the area (a – c). Clearly, if some farmers lose their entire crop due to, say, bad weather, they are worse off; however, *collectively* farmers can profit from events that reduce crop size—and they do, because the demand for most agricultural products is inelastic. Interestingly, if all farmers were hurt equally, say, losing one-third of their crop, each farmer would be better off. Of course, consumers would be worse off because the price of agricultural products would be higher.

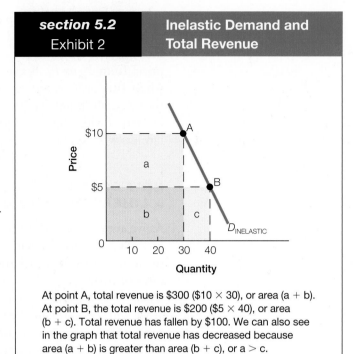

section 5.2
Exhibit 2

Inelastic Demand and Total Revenue

At point A, total revenue is $300 ($10 × 30), or area (a + b). At point B, the total revenue is $200 ($5 × 40), or area (b + c). Total revenue has fallen by $100. We can also see in the graph that total revenue has decreased because area (a + b) is greater than area (b + c), or a > c.

section 5.2
Exhibit 3

Elasticities and Total Revenue

a. Total Revenue and Inelastic Demand: A Reduction in Supply

b. Total Revenue and Inelastic Demand: An Increase in Supply

Alternatively, what if phenomenal weather has led to record wheat harvests or a technological advance has led to more productive wheat farmers? Either event would increase the supply from S_0 to S_1 in Exhibit 3(b). The increase in supply leads to a lower price, from P_0 to P_1. Because the demand for wheat is inelastic, the quantity sold of wheat rises proportionally less than the fall in the price. That is, in percentage terms, the price falls more than the quantity demanded rises. Each farmer is selling a few more bushels of wheat but the price of each bushel has fallen even more, so collectively wheat farmers will experience a decline in total revenue despite the good news.

HOW DOES PRICE ELASTICITY OF DEMAND CHANGE ALONG A LINEAR DEMAND CURVE?

As we showed earlier in the chapter, the slopes of demand curves can be used to estimate their *relative* elasticities of demand: The steeper that one demand curve is relative to another, the more inelastic it is relative to the other. However, beyond the extreme cases of perfectly elastic and perfectly inelastic curves, great care must be taken when trying to estimate the degree of elasticity of one demand curve from its slope. In fact, as we will see, a straight-line demand curve with a constant slope will change elasticity continuously as you move up or down it.

We can easily demonstrate that the elasticity of demand varies along a linear demand curve by using what we already know about the interrelationship between price and total revenue. Exhibit 4 shows a linear (constant slope) demand curve. In Exhibit 4(a), we see that when the price falls on the upper half of the demand curve from P_0 to P_1, and quantity demanded increases from Q_0 to Q_1, total revenue increases. That is, the new area of total revenue (area b + area c) is larger than the old area of total revenue (area a + area b). It is also true that if price increased in this region (from P_1 to P_0), total revenue would fall, because b + c is greater than a + b. In this region of the demand curve, then, there is a negative relationship between price and total revenue. As we discussed earlier, this is a characteristic of an elastic demand curve ($E_D > 1$).

section 5.2
Exhibit 4

Price Elasticity along a Linear Demand Curve

a. Elastic Range

b. Inelastic Range

The slope is constant along a linear demand curve, but the elasticity varies. Moving down along the demand curve, the elasticity is elastic at higher prices and inelastic at lower prices. It is unit elastic at its midpoint, the boundary between the inelastic and elastic ranges.

Exhibit 4(b) illustrates what happens to total revenue on the lower half of the same demand curve. When the price falls from P_2 to P_3 and the quantity demanded increases from Q_2 to Q_3, total revenue actually decreases because the new area of total revenue (area e + area f) is less than the old area of total revenue (area d + area e). Likewise, it is clear that an increase in price from P_3 to P_2 would increase total revenue. In this case, there is a positive relationship between price and total revenue, which, as we discussed, is characteristic of an inelastic demand curve ($E_D < 1$). Together, parts (a) and (b) of Exhibit 4 illustrate that, although the slope remains constant, the elasticity of a linear demand curve changes along the length of the curve—from relatively elastic at higher price ranges to relatively inelastic at lower price ranges.

In summary, Exhibit 5 illustrates how total revenue behaves over the entire range of demand. For example, when the price increases from $2 to $3, total revenue increases from $32 to $42—an increase in price increases total revenue, so demand is inelastic in this portion of the demand curve. But when the price increases from $8 to $9, the total revenue falls from $32 to $18, so demand is elastic in this portion of the demand curve.

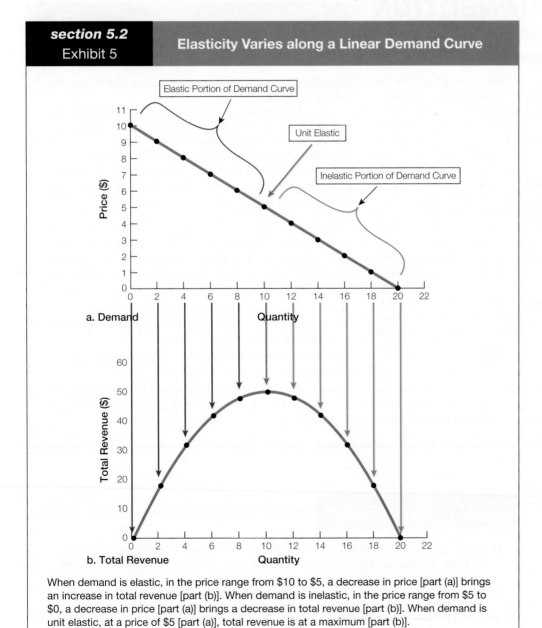

section 5.2
Exhibit 5

Elasticity Varies along a Linear Demand Curve

Elastic Portion of Demand Curve

Unit Elastic

Inelastic Portion of Demand Curve

a. Demand

b. Total Revenue

When demand is elastic, in the price range from $10 to $5, a decrease in price [part (a)] brings an increase in total revenue [part (b)]. When demand is inelastic, in the price range from $5 to $0, a decrease in price [part (a)] brings a decrease in total revenue [part (b)]. When demand is unit elastic, at a price of $5 [part (a)], total revenue is at a maximum [part (b)].

Specifically, when the price is high and the quantity demanded is low, this portion of the demand curve is elastic. Why? It is because a $1 reduction in price is a smaller percentage change when the price is high than when it is low. Similarly, an increase in 2 units of output is a larger percentage change when quantity demanded is lower. So we have a relatively small change in price leading to a proportionately greater change in quantity demanded—that is, demand is elastic on this portion of the demand curve.

Of course, the opposite is true when the price is low and the quantity demanded is high. Why? It is because a $1 change in price is a larger percentage change when the price is low and an increase in 2 units of output is a smaller percentage change when the quantity demanded is larger. That is, a relatively larger percentage change in price will lead to a relatively smaller change in quantity demanded—demand is relatively inelastic on this portion of the demand curve.

Business CONNECTION

CANADA'S OWN DOUGHNUTS AND THE MINIMUM WAGE

When former Ontario Premier Kathleen Wynne looked at her approval ratings in December 2017, she was concerned—they stood at 20 percent. A strong Liberal, whose party had been in power for nearly 18 years, she needed to try to gain more support to win the next election. An advocate of raising the minimum wage, she decided that the time was right. Unemployment was low, and the demand for labour in Ontario was generally solid. So Wynne's party introduced and she endorsed a raise in pay for minimum-wage earners to $14.00/hr from the $11.60/hr it had been for some years. Although 60 percent of voters seemed to support the raise, the backlash from smaller businesses was harsh.

Why were so many communities upset by franchisees laying off workers or cutting hours because of the wage hike? Over time, Tim Hortons has become closely associated with Canadians' values and their way of life. Marketing campaigns focus on hot chocolate and Tim Bits on a cold winter's day; they show charitable support for Little League hockey players. Kids in Little League are cute, and their parents dream of them becoming great players—scoring points for Team Canada or their favourite big-league hockey teams. Tim Hortons has a shop in almost every small town across Canada. Going for a Timmy's, Tim Bits, or a Double-Double are some of the first expressions new Canadians learn when they order a coffee. It is part of the Canadian identity.

But Tim Hortons is not just a cozy local doughnut shop—despite the marketing and its best efforts to occupy that space in every Canadian's heart. It's a franchise and it is part of a worldwide conglomerate of quick-service restaurants—Restaurant Brands International. It's operating in a highly competitive space, where small changes in profit margins make a big impact on the bottom line. Fast-food operations employ minimum-wage service workers. Raising the minimum wage could quickly lead to layoffs and fewer servers, because in such a competitive space, franchisees were forbidden from raising prices. Boycotts and protests quickly followed when franchisees cut payable hours for their servers. The Tim Hortons brand took a hit. Was it necessary?

1. Consider whether doughnuts have an elastic or inelastic demand profile? Would a price increase be harmful to total revenues? Why or why not?

2. Is competing by keeping prices low and cutting costs always the right strategy? Why or why not?

3. How do you see the determinants of price elasticity of demand impacting the price elasticity of demand for doughnuts?

SECTION CHECK

- If demand is price elastic ($E_D > 1$), total revenue will vary inversely with a change in price. If demand is price inelastic ($E_D < 1$), total revenue will vary in the same direction as a change in price.
- A linear demand curve is more price elastic at higher price ranges and more price inelastic at lower price ranges; it is unit elastic at the midpoint: $E_D = 1$.

Other Demand Elasticities

- What is the cross-price elasticity of demand?
- What is the income elasticity of demand?

WHAT IS THE CROSS-PRICE ELASTICITY OF DEMAND?

Price elasticities of demand are not the only elasticity calculation that economists use to better understand buyer behaviour. Sometimes the quantity of the good demanded is affected by the price of a related good (substitutes and complements). For example, if the price of potato chips falls, what is the impact, if any, on the quantity of soft drinks (a complement) demanded? Or if the price of soft drinks increases, to what degree will iced tea (a substitute) sales be affected? The **cross-price elasticity of demand** is a measure of the impact that a price change of one good will have on the quantity demanded of another good at a given price. Specifically, the cross-price elasticity of demand is defined as the percentage change in the quantity demanded of one good (good A) divided by the percentage change in price of another good (good B), or

cross-price elasticity of demand
a measure of the impact that a price change of one good will have on the quantity demanded of another good at a given price

$$\text{Cross-price elasticity of demand } (E_{AB}) = \frac{\text{Percentage change in quantity demanded of A}}{\text{Percentage change in the price of B}}$$

The cross-price elasticity of demand indicates not only the degree of the connection between the two variables but also whether the goods in question are substitutes or complements to one another.

Calculating the Cross-Price Elasticity of Demand

Let's calculate the cross-price elasticity of demand between sets of golf clubs and tennis racquets, where a 10 percent increase in the price of a set of golf clubs results in a 20 percent increase in the quantity of tennis racquets demanded. In this case, the cross-price elasticity of demand would be $+2$ ($+20$ percent $\div$ $+10$ percent $= +2$). Consumers responded to the increase in the price of golf clubs by buying fewer sets of golf clubs (moving along the demand curve for golf clubs) and increasing the quantity demanded of tennis racquets at every price (shifting the demand curve for tennis racquets). In general, if the cross-price elasticity is positive, we can conclude that the two goods are substitutes because the price of one good and the demand for the other move in the same direction.

For many golfers, the right set of clubs is only part of the equation—looking the part is just as important. Canadians spend billions of dollars annually on golf clubs and golf accessories.

As another example, let's calculate the cross-price elasticity of demand between sets of golf clubs and sleeves of golf balls, where a 10 percent decrease in the price of a set of golf clubs results in a 30 percent increase in the quantity of golf balls demanded. In this case, the cross-price elasticity of demand is -3 ($+30$ percent $\div$ -10 percent $= -3$). The quantity demanded of golf clubs increases as a result of the price decrease, and consumers then purchase additional sleeves of golf balls to use with their new golf clubs. Golf clubs and golf balls, then, are complements. In general, if the cross-price elasticity is negative, we can conclude that the two goods are complements because the price of one good and the demand for the other move in opposite directions.

Samot/Shutterstock.com

WHAT IS THE INCOME ELASTICITY OF DEMAND?

income elasticity of demand

a measure of the responsiveness of the quantity demanded of a good to a change in income

Even though the most widely employed demand relationship is that between price and quantity demanded, it is also sometimes useful to relate quantity demanded to income. The **income elasticity of demand** is a measure of the responsiveness of the quantity demanded of a good to a change in income. The income elasticity of demand coefficient not only expresses the degree of the connection between the two variables, but it also indicates whether the good in question is normal or inferior. Specifically, the income elasticity of demand is defined as the percentage change in the quantity demanded at a given price divided by the percentage change in income, or

$$\text{Income elasticity of demand } (E_I) = \frac{\text{Percentage change in quantity demanded}}{\text{Percentage change in income}}$$

Calculating the Income Elasticity of Demand

Let's calculate the income elasticity of demand for lobster, where a 10 percent increase in income results in a 15 percent increase in the quantity of lobster demanded at a given price. In this case, the income elasticity of demand is +1.5 (+15 percent ÷ +10 percent = +1.5). Lobster, then, is a normal good because an increase in income results in an increase in demand. In general, if the income elasticity is positive, then the good in question is a normal good because income and demand move in the same direction.

In comparison, let's calculate the income elasticity of demand for beans, where a 10 percent increase in income results in a 15 percent decrease in the demand for beans at each price. In this case, the income elasticity of demand is −1.5 (−15 percent ÷ +10 percent = −1.5). In this example, then, beans are an inferior good because an increase in income results in a decrease in the purchase of beans at a given price. In general, if the income elasticity is negative, then the good in question is an inferior good because the change in income and the change in demand move in opposite directions.

A second interpretation involving the income elasticity of demand coefficient involves the distinction between necessities and luxuries. In the case of a necessity, they are most often associated with an income elasticity of demand coefficient that is $0 < E_I < 1$. This means as income increases, the demand for necessities increases by a smaller proportion than the change in income. Classic examples of this would include the demand for utilities, fresh fruit or vegetables, and shampoo.

Luxuries are most often associated with an income elasticity of demand coefficient that is $E_I > 1$. This means that as income increases, not only does demand increase, it increases by a greater proportion than the increase in income. Common examples of this would include the demand for fine wine, designer clothing, and private education.

SECTION CHECK

- The cross-price elasticity of demand is the percentage change in the quantity demanded of one good divided by the percentage change in the price of another related good (complements and substitutes).
- The income elasticity of demand is the percentage change in quantity demanded divided by the percentage change in income (normal and inferior goods).

Price Elasticity of Supply

- What is the price elasticity of supply?
- What determines the price elasticity of supply?

WHAT IS THE PRICE ELASTICITY OF SUPPLY?

According to the law of supply, there is a positive relationship between price and quantity supplied, *ceteris paribus*. But by how much does quantity supplied change as price changes? It is often helpful to know the degree to which a change in price changes the quantity supplied. The **price elasticity of supply** measures the sensitivity of the quantity supplied to changes in the price of a good. In other words, it measures how responsive the quantity that sellers are willing and able to sell is to changes in the price. Specifically, the price elasticity of supply (E_S) is defined as the percentage change in the quantity supplied divided by the percentage change in price, or

price elasticity of supply
the measure of the sensitivity of the quantity supplied to changes in the price of a good

$$\text{Price elasticity of supply}\,(E_S) = \frac{\text{Percentage change in quantity supplied}}{\text{Percentage change in price}}$$

Calculating the Price Elasticity of Supply

The price elasticity of supply is calculated in much the same manner as the price elasticity of demand. Consider, for example, the case in which it is determined that a 10 percent increase in the price of carrots results in a 25 percent increase in the quantity of carrots supplied after, say, a few harvest seasons. In this case, the price elasticity is $+2.5$ ($+25$ percent $\div$ $+10$ percent $= +2.5$). This coefficient indicates that each 1 percent increase in the price of carrots induces a 2.5 percent increase in the quantity of carrots supplied.

The Ranges of the Price Elasticity of Supply

Economists delineate several ranges of the price elasticity of supply. As with the elasticity of demand, these ranges centre on whether the elasticity coefficient is greater than or less than one. Goods with a supply elasticity that is greater than one ($E_S > 1$) are said to be relatively elastic in supply. With that, a 1 percent change in price will result in a greater than 1 percent change in quantity supplied. In our earlier example, carrots were elastic in supply, because a 1 percent price increase resulted in a 2.5 percent increase in quantity supplied. An example of an elastic supply curve is shown in Exhibit 1(a).

Goods with a supply elasticity that is less than one ($E_S < 1$) are said to be inelastic in supply. This means that a 1 percent change in the price of these goods will induce a proportionately smaller change in the quantity supplied. This situation is shown in the supply curve in Exhibit 1(b).

Finally, there are two extreme cases of price elasticity of supply: perfectly inelastic supply and perfectly elastic supply. In a condition of perfectly inelastic supply, an increase in price will not change the quantity supplied. For example, in a sports arena in the short run (i.e., in a period too brief to adjust the structure), the number of seats available will be almost fixed, say at 20 000 seats. Additional portable seats might be available, but for the most part, even if there is a higher price, there will be only

a. Elastic Supply ($E_s > 1$)

A change in price leads to a larger percentage change in quantity supplied.

b. Inelastic Supply ($E_s < 1$)

A change in price leads to a smaller percentage change in quantity supplied.

c. Perfectly Inelastic Supply ($E_s = 0$)

The quantity supplied does not change regardless of the change in price.

d. Perfectly Elastic Supply ($E_s = \infty$)

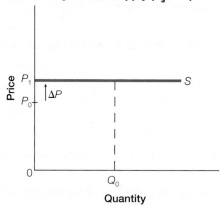

Even a small percentage change in price will change quantity supplied by an infinite amount.

20 000 seats available. We say that the elasticity of supply is zero, which describes a perfectly inelastic supply curve. Famous paintings, like Leonardo da Vinci's *Mona Lisa*, provide another example; there is only one original in existence and, therefore, only one can be supplied, regardless of price. An example of this condition is shown in Exhibit 1(c).

At the other extreme is a perfectly elastic supply curve, where the elasticity equals infinity, as seen in Exhibit 1(d). In a condition of perfectly elastic supply, nothing will be supplied at any price up to a certain level, but at some higher price, sellers would be willing to supply whatever quantity buyers wished to buy. In this case, if the price is below the market price at P_0, the quantity supplied will fall to zero. But at P_1, sellers will sell all that buyers wish to buy. However, most cases fall somewhere between the two extremes of perfectly elastic and perfectly inelastic.

WHAT DETERMINES THE PRICE ELASTICITY OF SUPPLY?

Time is usually critical in supply elasticities (as well as in demand elasticities) because it is more costly for producers to bring forth and release resources in a shorter period of time. For example, the higher wheat prices may cause farmers to grow more wheat, but big changes cannot occur until the next growing season. That is, immediately after harvest season, the supply of wheat is relatively inelastic, but over a longer period that extends over the next growing period, the supply curve becomes much more elastic. Hence, supply tends to be more elastic in the long run than in the short run, as shown in Exhibit 2.

Another example of a good whose supply is highly inelastic in the short run is rental units in most urban areas without rent controls. There is generally only a fixed number of rental units available in the short run. Thus, in the short run, an increase in demand will lead only to higher prices (rents). However, in the long run, these same higher prices (rents) provide an incentive to renovate and build new rental units.

In the short run, firms can increase output by using their existing facilities to a greater capacity, paying workers to work overtime, and hiring additional workers. However, firms will be able to increase output much more in the long run when they can build new factories. In addition, some new firms can enter in the long run. In other words, the quantity supplied will be much more elastic in the long run than in the short run.

Another factor that can influence the price elasticity of supply relates to the level of scarcity and sophistication of the resources and technology used in production. The more complicated the technology or rare the resources needed to produce a particular good or service, the more inelastic the supply. Resources that are very limited in supply—such as technology workers—and very sophisticated technology—such as computer-assisted design software—take longer for suppliers to acquire and activate in response to a price increase, thereby making price elasticity of supply more inelastic.

Alternatively, when production is associated with resources that are in abundant supply or technology that is simpler, producers are able to both acquire and activate needed resources and technology in a timely fashion, making price elasticity of supply appear to be more elastic.

section 5.4
Exhibit 2

Short-Run and Long-Run Supply Curves

For most goods, supply is more elastic in the long run than in the short run. For example, if price increases, firms have an incentive to produce more but are constrained by the size of their plants. In the long run, they can increase their capacity and produce more.

section

5.5

Elasticity and Taxes

● What is tax incidence?
● How does the relative elasticity of supply and demand determine the tax burden?

WHAT IS TAX INCIDENCE?

tax incidence
the analysis of the effect of a particular tax on the distribution of economic welfare

To varying degrees, all levels of government (federal, provincial/territorial, and municipal) use taxes to generate needed revenue. For example, the harmonized sales tax (HST) that is in effect in some jurisdictions is a consumption-based tax that is calculated as a percentage of the sale price of the product. Although the legislation that accompanies a tax designates who is required to pay the particular tax, the ultimate impact of the tax—also known as the *tax burden*—is less certain. In economics, the term **tax incidence** refers to the analysis of the effect of a particular tax on the distribution of economic welfare. In other words, tax incidence looks at the ultimate burden of a tax.

HOW DOES THE RELATIVE ELASTICITY OF SUPPLY AND DEMAND DETERMINE THE TAX BURDEN?

The relative elasticity of supply and demand determines the distribution of the tax burden for a good. As we will see, if demand has a lower elasticity than supply in the relevant tax region, the largest portion of the tax is paid by the consumer. However, if demand is relatively more elastic than supply in the relevant tax region, the largest portion of the tax is paid by the producer.

In Exhibit 1, the pre-tax equilibrium price is $1 and the pre-tax equilibrium quantity is Q_{BT}—the quantity before tax. If the government imposes a $0.50 tax on the seller, the supply curve shifts vertically by the amount of the tax (just as if an input price rose by $0.50).

In the case where demand is relatively less elastic than supply in the relevant region, almost the whole tax is passed on to the consumer, *ceteris paribus*. For example, in Exhibit 1(a), sellers are very responsive to changes in the price of the good (explaining the relatively flat supply curve), whereas consumers are relatively less responsive (explaining the relatively steep demand curve). In response to the tax, the price paid by consumers rises substantially, indicating that consumers bear most of the burden of the tax. With a post-tax equilibrium price of $1.40, consumers end up paying 40 cents more per unit compared to the per-tax equilibrium price. The price received by producers,

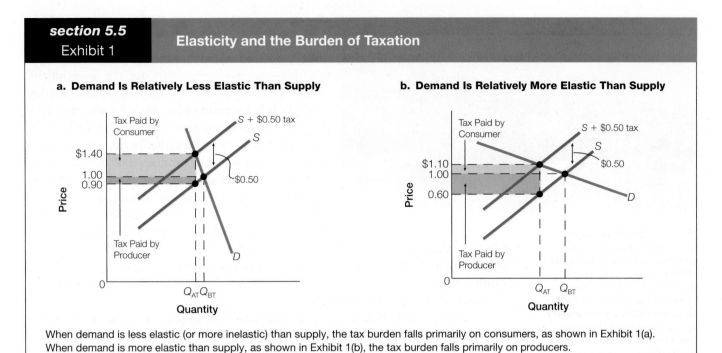

section 5.5
Exhibit 1

Elasticity and the Burden of Taxation

a. Demand Is Relatively Less Elastic Than Supply

b. Demand Is Relatively More Elastic Than Supply

When demand is less elastic (or more inelastic) than supply, the tax burden falls primarily on consumers, as shown in Exhibit 1(a). When demand is more elastic than supply, as shown in Exhibit 1(b), the tax burden falls primarily on producers.

however, does not fall by very much, indicating that sellers bear only a small burden of the tax. At 90 cents per unit ($1.40 − $0.50 = $0.90), the producer burden amounts to only 10 cents.

In Exhibit 1(b), demand is relatively more elastic than the supply in the relevant region. Here, we see that the greater burden of the same 50-cent tax falls on the producer, *ceteris paribus*. In response to the tax, the price paid by consumers does not rise very much, but the price received by producers falls substantially. With a post-tax equilibrium price of $1.10, the producer will receive only 60 cents per unit ($1.10 − $0.50 = $0.60), resulting in a 40-cent per-unit tax burden. Consumers, on the other hand, end up paying 10 cents more per unit compared to the pre-tax equilibrium price.

In general, then, the tax burden falls on the side of the market that is less elastic. Note that who actually pays the tax at the time of the purchase has nothing to do with who incurs the ultimate burden of the taxation—that depends on the relative elasticity.

Knowing how the relative elasticity of supply and demand determines the distribution of the tax burden for a good provides us with unique insight into the rationale behind a particular classification of taxes—sin taxes.

In April of 2018, a carton of 200 cigarettes in Canada ranged in price from as low as $96.36 in Quebec to as much as $139.83 in Manitoba. This variance in price from region to region is due to different rates of provincial/territorial and federal taxation. Generally, taxes on a carton of cigarettes represent between 60 and 80 percent of its price. Alcohol and gasoline, two other sin goods, experience similar tax treatment—half the retail price of beer is accounted for by various taxes and about 80 percent of the price of a bottle of alcohol is the result of tax. Recent studies have found that various federal, provincial/territorial, and local taxes account for approximately 35 percent of the price of a litre of gasoline.

The fact that goods such as alcohol, tobacco, and gasoline are highly inelastic makes them prime candidates for higher taxation. While the government may be accomplishing secondary social objectives through this punitive tax treatment, the ability to effectively generate needed revenue cannot be overlooked as the prime reason.

Why are these so-called sin goods subjected to such extreme tax treatment? To answer this, we need only to remind ourselves of the primary objective of taxation—revenue generation for the government. The reason why products such as alcohol, cigarettes, and gasoline are taxed so heavily is because they have the greatest ability to generate this much-needed tax revenue. As we discussed earlier in this section, when a tax is imposed on a product, the contractionary impact of the tax shifts the supply curve leftward, forcing price up and quantity sold down (review Section 5.5, Exhibit 1). For sin goods however, due to their highly inelastic demand, prices increase by much more than quantity sold declines (refer back to Section 5.5, Exhibit 1a). The fact that quantity sold falls by a relatively small amount means that the imposition of the tax has only a negligible impact on sales and therefore on the ability of the various levels of government to generate tax revenue.

A second example that will help us appreciate the impact of elasticity on market behaviour involves the methods by which governments enact drug policy. The Canadian government spends hundreds of millions of dollars a year in an effort to stop the flow of illegal drugs into and within Canada. Although these efforts are clearly targeted at suppliers, who really pay the higher enforcement and evasion costs? The government crackdown has increased the probability of apprehension and conviction for drug smugglers. That increase in risk for suppliers increases their cost of doing business—raising the cost of importing and distributing illegal drugs. This would shift the supply curve for illegal drugs to the left, from S_0 to S_1, as seen in Exhibit 2. For most drug users—addicts, in particular—the price of drugs like cocaine and heroin lies in the highly inelastic region of the demand curve. Because the demand for drugs is relatively inelastic in this region, the seller would be able to shift most of this cost onto the consumer (think of this as similar to the tax shift just discussed). The buyer now has to pay a much higher price, P_B, and the seller receives a slightly lower price, P_S. That is, enforcement efforts increase the price of illegal drugs, but only a small reduction in quantity demanded results from this price increase.

Increased enforcement efforts may have unintended consequences due to the fact that buyers bear the majority of the burden of this price increase. Tighter smuggling controls may, in fact, result in higher levels of burglary, muggings, and white-collar crime, as more cash-strapped buyers search for alternative ways of funding their increasingly expensive habit.

This is not to say that we should abandon our efforts against illegal drugs. Illegal drugs can impose huge personal and social costs—billions of dollars of lost productivity and immeasurable personal tragedy. However, solely targeting the supply-side can have unintended consequences. Policymakers may get their best results by focusing on a reduction in demand—changing user preferences. For example, if drug education leads to a reduction in the demand for drugs, the demand curve will shift

section 5.5
Exhibit 2

Government Effort to Reduce the Supply of Illegal Drugs

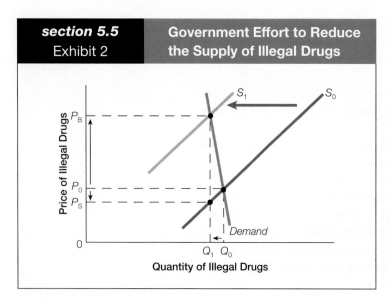

to the left—reducing the price and the quantity of illegal drugs exchanged, as seen in Exhibit 3. The remaining drug users, at Q_1, will now pay a lower price, P_1. This lower price for drugs will lead to fewer drug-related crimes, *ceteris paribus*.

It is also possible that the elasticity of demand for illegal drugs may be more elastic in the long run than the short run. In the short run, as the price rises, the quantity demanded falls less than proportionately because of the addictive nature of illegal drugs (this is also true for goods like tobacco and alcohol, as we have already discussed). However, in the long run, the demand for illegal drugs may be more elastic; that is, the higher price may deter many younger, and poorer, people from experimenting with illegal drugs.

section 5.5
Exhibit 3

Possible Effect of Education on Drug Demand

DEBATE

WILL TAXATION CONTROL CANNABIS USE?

For:
Canada has joined the few but growing number of nations that have made the recreational use of cannabis legal. As of October 17, 2018, the purchase of cannabis is no longer a criminal offence. Finance Minister Bill Morneau said protecting Canadians is the government's first concern with cannabis legalization.*

He noted that the taxation of cannabis would be consistent with the goal of keeping cannabis out of the hands of kids and out of the underground markets. Medical cannabis will remain untaxed, while recreational cannabis may be subject to a tax of about 10 percent.

Against:
In the case of cigarettes and alcohol, raising taxes does alter consumer choices. Smoking rates have fallen, and it

could be argued that this is because more has been done to point out the damaging effects on health, as well as a number of landmark legal settlements that have done much to reduce people's interest in cigarette smoking and production. The higher taxes on cigarettes just help to nudge the consumer in the right direction.

Some consumers, however, find ways to get around taxes. In the case of recreational cannabis, there is some speculation that if taxes are too high, people will continue to go underground or turn to suppliers who sell the product in areas where federal and provincial/territorial excise taxes are not levied.

Questions:
1. What is your stance on the legalization of cannabis? Do you think that the legalization of cannabis will indeed protect Canadians, and why?
2. Do you think that high taxes on recreational cannabis will serve to limit its use by consumers?
3. What are some ways in which government could control cannabis use so that it is enjoyed but not abused?

*"Budget 2018 outlines how cannabis will be taxed, grants money to fight opioid crisis," *Global News*, Leslie Young, February 27, 2018, https://globalnews.ca/news/4051344/federal-budget-2018-marijuana-tax-opioid-crisis.

SECTION CHECK

- *Tax incidence* refers to the analysis of the effect of particular taxes on the distribution of economic welfare.
- If demand is more elastic than supply, producers bear the greater burden of the tax; however, if supply is more elastic than demand, consumers bear the greater burden of the tax.

For Your Review

Section 5.1

1. In each case below, indicate which good you think has a relatively *higher* price elasticity of demand and identify the most likely reason, in terms of the determinants of the elasticity of demand (more substitutes, greater share of budget, or more time to adjust).

    a. cars or Chevrolets

    b. salt or housing

    c. natural gas this month or over the course of several years

2. How might your elasticity of demand for copying and binding services vary if your work presentation is next week versus in two hours?

3. For each of the following pairs, identify which one of the pair is likely to exhibit more elastic demand:

    a. shampoo; Paul Mitchell Shampoo

    b. air travel prompted by an illness in the family; vacation air travel

    c. paper clips; an apartment rental

    d. prescription heart medication; a generic headache remedy

4. Using the midpoint formula for calculating the elasticity of demand, if the price of a good fell from $42 to $38, what would be the elasticity of demand if the quantity demanded changed from

    a. 19 to 21?

    b. 27 to 33?

    c. 195 to 205?

5. Explain why using the midpoint formula for calculating the elasticity of demand gives the same result whether price increases or decreases, but using the initial price and quantity instead of the average does not.

6. During the Thanksgiving season, why is the price elasticity of demand for turkeys likely to be lower, but the price elasticity of demand for turkeys at a particular store likely to be greater when compared to other times of the year?

7. If the elasticity of demand for hamburgers equals −1.5 and the quantity demanded equals 40 000, predict what will happen to the quantity of hamburgers demanded when the price increases by 10 percent. If the price falls by 5 percent, what will happen?

Blueprint Problem

Using the midpoint formula for calculating the elasticity of demand, if the price of a good went from $16 to $10, what would be the elasticity of demand if the quantity demanded changed from 8 to 12 units? Interpret your results.

Blueprint Solution

To better visualize this question, consider plotting the data.

Calculate midpoint values:

Quantity: $\dfrac{(8 + 12)}{2} = 10$

Price: $\dfrac{(\$16 + \$10)}{2} = \$13$

To this visual representation, you can add the midpoints you will need to calculate the percentage change values for price and quantity demanded.

$$\text{Midpoint between two values} = \frac{\text{Sum of values}}{2}$$

Recall the formula for E_D and enter the required values:

$$E_D = \frac{\left(\dfrac{Q_B - Q_A}{Q\,\text{midpoint}}\right)}{\left(\dfrac{P_B - P_A}{P\,\text{midpoint}}\right)} = \frac{\left(\dfrac{12 - 8}{10}\right)}{\left(\dfrac{\$10 - \$16}{\$13}\right)} = \frac{0.4}{-0.46} = |-0.87| = 0.87$$

While the midpoint formula ensures E_D is the same regardless of the direction of the calculation, you still must enter the values consistently. Also, since the sign of the E_D coefficient relates to the inverse relationship between price and quantity demanded (law of demand), it is ignored in interpretation—therefore take the absolute value of E_D.

Since the value of E_D is less than 1, the interpretation of the response of quantity demanded to the change in price is *inelastic*.

Recall the reference value of 1 for interpreting E_D:

$E_D > 1$ elastic

$E_D < 1$ inelastic

$E_D = 1$ unit elastic

8. Good weather produces a bumper crop of apples. As a result, the price falls from $6 to $3 a basket and the quantity demanded increases from 600 to 1100 baskets a week. Over this price range, calculate the price elasticity of demand (using the midpoint method).

9. Bad weather spoils the orange crop. As a result, the price rises from $3 to $5 a basket and the quantity demanded decreases from 1500 to 900 baskets a week. Over this price range, calculate the price elasticity of demand (using the midpoint method).

10. Isabella always spends $50 on red roses each month and simply adjusts the quantity she purchases as the price changes. What can you say about Isabella's elasticity of demand for roses?

Section 5.2

11. The Wellington Aces football team wants to boost revenues from ticket sales next season. You are hired as an economic consultant and asked to advise the Aces whether to raise or lower ticket prices next year. If the elasticity of demand for Aces game tickets is estimated to be -1.6, what would you advise? If the elasticity of demand equals -0.4?

12. Evaluate the following statement: "Along a downward-sloping linear demand curve, the slope and therefore the elasticity of demand are both 'constant.'"

13. If the midpoint on a straight-line demand curve is at a price of $7, what can we say about the elasticity of demand for a price change from $12 to $10? What about from $6 to $4?

14. According to reliable sources, the Caesars Wexton is the only four-diamond hotel in the city of Wexton. The hotel owners hired an economist to advise them on improving the hotel's profitability. The economist suggested that the hotel owners could increase this year's revenue by raising prices. The owners asked, "Won't raising prices reduce the quantity of hotel rooms demanded and increase vacancies?" Why did the economist suggest increasing prices?

15. Assume the following weekly demand schedule for Extra Scoop Ice Cream.

a. When Extra Scoop Ice Cream lowers its price for a scoop of ice cream from $4 to $3, what happens to its total revenue?

b. Between a price of $4 and a price of $3, is the demand for the ice cream elastic or inelastic?

c. Between a price of $2 and a price of $1, is the demand for the ice cream elastic or inelastic?

16. A movie production company faces a linear demand curve for its film, and it seeks to maximize total revenue from the film's distribution. At what level should the price be set? Where is demand elastic, inelastic, or unit elastic? Explain.

Section 5.3

17. If a 10 percent decline in the price of WiFi service increases the quantity of mobile computing devices demanded by 20 percent and increases the quantity of WiFi service demanded by 15 percent, calculate the cross-price elasticity of demand between WiFi service and mobile computing devices.

18. How does the cross-price elasticity of demand tell you whether two goods are substitutes? Complements?

19. Indicate whether the products are normal, inferior, or neither based on the following estimates for the income elasticity of demand:

   a. 1.7

   b. −1.7

20. If a 10 percent rise in the price of coffee increases the quantity of tea demanded by 25 percent and decreases the quantity of coffee demanded by 20 percent, calculate the cross-elasticity of demand between coffee and tea.

21. Assume you had the following observations on Canadian intercity rail travel: Between 2016 and 2017, rail travel increased from 17.5 passenger kilometres per person to 19 passenger kilometres per person. At the same time, neither per kilometre railroad price or incomes changed, but the per kilometre price of intercity airline travel increased by 7.5 percent. Between 2017 and 2018, per capita incomes rose by approximately 13 percent, while the price of travel by rail and plane stayed constant. Intercity rail travel was 20 passenger kilometres per person in 2017 and 19.5 in 2018. Assuming the demand for travel didn't change between these periods:

   a. Calculate the income elasticity of demand for intercity rail travel.

   b. Calculate the cross-price elasticity of demand for intercity rail travel.

   c. Are air travel and rail travel substitutes or complements? Is intercity rail travel a normal or an inferior good?

22. Suppose the demand for designer jeans increased from 42 000 to 56 000 when per capita incomes rose from $65 000 to $71 500. Calculate the income elasticity of demand coefficient (remember to use the midpoint method). Are designer jeans considered a normal or inferior good? Explain why. Are the jeans considered a luxury or necessity? Explain why.

Section 5.4

23. Using the midpoint formula for calculating the elasticity of supply, if the price of a good rose from $95 to $105, what would be the elasticity of supply if the quantity supplied changed from

   a. 38 to 42?

   b. 78 to 82?

   c. 54 to 66?

24. Elasticity of demand in the market for one-bedroom apartments is 2.0, elasticity of supply is 0.5, the current market price is $1000, and the equilibrium number of one-bedroom apartments is 10 000. If the government imposes a price ceiling of $800 on this market, predict the size of the resulting apartment shortage.

25. The price elasticity of supply coefficient for tablet computers is estimated to be equal to 0.6. With current production volumes of 50 million units, what would be the expectation for production volumes in response to a 5 percent increase in the price of tablet computers? What about an 8 percent decline in the price of tablet computers?

Section 5.5

26. Mayor George Henry has a problem. He doesn't want to anger voters by taxing them because he wants to be re-elected, but the town of Gapville needs more revenue for its schools. He has a choice between taxing tickets to professional basketball games or food. If the demand for food is relatively inelastic while the supply is relatively elastic, and if the demand for professional basketball games is relatively elastic while the supply is relatively inelastic, in which case would the tax burden fall primarily on consumers? In which case would the tax burden fall primarily on producers?

27. If both supply curves and demand curves are more elastic in the long run than in the short run, how does the incidence of a tax change from the short run to the long run as a result? What happens to the revenue raised from a given tax over time, *ceteris paribus*?

28. As part of its national "Get-Fit" program, the government instituted a doughnut tax to be paid by doughnut producers. Before the tax, 6000 doughnuts were sold each month at a price of $1.50 per doughnut. After the tax, 5600 doughnuts are being sold every month. Consumers pay $2.00 a doughnut and producers receive $1.40 a doughnut.

    a. In a properly labelled demand/supply diagram, illustrate the impact of this seller tax on the doughnut market.

    b. What is the amount of the tax?

chapter 6

Consumer Choice and Market Efficiency

section 6.1

Consumer Behaviour

- What is utility?
- What is diminishing marginal utility?

WHAT IS UTILITY?

To more clearly define the relationship between consumer choice and resource allocation, economists developed a concept of **utility**—a measure of the relative levels of satisfaction that consumers get from the consumption of goods and services. Defining one **util** as equivalent to one unit of satisfaction, economists can indicate relative levels of consumer satisfaction that result from alternative choices. For example, for a java junkie who wouldn't dream of starting the day without a strong dose of caffeine, a cup of coffee might generate 150 utils of satisfaction, while a cup of herbal tea might generate only 10 utils.

Inherently, utility varies from individual to individual depending on specific preferences. For example, Jabari might get 5 utils of satisfaction from eating his first piece of apple pie, while Bara may derive only 4 utils of satisfaction from her first piece of apple pie.

Utility Is a Personal Matter

Economists recognize that it is not really possible to make interpersonal utility comparisons. That is, they know that it is impossible to compare the relative satisfactions of different people. The relative satisfaction gained by various people drinking coffee, for example, simply cannot be measured in comparable terms. Likewise, although we might be tempted to believe that a poorer person would derive greater utility from finding a $100 bill than would a richer person, we should resist the temptation. We simply cannot prove it. The poorer person may be monetarily poor because money and material things are not important to her, and the rich person may have become richer because of his lust for the things money can buy.

Total Utility and Marginal Utility

Economists recognize two different dimensions of utility: total utility and marginal utility. **Total utility** (*TU*) is the total amount of satisfaction derived from the consumption of a certain number of units of a good or service. In comparison, **marginal utility** (*MU*) is the extra satisfaction generated by an additional unit of a good that is consumed

utility
a measure of the relative levels of satisfaction that consumers get from the consumption of goods and services

util
one unit of satisfaction

total utility (*TU*)
total amount of satisfaction derived from the consumption of a certain number of units of a good or service

marginal utility (*MU*)
extra satisfaction generated by an additional unit of a good that is consumed in a particular time period

Why do most individuals take only one newspaper from covered, coin-operated newspaper racks when it would be so easy to take more? Do you think potato chips, candy, or specialty coffees could be sold profitably in the same kind of dispenser? Although ethical considerations keep some people from taking additional papers, the law of diminishing marginal utility is also at work here.

in a particular time period. For example, eating four slices of pizza in an hour might generate a total of 28 utils of satisfaction. The first three slices of pizza might generate a total of 24 utils, while the last slice might generate only 4 utils. In this case, the total utility of eating four slices of pizza is 28 utils and the marginal utility of the fourth slice is 4 utils. Notice in Exhibit 1(a) how total utility increases as consumption increases (we see more total utility after the fourth slice of pizza than after the third). But notice, too, that the increase in total utility from each additional unit (slice) is less than the unit before, which indicates the marginal utility. In Exhibit 1(b), we see how the marginal utility falls as consumption increases.

WHAT IS DIMINISHING MARGINAL UTILITY?

Although economists believe that total utility increases with additional consumption, they also argue that the incremental satisfaction—the marginal utility—that results from the consumption of additional units tends to decline as consumption increases. In other words, as an individual consumes more and more of a good, each successive unit

section 6.1
Exhibit 1

Total and Marginal Utility

a. Total Utility

Slices of Pizza (per day)	Total Utility (utils)	Marginal Utility (utils)
0	0	
1	10	10
2	18	8
3	24	6
4	28	4
5	30	2
6	30	0
7	28	−2

b. Marginal Utility

As you can see in Exhibit 1(a), the total utility from pizza increases as consumption increases. In Exhibit 1(b) marginal utility decreases as consumption increases. That is, as you eat more pizza, your satisfaction from each additional slice diminishes.

DEBATE

IS A GOVERNMENT-SUPPORTED PHARMACARE PROGRAM DESIRABLE FOR CANADA?

For:

The 2013 findings of a study conducted by Statistics Canada on prescription medication usage in Canada concluded that prescription drugs are the second most costly component of Canada's annual health-care expenditure (approximately 14% = $29 billion). Much of the cost is associated with the management of chronic diseases and conditions (for instance, heart disease and high cholesterol, hypertension, diabetes, and depression) and contraception.

Pharmaceuticals are big business, often generating huge profits. Some feel that having publically funded, universal access to health care in Canada and not including "pharmacare" is omitting a large chunk of the modern health-care equation. Government can negotiate huge deals and gain access to effective, efficiently produced generic and some brand-name drugs at much lower prices than the individual hospital, pharmacy, or patient would be able to do.

In 2017, Ontario introduced pharmacare for anyone under the age of 25 with OHIP+. Anyone over 65 or on income support already has access to approved generic prescription medications and medical services.

Supporting universal access to health care for Canadians is the right thing to do.

Against:

Many pharmaceuticals are covered under employee benefit plans, enabling patients to sometimes gain access to prescription medications that are not covered under government plans. Parents who work and have drug benefit plans through private insurers funded through their employers do not currently find access to medications to be burdensome for themselves or their children.

Senior citizens already have access to many publically funded prescription medications or drugs covered by their former employee benefit plans and under existing provincial support agencies. In some ways, it is a non-issue.

Brand-name drugs, which have involved years of research and large amounts of sunk costs, have high prices to ensure profitability. That's business. If people can afford to pay, either from their own pocket, or through their employer benefit plans, then that is their right. They work hard, they earn their pay and benefits, and should be able to pay for and access the most effective drugs money can buy, without government support or interference.

Questions:

1. Where do you stand in terms of the utility derived from a government-supported and administered pharmacare program that would form part of universal access to health care?

2. Do pharmaceutical companies have a right to make high profits from the sale of lifesaving or disease-managing medications?

3. What types of approaches to health-care access and expenditure do you think would be of benefit to Canadians?

---

generates less and less utility (or satisfaction). This concept is traditionally referred to as the **diminishing marginal utility**. Exhibit 1(b) demonstrates this graphically, where the marginal utility curve has a negative slope.

It follows from the law of diminishing marginal utility that as a person uses more and more units of a good to satisfy a given want, the intensity of the want, and the utility derived from further satisfying that want, diminishes. Think about it: If you are starving, your desire for that first slice of pizza will be great, but as you eat, you gradually become more and more full, reducing your desire for yet another piece.

diminishing marginal utility

the concept that as an individual consumes more and more of a good, each successive unit generates less and less utility (or satisfaction)

SECTION CHECK

- Utility is the level of satisfaction an individual receives from consumption of a good or service. Total utility measures the amount of satisfaction derived from all units consumed, while marginal utility measures the change in utility from consuming one additional unit of a good or service.
- The less and less satisfaction an individual enjoys as she or he consumes more and more of a good or service illustrates the concept of diminishing marginal utility.

Consumer Choice

- What is the "best" decision for consumers?
- What is the connection between the law of demand and the law of diminishing marginal utility?

Decisions about what to buy and how much to buy would be easy if we enjoyed everything to the same degree and if we had limitless funds. But that's not reality. In the real world, we like some things more than other things and we are usually forced to stay within a budget. Consumer choice theory shows us how to make optimal decisions.

WHAT IS THE "BEST" DECISION FOR CONSUMERS?

We established the fact that marginal utility diminishes as additional units of a good are acquired, but what significance does this fact have for consumers? Remember, consumers try to add to their own total utility, so when the marginal utility generated by the purchase of additional units of one good drops too low, it is rational for the consumer to purchase other goods rather than purchase more of the first good. In other words, a rational consumer will avoid making purchases of any one good beyond the point at which other goods will yield greater satisfaction for the amount spent—the "bang for the buck."

Marginal utility, then, is an important concept in understanding and predicting consumer behaviour, especially when combined with information about prices. By comparing the marginal utilities generated by the units of the goods that they desire as well as comparing the prices, rational consumers seek the combination of goods that maximizes their satisfaction for a given amount spent. In the next section, we will see how this concept works.

Consumer Equilibrium

To reach consumer equilibrium, consumers must allocate their incomes in such a way that the marginal utility per dollar's worth of any good is the same for every good. That is, the "bang for the buck" must be equal for all goods at consumer equilibrium. When this goal is realized, one dollar's worth of additional gasoline will yield the same marginal utility as one dollar's worth of additional bread or apples or movie tickets or soap. This concept will become clearer to you as we work through an example illustrating the forces present when consumers are not at equilibrium.

Given a fixed budget, if the marginal utilities per dollar spent on additional units of two goods are not the same, you can increase total satisfaction by buying more of one good and less of the other good. For example, consider the case of Paula, a hard-working college student faced with choosing between hamburgers and milkshakes that are priced at $2 and $1, respectively. She has $11 to spend for the week.

The marginal utility Paula derives from each of the two goods is presented in column B of Exhibit 1. If Paula was solely interested in utility she would choose five hamburgers and five milkshakes because that would maximize her total utility (70 + 33 = 103); that is, adding up all of the marginal utilities for all hamburgers (70 utils) and all milkshakes (33 utils). The only problem with this outcome is that it would cost Paula $15: $10 for the five hamburgers and $5 for the five milkshakes, thus exceeding her $11 per week budget by $4.

So what is the best way for Paula to spend her money? To answer this question, we need to remember that economic decisions are made at the margin. By equalizing the

section 6.2 Exhibit 1	Marginal Utility per Dollar Spent	

A	B	C
Quantity of Hamburgers Consumed Each Week	**Marginal Utility from Last Hamburger**	**($MU_{hamburger}/P_{hamburger}$)**
1	20	10
2	16	8
3	14	7
4	12	6
5	8	4
Quantity of Milkshakes Consumed Each Week	**Marginal Utility from Last Milkshake**	**($MU_{milkshake}/P_{milkshake}$)**
1	12	12
2	9	9
3	5	5
4	4	4
5	3	3

marginal utility per dollar spent for all goods, Paula will be able to ensure she is getting the best bang for her buck. To help Paula optimally allocate her budget, her marginal utility per dollar spent for each hamburger and milkshake is presented in column C of Exhibit 1.

In terms of her first purchase, since the first milkshake gives more marginal utility per dollar spent than the first hamburger (12 utils versus 10 utils), Paula will purchase a milkshake first. For her second purchase, the first hamburger's *MU* per dollar spent (10 utils) is greater than the second milkshake's *MU* per dollar spent (9 utils), so her second purchase will be a hamburger. What about her third purchase? Paula will purchase a second milkshake since its *MU* per dollar spent exceeds the *MU* per dollar spent of the next hamburger (9 utils versus 8 utils). As for the fourth, fifth, and sixth purchases, these will all be hamburgers, as the *MU* per dollar spent on the second, third, and fourth hamburgers is greater than the *MU* per dollar spent for the third milkshake (8 utils, 7 utils, and 6 utils, respectively, versus 5 utils). Lastly, Paula's final purchase will be a milkshake, since the third milkshake's *MU* per dollar spent is above the *MU* per dollar spent of the fifth hamburger (5 utils versus 4 utils). A summary of the results is presented in Exhibit 2.

In conclusion, Paula can accomplish an optimal allocation of her $11 budget by purchasing four hamburgers and three milkshakes. As seen in Exhibit 2, this combination of purchases will generate a total utility of 88 utils, a level of utility greater than any other possible combination of purchases Paula could afford for $11.

What this example shows is that, to achieve maximum satisfaction—**consumer equilibrium**—consumers have to allocate income in a way that balances the ratio of marginal utility to the price of the goods purchased. In other words, in a state of consumer equilibrium,

$$MU_1/P_1 = MU_2/P_2 = MU_3/P_3 = \ldots = MU_N/P_N$$

In this situation, each good provides the consumer with the same level of marginal utility per dollar spent.

consumer equilibrium
allocation of consumer income that balances the ratio of marginal utility to the price of the goods purchased

		section 6.2 Exhibit 2	**The Path to Consumer Equilibrium: A Summary of Purchases**			

Purchase	Item	MU per Dollar Spent	MU	TU	Remaining Income
1st	Milkshake	12	12	12	$11 − $1 = $10
2nd	Hamburger	10	20	32	$10 − $2 = $8
3rd	Milkshake	9	9	41	$8 − $1 = $7
4th	Hamburger	8	16	57	$7 − $2 = $5
5th	Hamburger	7	14	71	$5 − $2 = $3
6th	Hamburger	6	12	83	$3 − $2 = $1
7th	Milkshake	5	5	88	$1 − $1 = 0

WHAT IS THE CONNECTION BETWEEN THE LAW OF DEMAND AND THE LAW OF DIMINISHING MARGINAL UTILITY?

The law of demand states that when the price of a good is reduced, the quantity demanded will increase. But why is this the case? By examining the law of diminishing marginal utility in action, we can determine the basis for this relationship between price and quantity demanded. Indeed, the demand curve merely translates marginal utility into dollar terms.

For example, let's say that you are in consumer equilibrium when the price of a personal-sized pizza is $4 and the price of a plate of French fries is $1. Further, in equilibrium, the marginal utility on the last pizza consumed is 40 utils, and the marginal utility on the last plate of French fries is 10 utils. So in consumer equilibrium, the MU/P ratio for both the pizza and French fries is 10 utils per dollar.

$$\frac{MU_{\text{pizza}}}{P_{\text{pizza}}} = \frac{40 \text{ utils}}{\$4} = 10 \text{ utils/dollar} = \frac{10 \text{ utils}}{\$1} = \frac{MU_{\text{French fries}}}{P_{\text{French fries}}}$$

Now suppose the price of the personal-sized pizza falls to $2, *ceteris paribus*. Instead of the MU/P ratio of the pizza being 10 utils per dollar, it is now 20 utils per dollar (40 utils/$2). This calculation implies, *ceteris paribus,* that you will now buy more pizza at the lower price because you are getting relatively more satisfaction for each dollar that you spend on pizza.

$$\frac{MU_{\text{pizza}}}{P_{\text{pizza}}} = \frac{40 \text{ utils}}{\$2} = 20 \text{ utils/dollar} > 10 \text{ utils/dollar} = \frac{10 \text{ utils}}{\$1} = \frac{MU_{\text{French fries}}}{P_{\text{French fries}}}$$

In other words, because the price of the personal-sized pizza fell, you are now willing to purchase more pizzas. By buying more pizzas, you travel farther out along your marginal utility curve for pizzas, and as a result, the marginal utility for pizza falls. With that change, the ratio of marginal utility per dollar spent for both pizzas and French fries changes in the following way:

$$\frac{MU_{\text{pizza}}}{P_{\text{pizza}}} = \frac{20 \text{ utils}}{\$2} = 10 \text{ utils/dollar} = \frac{10 \text{ utils}}{\$1} = \frac{MU_{\text{French fries}}}{P_{\text{French fries}}}$$

So in consumer equilibrium, the *MU/P* ratio for both pizzas and French fries is again equal.

In other words, as the price of pizzas decreases, consumers will maximize total utility by buying more pizzas, therefore producing a negatively sloped demand curve.

SECTION CHECK

■ To maximize consumer satisfaction, income must be allocated so that the ratio of the marginal utility to the price is the same for all goods purchased.
■ A fall in a good's price will raise its marginal utility–price (*MU/P*) ratio above that of other goods purchased. This relatively greater *MU/P* ratio will lead a rational consumer to purchase more of this good at the expense of other goods.

Consumer and Producer Surplus

● What is consumer surplus?
● What is producer surplus?
● How do we measure the total gains from exchange?

WHAT IS CONSUMER SURPLUS?

In a competitive market, consumers and producers buy and sell at the market equilibrium price. However, what a consumer actually pays for a unit of a good is usually less than the amount she is *willing* to pay. For example, you would be willing and able to pay far more than the market price for a rope ladder to get out of a burning building. You would also be willing and able to pay more than the market price for a tank of gasoline if you ran out of gas on a desolate highway. **Consumer surplus** is the monetary difference between the price a consumer is willing and able to pay for an additional unit of a good and what the consumer actually pays—the market price. Consumer surplus for the entire market is the sum of all of the individual consumer surpluses for those consumers who have purchased the good.

consumer surplus
the monetary difference between the price a consumer is willing and able to pay for an additional unit of a good and the price the consumer actually pays; for the entire market, it is the sum of all of the individual consumer surpluses for those consumers who have purchased the good

Marginal Willingness to Pay Falls as More Is Consumed

Suppose it is a very hot day and iced tea is going for $1 per glass but Mark is willing to pay $4 for the first glass, $2 for the second glass, and $0.50 for the third glass, reflecting the law of demand. How much consumer surplus will Mark receive? First, it is important to note the general fact that if the consumer is a buyer of several units of a good, the earlier units will have greater marginal value and therefore create more consumer surplus, because *marginal willingness to pay* falls as greater quantities are consumed in any period. In fact, you can think of the demand curve as a marginal benefit curve—the additional benefit derived from consuming one more unit. Notice in Exhibit 1 that Mark's demand for iced tea has a step-like slope. This is demonstrated by Mark's willingness to pay $4 and $2 successively for the first two glasses of iced tea. Thus, Mark will receive $3 of consumer surplus for the first glass ($4 − $1) and $1 of

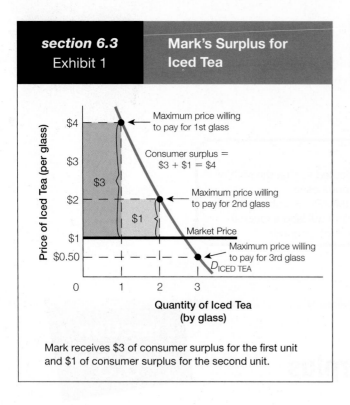

section 6.3
Exhibit 1

Mark's Surplus for Iced Tea

Mark receives $3 of consumer surplus for the first unit and $1 of consumer surplus for the second unit.

section 6.3
Exhibit 2

Consumer Surplus for Chocolate: A Smooth-Shaped Demand Curve

The area below the market demand curve but above the market price is called *consumer surplus*. It is represented by the shaded area. The market demand curve is smooth because many buyers purchase chocolate each year.

Imagine it is 30 degrees in the shade. Do you think you would get more consumer surplus from your first glass of iced tea than you would from a fifth glass?

consumer surplus for the second glass ($2 − $1), for a total of $4, as seen in Exhibit 1. Mark will not be willing to purchase the third glass because it would provide less value than its price warrants ($0.50 versus $1) and reduce consumer surplus as a result.

In Exhibit 2, we can easily measure the consumer surplus in the market by using a market demand curve rather than an individual demand curve. In short, the market consumer surplus is the area under the market demand curve and above the market price (area A in Exhibit 2). The market for chocolate contains millions of potential buyers, so we will get a smooth demand curve. That is, each of the millions of potential buyers has his or her own willingness to pay. Because the demand curve represents the marginal benefits consumers receive from consuming an additional unit, we can conclude that all buyers of chocolate receive at least some consumer surplus in the market, because the marginal benefit is greater than the market price—the shaded area in Exhibit 2.

Price Changes and Changes in Consumer Surplus

Imagine that the price of your favourite beverage fell because of an increase in supply. Wouldn't you feel better off? An increase in supply and a lower price will increase your consumer surplus for each of the units you were already consuming, and will also increase consumer surplus from increased purchases at the lower price. Conversely, a decrease in supply will cause an increase in price and will lower the amount of consumer surplus.

Exhibit 3 shows the gain in consumer surplus associated with, say, a technological advance that shifts the supply curve to the right. As a result, equilibrium price falls (from P_0 to P_1) and quantity rises (from Q_0 to Q_1). Consumer surplus then increases from area P_0AB to area P_1AC, or a gain

section 6.3
Exhibit 3

The Impact on Consumer Surplus of an Increase in Supply

As a result of the increase in supply, the price falls from P_0 to P_1. The initial consumer surplus at P_0 is the area P_0AB. The increase in the consumer surplus from the fall in price is P_0BCP_1.

in consumer surplus of P_0BCP_1. The increase in consumer surplus has two parts. First, there is an increase in consumer surplus because Q_0 can now be purchased at a lower price; this amount of additional consumer surplus is illustrated by area P_0BDP_1 in Exhibit 3. Second, the lower price makes it advantageous for buyers to expand their purchases from Q_0 to Q_1. The net benefit to buyers from expanding their consumption from Q_0 to Q_1 is illustrated by the area BCD. Similarly, if the market price rose, the quantity demanded would fall. The increase in price causes consumer surplus to decrease by P_0BCP_1.

In sum, consumer surplus measures the net gains that buyers perceive they receive, over and above the market price they must pay. So in this sense, it is a good measure of changes in economic well-being, if we assume that individuals make rational choices—self-betterment choices—and that individuals are the best judges of how much benefit they derive from goods and services.

WHAT IS PRODUCER SURPLUS?

As we have just seen, the difference between what a consumer would be willing and able to pay for a quantity of a good and what a consumer actually has to pay is called *consumer surplus*. The parallel concept for producers is called *producer surplus*. **Producer surplus** is the difference between what a producer is paid for a good and the cost of producing that unit of the good. Producers would never knowingly sell a good that is worth more to them than the asking price. Imagine selling coffee for half of what it cost to produce—you wouldn't be in business very long with that pricing strategy. The supply curve shows the minimum amount that sellers must receive to be willing to supply any given quantity. That is, the supply curve reflects that marginal cost curve to sellers, just like the demand curve is the marginal benefit curve to consumers. Because some units can be produced at a cost that is lower than the market price, the seller receives a surplus, or a net benefit, from producing those units.

For each unit produced, the producer surplus is the difference between the market price and the marginal cost of producing that unit. For example, in Exhibit 4, the market price is $4.50. Say the firm's cost is $2 for the first unit, $3 for the second unit, $4 for the third unit,

producer surplus
the difference between what a producer is paid for a good and the cost of producing that unit of the good; for the market, it is the sum of all of the individual sellers' producer surpluses—the area above the market supply curve and below the market price

section 6.3
Exhibit 4   **A Firm's Producer Surplus**

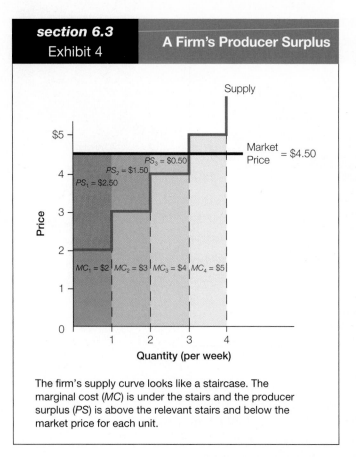

The firm's supply curve looks like a staircase. The marginal cost (*MC*) is under the stairs and the producer surplus (*PS*) is above the relevant stairs and below the market price for each unit.

and $5 for the fourth unit. Since producer surplus for a particular unit is the difference between the market price and the seller's cost of producing that unit, producer surplus would be as follows: The first unit would yield $2.50, the second unit would yield $1.50, the third unit would yield $0.50, while the fourth unit would add nothing to producer surplus, because the market price is less than the seller's cost.

When there are a lot of producers, the supply curve is more or less smooth, as in Exhibit 5. Total producer surplus for the market is obtained by summing all of the producer surpluses of all the sellers—the area above the market supply curve and below the market price up to the quantity actually produced—the shaded area in Exhibit 5. Producer surplus is a measurement of how much sellers gain from trading in the market.

Suppose there is an increase in demand and the market price rises, say from P_0 to P_1; the seller now receives a higher price per unit, so additional producer surplus is generated. In Exhibit 6, we see the additions to producer surplus. Part of the added surplus (area P_1DBP_0) is due to a higher price for the quantity already being produced (up to Q_0) and part (area DCB) is due to the expansion of output made profitable by the higher price (from Q_0 to Q_1). That is, there are gains to producers who would have supplied the output at the original price, P_0, and gains to the producers of added output who are drawn into the market at the higher market price, P_1. Similarly, a fall in the price from P_1 to P_0 would lead to a reduction in producer surplus of area P_1CBP_0.

Just as consumer surplus measures the net gains in economic well-being received by buyers, producer surplus measures the net gains in economic well-being received by sellers. Next, we see that maximizing total surplus (both consumer and producer surplus) will lead to an efficient allocation of resources.

section 6.3
Exhibit 5   **Market Producer Surplus**

The market producer surplus is the shaded area above the supply curve and below the market price up to the quantity produced, 50 000 units.

section 6.3
Exhibit 6
The Impact of an Increase in Demand on Producer Surplus

A higher price for quantity already being produced

Expansion of output from Q_0 to Q_1 made profitable because of higher price

A higher market price due to an increase in demand will increase total producer surplus. The initial producer surplus at P_0 is the area P_0AB. The increase in producer surplus from the higher price is area P_1CBP_0.

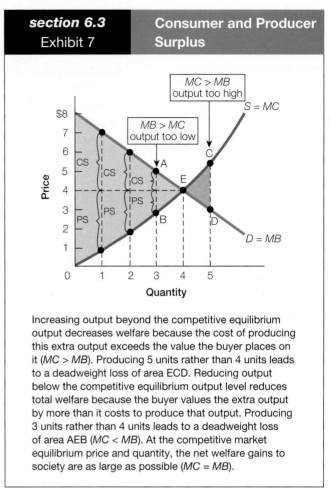

section 6.3
Exhibit 7

Consumer and Producer Surplus

$MC > MB$ output too high

$MB > MC$ output too low

Increasing output beyond the competitive equilibrium output decreases welfare because the cost of producing this extra output exceeds the value the buyer places on it ($MC > MB$). Producing 5 units rather than 4 units leads to a deadweight loss of area ECD. Reducing output below the competitive equilibrium output level reduces total welfare because the buyer values the extra output by more than it costs to produce that output. Producing 3 units rather than 4 units leads to a deadweight loss of area AEB ($MC < MB$). At the competitive market equilibrium price and quantity, the net welfare gains to society are as large as possible ($MC = MB$).

HOW DO WE MEASURE THE TOTAL GAINS FROM EXCHANGE?

With the tools of consumer and producer surplus, we can better analyze the total gains from exchange. The demand curve represents a collection of maximum prices that consumers are willing and able to pay for additional quantities of a good or service. It also shows the marginal benefits derived by consumers. The supply curve represents a collection of minimum prices that suppliers require to be willing and able to supply each additional unit of a good or service. It also shows the marginal cost of production. Both are shown in Exhibit 7. For example, for the first unit of output, the buyer is willing to pay up to $7 and the seller would have to receive at least $1 to produce that unit. However, the equilibrium price is $4, as indicated by the intersection of the supply and demand curves. It is clear that the two would gain from getting together and trading that unit because the consumer would receive $3 of consumer surplus ($7 − $4) and the producer would receive $3 of producer surplus ($4 − $1).

Both would also benefit from trading the second and third units of output—in fact, both would benefit from trading every unit up to the market equilibrium output. That is, buyers purchase each good, except for the very last unit, for less than the maximum amount that they would have been willing to pay; sellers receive, except for the very last unit, more than the minimum price that they would have been willing to accept to supply the good. Once the equilibrium output is reached at the equilibrium price, all of the mutually beneficial trade opportunities between the suppliers and the demanders will have taken place, and the sum of consumer surplus and producer surplus

total welfare gains
the sum of consumer and producer surplus

is maximized. This is where the marginal benefit to buyers is equal to the marginal cost to producers. Both buyers and sellers are better off from each of the units traded than they would have been if they had not exchanged them.

It is important to recognize that, in this case, the **total welfare gains** to the economy from trade in this good is the sum of the consumer and producer surplus created. That is, consumers benefit from additional amounts of consumer surplus and producers benefit from additional amounts of producer surplus. Improvements in welfare come from additions to both consumer and producer surplus. In competitive markets, where there are large numbers of buyers and sellers, at the market equilibrium price and quantity, the net gains to society are as large as possible. Not producing the efficient level of output leads to what economists call a **deadweight loss**. A deadweight loss is the net loss of total surplus that results from the misallocation of resources.

deadweight loss
net loss of total surplus that results from the misallocation of resources

Why would it be inefficient to produce only three units? The demand curve in Exhibit 7 indicates that the buyer is willing to pay $5 for the third unit. The supply curve shows that it costs the seller only $3 to produce that unit. That is, as long as the buyer values the extra output by more than it costs to produce that unit, total welfare would increase by expanding output. In fact, if output is expanded from three units to four units, total welfare (the sum of consumer and producer surpluses) will increase by area AEB in Exhibit 7.

What if five units are produced? The demand curve shows that the buyer is willing to pay only $3 for the fifth unit. However, the supply curve shows that it would cost about $5.50 to produce the fifth unit. So, increasing output beyond equilibrium decreases total welfare because the cost of producing this extra output is greater than the value the buyer places on it. If output is reduced from five units to four units, total welfare will increase by the area ECD in Exhibit 7.

Business *CONNECTION*

AMAZON PRIME DAY—NOW BIGGER THAN BLACK FRIDAY

It took just three years for Amazon Prime Day—the second Tuesday in July every year—to become a bigger retailing event than Black Friday.

In the past, sales were usually "end of season" affairs, where people could purchase whatever was left on store shelves at a big discount. Old inventory or slightly damaged products could be sold before the new seasonal merchandise was brought in.

In the United States, Black Friday—which is the day after American Thanksgiving—has traditionally been the day that more Americans went out to look for holiday gifts. They were in a spending mood and ready to buy. Retailers soon started to offer deep discounts on selected merchandise to attract customers into their stores. At the end of the day, they hoped to be "in the black"—having made a good profit, rather than being "in the red." With the advent of online retailing, Black Friday is followed by Cyber Monday, which is all about computers and electronics, and Giving Tuesday, when people are encouraged to give to charities. With online retailing, the Black Friday series of shopping events has become a worldwide phenomenon and key part of the retailing year.

New technology is enabling some new players to shake up those patterns. Many homeowners are getting smart technologies that control lighting, music, security, and more. Amazon has already captured a big share of this new market with its Echo and Amazon Prime subscription membership.

Once a consumer has an Echo device, an Amazon Prime membership is usually the next purchase. With it, users can access the benefits of that membership, which can include access to more and better music, easier shopping and shipping experiences, faster delivery, and so on. Now Prime members can shop and get discounts and deals on Prime Day. Prime Day started in 2015 and was somewhat disappointing. After just three years, though, the 2018 Prime Day was Amazon's biggest shopping event yet, with more than 100 million products sold.

1. Can you think of how your favourite retailers capitalize on the consumer surplus to boost sales?

2. What is the benefit of making access to sales seem to be "exclusive"?

3. How might retailers start to capture a bit more of the consumer surplus and turn it into a producer surplus?

In a competitive equilibrium, supply equals demand at the equilibrium. This means that the buyers value the last unit of output consumed by exactly the same amount that it cost to produce. If consumers valued the last unit by more than it cost to produce, welfare could be increased by expanding output. If consumers valued the last unit by less than it cost to produce, then welfare could be increased by producing less output.

In sum, *market efficiency* occurs when we have maximized the sum of consumer and producer surplus, when the marginal benefit of the last unit consumed is equal to the marginal cost of productivity, $MB = MC$.

SECTION CHECK

- The difference between how much a consumer is willing and able to pay and how much a consumer has to pay for a unit of the good is called *consumer surplus*. An increase (decrease) in supply will lead to an increase (decrease) in consumer surplus.
- Producer surplus is the difference between what a producer is paid for a good and the cost of producing that good. An increase (decrease) in demand will lead to an increase (decrease) in producer surplus.
- The economy's total welfare gains from exchange can be measured by the sum of consumer and producer surplus.

For Your Review

Section 6.1

1. If someone says, "You'd have to pay me to eat one more bite," what do we know about that person's marginal utility? What do we know about that person's total utility?

2. The following table shows Rene's total utility from eating escargot. Fill in the blanks that show the marginal utility that Rene derives from eating escargot.

Escargot		
Per Day	Total Utility	Marginal Utility
1	10	_____
2	18	_____
3	24	_____
4	28	_____
5	30	_____
6	30	_____

3. At the local ski resort, the rates for time on the slopes are as follows:

$$\text{4-hour pass} = \$23$$

$$\text{Full-day pass (8 hours)} = \$33$$

How does this pricing policy relate to what we know about marginal utility?

4. Why would you not continue to consume a good in the range where there was diminishing total utility?

5. Where possible, complete the following table by filling in the empty cells.

Number of Smartphone Apps.	Total Utility	Marginal Utility
0		—
1	12	
2	22	
3		7
4		4
5	33	
6		–2

6. Suppose it is "All You Can Eat" night at your favourite restaurant. Once you've paid $9.95 for your meal, how do you determine how many helpings to consume? Should you continue eating until your food consumption has yielded $9.95 worth of satisfaction? What happens to the marginal utility from successive helpings as consumption increases?

Section 6.2

7. Brandy spends her entire weekly budget of $20 on soft drinks and pizza. A soft drink and a slice of pizza are priced at $1 and $2, respectively. Brandy's marginal utility from soft drink and pizza consumption is 6 utils and 4 utils, respectively. What advice could you give Brandy to help her increase her overall satisfaction from the consumption of soft drinks and pizza? What will happen to the marginal utility per dollar from soft drink consumption if Brandy follows your advice? What will happen to the marginal utility per dollar from pizza consumption?

8. Suppose you were studying late one night and you were craving a Domino's pizza. How much marginal utility would you receive from the delivered pizza? How much marginal utility would you receive from a pizza that was delivered immediately after you finished a five-course holiday dinner? Where would you be more likely to eat more pizza in a single sitting, at home or at a crowded party (particularly if you're not sure how many pizzas have been ordered)? Use marginal utility analysis to answer the last question.

Blueprint Problem

The utility derived from consuming various quantities of pasta and sushi are presented in the following table.

Pasta		Sushi	
Servings of Pasta	Total Utility	Servings of Sushi	Total Utility
0	0	0	0
1	20	1	14
2	35	2	25
3	44	3	31
4	49	4	35
5	51	5	37

Suppose the price for a serving of pasta is $5 and the price for a serving of sushi is $4. If Elaine has a limited budget of $27, how many servings of pasta and sushi will she purchase in an effort to achieve consumer equilibrium?

Blueprint Solution

Pasta				Sushi			
Servings	TU	MU	MU/P	Servings	TU	MU	MU/P
0	0	—	—	0	0	—	—
1	20	20	4	1	14	14	3.5
2	35	15	3	2	25	11	2.75
3	44	9	1.8	3	31	6	1.5
4	49	5	1	4	35	4	1
5	51	2	0.4	5	37	2	0.5

Recall the condition that will bring our consumer to consumer equilibrium:

$$\frac{MU_{pasta}}{P_{pasta}} = \frac{MU_{sushi}}{P_{sushi}}$$

In order to use this condition to bring our consumer to the optimal combination of pasta and sushi, the *MU* per dollar spent for each serving of both pasta and sushi needs to be computed. It is suggested that this is done in a table, such as this one presented above.

To ensure that our consumer reaches consumer equilibrium, each purchase needs to be evaluated.

Consider the first purchase; since the first serving of pasta offers more *MU* per dollar spent than the first serving of sushi (4 utils vs. 3.5 utils), the consumer will purchase pasta. As for the second purchase, here the first serving of sushi offers more *MU* per dollar spent than the second serving of pasta (3.5 utils vs. 3 utils), so the consumer will purchase the first serving of sushi.

> Notice what is being compared in the second purchase—the first serving of sushi (that has yet to be bought) against the second serving of pasta (given that the first serving was bought in the first purchase).

In terms of the third purchase, since the *MU* per dollar spent for the second serving of pasta exceeds that for the second serving of sushi, the consumer will purchase a second serving of pasta. For the fourth purchase, the second serving of sushi produces more *MU* per dollar spent compared to the third serving of pasta, so the consumer will purchase the second serving of sushi. As for the fifth and sixth purchases, using the same reasoning as above, the consumer would purchase the third serving of pasta followed by the third serving of sushi.

To summarize these purchases and illustrate their impact on the consumer's budget, total utility, and marginal utility enjoyed, a table such as the following could be constructed.

Purchase	Item	Budget Remaining	MU (utils)	TU (utils)
1st	Pasta	$27 − $5 = $22	20	20
2nd	Sushi	$22 − $4 = $18	14	34
3rd	Pasta	$18 − $5 = $13	15	49
4th	Sushi	$13 − $4 = $9	11	60
5th	Pasta	$9 − $5 = $4	9	69
6th	Sushi	$4 − $4 = 0	6	75

> Note that the budget is exhausted in equilibrium.

> Note the total amount of utility:
> 3 servings of pasta (44 utils of utility) + 3 servings of sushi (31 utils of utility) = 75 utils of utility

9. The table below details the amount of utility a typical student derives from consuming cups of coffee and muffins. The price of a cup of coffee is $2, the price of a muffin is $1, and the student has a total of $9 to spend (and spends it all). Based on all this information, how many cups of coffee and muffins will our typical student purchase in consumer equilibrium?

Cups of Coffee		Muffins	
Number of Cups	Total Utility	Number of Muffins	Total Utility
0	0	0	0
1	16	1	6
2	29	2	10
3	40	3	11
4	49	4	11
5	54	5	9

10. Using the data from problem 9, what would happen to our utility-maximizing student's behaviour if the price of a muffin decreased to $0.50 (all other information remains constant)?

11. Complete the following table by filling in the missing cells.

Hockey Games			Football Games		
Number	TU	MU	Number	TU	MU
0	0	—	0		—
1	20		1		18
2	36		2	30	
3		12	3	36	
4		10	4		6
5	66	8	5	45	
6	72		6		0

If the price of a hockey ticket is $16, the price of a football ticket is $12, and local sports fans have a budget of $88, determine how many hockey games and football games they will attend using the utility-maximizing rule.

Section 6.3

12. Refer to the following exhibit.

a. If the price of each karate lesson is P_0, the consumer surplus is equal to what area?

b. If the price falls from P_0 to P_1, the change in consumer surplus is equal to what area?

13. Steve loves potato chips. His weekly demand curve is shown in the following exhibit.

a. How much is Steve willing to pay for one bag of potato chips?

b. How much is Steve willing to pay for a second bag of potato chips?

c. If the actual market price of potato chips is $2.50 and Steve buys five bags as shown, what is the value of his consumer surplus?

d. What is Steve's total willingness to pay for five bags?

14. If a freeze ruined this year's lettuce crop, show what would happen to consumer surplus.

15. If demand for apples increased as a result of a news story that highlighted the health benefits of two apples a day, what would happen to producer surplus?

16. How is total surplus (the sum of consumer and producer surpluses) related to the efficient level of output? Using a supply and demand curve, demonstrate that producing less than the equilibrium output will lead to an inefficient allocation of resources—a deadweight loss.

17. Suppose Phil's supply curve for widgets is as follows: At $20, he will supply 1; at $30, he will supply 2; at $40, he will supply 3; at $50, he will supply 4; and at $60, he will supply 5.

    a. If the price of widgets is $40, what is his producer surplus?

    b. If the price of widgets rises from $40 to $50, how much will his producer surplus change?

chapter

7

Production and Costs

section

7.1

Profits: Total Revenues Minus Total Costs

- What are explicit and implicit costs?
- What are profits?
- What are sunk costs?

WHAT ARE EXPLICIT AND IMPLICIT COSTS?

As we discussed in Chapter 1, costs exist because resources are scarce and have competing uses—to produce more of one good means forgoing the production of another good. The cost of producing a good is measured by the worth of the most valuable alternative that was given up to obtain the resource. As you may recall, this is called the *opportunity cost*.

In Chapter 2, the production possibilities curve highlighted this trade-off. Recall that the opportunity cost of producing additional shelter was the units of food that had to be sacrificed. Other examples of opportunity costs abound: Paper used in this text could have been used in other books or for hundreds of other uses, and the steel used in the construction of a new building could have been used in the production of an automobile or a washing machine.

But what exactly makes up a firm's costs? Let's look at the two distinct components that make up the firm's costs: explicit costs and implicit costs.

Explicit Costs

explicit costs

the opportunity costs of production that require a monetary payment

Explicit costs are the opportunity costs of production that require a monetary payment—the out-of-pocket expenses for labour services, raw materials, fuel, transportation, utilities, advertising, and so on. It is important to note that the explicit costs are opportunity costs to the firm. For example, money spent on electricity cannot be used for advertising. Remember, in a world of scarcity, we are always giving up something to get something else. Trade-offs are pervasive. The costs that we have discussed so far are relatively easy to measure and an economist and an accountant would most likely arrive at the same amounts. But that will generally not be the case.

Implicit Costs

Some of the firm's (opportunity) costs of production are implicit. **Implicit costs** do not require monetary payment. This is where the economist's and the accountant's ideas of costs diverge because accountants do not include implicit costs. For example, whenever an investment is made, opportunities to invest elsewhere are forgone. This lost opportunity is an implicit cost that economists include in the total cost of the firm, even though no money is expended. A typical farmer or small business owner may perform work without receiving formal wages, but the value of the alternative earnings forgone represents an implicit opportunity cost to the individual. Because other firms could have used the resources, what the resources could have earned elsewhere is an implicit cost to the firm. It is important to emphasize that whenever we are talking about costs—explicit or implicit—we are talking about opportunity costs.

To better delineate the difference between explicit and implicit costs, consider whether the following statement is true or false: "A company located in a growing urban area with rising rents can protect itself against these rising costs by owning the building it occupies." This statement is not entirely true. The company is protected against having to pay the rising rents (explicit cost) by owning the building it occupies. However, if the company owns the building and rents increase, so does the opportunity cost of owning the building. That is, by occupying the building, the company is giving up the new higher rents it could receive from renters if it leased out the space. So, even though the company pays zero rent by owning the building, the rent that it could receive by leasing it to another company is a very real economic cost (but not an accounting cost) to the firm.

implicit costs
the opportunity costs of production that do not require a monetary payment

WHAT ARE PROFITS?

Economists generally assume that the ultimate goal of the firm is to maximize **profits**, that is, to maximize the difference between total revenue and total cost. In other words, firms try to maximize the difference between what they give up for their inputs—their total costs (explicit and implicit)—and the amount they receive for their goods and services—their total revenue. Like revenues and costs, profits refer to flows over time. When we say that a firm earned $5 million in profits, we must clarify the time period in which the profits were earned—a week, month, year, and so on.

profits
the difference between total revenue and total cost

Accounting Profits vs. Economic Profits

A firm can make a profit in the sense that the total revenues that it receives exceed the explicit costs that it incurs in the process of doing business. We call these **accounting profits**—profits as accountants record them are determined by total revenues minus total explicit costs. In other words, accounting profits do not include implicit costs.

Economists prefer an alternative way of measuring profits; **economic profits** are determined by total revenue minus all costs (both explicit and implicit). In calculating a firm's total costs, economists include the implicit costs—as well as the explicit costs.

Summing up, measured in terms of accounting profits like those reported in real-world financial statements, a firm has a profit if its total revenues exceed explicit costs.

accounting profits
total revenues minus total explicit costs

economic profits
total revenues minus explicit and implicit costs

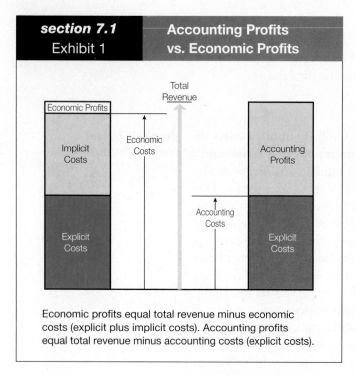

section 7.1
Exhibit 1

Accounting Profits vs. Economic Profits

Economic profits equal total revenue minus economic costs (explicit plus implicit costs). Accounting profits equal total revenue minus accounting costs (explicit costs).

In terms of economic profits, a firm has a profit if its total revenues exceed its total opportunity cost—both its explicit costs and implicit costs. Exhibit 1 illustrates the difference between accounting profits and economic profits.

A Zero Economic Profit Is a Normal Profit

As we just discussed, an economic profit is less than an accounting profit because economic profits include implicit as well as explicit costs. In fact, an economist considers a zero economic profit to be a normal profit. Recall that zero economic profit means that the firm is covering both explicit and implicit costs—the total opportunity costs of its resources. In other words, the firm's total revenue is sufficient to compensate the time and money that owners have put into the business. For example, suppose you became a farmer and made $80 000 per year. Initially, you had to invest $1 million for the property, seed, and equipment. However, if you had put that money in the bank at, say, 3 percent interest, you would have made $30 000 per year, so you have an implicit cost of $30 000 per year in lost interest. In addition, you have an implicit cost of $50 000 per year because you did not take the job you were offered at the tractor dealership. So an accountant would have you making an economic profit of $80 000, but an economist would say you made zero economic profit because your total revenue minus total costs (explicit + implicit costs) is zero. But even though your profits are driven to zero, your revenue from farming compensates you for your total costs, so you stay in business. This is clearly different from making zero accounting profits, when revenues would cover only the explicit costs. (We will return to this important point in the next chapter.)

WHAT ARE SUNK COSTS?

We have just seen how opportunity costs are often hidden, as in the case of implicit costs. However, there is another type of cost that should be discussed—sunk costs. **Sunk costs** are costs that have already been incurred and cannot be recovered. Suppose, for example, that you bought a DVD that looked interesting, but when you got home and played it you wished you hadn't. Now your friend comes over and says he likes that DVD and will buy it from you for $5. You say "no way" because you paid $15 for the DVD. Are you acting rationally? Economists believe that what you paid for the DVD is now irrelevant. Now, you must decide whether you would rather have the $5 or the DVD. If you decide to keep the DVD, the cost is the $5 you could have received from your friend—the rest is sunk.

Or suppose a doughnut shop has a one-year lease and after three months the owner decides that the shop would do much better by relocating to a new mall that has just opened. Should the doughnut shop just stay put until the end of the year because it is legally obligated to pay the 12-month lease? No, the nonrefundable lease payment is sunk and irrelevant to the decision to relocate. The decision to relocate should be based on the prospects of future profits regardless of the length of the current lease. In short, sunk costs are irrelevant for any future action because they have already been incurred and cannot be recovered.

sunk costs

costs that have been incurred and cannot be recovered

Business *CONNECTION*

THE IMPORTANCE OF WATCHING *ALL* COSTS

Many businesses fail because they focus on revenues and forget to watch and understand all of their costs. The key word here is *all*, because although some costs are obvious and can readily be identified, others are not so apparent. In fact, some time may pass between a business incurring a cost and realizing the impact. In economics, we give the label *explicit costs* to incurred costs that are paid directly with cash, a debit card, a credit card, or a cheque and can easily be identified as corresponding to particular units of land, buildings, materials, machinery or equipment, or labour. Sometimes these are also referred to as *accounting costs* because they can be readily identified, measured, recorded, interpreted, and communicated to others—an important role of accounting. Accounting costs reflect historical costs, and planning (or forecasting) requires interpreting historical costs into the future.

There is, however, another set of costs that are not easily identified, that many business operators forget to take into account in making business decisions, and that many students forget about, too. These costs are referred to as *implicit costs*. They are *implicit* because they are not usually apparent unless we carefully consider what we are giving up to obtain a good or service. Take, for example, our education. Our explicit costs include tuition fee payments to the college or university and the cost of textbooks and other school supplies. Our implicit costs—what we gave up to pursue an education—vary, based on individual circumstances. For some of us, the implicit costs include the wages we could have earned working at a job; for others, it's the interest on the savings that we no longer have in the bank.

There is another set of costs, known as *sunk costs*. These are costs that a firm is required to undertake but will not be able to recover, such as the cost of repairing a leaky roof or cleaning up after a flood—costs that are rare and generally cannot be passed on to the customer. If firms do try to pass the costs on, they very well might push the product price into an uncompetitive level.

Business operators who take into account that total economic costs include both explicit and implicit costs, with the reality of sunk costs, realize that over time, if they are really to make a profit, the revenue obtained from their business activities must cover these costs and that they will need to interpret opportunity costs in making decisions on future activities. For example, assume a Canadian toy manufacturer's main plant is close to its operational capacity as it runs two eight-hour shifts. The manufacturer is considering three courses of action: (1) running two ten-hour shifts, (2) building and expanding its plant across town, or (3) outsourcing its manufacturing to Southeast Asia. In considering the explicit costs, it would look at all historical costs and forecast future costs of the overtime in option 1 and construction/transportation costs in option 2. In option 3, it would look at the explicit costs of added transportation and perhaps training, but the manufacturer would also have to compare the opportunity costs of manufacturing in-house versus outsourcing. The possibility of losing control of intellectual property and having to deal with counterfeit production might also be of concern. Looking only at the historical/accounting costs, a firm would limit its success, not putting itself in a position to think of alternatives when the market changes.

Businesspeople who are fully aware of all costs are more likely to set realistic prices for goods and services to ensure that the revenues received cover all explicit and all implicit costs, as well as an amount to provide a profit.

1. It is becoming clear that highly skilled and knowledgeable workers could soon be replaced by machinery and robots. What is your position regarding replacing skilled workers with robots?

2. In Thailand, slave labour is employed to peel and prepare shrimp for worldwide consumption. If you were a Canadian shrimp wholesaler, would you buy Thai-processed shrimp?

3. If your company has to compete with shrimp wholesalers who buy from owners of slaves, who can therefore charge lower prices, how might you compete?

DEBATE

SHOULD GREENBELT LEGISLATION BE DROPPED?

For:
When cities are undergoing rapid periods of development and expansion, pressure is often brought to bear to have areas beyond the city limits rezoned for various uses. Farmland and underused scrublands can then be purchased for subdivisions, public buildings, shopping centres, schools, and industrial facilities.

Most landowners will not take the first offer that a developer makes for their land. In the case of farmland, a farmer may continue to work the land, raise crops or livestock, and make a good living. As other farms sell to developers who build more housing or whole communities, more people are attracted to the newly developed area. The value of the land that the farmer holds begins to rise at a faster

(continued)

rate than the value of the living the farmer can make from the land.

Given the low margins that farmers have in a competitive agricultural industry, there is not always a lot of income associated with farming. While there may still be sentimental value attached to the farmer's homestead, the romance of the "family farm" begins to fade. The new generation begins to leave the farms, showing little interest in working them. In time, selling the farm becomes the best way for the farmer to realize the value from the land.

Recently, in an area northwest of Toronto, a farmer sold the family's 61-hectare property for $97 million. By holding out for a good price, that farmer became a multimillionaire.

The opportunity cost of farming near urban centres has just become too high to be concerned about preserving greenbelts.

Against:

Science is showing that human beings benefit from the preservation of natural ecosystems. Environmentalists, concerned about poorly managed urban expansion, say the land is effectively being destroyed, leading to ecosystem collapse and the decline of many important plant and animal species. "Hardscaping," the widespread introduction of man-made elements such as brick, concrete, and stone buildings and paved roads, has been linked to global warming.

In a bid to slow down this destruction, governments should rezone land such as farmland as greenbelts, or purchase and maintain large tracts of land for national or provincial parks. As our ability to accurately account for the value of having and maintaining our ecosystem improves, it is in the public interest to support healthy ecosystems and parks.

Questions:

1. Should governments allow rezoning of undeveloped green spaces for more housing or commercial development?
2. Are greenbelts contributing to lower housing prices, resulting in many people being able to own a home?
3. How can opportunity cost be used to justify greenbelts or, alternatively, justify development?

SECTION CHECK

- Total cost consists of explicit costs and implicit costs. Explicit costs are the opportunity costs of production that require a monetary payment, while implicit costs are the opportunity costs that do not represent an outlay of money.
- Profits are the difference between the total revenues of a firm and its total costs. Accounting profits are revenues minus explicit costs, while economic profits are revenues minus total opportunity costs—both explicit and implicit.
- Sunk costs are irretrievable and irrelevant to the firm once they have been incurred.

section 7.2

Production in the Short Run

- What is the difference between the short run and the long run?
- How does production in the short run behave?
- What is the relationship between average and marginal amounts?

WHAT IS THE DIFFERENCE BETWEEN THE SHORT RUN AND THE LONG RUN?

Of fundamental importance for cost and production behaviour is the extent to which a firm is able to adjust inputs as it varies output. Since it takes more time to vary some inputs than others, we must distinguish between the short run and the long run. The **short run** is defined as a period too brief for some production inputs to be varied. For example, the current size of a plant cannot be altered and new equipment cannot

short run

a period too brief for some production inputs to be varied be obtained or built overnight. If demand increases for the firm's product and the firm chooses to produce more output in the short run, it must do so with its existing equipment and factory. Inputs like buildings and equipment that do not change with output are called *fixed* inputs.

The **long run** is a period of time over which all production inputs are variable and can change as output changes. The long run can vary considerably from industry to industry. For a chain of coffeehouses that wants to add a few more stores, the long run may be only a few months. In other industries, like the automobile or steel industry, the long run might be a couple of years, as a new plant or factory in this type of industry will take much longer to build.

long run
a period over which all production inputs are variable

HOW DOES PRODUCTION IN THE SHORT RUN BEHAVE?

Exhibit 1 shows how the quantity of bagels produced by Moe's Bagel Shop per hour varies with the number of workers. This relationship between the quantity of inputs (workers) and the quantity of outputs (bagels) is called the **production function**. Suppose that Moe's Bagel Shop has just one input that is variable, labour, whereas the size of the bagel shop is fixed in the short run. **Total product (*TP*)** is the total amount of a good produced by a firm. In this case, total product is the total amount of bagels generated by Moe's shop, as the level of the variable input, labour (*L*), is increased. Common sense suggests that total product will start at a low level and increase—perhaps rapidly at first, and then more slowly—as the amount of the variable input increases. It will continue to increase until the quantity of the variable input (labour) becomes so large in relation to the quantity of other inputs—like the size of the bagel shop—that further increases in output become more and more difficult or even impossible.

In column (2) of Exhibit 1, we see that as we increase the number of workers in Moe's Bagel Shop, Moe is able to produce more bagels. The addition of the first worker results in a total output of 10 bagels per hour. When Moe adds a second worker, bagel output climbs to 22, an increase of 12 bagels per hour. Total product continues to increase even with the sixth worker hired, but you can see that it has slowed considerably, with the sixth worker increasing total product by only one bagel per hour. Beyond this point, additional workers result in a decline in total bagel output as workers bump

production function
the relationship between the quantity of inputs and the quantity of outputs produced

total product (*TP*)
the total output of a good produced by the firm

section 7.2 Exhibit 1	Moe's Production Function with One Variable Input, Labour

Variable Input Labour (L) (workers) (1)	Total Product (TP) of Labour (bagels per hour) (2)	Average Product of Labour (bagels per hour) TP/L (3)	Marginal Product of Labour (bagels per hour) ΔTP/ΔL (4)
0	0	—	
1	10	10.0	10
2	22	11.0	12
3	36	12.0	14
4	46	11.5	10
5	50	10.0	4
6	51	8.5	1
7	50	7.1	−1

into each other in the small bagel shop. This outcome can be seen in Exhibit 1, column 2, by the total product number declining from 51 to 50, and in Exhibit 2(a), where the total product curve becomes downward sloping.

Average Product

average product (AP)
the total product divided by the number of units of the variable input used to produce it

Average product (AP) is the total product divided by the number of units of the variable input used to produce it. This concept is shown in column 3 in Exhibit 1 and is illustrated by the *AP* curve in Exhibit 2(b). If labour (*L*) was used to represent the variable input, average product would be

$$AP = \frac{TP}{L}$$

An examination of average product in column 3 in Exhibit 1 reveals that the first three variable inputs (workers one, two, and three) generate increasing average product, while the remaining variable inputs (workers four, five, six, and seven) generate declining average product. When the bagel shop has three workers, average product is at its maximum; this is referred to as the *point of diminishing average product.*

Marginal Product

marginal product (MP)
the change in total product resulting from a unit change in variable input

The **marginal product (MP)** of any single input is defined as the change in total product resulting from a unit change in the amount of variable input used. This concept is shown in column (4) in Exhibit 1, and is illustrated by the *MP* curve in Exhibit 2(b). As you can see in Exhibit 2(b), the *MP* curve first rises and then falls.

If labour is again used to represent the variable input, marginal product would be

$$MP = \frac{\Delta TP}{\Delta L}$$

section 7.2 Exhibit 2	**Total Product, Average Product, and Marginal Product**

a. Total Product

b. Average and Marginal Product

In Exhibit 2(a), we see that total output increases as the amount of the variable input, labour, is increased—usually more rapidly at first and then more slowly. In Exhibit 2(b), we see that the marginal product first rises (increasing marginal product) as workers are added to the fixed input (e.g., a machine), which is thus used more efficiently. Then the marginal product falls; the crowding of the fixed input with more and more workers causes marginal product to fall. Lastly, negative marginal product occurs where additional inputs cause output to fall. Also in Exhibit 2(b), we see the average product curve. Average product initially increases, but eventually declines. The average product curve intersects the marginal product curve at the maximum amount of average product.

The Rise in Marginal Product   The initial rise in the marginal product is the result of more effective use of fixed inputs (the bagel shop) as the number of workers increases (due to specialization and division of labour). For example, certain types of capital equipment may require a minimum number of workers for efficient operation, or perhaps any operation at all. With a small number of workers (the variable factors), some machines cannot operate at all, or only at a very low level of efficiency. As additional workers are added, machines are brought into efficient operation, and thus the marginal product of the workers rises. Similarly, if one person tried to operate a large department store alone—doing work of all types necessary in the store—her energies would be spread so thinly in so many directions that total output (sales) might be less than if she was operating a smaller store (working with less capital). As successive workers are added, up to a certain number, each worker adds more to total product than the previous one and the marginal product rises. This area of increasing marginal product is seen in the first shaded area in Exhibit 2(b) where the marginal product curve is rising.

The Fall in Marginal Product   But why does marginal product then fall? The answer is **diminishing marginal product**, which stems from the crowding of the fixed input. Specifically, as the amount of a variable input is increased, the amount of other (fixed) inputs being held constant, a point ultimately will be reached beyond which marginal product will decline. Beyond this point, output increases, but at a decreasing rate. It is the crowding of the fixed input with more and more workers that causes the decline in the marginal product. Too many workers in a store make it more difficult for customers to shop; too many workers in a factory get in each other's way. Adding more and more of a variable input to a fixed input will eventually lead to diminishing marginal product.

The point of this discussion is that production functions conform to the same general pattern as that shown by Moe's Bagel Shop in column (3) of Exhibit 1 and illustrated in Exhibit 2(b). In column 4 in Exhibit 1, we see that as we increase the number of workers in Moe's Bagel Shop, Moe is able to produce more bagels. The first worker is able to produce 10 bagels per hour. When Moe adds a second worker, total bagel output climbs to 22, an increase of 12 bagels per hour. When Moe hires a third worker, bagel output increases again, a third worker's marginal production (14 bagels per hour) is greater than that of the first and second worker. However, when Moe hires a fourth worker, while bagel output still increases, the marginal production of the fourth worker is less than that of the third worker. In fact, the marginal product continues to drop as more and more workers are added to the bagel shop. This is diminishing marginal product at work.

Note that it is not because the fourth worker is not as "good" as the third worker that marginal product fell. Even with identical workers, the increased "crowding" of the fixed input causes marginal output to eventually fall. This area of *diminishing marginal product* is seen in the middle shaded area in Exhibit 2(b), where the marginal product curve is declining but is still above the horizontal axis.

A firm never *knowingly* allows itself to reach the point where the marginal product becomes negative, the situation in which the use of additional variable input units actually reduces total product. In such a situation, there are so many units of the variable input—inputs with positive opportunity costs—that efficient use of the fixed input units is impaired. In such a situation, *reducing* the number of workers would actually *increase* total product. This area of negative marginal product is seen in the final shaded area in Exhibit 2(b), where the marginal product curve is below the horizontal axis.

diminishing marginal product
as a variable input increases, with other inputs fixed, a point will be reached where the additions to output will eventually decline

How many workers could be added to this jackhammer and still be productive (not to mention safe)? If more workers were added, how much output would be derived from each additional worker? There may be slightly more total output from the second worker because the second worker will be using the jackhammer while the first worker is taking a break from "the shakes." However, the fifth or sixth worker would clearly not create any additional output, as workers would just be standing around waiting for their turn. That is, the marginal product (additional output) would eventually fall because of diminishing marginal product.

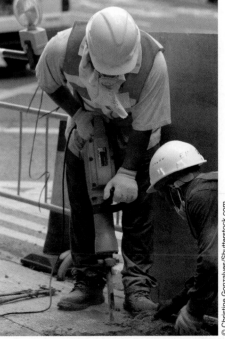

© Christine Gonzalves/Shutterstock.com

WHAT IS THE RELATIONSHIP BETWEEN MARGINAL AND AVERAGE AMOUNTS?

The relationship between the marginal and the average is simply a matter of arithmetic; when a number (the marginal product) being added into a series is smaller than the previous average of the series, the new average will be lower than the previous one. Likewise, when the marginal number is larger than the average, the average will rise. For example, if you have taken two economics exams and received 90 percent on your first exam and 80 percent on your second exam, you have an 85 percent average. If after some serious studying, you get 100 percent on the third exam (the marginal exam), what happens to your average? It rises to 90 percent.

Because the marginal is greater than the average, it "pulls" the average up. However, if the score on your third (marginal) exam is lower, 70 percent, your average will fall to 80 percent because the marginal is below the average.

We can now use this reasoning to better understand our per-unit measures of productivity. The reason the average product curve is initially rising is because the marginal product curve is initially above it; the higher marginal product has the effect of "pulling" average product up. The reason why the average product curve eventually declines is because the marginal product curve falls below it, thereby "pulling" average product down.

SECTION CHECK

- The *short run* is defined as a period too brief for some inputs to be varied, whereas the *long run* is a period of time long enough to allow the firm to adjust all inputs. Inputs such as buildings and equipment that do not change with output in the short run are called *fixed inputs*.
- Total output increases as variable inputs are increased. Marginal product initially rises, but eventually declines as variable inputs are added. Finally, negative marginal product can occur, indicating a fall in total output.
- Adding a marginal amount affects the value of the average amount—the average will rise (fall) when the marginal amount is larger (smaller) than the initial average.

section 7.3

Costs in the Short Run

- What are fixed costs, variable costs, and total costs?
- What are average costs?
- What is marginal cost?

In the last section we learned about the relationship between a firm's inputs and its level of output. But that is only one part of the discussion; we must also consider how much it will cost the firm to use each of these inputs in production. In this section, we will examine the short-run costs of the firm—what they are and how they vary with the output levels that are produced. The short-run total costs of a business fall into two distinct categories: fixed costs and variable costs.

WHAT ARE FIXED COSTS, VARIABLE COSTS, AND TOTAL COSTS?

Fixed costs are those that do not vary with the level of output in the short run. For example, the rent on buildings or equipment is usually fixed for at least some period of time; whether the firm produces lots of output or little output, the rent stays the same. Insurance premiums, property taxes, and interest payments on debt used to finance capital equipment are other examples of fixed costs—they have to be paid even if no output is produced. In the short run, fixed costs cannot be avoided. The only way a firm can avoid a fixed cost is by going out of business. The sum of the firm's fixed costs is called the **total fixed cost (*TFC*)**.

   Variable costs vary with the level of output. As more variable inputs like labour and raw materials are added, output increases. The variable cost, the expenditures for wages and raw materials, increases as output increases. The sum of the firm's variable costs is called **total variable cost (*TVC*)**. The sum of the total fixed costs and total variable costs is called the firm's **total cost (*TC*)**.

WHAT ARE AVERAGE COSTS?

Although we are often interested in the total amount of costs incurred by the firm, sometimes we find it convenient to discuss these costs on a per-unit-of-output, or an average, basis. For example, if Pizza Shack Company has $1600 in total fixed cost and $2400 in total variable cost, its total cost is $4000. If it produces 800 pizzas in the time period in question, its total cost per unit of output equals $5 ($4000 total cost (*TC*) divided by 800 units of output). We call this per-unit total cost the **average total cost (*ATC*)**—*TC/q*. Likewise, we might talk about the per-unit fixed cost of output, or **average fixed cost (*AFC*)**—*TFC/q*. In the case of Pizza Shack, the average fixed cost, or *AFC,* would equal $2 ($1600 is the fixed cost divided by 800 units of output (*q*)). Similarly, we can speak of per-unit variable cost, or **average variable cost (*AVC*)**—*TVC/q*. In this example, the average variable cost would equal $3 ($2400 is the variable cost divided by 800 units of output).

WHAT IS MARGINAL COST?

To this point, six different short-run cost concepts have been introduced: total cost, total fixed cost, total variable cost, average total cost, average fixed cost, and average variable cost. All of these concepts are relevant to a discussion of firm behaviour and profitability. However, the most important single cost concept has yet to be mentioned: marginal (or additional) cost. You may recall this concept from Chapter 1, where we highlighted the importance of using marginal analysis—that is, analysis that focuses on *additional* or marginal choices. Specifically, **marginal cost (*MC*)** shows the change in total costs resulting from a one-unit change in output ($\Delta TC/\Delta q$). Put a bit differently, marginal cost is the cost of producing one more unit of output. As such, marginal costs are really just a very useful way to view variable costs—costs that vary as output varies. Marginal cost represents the added labour, raw materials, and miscellaneous expenses that are incurred in making an additional unit of output. Marginal cost is the additional, or incremental, cost associated with the "last" unit of output produced.

The Relationships among the Different Costs

Exhibit 1 summarizes the definitions of the seven different short-run cost concepts introduced in this chapter. To further clarify these concepts and to illustrate the relationships among them, we will now return to our discussion of the costs faced by Pizza Shack.

fixed costs
costs that do not vary with the level of output in the short run

total fixed cost (*TFC*)
the sum of the firm's fixed costs

variable costs
costs that vary with the level of output

total variable cost (*TVC*)
the sum of the firm's variable costs

total cost (*TC*)
the sum of the firm's total fixed costs and total variable costs

average total cost (*ATC*)
a per-unit cost of operation; total cost divided by output

average fixed cost (*AFC*)
a per-unit measure of fixed costs; fixed costs divided by output

average variable cost (*AVC*)
a per-unit measure of variable costs; variable costs divided by output

marginal cost (*MC*)
the change in total costs resulting from a one-unit change in output

section 7.3
Exhibit 1
A Summary of the Short-Run Cost Concepts

Concept	Abbreviation	Definition
Total fixed cost	TFC	Costs that are the same at all output levels in the short run (e.g., insurance, rent).
Total variable cost	TVC	Costs that vary with the level of output (e.g., hourly labour, raw materials).
Total cost	TC	The sum of the firm's total fixed costs and total variable costs at a level of output ($TC = TFC + TVC$).
Marginal cost	MC	The added cost of producing one more unit of output; change in TC associated with one more unit of output ($\Delta TC/\Delta q$).
Average total cost	ATC	TC per unit of output; TC divided by output (TC/q).
Average fixed cost	AFC	*TFC per unit of output; TFC divided by output (TFC/q).*
Average variable cost	AVC	TVC per unit of output; TVC divided by output (TVC/q).

Exhibit 2 presents the costs incurred by Pizza Shack at various levels of output. Note that the total fixed cost is the same at all output levels and that at very low output levels (four or fewer units in the example), total fixed cost is the dominant portion of total costs. At high output levels (eight or more units in the example), total fixed cost becomes quite small relative to total variable cost. As the firm increases its output, it spreads its total fixed cost across more units; as a result, average fixed cost declines continuously.

It is often easier to understand the cost concepts by examining graphs that show the levels of the various costs at different output levels. The graph in Exhibit 3 shows the first three cost concepts: fixed, variable, and total costs for Pizza Shack. The total fixed cost (TFC) curve is always a horizontal line because, by definition, fixed costs are the same at all output levels in the short run—even at zero level of output. In Exhibit 3, notice that $TVC = 0$ when $q = 0$; if there is no output being produced, there are no variable costs.

The total cost (TC) curve is the summation of the total variable cost (TVC) and total fixed cost (TFC) curves. Because the total fixed cost curve is horizontal, the total cost curve lies above the total variable cost curve by a fixed (vertical) amount.

Exhibit 4 shows the average fixed cost curve, the average variable cost curve, the average total cost curve, and the associated marginal cost curve for Pizza Shack. In this

section 7.3
Exhibit 2
Cost Calculations for Pizza Shack Company

Hourly Output (q)	Total Fixed Cost (TFC)	Total Variable Cost (TVC)	Total Cost (TC = TVC + TFC)	Marginal Cost (MC = ΔTC/Δq)	Average Fixed Cost (AFC = TFC/q)	Average Variable Cost (AVC = TVC/q)	Average Total Cost (ATC = TC/q or AFC + AVC)
0	$40	$ 0	$ 40	—	—	—	—
1	40	10	50	$10	$40.00	$10.00	$50.00
2	40	18	58	8	20.00	9.00	29.00
3	40	25	65	7	13.33	8.33	21.67
4	40	33	73	8	10.00	8.25	18.25
5	40	43	83	10	8.00	8.60	16.60
6	40	56	96	13	6.67	9.33	16.00
7	40	73	113	17	5.71	10.43	16.10
8	40	94	134	21	5.00	11.75	16.75
9	40	120	160	26	4.44	13.33	17.78
10	40	152	192	32	4.00	15.20	19.20

section 7.3
Exhibit 3

Total, Variable, and Fixed Costs for Pizza Shack

The total fixed cost (*TFC*) curve is, by definition, a horizontal line. The total cost (*TC*) curve is the vertical summation of the total variable cost (*TVC*) and total fixed cost (*TFC*) curves. Notice that *TVC* = 0 when *q* = 0 and that *TFC* = \$40 even when there is no output being produced.

section 7.3
Exhibit 4

Average and Marginal Costs for Pizza Shack

The marginal cost (*MC*) curve always intersects the average total cost (*ATC*) and average variable cost (*AVC*) curves at those curves' minimum points. Average fixed cost (*AFC*) curves always decline and approach but never reach zero. The *ATC* curve is the vertical summation of the *AFC* and *AVC* curves; it reaches its minimum (lowest unit cost) point at a higher output than the minimum point of the *AVC* curve.

exhibit, note how the average fixed cost (*AFC*) curve constantly declines, approaching but never reaching zero. Remember, the *AFC* is simply *TFC/q*, so as output expands, *AFC* declines because the total fixed cost is being spread over successively larger volumes of output. Also observe how the marginal cost (*MC*) curve crosses the average variable cost (*AVC*) and average total cost (*ATC*) curves at their lowest points. At higher output levels, high marginal costs pull up the average variable cost and average total cost curves, whereas at low output levels, low marginal costs pull the curves down. In the next section, we will explain why the marginal cost curve intersects the average variable cost curve and the average total cost curve at their minimum points.

section 7.4

The Shape of the Short-Run Cost Curves

- What is the relationship between marginal costs and marginal product?
- Why is the average total cost curve U-shaped?
- What is the relationship between marginal cost and average variable and average total cost?

WHAT IS THE RELATIONSHIP BETWEEN MARGINAL COSTS AND MARGINAL PRODUCT?

The behaviour of marginal costs bears a definite relationship to marginal product (*MP*). Say, for example, that the variable input is labour. Initially, as the firm adds more workers, the marginal product of labour tends to rise. When the marginal product of labour is rising, marginal costs are falling, because each additional worker adds more to the total product than the previous worker. Thus, the increase in total cost resulting from the production of another unit of output—marginal cost—falls. However, when marginal product of labour is declining, marginal costs are rising, because additional workers are adding less to total output.

In sum, if an additional worker's marginal product is lower (higher) than that of previous workers, marginal costs increase (decrease), as seen in Exhibit 1. In Area (a) of the two graphs in Exhibit 1, we see that as marginal product rises, marginal costs fall; in Area (b), we see that as marginal product falls, marginal costs rise. For example, if we are producing only a few bagels in our bagel shop, we have some idle resources like equipment: toasters, cash registers, and so on. At this point, the marginal product of an extra worker is large and the marginal cost of

section 7.4 Exhibit 1	Marginal Product and Marginal Costs

An inverse relationship exists between marginal product (*MP*) and marginal cost (*MC*). When marginal product is rising, marginal cost must fall, and when marginal product falls, marginal cost must rise.

producing one more bagel is small. However, when the bagel shop is crowded, with many bagels being produced by many workers and the equipment being used to capacity, the marginal product of hiring another worker is low. Why? Because the new worker has to work in crowded conditions where she may be bumping into other workers as she waits to use a toaster or cash register. In short, when the number of bagels produced is high, the marginal product of another worker is low and the marginal cost of an additional bagel is large.

WHY IS THE AVERAGE TOTAL COST CURVE U-SHAPED?

The average total cost curve is usually U-shaped, as seen in Exhibit 2. Why is this? At very small levels of output and very large levels of output, average total cost is very high. The reason for the high average total cost when the firm is producing a very small amount of output is the high average fixed cost—when the output rate of the plant is small relative to its capacity, the plant is being underutilized. But as the firm expands output beyond this point, the average total cost falls. Why? Remember that $ATC = AFC + AVC$, and average fixed cost always falls when output expands because the fixed costs are being spread over more units of output. Thus, it is the declining AFC that is primarily responsible for the falling ATC.

The average total cost rises at high levels of output because of diminishing marginal product. For example, as more and more workers are put to work using a fixed quantity of machines, the result may be crowded working conditions and/or increasing maintenance costs as equipment is used more intensively, or older, less-efficient machinery is called on to handle the greater output. In fact, diminishing marginal product sets in at the very bottom of the marginal cost curve, as seen in Exhibit 2. That is, diminishing marginal product causes the marginal cost to increase, eventually causing the average variable cost and the average total cost curves to rise. At very large levels of output, where the plant approaches full capacity, the fixed plant is overutilized, and this leads to high marginal cost that causes a high average total cost.

WHAT IS THE RELATIONSHIP BETWEEN MARGINAL COST AND AVERAGE VARIABLE AND AVERAGE TOTAL COST?

Certain relationships exist between marginal cost and average variable and average total cost. For example, when average variable cost is falling, marginal cost must be less than average variable cost; and when average variable cost is rising, marginal cost is greater than average variable cost. Marginal cost is equal to average variable cost at the lowest point of the average variable cost curve, as seen in Exhibit 3. In the left-hand

section 7.4
Exhibit 2

U-Shaped Average Total Cost Curve

At low levels of output, ATC is high because AFC is high—the fixed plant is underutilized. At high levels of output (close to capacity), the fixed plant will be overutilized, leading to high MC and, consequently, high ATC. It is diminishing marginal product that causes the MC, and eventually the AVC and ATC, to rise.

section 7.4
Exhibit 3

Marginal Cost and Average Variable Cost

The marginal cost curve crosses the average variable cost curve at its minimum point.

The marginal cost curve crosses the average total cost curve at its minimum point.

(shaded) portion of Exhibit 3, marginal cost is less than average variable cost and average variable cost is falling. On the right-hand side, marginal cost is greater than average variable cost and average variable cost is rising. The same relationship holds for the marginal cost curve and the average total cost curve. In the left-hand (shaded) portion of Exhibit 4, marginal cost is less than average total cost and average total cost is falling. On the right-hand side, marginal cost is greater than average total cost and average total cost is rising.

SECTION CHECK

- An inverse relationship exists between marginal product and marginal cost—as marginal product increases, marginal cost must fall, and when marginal product falls, marginal cost must rise.
- Average total cost declines with expanding output as average fixed costs decline, but then increases as output expands due to increasing marginal cost.
- When marginal cost is less than (greater than) an average cost, the average cost must be falling (rising); when marginal cost is greater than (less than) an average cost, the average cost must be rising (falling).

section
7.5

Cost Curves: Short Run and Long Run

- How is the long-run average total cost curve created?
- What are economies of scale?
- Why would cost curves shift?

Over long enough periods of time, firms can vary all of their productive inputs. For example, time provides an opportunity to replace more expensive labour inputs with lower-cost capital (like larger plants or newer, more sophisticated equipment). However, in the short run, a company cannot vary its plant size and equipment. These inputs are fixed in the short run, so the firm can expand output only by employing more variable inputs (e.g., workers and raw materials) in order to get extra output from the existing factory. For example, if a company has to pay lots of workers overtime wages to get expanded output in the short run, over longer periods, new highly automated machinery may be introduced that conserves on expensive labour. That is, in the long run (perhaps several years), the company can expand the size of its factories, build new ones, or shut down unproductive ones. Of course, the time it takes for a firm to get to the long run varies from firm to firm. For example, it may take only a couple of months to build a new coffee shop, whereas it may take a few years to build a new automobile plant.

HOW IS THE LONG-RUN AVERAGE TOTAL COST CURVE CREATED?

In Exhibit 1, the firm has three possible plant sizes—a small plant, $SRATC_1$, a medium-sized plant, $SRATC_2$, and a large plant, $SRATC_3$. As we move along the *LRATC* (the blue line) in Exhibit 1, the factory size changes with the quantity of output. Certain relationships among the successive curves should be emphasized. For very small output levels, q_1, costs are lowest with plant size $SRATC_1$, point A. Costs with plant size $SRATC_2$ (the medium plant size) are relatively high for these low levels of output because the plant's fixed costs are far too high for low levels of output; machinery, buildings, and so on would be poorly utilized. In Exhibit 1, we can see that if q_1 output is produced with plant size $SRATC_2$, the plant would be operating below capacity, point B, and the cost would be higher at $10 per unit rather than at $8 per unit, at point A. However, if the firm planned to produce output level q_2, costs with plant size $SRATC_2$ are lower than those with $SRATC_1$. If output levels in this range were produced with the smaller plant, $SRATC_1$, the plant would be operating beyond designed capacity, point D, and the cost would be higher at $8 per unit rather than at $5 per unit, at point C. That is, plant $SRATC_2$, designed for a larger volume of output than the small plant, would minimize costs for producing quantity q_2.

If a straight line was extended upward from the horizontal output axis on a graph containing the various *SRATC* curves for different-sized plants, the point

By having several screens in one complex, a cinema company can cut down on advertising and employee costs as well as rent. Because of economies of scale, it may be less expensive to have eight screens in one building with one concession area than eight separate theatres, each with one screen and a concession area.

section 7.5
Exhibit 1

Short- and Long-Run Average Total Costs

In the short run, some inputs are fixed, like the size of the physical plant or certain machinery. In the long run, firms can increase their capital inputs as well as their inputs that are variable in the short run, in some cases lowering average costs per unit. The curve thus has a shallower U-shape than the short-run average total cost curves. In the long run, all inputs are variable. The *LRATC* is the solid blue line that traces out the three different possible plant sizes, $SRATC_1$, $SRATC_2$, and $SRATC_3$. The *LRATC* shows the lowest average total cost for producing each output in the long run.

at which it first struck an *SRATC* curve would indicate the relevant value of *LRATC* for that output level. Thus, in Exhibit 1, for low levels of output, q_1, the lowest average cost point is on curve $SRATC_1$; at output, q_2, it is on $SRATC_2$, and so on. The *LRATC* curve is identical with *SRATC* at the solid scalloped portion of the three short-run cost curves. When there are many possible plant sizes, the successive *SRATC* curves will be close to one another, and the *LRATC* curve will be smooth and U-shaped like the dark solid blue line in Exhibit 1.

The *LRATC* curve is often called a *planning curve,* since it represents the cost data relevant to the firm when it is planning policy relating to scale of operations, output, and price over a long period of time. At a particular time, a firm already in operation has a certain plant and must base its current price and output decisions on the costs with the existing plant. However, when the firm considers the possibility of adjusting its scale of operations, long-run cost estimates are necessary.

section 7.5
Exhibit 2

A Typical Long-Run ATC

All firms are different but most firms will probably have a long-run *ATC* that declines at low levels of output and then remains constant and eventually will rise at the higher levels of output. The minimum efficient scale is the lowest level of output at which average total costs are minimized.

WHAT ARE ECONOMIES OF SCALE?

By examining the long-run average total cost in Exhibit 2, we can see three possible production patterns. When *LRATC* falls as output expands, we say that there are **economies of scale** present. And when the *LRATC* does not vary with output, the firm is facing **constant returns to scale**. And when *LRATC* rises as output expands, we say that the firm is facing **diseconomies of scale**.

The typical firm in an industry may well experience economies of scale at low levels of output, constant returns to scale at higher levels of output, and diseconomies of scale at still higher levels of output, as seen in Exhibit 2. At the **minimum efficient scale**, a plant has exhausted its economies of scale and constant returns to scale begin. This is shown in Exhibit 2. In this constant returns to scale range (the flat portion of the *LRATC*), firms of differing size can compete on a roughly equal basis as far as costs are concerned—that is, larger firms have no cost advantage over firms that are operating at the minimum efficient scale.

The Causes of Economies and Diseconomies of Scale

As we have just seen, economies of scale exist when there is a reduction in the firm's long-run average costs as output expands. This may occur because a firm can use mass production techniques like assembly-line production or capture gains from labour specialization that might not be possible if the firm was producing at lower levels of output. For example, workers might experience greater proficiency gains if they concentrated on a few specific tasks rather than on many different tasks; that is, people who try to do everything may end up doing nothing very well. As well, larger firms may also enjoy cost advantages relative to smaller competitors when borrowing money or when purchasing inputs.

Recall that diseconomies of scale exist when there is an increase in the firm's long-run average costs as output expands. This may occur as the firm finds it increasingly difficult to handle the complexities of large-scale management. For example, information and coordination problems tend to increase when a firm becomes very large. As well, workers may feel alienated in a large plant and hence productivity and creativity may be stifled.

WHY WOULD COST CURVES SHIFT?

Any cost curve is based on the assumption that input prices, taxes, regulation, and technology are constant. When these factors change, the cost curves of the firm will shift. For example, in Exhibit 3(a) we see how a per-unit tax increases the marginal cost of each unit of output, shifting the *MC* curve and the *ATC* up by the tax amount. The tax does not affect the firm's fixed cost because it is a tax on units produced. If a licence-to-operate fee increased, it would act like a fixed cost and affect only the average total cost curve—shifting *ATC* up by the amount of the fee increase. Improved technology will reduce marginal costs, shifting *MC* downward along with *ATC*, as in Exhibit 3(b).

economies of scale
occur in an output range where LRATC falls as output increases

constant returns to scale
occur in an output range where LRATC does not change as output varies

diseconomies of scale
occur in an output range where LRATC rises as output expands

minimum efficient scale
the output level where economies of scale are exhausted and constant returns to scale begin

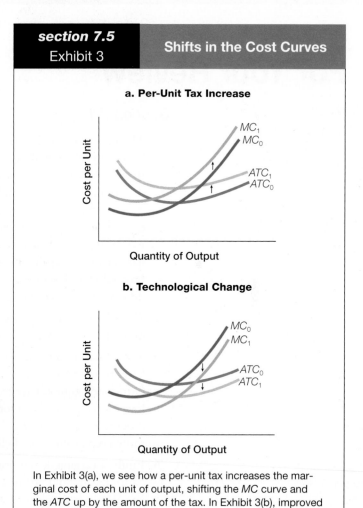

section 7.5
Exhibit 3

Shifts in the Cost Curves

a. Per-Unit Tax Increase

Cost per Unit

MC_1
MC_0
ATC_1
ATC_0

Quantity of Output

b. Technological Change

Cost per Unit

MC_0
MC_1
ATC_0
ATC_1

Quantity of Output

In Exhibit 3(a), we see how a per-unit tax increases the marginal cost of each unit of output, shifting the *MC* curve and the *ATC* up by the amount of the tax. In Exhibit 3(b), improved technology will reduce marginal costs, shifting *MC* downward along with *ATC*.

SECTION CHECK

- In the long run, firms can vary inputs that are fixed in the short run, such as plant size and equipment, and in some cases, lowering average costs per unit. The long-run average total cost curve shows the lowest average total cost for producing each output in the long run.
- At low output levels, when all inputs can be varied, some firms will experience economies of scale, where their per-unit costs are decreasing as output increases. In intermediate output ranges, firms may exhibit roughly constant returns to scale; in this range, their per-unit costs remain stable as output increases. Firms that expand all inputs beyond a certain point will encounter diseconomies of scale, incurring rising per-unit costs as output grows in the long run.
- Input prices, taxes, technology, and regulation can shift the cost curves.

For Your Review

Section 7.1

1. The year 2015 marked the tenth anniversary of Ontario's Greenbelt. As the world's largest greenbelt at almost 810 000 hectares of working countryside, it spans across the Greater Golden Horseshoe and extends to the tip of the Bruce Peninsula. As the amount of land around Toronto and its adjacent suburbs continues to fall well short of that needed to satisfy both the needs of local agricultural interests and of city dwellers looking for a more affordable place to live, the policy of keeping this productive farmland and environmentally sensitive land officially off-limits to developers has become a growing issue. What happens to the cost of farming and environmental protection as developers continue to offer more and more money for the right to develop this key land resource?

2. What happens to the cost of growing strawberries on your own land if a housing developer offers you three times what you thought your land was worth?

3. The salmon fishery on Vancouver Island has historically been one of the world's richest. Over the past few years, poor returns of salmon to the island and competition from farm-raised salmon have reduced the economic returns to the anglers. One response to lower revenues has been for anglers to use family members instead of hiring crew "in order to reduce their costs." Evaluate this business strategy. Will employing relatives really keep profits from falling? Under what conditions is this a good strategy?

4. Emily, an energetic ten-year-old, set up a lemonade stand in front of her house. One Saturday, she sold 50 cups of lemonade at 50 cents each to her friends, who were hot and thirsty from playing. These sales generated $25 in total revenues for Emily. Emily was pleased because she knew that her total costs—lemonade mix, cups, and so on— were only $5. As she was closing up shop for the day, her neighbour, an accountant, stopped by to say hello. Emily told him about her successful day. He said, "What a great job! You made a $20 profit!" Excited, Emily rushed into the house to tell her mother, an economist, the great news. Will Emily's mother agree with the accountant's calculation of Emily's profits? If not, why?

Section 7.2

5. Willie's Water Park Short-Run Production Function

Labour (workers)	Total Product (visits per hour)	Marginal Product
0		—
1		10
2		12
3		9
4		8
5		4
6		−2

a. Fill in the Total Product column.

b. Willie's Water Park experiences diminishing marginal product beginning with which worker?

c. Willie's Water Park experiences diminishing total product beginning with which worker?

6. Harry's Hat Company makes hats "for discerning gentlemen."

With Three Machines			With Four Machines		
Labour	Total Product (hats)	Marginal Product (hats)	Labour	Total Product (hats)	Marginal Product (hats)
1 day	8		1 day	9	
2 days	18		2 days	20	
3 days	30		3 days	35	
4 days	45		4 days	55	
5 days	57		5 days	76	
6 days	67		6 days	88	
7 days	72		7 days	95	

a. Fill in the Marginal Product columns of these tables.

b. At what point does diminishing marginal product set in with three machines? With four?

c. Why is the point of diminishing marginal product different in each case?

7. Fill in the rest of the production function for Candy's Candies from the information provided.

Labour (workers)	Total Product (kilograms)	Marginal Product (kilograms)
0		
1	20	
2	44	
3	62	
4		12
5		6
6	78	

a. Candy's Candies begins to experience diminishing marginal product with which worker?

b. Does Candy's Candies ever experience negative marginal product? If so, with the addition of which worker?

8. What is diminishing marginal product? What causes it?

9. Suppose your firm's total product curve includes the following data: One worker can produce 8 units of output; two workers, 20 units; three workers, 34 units; four workers, 50 units; five workers, 60 units; six workers, 70 units; seven workers, 76 units; eight workers, 78 units; and nine workers, 77 units.

a. What is the marginal product of the seventh worker?

b. When does the law of diminishing product set in?

c. Under these conditions, would you ever choose to employ nine workers?

10. Why does the law of diminishing marginal product imply the law of increasing costs?

Section 7.3

Blueprint Problem

Fran's Flowers has fixed costs of $8. Complete the following cost of production table for Fran's Flowers.

Output	TVC	TFC	TC	AVC	AFC	ATC	MC
0	$0.00			—	—	—	—
1	$6.00						
2	$9.00						
3	$10.00						
4	$15.00						
5	$22.00						
6	$31.00						
7	$42.00						
8	$55.00						
9	$70.00						
10	$87.00						

Blueprint Solution

[1]Fixed costs do not change as output changes, therefore fixed costs remain constant at $8.

[2]Having determined *TFC*, we can calculate total cost [$TC = TVC + TFC$].

Output	TVC	TFC	TC	AVC	AFC	ATC	MC
0	$0.00	$8.00[1]	$8.00[2]	—	—	—	—
1	$6.00	$8.00	$14.00	$6.00	$8.00	$14.00	$6.00
2	$9.00	$8.00	$17.00	$4.50	$4.00	$8.50	$3.00
3	$10.00	$8.00	$18.00	$3.33	$2.67	$6.00	$1.00
4	$15.00	$8.00	$23.00	$3.75	$2.00	$5.75	$5.00
5	$22.00	$8.00	$30.00	$4.40	$1.60	$6.00	$7.00
6	$31.00	$8.00	$39.00	$5.17	$1.33	$6.50	$9.00
7	$42.00	$8.00	$50.00	$6.00	$1.14	$7.14	$11.00
8	$55.00	$8.00	$63.00	$6.88	$1.00	$7.88	$13.00
9	$70.00	$8.00	$78.00	$7.78	$0.89	$8.67	$15.00
10	$87.00	$8.00	$95.00	$8.70	$0.80	$9.50	$17.00

$$MC = \frac{\Delta TC}{\Delta q}$$

For example, as output increases from 0 to 1 (a change of 1), *TC* increases from $8 to $14 (a change of $6).

$$MC = \frac{\$6}{1} = \$6$$

AVC and *AFC* values are determined by dividing the corresponding total cost value by quantity produced.

Note: The initial values are indeterminate because you cannot divide by zero.

ATC values can be determined two ways:
1. *TC/q*
2. *AVC + AFC*

11. Complete the following table describing the short-run daily costs of the Attractive Magnet Co. for 2018.

Output	Total Fixed Costs	Total Variable Costs	Total Costs	Average Fixed Costs	Average Variable Costs	Average Total Costs	Marginal Costs
1	$100	$30	$130	$100	$30	$130	$30
2					25		
3					20		
4					16		
5					18		
6					21		
7					24		
8		218	318				

12. A one-day ticket to visit the Screaming Coasters theme park costs $36, but you can also get a two-consecutive-day ticket for $40. What is the average cost per day for the two-day ticket? What is the marginal cost of the second consecutive day?

13. As a movie exhibitor, you can choose between paying a flat fee of $5000 to show a movie for a week and paying a fee of $2 per customer. Will your choice affect your fixed and variable costs? How?

14. What is likely to happen to your marginal costs when adding output requires working beyond an eight-hour day, if workers must be paid time-and-a-half wages beyond an eight-hour day?

15. Suppose an oil producer's average total cost of producing a barrel of oil has been $20 a barrel and the oil producer can sell that oil to a distributor for $23 a barrel. On average, this seems like a profitable business. Should the oil producer expand production given this profitability?

16. Fill in the rest of the cost function for Bob's Bowling Balls.

Output	Total Fixed Costs	Total Variable Costs	Total Costs	Average Fixed Costs	Average Variable Costs	Average Total Costs	Marginal Costs
1	$200	$60	$	$	$	$	$
2		100					
3		120					
4		128					
5		180					
6		252					
7		366					
8		536					

17. If your college or university pays lecture note-takers $20 per hour to take notes in your economics class and then sells subscriptions for $15 per student, is the cost of the lecture note-taker a fixed or variable cost of selling an additional subscription?

18. The Lighthouse Safety Vest Co. makes flotation vests for recreational boaters. The company currently employs 50 people and produces 12 000 vests per month. Lighthouse managers know that when they hire one more person, monthly vest production will increase by 200 vests. They pay workers $1600 per month.

    a. What is the marginal product of the 51st worker?

    b. What is the marginal cost to produce one more vest? (*Hint:* Think of the marginal cost as the additional worker's pay divided by the changes in output.)

    c. If labour is the only variable factor of production, will the average variable cost of production rise or fall as a result of hiring a 51st worker? Why?

    d. What happens to the marginal cost of a vest when the 52nd worker is added and the marginal product drops to 160 vests per month?

Section 7.4

19. Use the graph below to answer the following questions.

     a. Curve A represents which cost curve?

     b. Curve B represents which cost curve?

     c. Curve C represents which cost curve?

     d. Curve D represents which cost curve?

     e. Why must curve D pass through the minimum points of both curve B and curve C?

     f. What significance does the point have where curve A intersects curve D?

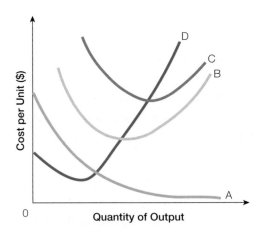

20. Illustrate how the shape of the marginal product curve relates to the shape of the marginal cost curve.

21. Use the following graph to answer the questions below.

     a. At what level is *AVC* at its minimum? Why is it at its minimum at this point?

     b. At what level is *ATC* at its minimum? Why is it at its minimum at this point?

     c. At what level is *MC* at its minimum? Why is it at its minimum at this point?

Section 7.5

22. You have the following information about long-run total cost for the following firms:

Quantity	Arnold's Apples LRTC	Belle's Bananas LRTC	Cam's Cantaloupes LRTC
1	120	33	42
2	140	72	68
3	160	117	98
4	180	168	132
5	200	225	170
6	220	288	212
7	240	357	258

a. Do any of these firms experience constant returns to scale? How do you know?

b. Do any of these firms experience diseconomies of scale? How do you know?

c. Do any of these firms experience economies of scale? How do you know?

23. Refer to the cost curve below.

a. What is the lowest level of output at which the efficient scale of production is reached in the long run?

b. In the short run described by *SRATC*, what is the efficient output level?

c. When the firm is producing at the level of output described by D, will it be experiencing constant returns to scale, economies of scale, or diseconomies of scale?

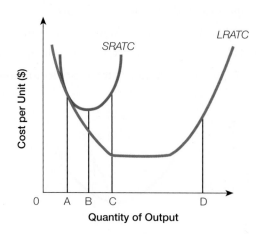

24. Suppose the following table details the cost structure for an Internet modem manufacturer.

Output	TVC_0	TVC_1	AVC_0	AVC_1	MC_0	MC_1
0	0		—		—	
1	10		10		10	
2	18		9		8	
3	21		7		3	
4	26		6.5		5	
5	35		7		9	
6	51		8.5		16	
7	77		11		26	

If the cost of the inputs needed to produce Internet modems increases by 50 percent, calculate TVC_1, AVC_1, and MC_1. Graph the results for AVC_1 and MC_1 against the original AVC and MC curves (AVC_0 and MC_0).

25. Determine the effect (increase, decrease, or unchanged) of the following changes of MC, AVC, and ATC.

Change	AVC	MC	ATC
a. The government imposes a tax that is applied to every unit produced.			
b. The price of rent increases.			
c. New technology that improves productivity is introduced.			
d. The cost of labour increases.			
e. The cost of materials used in manufacturing decreases.			
f. Property taxes increase.			

26. Buffalo Bill has a potato chip company, Buffalo's Chips. He is currently losing money on every bag of chips he sells. Mrs. Bill, who has just completed an economics class, tells Buffalo Bill he could make a profit if he added more machines and produced more chips. How could this be possible? What is Mrs. Bill assuming about the output range in which Buffalo Bill is currently producing?

section

8.1 The Four Major Market Structures

- What are the four major market structures?
- What are the characteristics of a perfectly competitive market?
- Why is it useful to study the perfectly competitive market structure?

WHAT ARE THE FOUR MAJOR MARKET STRUCTURES?

Economists have identified four major market structures in which firms operate: perfect competition, monopoly, monopolistic competition, and oligopoly. Each structure or environment has certain key characteristics that distinguish it from the other structures. In practice, it is sometimes difficult to decide precisely which structure a given firm or industry most appropriately fits, since the dividing line between the structures is not entirely crystal clear.

Perfect Competition

A competitive market is a market situation in which there is a large number of buyers and sellers—perhaps thousands or very conceivably millions. In addition, no single firm produces more than an extremely small proportion of total output. This means that no single firm can influence the market price or quantity. Firms are price takers; they must accept the price for the product as determined by the forces of demand and supply. Individually, they are too small and powerless to alter prices.

Firms in perfect competition sell a homogeneous or standardized product. In the wheat market, which approximates the conditions of perfect competition, it is not possible to determine any significant and consistent qualitative differences in the wheat produced by different farmers. New firms can easily enter the market.

Monopoly

On the other end of the continuum of market environments is pure monopoly. In this market structure, there is one firm (a single seller) that produces a good or service that has no close substitutes, and there are significant barriers to potential entrants into the market. Examples of monopoly include government-owned or government-regulated public utilities (electric, water, and natural gas suppliers) and Facebook as a social networking tool.

Monopolistic Competition

Monopolistic competition falls between perfect competition and monopoly. Monopolistic competition is a market structure where firms have both an element of competition and an element of monopoly power. Because each firm's product is differentiated at least slightly from that of other competitors, it has some monopoly power. For example, in a given city of 100 000 there may be 100 restaurants, each slightly different in the type of food that it sells, the services that it provides, and the hours that it stays open. However, because there are so many competing restaurants vying for your business it also has an element of competitive markets. The same is true for service stations and retail businesses such as furniture stores.

Oligopoly

Like monopolistic competition, oligopoly also falls between perfect competition and monopoly. Oligopoly exists when a *few* firms produce similar or identical goods, as opposed to one firm (monopoly) or many firms (competitive market). Unlike pure monopoly, oligopoly allows for some competition between firms; unlike competition, firms in oligopolistic environments have a significant share of the total market for the good being produced.

The oligopolist is very conscious of the actions of competing firms. In this respect, the oligopoly structure differs from other structures. In perfect competition, Farmer Jones does not worry about what Farmer Smith does, since neither of them is big enough to have any influence on overall market conditions. In monopoly, there is no other firm to worry about. In true monopolistic competition, there are many relatively small firms, so again a firm usually does not worry much about its impact on the behaviour of a competing firm. In oligopoly, though, a firm's behaviour is closely related to that of its competitors. General Motors' pricing decisions influence the pricing decisions of Ford, Chrysler, and other manufacturers, including ones located in other countries. The oligopolist does have some control over price and thus is a price setter. Note that the oligopoly may involve a standardized product (like steel, aluminum, or crude oil) or a differentiated one (such as automobiles, refrigerators, or personal computers).

Exhibit 1 provides an overview of the various market structures; for added insight, the structures have been placed in order on a continuum (or ruler). While no significance should be attributed to the left versus the right side of the continuum, the positioning of pure monopoly at one end of the continuum and perfect competition at the other is significant. By locating perfect competition and pure monopoly at opposite ends of the continuum, it can be understood that the opposite characteristics that define pure

Can the owner of this orchard charge a noticeably higher price for the same quality of apples? What if she charges a lower price for the same-quality apples? How many apples can she sell at the market price?

© BRUCE HEINEMANN/PHOTODISC/GETTY IMAGES

section 8.1 Exhibit 1	**Characteristics of the Four Major Market Structures**			
Characteristic	*Perfect Competition*	*Monopolistic Competition*	*Oligopoly*	*Pure Monopoly*
Number of firms	Very many	Many	A few	One
Type of product	Homogeneous	Differentiated	Homogeneous or differentiated	Homogeneous
Barriers to entry or exit from industry	No substantial barriers	Minor barriers	Considerable barriers	Extremely great barriers
Examples	Agriculture	Retail trade	Banking	Public utilities

SOURCE: From Sexton, *Exploring Economics*, 6E. ©2013 South-Western, a part of Cengage, Inc. Reproduced by permission, www.cengage.com/permissions.

monopoly define perfect competition. For example, looking at the *Number of Firms* characteristic, the perfectly competitive market consists of very many producers—the largest number of producers of any market structure, while the purely monopolized market consists of one producer—the fewest number of producers of any market structure. This relationship of opposites remains intact for all but one of the characteristics.

Another key feature of Exhibit 1 is the positioning of the oligopoly and monopolistic competition market structures. The oligopoly market structure is located closer to pure monopoly than it is to perfect competition. This tells us that, while the oligopoly market structure is a mixture of monopolistic and competitive principles, it is predominantly monopolistic. Alternatively, the positioning of the monopolistic competition market structure closer to the perfect competition end of the continuum indicates that this structure is predominantly competitive. For example, looking at the *Barriers to entry or exit from industry* characteristic, the monopolistic competition structure exhibits only minor barriers (an increase from the perfectly competitive structure that experiences no substantial barriers to entry or exit), while the oligopolistic market structure experiences considerable barriers (a further increase in this characteristic toward the pure monopoly experience of extremely great barriers to entry or exit).

WHAT ARE THE CHARACTERISTICS OF A PERFECTLY COMPETITIVE MARKET?

This chapter examines perfect competition, a market structure characterized by (1) many buyers and sellers, (2) an identical (homogeneous) product, and (3) easy market entry and exit. Let's examine these characteristics in greater detail.

Many Buyers and Sellers

In **perfect competition**, there are many buyers and sellers, all selling a homogeneous product; market entry and exit are easy, and no one firm can affect the market price. Because each firm is so small in relation to the industry, its production decisions have no impact on the market—each regards price as something over which it has little control. A perfectly competitive firm is called a **price taker** because it takes the price that

perfect competition
a market with many buyers and sellers, all selling a homogeneous product; market entry and exit is easy, and no firm can affect the market price

price taker
A perfectly competitive firm takes the price that it is given by the intersection of the market demand and market supply curves.

it is given by the intersection of the market demand and market supply curves. That is, it must take the price given by the market because its influence on price is insignificant. If the price of apples in the apple market is $2 a kilogram, then individual apple farmers will receive $2 per kilogram for their apples. Similarly, no single buyer of apples can influence the price of apples because each buyer purchases only a small amount of the apples traded. We will see how this works in more detail in Section 8.2.

Identical (Homogeneous) Products

Consumers believe that all firms in perfectly competitive markets *sell identical (or homogeneous) products*. For example, in the wheat market, it is not possible to determine any significant and consistent qualitative differences in the wheat produced by different farmers. Another way of describing what firms in a perfectly competitive market sell is to realize their output as perfect substitutes for each other. That is, the wheat produced by Farmer Jones looks, feels, smells, and tastes like that produced by Farmer Smith. In short, a tonne of wheat is a tonne of wheat.

Easy Entry and Exit

Product markets characterized by perfect competition have no significant *barriers to entry or exit*. This means that it is fairly easy for entrepreneurs to become suppliers of the product or, if they are already producers, to stop supplying the product. "Fairly easy" does not mean that any person on the street can instantly enter the business, but rather that the financial, legal, educational, and other barriers to entering the business are modest, so that large numbers of people can overcome the barriers and enter the business in any given time period if they so desire. If buyers can easily switch from one seller to another and sellers can easily enter or exit the industry, then we have met the perfectly competitive condition of easy entry and exit. Because of this easy market entry, perfectly competitive markets generally consist of a large number of small suppliers.

WHY IS IT USEFUL TO STUDY THE PERFECTLY COMPETITIVE MARKET STRUCTURE?

A perfectly competitive market is approximated most closely in highly organized markets for securities such as the Toronto Stock Exchange and the markets for agricultural products such as wheat and corn. For example, there are literally hundreds of thousands of farms across Canada growing a variety of agricultural products. In 2017 alone, Canadian farmers produced close to 30 million tonnes of wheat, 21.3 million tonnes of canola, 14.1 million tonnes of corn for grain, and 7.7 million tonnes of soybeans. However, whether the corn was grown in Ontario or Quebec, domestic and international consumers considered the output for each individual farm to be virtually identical. The Toronto Stock Exchange (TSX), along with the TSX Venture Exchange (TSXV), lists nearly 4000 companies. Other than the fees associated with "going public," there are few restrictions preventing any company from listing themselves on the TSX/TSXV and therefore entering this market.

You can legitimately ask the question: If perfectly competitive and monopolistic firms are rare and monopolistically competitive and oligopoly firms are common, why do we start our study of market structures with the former first? What we will learn from the perfectly competitive model about costs, entry, exit, and efficiency are important concepts for imperfectly competitive firms. Although all of the criteria for a perfect competitive market are rarely met, a number of markets come close to satisfying them. Even when all the assumptions don't hold, it is important to note that studying the model of perfect competition is useful because there are many markets that resemble perfect competition—that is, markets in which firms face very elastic (flat) demand curves and relatively easy entry and exit. The model also gives us a standard of comparison. In other words, we can make comparisons with the perfectly competitive model to help us evaluate what is going on in the real world.

SECTION CHECK

- There are four major market structures: perfect competition, monopoly, monopolistic competition, and oligopoly.
- A perfectly competitive market has the following characteristics: many buyers and sellers, so that neither buyers nor sellers have control over price; a homogeneous product—consumers believe that all firms sell virtually identical products; no significant barriers to entry or exit.
- Studying the perfectly competitive market structure provides us with important information about how markets operate (entry, exit, costs, and efficiency) that can be applied to imperfect market structures. In addition, the perfectly competitive structure can give us a point of comparison to evaluate real-world markets.

section 8.2 An Individual Price Taker's Demand Curve

- What does the individual price taker's demand curve look like?
- What effect will a change in market price have on an individual price taker's demand curves?

WHAT DOES THE INDIVIDUAL PRICE TAKER'S DEMAND CURVE LOOK LIKE?

Perfectly competitive firms are price takers; that is, they must sell at the market-determined price, where the market price and output are determined by the intersection of the market supply and demand curves, as seen in Exhibit 1(a). Individual wheat farmers know that they cannot dispose of their wheat at any figure higher than the current market price; if they attempt to charge a higher price, potential buyers would simply make their purchases from other wheat farmers. And the farmers certainly would not knowingly charge a lower price because they could sell all they want at the market price.

Likewise, in a perfectly competitive market, individual sellers can change their output and it will not alter the market price. This is possible because of the large number of sellers who are selling identical products. Each producer provides such a small fraction of the total supply that a change in the amount it offers does *not* have a noticeable effect on market equilibrium price. In a perfectly competitive market, then, an individual firm can sell as much as it wants on the market at the prevailing price; the demand, as seen by the seller, is perfectly elastic.

section 8.2
Exhibit 1

Market and Individual Firm Demand Curves in Perfect Competition

a. Market Supply and Demand Curves

b. Individual Firm Demand Curve

At the market price for wheat, $5, the individual farmer can sell all the wheat he wishes. Because each producer provides only a small fraction of industry output, any additional output will have an insignificant impact on market price. The firm's demand curve is perfectly elastic at the market price.

It is easy to construct the demand curve for an individual seller in a perfectly competitive market. Remember, she won't charge more than the market price because no one will buy the good, and she won't charge less because she can sell all she wants at the market price. Thus, the farmer's demand curve is horizontal over the entire range of output that she could possibly produce. If the prevailing market price of the product is $5, the farmer's demand curve will be represented graphically by a horizontal line at the market price of $5, as shown in Exhibit 1(b).

WHAT EFFECT WILL A CHANGE IN MARKET PRICE HAVE ON AN INDIVIDUAL PRICE TAKER'S DEMAND CURVES?

To say that producers under perfect competition regard price as a given is not to say that price is constant. The *position* of the firm's demand curve varies with every change in the market price. In Exhibit 2, we see that when the market price for wheat increases, perhaps as a result of an increase in market demand, the price-taking firm will receive a higher price for all of its output. Or when the market price decreases, say as a result of a decrease in market demand, the price-taking firm will receive a lower price for all of its output.

In effect, sellers are provided with current information about market demand and supply conditions as a result of price changes. It is an essential aspect of the perfectly competitive model that sellers respond to the signals provided by such price movements, so they must alter their behaviour over time in the light of actual experience, revising their production decisions to reflect changes in market price. In this respect, the perfectly competitive model is very straightforward; it does not assume any knowledge on the part of individual sellers about market demand and supply—they only have to know the price of the good they sell.

section 8.2
Exhibit 2

Market Prices and the Position of a Firm's Demand Curve

The position of the firm's demand curve will vary with every change in the market price.

SECTION CHECK

- Individual sellers won't sell at a higher price than the going market price because buyers can purchase the same good from someone else at the going market price, nor will they sell for less than the going market price because they are so small relative to the market that they can sell all they want at the going market price. Therefore, the individual price taker's demand curve is horizontal over the entire range of output.
- The position of the individual firm's demand curve varies directly with the market price.

section 8.3

Profit Maximization

- What is total revenue?
- What are average revenue and marginal revenue?
- How do firms maximize profits?

The objective of the firm is to maximize profits. To maximize profits the firm wants to produce the amount that maximizes the difference between its total revenues and total costs. In this section, we will examine the different ways to look at revenue in a perfectly competitive market: total revenue, average revenue, and marginal revenue.

WHAT IS TOTAL REVENUE?

total revenue (*TR*)
the product price times the quantity sold

Total revenue (*TR*) equals the product price (P) times the quantity (q) sold ($TR = P \times q$); it is the revenue that the firm receives from the sale of its product. For example, if a farmer sells 10 tonnes of wheat a day for $5 a tonne, his total revenue is $50 ($5 \times 10$ tonnes). (Note: We will use the small letter q to denote the single firm's output and reserve the large Q for the output of the entire market. For example, q would be used to represent the output of one potato grower, whereas Q would be used to represent the output of all potato growers in the potato market.)

section 8.3 Exhibit 1	Revenues for a Perfectly Competitive Firm			
Quantity (q)	Price (P)	Total Revenue (TR = P × q)	Average Revenue (AR = TR/q)	Marginal Revenue (MR = ΔTR/Δq)
1	$5	$ 5	$5	$5
2	5	10	5	5
3	5	15	5	5
4	5	20	5	5
5	5	25	5	

WHAT ARE AVERAGE REVENUE AND MARGINAL REVENUE?

Average revenue (*AR*) equals total revenue divided by the number of units sold (*TR*/*q*, or [*P* × *q*]/*q*). For example, if the farmer sells 10 tonnes at $5 a tonne, total revenue is $50 and average revenue is $5 ($50/10 tonnes = $5 per tonne). So, in perfect competition, average revenue is equal to the price of the good.

    Marginal revenue (*MR*) represents the increase in total revenue that results from the sale of one more unit. In a perfectly competitive market, because additional units of output can be sold without reducing the price of the product, marginal revenue is constant at all outputs and equal to average revenue. For example, if the price of wheat per tonne is $5, the marginal revenue is $5. Because total revenue is equal to price multiplied by quantity (*TR* = *P* × *q*), as we add one additional unit of output, total revenue will always increase by the amount of the product price, $5. Marginal revenue facing a perfectly competitive firm is equal to the price of the good.

    The relationship between marginal revenue, price, and average revenue is clearly illustrated in the calculations presented in Exhibit 1. In perfect competition, then, we can draw the following conclusion:

$$P = MR = AR.$$

average revenue (AR)
total revenue divided by the number of units sold

marginal revenue (MR)
the increase in total revenue that results from the sale of one more unit

HOW DO FIRMS MAXIMIZE PROFITS?

Now that we have discussed both the firm's cost curves (Chapter 7) and the firm's revenues, we are ready to see how a firm maximizes its profits. A firm's profits equal its total revenues minus its total costs. But at what output level will a firm produce and sell in order to maximize profits? There are two methods for identifying this output: the marginal approach and the total cost–total revenue approach. In all types of market environments, firms will maximize profits at the output that maximizes the difference between total revenue and total costs, which is at the same output level where marginal revenue equals marginal costs.

Equating Marginal Revenue and Marginal Cost

The importance of equating marginal revenue and marginal costs is seen in Exhibit 2. As output expands beyond zero up to q^*, the marginal revenue derived from each unit of the expanded output exceeds the marginal cost of that unit of output, so the

section 8.3
Exhibit 2

Finding the Profit-Maximizing Level of Output

At any output below q^*, like at $q_{\text{TOO LITTLE}}$, the marginal revenue (MR) from expanding output exceeds the added costs (MC) of that output, so additional profits can be made by expanding output. Beyond q^*, like at $q_{\text{TOO MUCH}}$, marginal costs exceed marginal revenue, so output expansion is unprofitable and output should be reduced. The profit-maximizing level of output is at q^*, where the profit-maximizing output rule is followed—the firm should produce the level of output where $MR = MC$.

expansion of output creates additional profits. This addition to profit is shown as the left-most shaded section in Exhibit 2. As long as marginal revenues exceed marginal costs, profits continue to grow. For example, if the firm decides to produce $q_{\text{TOO LITTLE}}$, the firm sacrifices potential profits because the marginal revenue from producing more output is greater than the marginal cost. Only at q^*, where $MR = MC$, is the output level just right—not too large, not too small. Further expansion of output beyond q^* will lead to losses on the additional output (decrease the firm's overall profits) because $MC > MR$. For example, if the firm produces $q_{\text{TOO MUCH}}$, the firm incurs losses on that output produced beyond q^*; the firm should reduce its output. Only at output q^*, where $MR = MC$, can we find the profit-maximizing level of output. The **profit-maximizing output rule** says a firm should always produce at the level of output where its $MR = MC$.

Profit-Maximizing Output Rule

$$MR = MC$$

profit-maximizing output rule

A firm should always produce at the level of output where MR = MC.

The Marginal Approach

We can use the data in Exhibit 3 to find Farmer John's profit-maximizing position. In the table in Exhibit 3, columns 5 and 6 show the marginal revenue and marginal cost, respectively. We see that output levels of one and two tonnes produce outputs that have marginal revenues that exceed marginal cost—John certainly wants to produce those units and more. That is, as long as marginal revenue exceeds marginal costs, producing and selling those units adds more to revenues than to costs; in other words, they add to profits. However, once he expands production beyond four units of output, John's marginal revenues are less than his marginal costs and his profits begin to fall. Clearly, Farmer John should not produce beyond four tonnes of wheat.

The Total Cost–Total Revenue Approach

Let us take another look at profit maximization using the table in Exhibit 3. Comparing columns 2 and 3, the calculations of total revenues and total costs, respectively, we see that Farmer John maximizes his profits at output levels of three or four tonnes, where he will make profits of $4. In column 4, "Profit," you can see that there is no higher level of profit at any of the other output levels.

In the next section we will use the profit-maximizing output rule to see what happens when changes in the market cause the price to fall below average total cost and even below average variable costs. We will introduce the four-step method to determine whether the firm is making an economic profit, minimizing its losses, or should temporarily shut down.

section 8.3 Exhibit 3	Cost and Revenue Calculations for a Perfectly Competitive Firm

Quantity (1)	Total Revenue (2)	Total Cost (3)	Profit (TR – TC) (4)	Marginal Revenue (ΔTR/Δq) (5)	Marginal Cost (ΔTC/Δq) (6)
0	$ 0	$ 2	–$2		
1	5	4	1	$5	$2
2	10	7	3	5	3
3	15	11	4	5	4
4	20	16	4	5	5
5	25	22	3	5	6

SECTION CHECK

- Total revenue is price times the quantity sold ($TR = P \times q$).
- Average revenue is total revenue divided by the quantity sold ($AR = TR/q$). Marginal revenue is the change in total revenue from the sale of an additional unit of output ($MR = \Delta TR/\Delta q$). In a competitive industry, $P = AR = MR$.
- The profit-maximizing output rule says a firm should always produce where $MR = MC$. When $MR > MC$, the seller should expand production because producing and selling those units adds more to revenues than to costs, or increases profits. However, if $MR < MC$, the seller should decrease production.

Short-Run Profits and Losses

section

8.4

- How do we determine whether a firm is generating an economic profit or loss?
- What is the individual firm's short-run supply curve?
- Can we review the short-run production decisions of an individual competitive firm?

In the previous section, we discussed two methods of determining the profit-maximizing output level for a perfectly competitive firm. However, producing at this profit-maximizing level does not mean that a firm is actually generating profits; it merely means that a firm is maximizing its profit opportunity at a given price level.

HOW DO WE DETERMINE WHETHER A FIRM IS GENERATING AN ECONOMIC PROFIT OR LOSS?

Determining whether a firm is generating economic profits, economic losses, or zero economic profits at the profit-maximizing level of output, q^*, can be done in four easy steps. First, we will walk through these steps and then, in Exhibit 1, we will apply the method to three different situations for a hypothetical firm in the short run.

The Four-Step Method for Perfect Competition

1. The first step is to find the profit-maximizing level of output (q^*). To do this, find where marginal revenues equal marginal costs and proceed straight down to the horizontal quantity axis to find the profit-maximizing output level.

2. The second step is to determine the total revenue (TR) being generated at q^*. To do this, go straight up from q^* to the demand curve and then to the left to find the market price, P^*. Once you have identified P^* and q^*, you can find total revenue at the profit-maximizing output level, because $TR = P \times q$.

3. The third step is to find total costs (TC) at q^*. Again, go straight up from q^* to the average total cost (ATC) curve and then left to the vertical axis to compute the average total cost *per unit*. If we multiply average total costs by the output level, we can find the total costs ($TC = ATC \times q$).

4. The final step is to determine the amount of either profit or loss at q^*. If total revenue (from step 2) is greater than total costs (from step 3) at q^*, the firm is generating economic profits. If total revenue is less than total costs at q^*, the firm is generating economic losses. If total revenue is equal to total cost at q^*, there are zero economic profits (or a normal rate of return). Alternatively, to find total economic profits, we can take the product price at P^* and subtract the average total cost at q^*. This will give us per-unit profit. If we multiply this by output, we will arrive at total economic profit: $(P^* - ATC) \times q^* = $ Total economic profit.

Remember, the cost curves include implicit and explicit costs—that is, we are covering the opportunity costs of our resources. So even if there are zero economic profits, no tears should be shed, because the firm is covering both its implicit and explicit costs. Because firms are also covering their implicit costs, or what they could be producing with these resources in another endeavour, economists sometimes call this zero economic profit *a normal rate of return*. That is, the owners are doing as well as they could elsewhere, in that they are getting the normal rate of return on the resources they invested in the firm.

The Four-Step Method in Action

In Exhibit 1, there are three different short-run equilibrium positions; in each case, the firm is producing at a level where marginal revenue equals marginal costs. Each of these alternatives shows that the firm is maximizing profits or minimizing losses in the short run.

section 8.4
Exhibit 1

Short-Run Profits, Losses, and Zero Economic Profits

a. Economic Profit

b. Economic Loss

c. Zero Economic Profits

In Exhibit 1(a), the firm is earning short-run economic profits of $120; in Exhibit 1(b), the firm is suffering losses of $80; and in Exhibit 1(c), the firm is making zero economic profits, with the price just equal to the average total cost in the short run.

Assume that three alternative prices—$6, $4, and $4.90—are available for a firm with given costs. In Exhibit 1(a), the firm receives $6 per unit at an equilibrium level of output ($MR = MC$) of 120 units. Total revenue ($P \times q^*$) is $6 × 120, or $720. The average total cost at 120 units of output is $5, and the total cost ($ATC \times q^*$) is $600. Following the four-step method, we can calculate that this firm is earning total economic profits of $120. Or we can calculate total economic profit by using the following equation: $(P^* - ATC) \times q^* = (\$6 - \$5) \times 120 = \$120$.

In Exhibit 1(b), the market price is $4 per unit. At the equilibrium level of output, the firm is now producing 80 units of output at an average total cost of $5 per unit. The total revenue is now $320 ($4 × 80), and the total costs are $400 ($5 × 80). We can see that the firm is now incurring total economic losses of $80. Or we can calculate total economic profit by using the following equation: $(P^* - ATC) \times q^* = (\$4 - \$5) \times 80 = -\$80$.

In Exhibit 1(c), the firm is earning zero economic profits, or a normal rate of return. The market price is $4.90, and the average total cost is $4.90 per unit for 100 units of output. In this case, economic profits are zero because total revenue, $490, minus total cost, $490, is equal to zero. This firm is just covering all its costs, both implicit and explicit. Or we can calculate total economic profit by using the following equation: $(P^* - ATC) \times q^* = (\$4.90 - \$4.90) \times 100 = \$0$.

Evaluating Economic Losses in the Short Run

A firm generating an economic loss faces a tough choice: Should it continue to produce or shut down its operation in the short run? To make this decision, we need to add another variable to our discussion of economic profits and losses: average variable costs. Variable costs are those costs that vary with output, such as wages, raw materials, transportation, and electricity. If a firm cannot generate enough revenues to cover its variable costs, then it will have larger losses if it operates than if it shuts down (losses in that case = fixed costs). Thus, a firm will not produce at all unless the price is greater than its average variable costs.

Operating at a Loss   At price levels greater than or equal to average variable costs, a firm may continue to operate in the short run even if average total costs—variable and fixed costs—are not completely covered. That is, the firm may continue to operate even though it is experiencing an economic loss. Why? Because fixed costs continue whether the firm produces or not; it is better to earn enough to cover a portion of fixed costs rather than earn nothing at all.

For example, a restaurant may decide to stay open for lunch even with few customers if its revenues can cover variable costs. Many of a restaurant's costs are fixed—rent, insurance, kitchen appliances, pots, pans, tableware, and so on. These are sunk costs in the short run, so shutting down for lunch would not reduce these costs; the restaurant can ignore them when making its business strategy decisions.

The restaurant's lunch decision hinges on whether the revenue from the few lunchtime customers can cover the variable costs like staff and extra food. If the restaurant owner cannot cover the variable costs at lunchtime, she shuts down for lunch.

In Exhibit 2, price is less than average total cost but more than average variable cost. In this case, the firm

section 8.4
Exhibit 2

Short-Run Losses: Price above *AVC* but below *ATC*

P > AVC
Do not shut down

MC ATC
AVC
P   P = MR = AR
Shutdown Point

Price

Quantity
(firm)

In this case, the firm operates in the short run but incurs a loss because P < ATC. Nevertheless, P > AVC, and revenues cover variable costs and partially defray fixed costs. This firm will leave the industry in the long run unless prices are expected to rise in the near future, but in the short run it continues to operate at a loss as long as P > AVC.

P < AVC
Shut down

Price

MC   ATC
AVC

P   P = MR = AR
        Shutdown Point

0

Quantity (firm)

Because its average variable costs exceed price at all levels of output, this firm would cut its losses by discontinuing production.

produces in the short run, but at a loss. To shut down would make this firm worse off because it can cover at least *some* of its fixed costs with the excess of revenue over its variable costs.

The Decision to Shut Down Exhibit 3 illustrates a situation in which the price a firm is able to obtain for its product is below its average variable costs at all ranges of output. In this case, the firm is unable to cover even its variable costs in the short run. Because the firm is losing even more than the fixed costs it would lose if it shut down, it is more logical for the firm to cease operations. So if $P < AVC$, the firm can cut its losses by shutting down.

For example, the owner of a miniature golf course at a summer resort may shut down for the winter months because of insufficient demand. But the fixed costs are still incurred year-round. The miniature golf course will shut down if $TR < VC$, or $(P \times q) < VC$. If we divide both sides by q, the firm will shut down if $P < AVC$, or $(P \times q)/q < VC/q$. So the course will shut down when its total revenues do not cover its variable costs.

We must be careful to distinguish between a firm's decision to temporarily shut down and a permanent exit from the market. We reserve the language "shut down" to describe a firm that has made a short-run decision not to produce any output in the specific time period because of current market conditions. Exit, on the other hand, is a long-run decision to leave the market permanently. Remember, the firm cannot avoid fixed costs in the short run, but it can in the long run. That is, in the short run, a firm may shut down, but it still has to pay its fixed costs. In the long run, a firm that exits does not have to pay fixed or variable costs.

WHAT IS THE INDIVIDUAL FIRM'S SHORT-RUN SUPPLY CURVE?

As we have just seen, at all prices above minimum AVC, a firm produces in the short run even if average total cost (ATC) is not completely covered, and at all prices below the minimum AVC, the firm shuts down. The firm produces above the minimum of the AVC even if it is incurring economic losses because it can still earn enough in total revenues to cover all of its average variable costs and a portion of its fixed costs—this is better than not producing, and earning nothing at all.

short-run supply curve
As a cost relationship, this curve shows the marginal cost of producing any given output; as a supply curve, it shows the equilibrium output that the firm will supply at various prices in the short run.

For an individual competitive seller, the **short-run supply curve**, as a cost relationship, shows the marginal cost of producing any *given output*; as a supply curve, it shows the *equilibrium output* that the firm will supply at various prices in the short run. In graphical terms, the short-run supply curve is identical to the portion of the MC curve that lies above the minimum of the AVC curve. This is illustrated by the thick line in Exhibit 4. The declining portion of the MC curve has no significance for supply, because if the price falls below average variable costs, the firm is better off shutting down—producing no output. Beyond the point of lowest AVC, the marginal costs of successively larger amounts of output are progressively greater, so the firm will supply larger and larger amounts only at higher prices. The absolute maximum that the firm can supply, regardless of price, is the maximum quantity that it can produce with the resources it currently has.

Deriving the Short-Run Market Supply Curve

The **short-run market supply curve** is the horizontal summation of the individual firms' supply curves (i.e., the portion of the firms' *MC* above *AVC*) in the market. Because the short run is too brief for new firms to enter the market, the market supply curve is the horizontal summation of *existing* firms. For example, in Exhibit 5, at P_0, each of the 1000 identical firms in the industry produces 50 tonnes of wheat per day at point a, in Exhibit 5(a) and the quantity supplied in the market is 50 000 tonnes of wheat, point A, in Exhibit 5(b). We can again sum horizontally at P_1; the quantity supplied for each of the 1000 identical firms is 80 tonnes of wheat per day at point b in Exhibit 5(a), so the quantity supplied for the industry is 80 000 tonnes of wheat per day, point B in Exhibit 5(b). Continuing this process gives us the market supply curve for the wheat market. In a market of 1000 identical wheat farmers, the market supply curve is 1000 times the quantity supplied by each firm, as long as the price is above *AVC*.

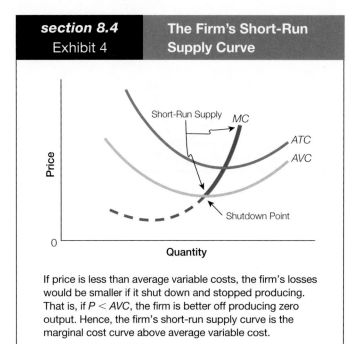

section 8.4
Exhibit 4

The Firm's Short-Run Supply Curve

If price is less than average variable costs, the firm's losses would be smaller if it shut down and stopped producing. That is, if $P < AVC$, the firm is better off producing zero output. Hence, the firm's short-run supply curve is the marginal cost curve above average variable cost.

short-run market supply curve
the horizontal summation of the individual firms' supply curves in the market

section 8.4
Exhibit 5

Deriving the Short-Run Market Supply Curve

a. Individual Firm Supply Curve for Wheat

b. Market Supply Curve for Wheat

The short-run market supply curve is the horizontal summation of the individual firm's supply curves (the firm's marginal cost curve above *AVC*) in Exhibit 5(a). In a market of 1000 identical wheat farmers, the market supply curve is 1000 times the quantity supplied by each firm in Exhibit 5(b).

section 8.4
Exhibit 6
The Short-Run Output Decision

CAN WE REVIEW THE SHORT-RUN PRODUCTION DECISIONS OF AN INDIVIDUAL COMPETITIVE FIRM?

Consider the firm represented by the revenue and cost curves presented in Exhibit 6. At the various market prices—P_1, P_2, P_3, and P_4—what would be the firm's short-run output decisions?

At a market price of P_1, the firm would not cover its average variable costs—the firm would produce zero output because the firm's losses would be smaller if it shut down and stopped producing. At a market price of P_2, the firm would produce at the loss-minimizing output of q_2 units. It would operate rather than shut down because it could cover all of its average variable costs and some of its fixed costs. At a market price of P_3, the firm would produce q_3 units of output and make zero economic profits (a normal rate of return). Finally, at a market price of P_4, the firm would produce q_4 units of output and be making short-run economic profits.

Business *CONNECTION*

A KEY FACTOR IN PERFECT COMPETITION—MANAGING COSTS

In economics, we teach perfect competition to illustrate that on one end of the economic spectrum is a market where neither consumers nor producers have any power in setting price—the market sets the price. On the other end of the spectrum are pure monopolies, where the power rests with the producer. In perfect competition, we are all price takers and we compete only on price. In fact, perfect competition happens only in theory—can you think of any product or service that is purchased solely on price? The other 3Ps (product, price, and promotion) have no place in the perfectly competitive market.

In business, the basic decisions that owners/managers must make are how many units to produce and at what price. Given that in perfect competition the price decision is made for producers (and consumers) in the market, the only decision left is how much to produce. Remember that a firm's revenue equals price times quantity and profits are revenues less expenses. So for a firm to maximize its profit, it has to produce or sell the amount that achieves the lowest costs. If it makes too many at the given price, it will have a surplus and be forced to lower prices to sell. In this case, it won't be maximizing profit—it will be minimizing losses instead. On the other hand, if it doesn't make as much as the market demands, the market will bid up the price due to the shortage, and in the short term, some other firm will benefit from selling the added quantity.

The biggest mistake entrepreneurs make in understanding the basics of business is to think that the more they sell, the more profits they'll make. It's critical to understand that revenues and profits are not the same and that when businesses are able to make more products on the economies of scale side (where average costs fall because of an increase in the scale of production) or without saturating the market, they will both lower their costs and increase their profits. However, if they produce while on the diseconomies of scale side (where firms expand too much), they will drive up their costs and eventually find themselves making up the loss from their available financial resources. Once those resources are exhausted, the business may fail.

Success, whether for businesses or for consumers, is not based on increasing revenues but rather on controlling expenses. Businesses in highly competitive markets absolutely need to be aware at what level of production their costs are the lowest, and unless the market changes or they can lower costs further, deviating from that level of production may have dire long-term consequences.

1. Can you think of any business that competes in an absolutely perfectly competitive market in which price is the only deciding factor? Can you describe the attributes of that product?

2. Why do you think firms that are competing strictly on price tend to be large firms? Why can't smaller firms compete with these large firms? Do you see this as a barrier to entry for smaller firms, and if so, how can smaller firms compete (or can they)?

3. If a firm is competing in a perfectly competitive market, should the firm be more concerned about revenues or about profits? Why?

- The profit-maximizing output level is found by equating $MR = MC$ at q^*. If at q^* the market price is greater than the ATC for the firm, it is making an economic profit. If at q^* the market price is less than ATC, the firm is incurring an economic loss. If at q^* the market price is equal to ATC, the firm is making zero economic profits; that is, making a normal rate of return.
- The portion of the MC curve that lies above the minimum of the AVC curve is the short-run supply curve for the individual competitive seller.
- As market price rises, the output decisions of a competitive firm evolve from not producing at all (shutting down), to operating at an economic loss, to economically breaking even, to generating an economic profit.

Long-Run Equilibrium

- What happens to economic profits and losses in the long run?
- What is the long-run equilibrium for the competitive firm?

WHAT HAPPENS TO ECONOMIC PROFITS AND LOSSES IN THE LONG RUN?

If farmers are able to make economic profits producing wheat, what will their response be in the long run? Farmers will increase the resources that they devote to the lucrative business of producing wheat. Suppose Farmer John is making an economic profit (he is earning an above-normal rate of return) producing wheat. To make even more profits, he may take land out of producing other crops and plant more wheat. Other farmers or people who are holding land for speculative purposes might also decide to plant wheat on their land.

As the word gets out that wheat production is proving profitable, there will be a supply response—the market supply curve will shift to the right as more firms enter the industry and existing firms expand, as in Exhibit 1(a). With this shift, the quantity of wheat supplied at any given price is greater than before. It may take a year or even longer, of course, for the complete supply response to take place, simply because it takes some time for information to spread on profit opportunities, and still more time to plant, grow, and harvest the wheat. Note that the impact of increasing supply, other things equal, is to reduce the equilibrium price of wheat. Suppose that, as a result of the supply response, the price of wheat falls from P_0 to P_1.

The impact of the change in the market price of wheat, over which John has absolutely no control, is very simple. If his costs have not changed, he will move from making a profit ($P_0 > ATC$) to zero economic profits ($P_1 = ATC$), as seen in Exhibit 1(b). In long-run equilibrium, perfectly competitive firms make zero economic profits. Remember, zero economic profits means that the firm is actually earning a normal return on the use of its capital. Zero economic profits is an equilibrium or stable situation because any positive economic (above-normal) profits signal resources to enter the industry, beating down prices and thus revenues to the firm. Any economic losses signal resources to leave the industry, causing market supply reductions that lead to increased prices and

section 8.5
Exhibit 1

Profits Disappear with Entry

a. Market

b. Individual Firm

As the industry-determined price of wheat falls, Farmer John's marginal revenue curve shifts downward from mr_0 to mr_1 in Exhibit 1(b). A new profit-maximizing ($MC = MR$) point is reached at q_1. When the price is P_0, Farmer John is making a profit because $P_0 > ATC$. But when the market supply increases, causing the market price to fall to P_1, Farmer John's profits disappear because $P_1 = ATC$.

section 8.5
Exhibit 2

Losses Disappear with Exit

a. Individual Firm

b. Market

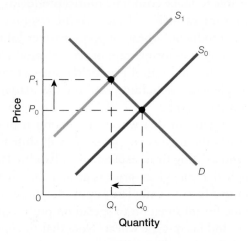

When firms in the industry suffer losses, some firms will exit in the long run, shifting the market supply curve to the left from S_0 to S_1. This causes market price to rise from P_0 to P_1 and market output to fall from Q_0 to Q_1. When the price is P_0 the firm is incurring a loss, because ATC is greater than P_0 at q_0. When the market supply decreases from S_0 to S_1, it causes the market price to rise and the firm's losses disappear, because $P_1 = ATC$.

higher firm revenues for the remaining firms. For example, in Exhibit 2 we see a firm that continues to operate despite its losses—ATC is greater than P_0 at q_0. With losses, however, some firms will exit the industry, causing the market supply curve to shift from S_0 to S_1 and driving up the market price to P_1. This price increase reduces the losses for the firms remaining in the industry, until the losses are completely eliminated at P_1. The remaining firms will maximize profits by producing at q_1 units of output, where profits and losses are zero. Only at zero economic profits is there no tendency for firms to either enter or exit the industry.

WHAT IS THE LONG-RUN EQUILIBRIUM FOR THE COMPETITIVE FIRM?

The long-run competitive equilibrium for a perfectly competitive firm is graphically illustrated in Exhibit 3. At the equilibrium point (where $MC = MR$), short-run and long-run average total costs are also equal. The average total cost curves touch the marginal cost and marginal revenue (demand) curves at the equilibrium output point. Because the marginal revenue curve is also the average revenue curve, average revenues and average total costs are equal at the equilibrium point. The long-run equilibrium in perfect competition depicted in Exhibit 3 has an interesting feature. Note that the equilibrium output occurs at the lowest point on the average total cost curve. As you may recall, this occurs because the marginal cost curve must intersect the average total cost curve at the latter curve's lowest point. Hence, the equilibrium condition in the long run in perfect competition is for firms to produce at that output that minimizes average total costs—that is, the firm is operating at its minimum efficient scale. At this long-run equilibrium, all firms in the industry are earning zero economic profit; consequently, new firms have no incentive to enter the market, and existing firms have no incentive to exit the market.

section 8.5 Exhibit 3	**The Long-Run Competitive Equilibrium**

Quantity of Wheat
(tonnes per year)

In the long run in perfect competition, a stable situation or equilibrium is achieved when economic profits are zero. In this case, at the profit-maximizing point where $MC = MR$, short-run and long-run average total costs are equal. Industry-wide supply shifts would change prices and average revenues and wipe out any losses or profits that develop in the short run, leading to the situation depicted above.

DEBATE

IS "PERFECT" COMPETITION IMPERFECT IN THE LONG TERM?

For:
In a perfectly competitive market, goods trade on price alone—not on product differentiation, convenience, or promotional advertising. Innovation raises costs, and there's no incentive for producers to innovate if they can't recover those costs. Those who try to innovate will only increase their costs, and eventually they'll be driven out of the market. Economies that work at this level will sustain themselves only as long as the resource involved is available. When scarcity starts to set in, they are unprepared to adapt. There is a social cost to this approach—greater wealth is based on value-added, and without adding value, an economy develops at less than a socially optimal level. So surely a form of competition that stifles innovation is imperfect in the long term? In this market, the marginal social costs (the costs to society of producing more of the item) exceed the marginal private costs of the producers. Can you provide examples of where these two costs come into conflict and how they might be played out in the market to back up your position?

Against:
One point worth considering is that the goods that trade in perfectly competitive markets tend to be very basic and homogeneous in nature—most likely commodities and raw resources. Economies that generally trade in raw resources are usually not innovative to start with. Over the long term, though, firms have to innovate to lower their costs, and in that way they contribute to long-term economic development. While it may be true that innovation is slower in markets that are perfectly competitive, innovation nevertheless develops. Firms in perfectly competitive markets have found ways to innovate while maintaining competitive margins, and such firms are generally efficient and lower-cost producers. Surely perfect competition is as perfect as those involved want it to be, for the short term as well the long term. Can you provide examples where firms in perfectly competitive markets can innovate and where this has been socially beneficial?

section 8.6

Long-Run Supply

● What are constant-cost industries?
● What are increasing-cost and decreasing-cost industries?
● How is perfect competition economically efficient?

The preceding sections have considered the costs of an individual, perfectly competitive firm as it varies output, on the assumption that the prices paid for inputs (costs) are given. However, when the output of an entire industry changes, the likelihood is greater of changes occurring in costs. But how will the changes in the number of firms in an industry affect the input costs of individual firms? In this section we develop the long-run supply curve (*LRS*). As we will see, the shape of the long-run supply curve depends on the extent to which input costs change when there is entry or exit of firms in the industry. We will look at two possible types of industries when considering long-run supply: constant-cost industries and increasing-cost industries.

WHAT ARE CONSTANT-COST INDUSTRIES?

constant-cost industry
An industry where input prices (and cost curves) do not change as industry output changes.

In a **constant-cost industry**, input prices do not change as industry output changes. The industry may not use inputs in sufficient quantities to affect input prices. For example, say the firms in the industry use a lot of unskilled labour but the industry is small. So, as output expands, the increase in demand for unskilled labour will not cause the market wage for unskilled labour to rise. Similarly, suppose a paper-clip maker decides to double its output. It is highly unlikely that its demand for steel will have an impact on steel prices because its demand for the input is so small.

Once long-run adjustments are complete, by necessity each firm operates at the point of lowest long-run average total costs because supply shifts with entry and exit, eliminating profits. Therefore, each firm supplies the market with the quantity of output that it can produce at the lowest possible long-run average total cost.

In Exhibit 1, we can see the impact of an unexpected increase in market demand. Suppose that recent reports show that blueberries can lower cholesterol, lower blood pressure, and significantly reduce the risk of all cancers. The increase in market demand for blueberries leads to a price increase from P_0 to P_1 as the firm increases output from

section 8.6
Exhibit 1
Demand Increase in a Constant-Cost Industry

a. Initial Equilibrium

b. Short-Run Profits

c. Long-Run Entry and No Economic Profits

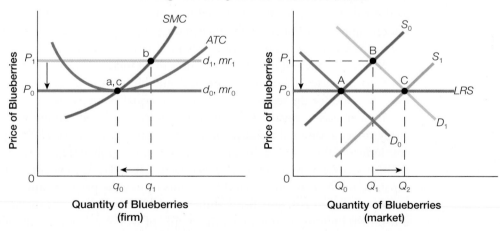

An unexpected increase in market demand for blueberries leads to an increase in the market price at point b. The new market price leads to positive profits for existing firms, which attracts new firms into the industry, shifting market supply from S_0 to S_1 at point c. This increased short-run industry supply curve intersects D_1 at point C. Each firm (of a new larger number of firms) is again producing at q_0 and earning zero economic profit.

q_0 to q_1, and blueberry industry output increases from Q_0 to Q_1, as seen in Exhibit 1(b). The increase in market demand generates a higher price and positive profits for existing firms in the short run. The existence of economic profits will attract new firms into the industry, causing the short-run supply curve to shift from S_0 to S_1 and lowering price until excess profits are zero. This shift results in a new equilibrium, point C in Exhibit 1(c). Because the industry is one of constant costs, industry expansion does not alter firms' cost curves, and the industry long-run supply curve is horizontal. That is, the long-run equilibrium price is at the same level that prevailed before demand increased; the only long-run effect of the increase in demand is an increase in industry output, as more firms enter that are just like existing firms, as Exhibit 1(c) indicates. However, the long-run supply curve does not have to be horizontal. The long-run supply curve is horizontal when the market has free entry and exit, there are a large number of firms with identical costs, and input prices are constant. Because these strong assumptions do not generally hold, we will now discuss when the long-run supply curve has a positive or negative slope. Studies have shown that retail trade may fall into the category of a constant-cost industry because output can be expanded or contracted without a noticeable impact on input prices. The same may be true of publishing and content businesses such as AOL.

WHAT ARE INCREASING-COST AND DECREASING-COST INDUSTRIES?

An Increasing-Cost Industry

increasing-cost industry
an industry where input prices rise (and cost curves rise) as industry output rises

In the **increasing-cost industry**, input prices rise (and cost curves rise) as industry output rises. In this more likely scenario, the cost curves of the individual firms rise as the total output of the industry increases. Increases in input prices (upward shifts in cost curves) occur as larger quantities of factors are employed in the industry. When an industry utilizes a large portion of an input whose total supply is not huge, input prices will rise when the industry uses more of the input.

Increasing-cost conditions are typical of "extractive" industries, such as agriculture, fishing, mining, and lumbering, which utilize large portions of the total supply of specialized natural resources such as land and mineral deposits. As the output of such an industry expands, the increased demand for the resources raises the prices that must be paid for their use. Because additional resources of a given quality cannot be produced, greater supplies can only be obtained (if at all) by luring them away from other industries or by using lower-quality (and less-productive, thus higher-cost) resources.

Wheat production is a typical example of an increasing-cost industry. As the output of wheat increases, the demand for land suitable for the production of wheat rises, so the price paid for the use of land of any given quality increases.

If there was a construction boom in a fully employed economy, would it be more costly to get additional resources like workers and raw materials? Yes, in an increasing-cost industry, the industry can produce more output only if it gets a higher price, because the firm's costs of production rise as output expands. As new firms enter and output expands, the increase in demand for inputs causes the price of inputs to rise—the cost curves of all construction firms shift upward as the industry expands. Or consider a downtown building boom where the supply of workers who are willing to work on tall skyscrapers is very inelastic; a very steep supply of labour curve. The high demand for these few workers causes their wages to rise sharply and the cost of skyscrapers to rise. The industry can produce more output but only at a higher price, enough to compensate the firm for the higher input costs. In an increasing-cost industry, the long-run supply curve is upward sloping.

For example, in Exhibit 2, we see that an unexpected increase in the market demand for wheat will shift the market demand curve from D_0 to D_1. Consequently, price will increase from P_0 to P_1 in the short run and the industry output will increase from Q_0 to Q_1. The typical firm (farm) will have positive short-run profits and expand output. With the presence of short-run economic profits, new firms will enter the industry, shifting the short-run market supply curve to the right from S_0 to S_1. The prices of inputs, like farmland, fertilizer, seed, farm machinery, and so on, will be bid up by competing farmers, causing the farm's marginal and long-run average cost curves to rise. The cost increases mean that the market supply curve shifts right less than it would in a constant-cost industry. This leads to an upward-sloping long-run industry supply curve, as seen in Exhibit 2.

section 8.6
Exhibit 2

Increasing-Cost Industry

Another example of an increasing-cost industry can be found by looking at the National Hockey League (NHL). The 1990s saw the NHL undergo ambitious expansion with the addition of numerous teams in the southern United States. This growth in turn created increased demand for professional calibre hockey players, as new teams worked to become competitive with existing teams. That is, as the number of professional hockey teams increased, the team's costs increased, *ceteris paribus*. This created the situation of an upward-sloping long-run industry supply curve.

Whether the industry is one of constant cost or increasing cost, the basic point is the same. The long-run supply is usually more elastic than the short-run supply because in the long run, firms can enter and exit the industry.

A Decreasing-Cost Industry

It is also possible that an expansion in the output of an industry can lead to a reduction in input costs and shift the *MC* and *ATC* curves downward, and the market price falls because of *external economies of scale*. We use the term *external* because the cost decreases are external to the firm; no one firm can gain by its own expansion. That is, the gains occur when the total industry's output expands. A **decreasing-cost industry** is an industry where input prices fall (and cost curves fall) as industry output rises. As a result, the new long-run market equilibrium has more output at a lower price— that is, the long-run supply curve is downward sloping.

decreasing-cost industry
an industry where input prices fall (and cost curves fall) as industry output rises

Consider a new mining region, developed in an area remote from railroad facilities back in the days before motor vehicles. As long as the total output of the mines was small, the ore was hauled by wagon, an extremely expensive form of transportation. But when the number of mines increased and the total output of the region rose substantially, it became feasible to construct a railroad to service the area. The railroad lowered transportation costs and reduced the costs of all firms in the industry. As a practical matter, decreasing-cost industries are rarely encountered, at least over a large range of output. However, some industries may operate under decreasing-cost conditions in the short intervals of output expansion when continued growth makes possible the supply of materials or services at reduced cost. A larger industry might benefit from improved transportation or financial services, for example.

This situation might occur in the computer industry. The firms in the industry may be able to acquire computer chips at a lower price as the industry's demand for computer chips rises. Why? Perhaps it is because the computer chip industry can employ cost-saving techniques that become more economical at higher levels of output. That is, the marginal and average costs of the firm fall as input prices fall because of expanded output in the industry.

HOW IS PERFECT COMPETITION ECONOMICALLY EFFICIENT?

Perfect Competition and Productive Efficiency

In this chapter, we have seen that a firm in a perfectly competitive market produces at the minimum of the *ATC* curve in the long run and charges a price consistent with that cost (recall Section 8.5, Exhibit 3). Because competitive firms are producing using the least-cost method, the minimum amount of resources is being used to produce a given level of output. This leads to lower product prices for consumers. In short, since perfect competition requires a firm to operate at the minimum of its *ATC* curve, perfect competition ensures a good or service is produced at the lowest possible cost— **productive efficiency.**

productive efficiency
where a good or service is produced at the lowest possible cost

Perfect Competition and Allocative Efficiency

Productive efficiency alone does not guarantee that markets are operating efficiently— society must also produce the goods and services that society wants most. This leads us to what economists call **allocative efficiency**, where $P = MC$ and production is allocated to reflect consumer preferences.

At the intersection of market supply and market demand, we find the competitive equilibrium price, P^*, and the competitive equilibrium output, Q^*. In competitive markets, market supply equals market demand and $P = MC$. When $P = MC$, buyers value the last unit of output by the same amount that it cost sellers to produce it. If buyers value the last unit by more than the marginal cost of production, resources are not being allocated efficiently, like at Q_0 in Exhibit 3(a). Think of the demand curve as the marginal benefit curve ($D = MB$) and the supply curve as the marginal cost curve ($S = MC$). According to the rule of rational choice, we should pursue an activity as long as the expected marginal benefits are greater than the expected marginal costs. For example in Exhibit 3(a), if Q_0 is produced, society is experiencing a reduction in total welfare because the marginal benefits from producing additional units are greater than the marginal costs. Society would gain from an expansion of output up to Q^*. That is, at Q_0, resources are not being allocated efficiently, and output should be expanded. This loss of total welfare is commonly referred to as a *deadweight loss* (the shaded area in Exhibit 3[a]).

allocative efficiency
where $P = MC$ and production is allocated to reflect consumer preferences

We can also produce too much output. For example, if output is expanded beyond Q^*, as it is in Exhibit 3(b), the cost to sellers for producing the good is greater than the marginal benefits to consumers. Society would gain from a reduction in output back to Q^*. Once the competitive equilibrium is reached, the buyers' marginal benefit equals the sellers' marginal cost; that is, in a competitive market, producers efficiently use their resources (labour, machinery, and other inputs) to produce what consumers want. In this sense, perfect competition achieves *allocative efficiency*. When such an allocative efficient equilibrium is not achieved, society experiences a loss in total welfare—a deadweight loss (the shaded area in Exhibit 3[b]).

section 8.6
Exhibit 3
Allocative Efficiency and Perfect Competition

a. Producing Less than the Competitive Level of Output Lowers Welfare

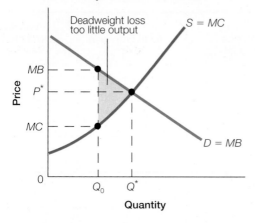

b. Producing More than the Competitive Level of Output Lowers Welfare

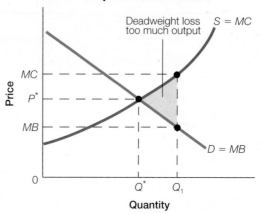

The demand curve measures the marginal benefits to the consumer and the supply curve measures the marginal cost to the sellers. At P^* and Q^*, resources are being allocated efficiently—the marginal benefits of those resources are equal to the marginal cost of those resources. At this point the sum of consumer and producer surplus is maximized. If Q_0 is produced, then the marginal benefits from producing additional units are greater than the marginal costs. Society gains from expanding output up to the point where $MB = MC$ at Q^*. If output is expanded beyond Q^*, $MC > MB$, society gains from a reduction in output, back to Q^*.

SECTION CHECK

- In constant-cost industries, the cost curves of the firm are not affected by changes in the output of the entire industry. Such industries are usually very small demanders of resources in the market.
- In an increasing-cost industry, the cost curves of the individual firms rise as total output increases, whereas in a decreasing-cost industry, the cost curves decline as total output increases. The increasing-cost case is the most typical.
- Perfect competition long-run equilibrium achieves productive efficiency (production at least-possible cost), allocative efficiency ($P = MC$), and production allocated to reflect consumers' wants, thereby making perfect competition economically efficient.

For Your Review

Section 8.1

1. Why does the fact that perfectly competitive firms are small relative to the market make them price takers?

2. Based on the information provided in the following table, which of the industries described in the table are perfectly competitive? Check-mark the perfectly competitive market characteristics that each industry possesses and indicate whether it is a perfectly competitive market.

Industry	Many Firms and Buyers	Identical Products	Ease of Entry and Exit	Perfectly Competitive Market
Montreal taxi business: City issues a limited number of permits.				
Commercial aircraft company: The costs of starting such a business are significant.				
Window-washing business: Low cost of entry and limited specialized training.				
Fast-food business: Restaurant chains produce meals that are distinctive.				
Broccoli farming: There are many producers of broccoli, which requires no special growing conditions.				

3. Industry councils promote the consumption of particular types of farm products. These groups urge us to "Drink Milk" and "Get Cracking." Very little advertising is done by individual farmers. Using your understanding of the perfectly competitive market, explain this advertising strategy.

Section 8.2

4. Using the above exhibit:

   a. Illustrate the relationship between a perfectly competitive firm's demand curve and the market supply and demand curve.

   b. Illustrate the effects of an increase in market demand on a perfectly competitive firm's demand curve.

5. Why would a perfectly competitive firm not try to raise or lower its price?

6. Suppose Spartan Orchards is one of over a thousand perfectly competitive apple growers in Canada. The following graph shows the market demand and supply curves.

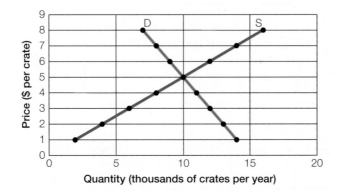

In a properly labelled diagram, draw Spartan Orchard's demand curve for apples. What is the predominant feature of this individual perfectly competitive firm's demand curve?

Blueprint Problem

Suppose the following table describes the costs of production for Carl's Calculators, a perfectly competitive firm.

Output (q)	TVC	TFC	TC	AVC	AFC	ATC	MC
0	$0.00	$40.00	$40.00	—	—	—	—
1	$10.00	$40.00	$50.00	$10.00	$40.00	$50.00	$10.00
2	$16.00	$40.00	$56.00	$8.00	$20.00	$28.00	$6.00
3	$20.00	$40.00	$60.00	$6.67	$13.33	$20.00	$4.00
4	$29.00	$40.00	$69.00	$7.25	$10.00	$17.25	$9.00
5	$44.00	$40.00	$84.00	$8.80	$8.00	$16.80	$15.00
6	$66.00	$40.00	$106.00	$11.00	$6.67	$17.67	$22.00
7	$104.00	$40.00	$144.00	$14.86	$5.71	$20.57	$38.00

a. If Carl sells each calculator for $19, determine profit-maximizing output using the total approach.

b. At the same market clearing price of $19, determine Carl's profit-maximizing output using the marginal approach. Use the four-step method and detail the steps.

c. At what market clearing price would Carl's Calculators achieve economic breakeven?

d. Below which market clearing price would Carl's Calculators be better off shutting down?

Blueprint Solution

a.

> Given that Carl is selling each calculator for \$19, total revenue (*TR*) can be determined.
>
> $TR = P \times q$

Output (q)	TR	TC	Total Profit
0	\$0	\$40.00	–\$40.00
1	\$19	\$50.00	–\$31.00
2	\$38	\$56.00	–\$18.00
3	\$57	\$60.00	–\$3.00
4	\$76	\$69.00	\$7.00
5	\$95	\$84.00	\$11.00
6	\$114	\$106.00	\$8.00
7	\$133	\$144.00	–\$11.00

> By determining total profit (*TR – TC*), the total approach reveals that q^* is 5 calculators.

b.

Output	MR	MC	Interpretation
0	—	—	
1	\$19.00	\$10.00	Produce
2	\$19.00	\$6.00	Produce
3	\$19.00	\$4.00	Produce
4	\$19.00	\$9.00	Produce
5	\$19.00	\$15.00	Produce
6	\$19.00	\$22.00	Do not produce
7	\$19.00	\$38.00	Do not produce

> Being a rational decision maker, Carl will produce only the number of calculators that will give him positive net benefit (*MR > MC*). This rational decision rule will lead Carl to produce a total of 5 calculators.

> The individual perfectly competitive firm experiences constant *MR* over the entire range of output.

Step 1: $MR = MC$ at 5 calculators (actually in this example, MR is as close to MC without exceeding it)

Step 2: $TR = P^* \times q^* = \$19 \times 5 = \$95$

Step 3: $TC = ATCq^* \times q^* = \$16.80 \times 5 = \$84$

Step 4: Total profit $= TR - TC = \$95 - \$84 = \$11$. Or you can calculate total economic profit by using the following equation: $(P^* - ATC) \times q^* = (\$19.00 - \$16.80) \times 5 = \$11.00$.

c. Economic breakeven price is $16.80.

> If Carl is forced to sell each calculator he produces for $16.80, the profit-maximizing output (q^*) would be 5. If Carl produces 5 calculators, the average total cost (ATC) of making one calculator will be $16.80. Confirm this by looking up the ATC for $q = 5$ in the cost of production table at the start of the question.
>
> Calculate total economic profit using the equation:
>
> $$(P^* - ATC) \times q^* = (\$16.80 - \$16.80) \times 5 = \$0$$
>
> As a result, at $16.80, Carl is just covering his implicit and explicit costs of production and therefore achieving *economic breakeven*.
>
> It is also interesting to notice that the economic breakeven price is also the minimum value of the average total cost (ATC) curve.

d. If the price of calculators was to fall below $6.67, Carl would be better off *shutting down*.

> Recall the shut-down condition: A firm will shut down if $P < AVC$. Suppose the price of calculators fell to $5 (thus invoking the shut-down condition). At $5, the profit-maximizing level of output (q^*) appears to be 3, but why is this incorrect and why is Carl better off producing zero calculators if their price is $5?
>
> Calculate total economic profit using the equation:
>
> $$(P^* - ATC) \times q^* = (\$5 - \$20) \times 3 = -\$45$$
>
> If Carl instead decided not to produce any calculators ($q^* = 0$), his loss would only be $40 (confirm this by looking up the TC for $q = 0$ in the cost of production table at the start of the question).
>
> Being a rational decision maker and faced with the decision of losing either $40 or $45, Carl would choose to lose the lower amount and therefore choose to shut down.

Section 8.3

7. Given the data below, determine *AR*, *MR*, *P*, and the short-run profit-maximizing (loss-minimizing) level of output.

Output	Total Cost	Total Revenue
0	$ 30	$ 0
1	45	25
2	65	50
3	90	75
4	120	100
5	155	125

8. Complete the following table for a perfectly competitive firm, and indicate its profit-maximizing output.

Quantity	Price	Total Revenue	Marginal Revenue	Total Cost	Marginal Cost	Total Profit
6	$10	$	$	$30	$3	$30
7				35		
8				42		
9				51		
10				62		
11				75		
12				90		

9. At a price of $5, the profit-maximizing output for a perfectly competitive firm is 1000 units per year. If the average total cost is $3 per unit, what will be the firm's profit? If the average total cost is $6 per unit, what will be the firm's profit? What is the relationship between profit, price, and average total cost?

10. Use the following diagram to answer questions (a) through (d).

a. How much would a perfectly competitive firm produce at each of the indicated prices?

b. At which prices is the firm earning economic profits? Zero economic profits? Negative economic profits?

c. At which prices would the firm shut down?

d. Indicate what this firm's supply curve would be.

11. a. Complete the following table and identify the profit-maximizing output.

Quantity	Price	Total Revenue	Marginal Revenue	Marginal Cost	Total Profit
10	$12	$120	$12	$ 8	$25
11	12			9	
12	12			11	
13	12			12	
14	12			14	

b. What is true about marginal revenue and marginal costs when profit is maximized?

c. What would be the profit-maximizing level of output if the price fell to $9?

Section 8.4

12. Why would a profit-maximizing, perfectly competitive firm continue to operate for a period of time if price was greater than average variable cost but less than average total cost?

13. The diagram below applies to a perfectly competitive firm.

a. According to the diagram, what is the current market clearing price facing this producer and how many units are being produced at this price?

b. At the indicated market clearing price, what are the economic profits or losses of the firm?

c. Suppose the market clearing price falls to $25. What are the economic profits or losses of the firm? Should the firm continue to produce in the short run to maximize profits (or minimize losses)? Explain.

d. Suppose the market clearing price falls to $10. Should the firm continue to produce in the short run to maximize profits (or minimize losses)? Explain.

14. Discuss the following questions.
    a. Why must price cover *AVC* if firms are to continue to operate?
    b. If the firm is covering its *AVC* but not all its fixed costs, will it continue to operate in the short run? Why or why not?
    c. Why is it possible for price to remain above the average total cost in the short run but not in the long run?

15. Evaluate the following statements. Determine whether each is true or false and explain your answer.
    a. If economic profits are zero, firms will exit the industry in the long run.
    b. A firm cannot maximize profits without minimizing costs.
    c. If a firm is minimizing costs, it must be maximizing profits.

Section 8.5

16. Explain why the following conditions are typical under perfect competition in the long run.
    a. $P = MC$
    b. $P = $ Minimum *ATC*

17. Describe what would happen to the industry supply curve and the economic profits of the firms in a competitive industry if those firms were currently earning economic profits. What if they were currently earning economic losses?

18. The following graph shows the output for Pat, a profit-maximizing corn farmer.

    a. Suppose the corn market consists of 1000 farms, including and identical to Pat's. In the table below, determine the market supply in column 2.

(1)	(2)	(3)
Price ($)	Market Supply (tonnes per year)	Market Demand (tonnes per year)
2		19000
4		18000
6		17000
8		16000
10		15000

    b. If the market demand for corn is as shown in column 3 of the table in part (a), at equilibrium price how much will Pat produce? Is she generating a profit or a loss? How much will the market produce? Is the market generating a profit or a loss?

    c. Given the results from part (b), what will happen to the corn market in the long run?

Section 8.6

19. Use the following diagrams to answer (a) and (b).

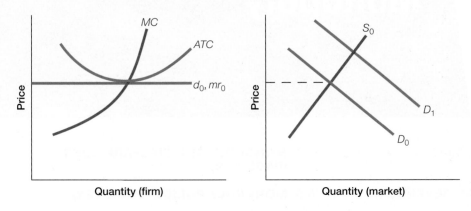

a. Show the effect of this increase in demand on the perfectly competitive firm's price, marginal revenue, output, and profits in the short run.

b. Show the long-run effects of this increase in demand for the industry, and the effects on a perfectly competitive firm's price, marginal revenue, output, and profits for a constant-cost industry.

20. Graph and explain the adjustments to long-run equilibrium when market demand decreases in a constant-cost industry.

21. Given the industry description, identify each of the following as an increasing-cost or constant-cost industry.

a. Major League Baseball: Uses the majority of pitchers. As the number of pitchers used increases, the quality declines.

b. Fast-food restaurants: Use a relatively small share of land and unskilled labour in most cities.

c. Trucking industry: Uses a large number of trained and experienced drivers, especially long-distance drivers.

chapter
9
Monopoly

section 9.1

Monopoly: The Price Maker

- What is a monopoly?
- What are the sources of monopoly power?

WHAT IS A MONOPOLY?

This chapter examines monopolies, a market structure that can be characterized by (1) only one seller of a product, (2) no close substitutes, and (3) barriers to entry that prevent competition. Let's examine these characteristics in greater detail.

Single Seller

monopoly
a market with only one seller of a product that has no close substitute and there are natural and legal barriers to entry that prevent competition

price maker
a monopolistic firm that sets the price of its product so as to maximize its profits

A true or pure **monopoly** exists where there is a market with only one seller of a product that has no close substitute and there are natural or legal barriers to entry that prevent competition. In a monopoly, the firm and "the industry" are one and the same. Consequently, the firm sets the price of the good because the firm faces the industry demand curve and can pick the most profitable point on that demand curve.

A monopolist is a **price maker** (rather than a price taker) that sets the price of its product so as to maximize its profits. Take for example the market for cable television in Canada. Depending on where you live in the country, you can get cable television services from only one provider. Whether that provider is Rogers, Shaw, Cogeco, or EastLink, cable companies are prevented from competing with each other within the same market by the Canadian Radio-television and Telecommunications Commission (CRTC). Therefore, due to their single-seller status in the cable television market, cable companies could be considered monopolists.

Unique (Heterogeneous) Product

Since a true monopolist exists alone, without any competition, the good or service that is produced by the monopolist is without any substitute—the product is unique. For example, while other forms of power generation exist, the vast majority of household products (refrigerator, television, computer, etc.) require electricity to operate. Therefore, it could be said that electricity is a product without a reasonable alternative, that it is a unique source of consumer energy. As a result, local electricity utilities, which are the exclusive providers of this very unique product, could be considered to be monopolists.

Barriers to Entry

If a monopolist is to maintain its exclusive ownership of the manufacturing of a particular product and therefore maintain the product's uniqueness in the marketplace, other producers have to be prevented from entering. Monopolists successfully accomplish this through a variety of barriers to entry. For example, the Liquor Control Board of Ontario (LCBO), with its distribution and retail network of over 600 stores, is (with few exceptions) the only retailer with a licence to sell distilled spirits in the province of Ontario. The impact of this provincial regulation is that no other retailer can enter the distilled spirits market in Ontario, making the LCBO a monopolist.

The Ontario government is not alone in using this tactic of monopolizing the distribution and/or retailing of alcoholic beverages. In fact, the majority of Canadian provincial governments exercise either complete or partial monopolization when it comes to the retailing and/or distribution of alcohol (beer, wine, and spirits). For example, in British Columbia, the Liquor Distribution Branch (LDB) has the sole right to purchase beverage alcohol. It is responsible for the importation, distribution, wholesaling, and retailing of beverage alcohol, and operates government liquor stores and distribution centres in the province.

In Saskatchewan, the Saskatchewan Liquor and Gaming Authority (SLGA) is responsible for the distribution, control, and regulation of liquor and gaming across the province. The SLGA operates 79 liquor stores and has granted 188 small businesses in Saskatchewan a franchise to sell beverage alcohol on its behalf. The Yukon Liquor Corporation controls the purchase and sale of all beverage alcohol products through the operation of six retail stores. Prince Edward Island Liquor Control Commission (PEILCC) operates 19 board-controlled liquor outlets and one agency outlet.*

Pure Monopolies Are Rare

In discussing the key characteristics of monopolies, various examples have been given to illustrate the existence of these features in the marketplace. However, you should remember that few goods and services are actually produced by monopolies. One might think of a small community with a single bank, a single newspaper, or a single grocery store. Even in these situations, however, most people can bank out of town, use a substitute financial institution, buy out-of-town newspapers or read them on the Web, go to a nearby town to buy groceries, and so on. Near-monopoly conditions exist, but absolute total monopoly is rather unusual.

One area where there is typically only one producer of goods and services within a market area is public utilities. In any given market, usually only one company provides natural gas or supplies water. Moreover, governments themselves provide many

As the sole retailer licensed to sell distilled spirits in the province of Ontario, the LCBO is an example of a monopolist.

© Jill Morgan/Alamy Stock Photo

---

*Kirkwood Diamond Canada, http://www.kirkwooddiamond.com/Markets/LiquorBoards/ProvincialLiquorBoards.aspx.

DEBATE

SHOULD NORTHERN AND RURAL BUS ROUTES BE SERVED BY ONE PROVIDER?

For:

Greyhound Canada had a monopoly in northern and rural communities across Canada up until mid-2018. It was often the only bus service that many Canadians could access when they wanted to travel between cities and towns in rural Canadian communities. In exchange for the monopoly rights to run the only buses between certain communities, Greyhound or similar services were able to subsidize those services with the profits it earned from the high-population southern Ontario and southern British Columbia corridors. It also had the opportunity to review applications from potential competitors to ensure it kept its own routes and services secure.

Greyhound received regulated monopoly status because it was perceived to be the only way to serve remote communities. There was no critical mass of customers to make competitive services viable. When Greyhound pulled its service in mid-2018, the government of Alberta, for example, offered fully government-operated bus services to fill the void, providing city-to-city bus services in rural parts of Alberta.

Without Greyhound, rural and northern customers who can't afford or don't normally need a car could be left without any transportation options. A bus service has a minimum efficient scale, and so, some governments have now had to step in. The minimum efficient scale is just not achievable in some smaller communities. Without a government service or a regulated monopoly transportation provider, northern and rural communities will continue to have little or no transit options.

Against:

Greyhound benefited from provincial government grants and monopoly rights to operate in what Greyhound said were unprofitable areas. Along with those unprofitable areas, though, Greyhound has access to the more lucrative routes such as Toronto to Ottawa and Toronto to Montreal. However, in practice, according to customers in the northern and rural communities it served, Greyhound offered poor service—once or twice a day, or even per week—and took government subsidies without really being accountable for good service.

In mid-2018, Greyhound announced it would no longer serve these northern and rural communities.

Advocates for more competition from other bus companies or from the increasingly popular ride-hailing apps say that it's time for a change. The town of Innisfil in Ontario switched its public transit strategy to include ride-sharing services. The town negotiated with services such as Uber for specific rates and reliable rides between key areas of the town. It works well as an alternative to developing heavily subsidized bus systems. Ride-hailing services are efficient, matching drivers and riders.

Questions:

1. Greyhound said that providing service to rural and northern communities was very unprofitable and not workable. Would competition really be possible in this case?
2. Consider minimally efficient scale in transportation. Is it possible to have a useful transit system in smaller communities? Consider how new technologies may change the game for transit.

---

services for which they are often the sole providers—sewer services, fire and police protection, and military protection. Most of these situations resemble a pure monopoly. Again, however, for most of the goods and services mentioned above, substitute goods and services are available. People heating their homes with natural gas can switch to electric heat (or vice versa). In some areas, one can even substitute home-collected rainwater or well water for that provided by the local water company.

Although the purist might correctly deny the existence of monopoly, the situations where monopoly conditions are closely approximated are numerous enough to make the study of monopoly more than a theoretical abstraction; moreover, the study of monopoly is useful in clarifying certain desirable aspects of perfect competition.

WHAT ARE THE SOURCES OF MONOPOLY POWER?

There are several ways that a monopolist may make it virtually impossible for other firms to overcome barriers to entry. For example, a monopolist might prevent potential rivals from entering the market through legal barriers, through economies of scale, or by controlling important inputs.

Legal Barriers

In the case of legal barriers, the government might franchise only one firm to operate an industry, as is the case for postal services in most countries. The government can also provide licensing designed to ensure a certain level of quality and competence. People in many industries require government licensing, such as medical doctors, nurses, electricians, and plumbers.

Also, the government could give a company a patent to encourage inventive activity. It can cost millions of dollars to develop a new drug or a computer chip and without a patent to recoup some of these costs, there would certainly be less inventive activity. As long as the patent is in effect, the company has the potential to enjoy monopoly profits for many years. After all, why would a firm engage in costly research if any other company could free-ride off its discovery and produce and sell the new drug or computer chip?

Economies of Scale

The situation in which one large firm can provide the output of the market at a lower cost than two or more smaller firms is called a **natural monopoly**. With a natural monopoly, it is more efficient to have one firm produce the good. The reason for the cost advantage is economies of scale; that is, *ATC* falls as output expands throughout the relevant output range, as seen in Exhibit 1. Public utilities, such as water, natural gas, and electricity, are examples of natural monopoly. It is less costly for one firm to lay down pipes and distribute water than for a number of firms to lay down a maze of competing pipes. That is, a single firm can supply water more efficiently than a large number of competing firms.

natural monopoly
a firm that can produce at a lower cost than a number of smaller firms could

Control over an Important Input

Another barrier to entry could occur if a firm had control over an important input. For example, from the late nineteenth century to the early 1940s, the Aluminum Company of America (Alcoa) had a monopoly in the production of aluminum in the United States. Its monopoly power was guaranteed because of its control over an important ingredient in the production of aluminum—bauxite. However, the ownership of key resources is rarely the source of monopoly power. Many goods are traded internationally, and resources are owned by many different people around the world. It is uncommon that a firm would control the worldwide supply of a resource that did not have a close substitute.

section 9.1
Exhibit 1   **Economies of Scale**

Exhibit 1 shows a firm that has economies of scale over the relevant range of output with declining average total costs. If one firm can produce the total output at a lower cost than several small firms, it is called a *natural monopoly*.

SECTION CHECK

- A pure monopoly exists where there is only one seller of a product for which no close substitute is available.
- Sources of monopoly power include legal barriers, economies of scale, and control over important inputs.

Demand and Marginal Revenue in Monopoly

- How does the demand curve for a monopolist differ from that of a perfectly competitive firm?
- Why is marginal revenue less than price in a monopoly?
- What is the relationship between the elasticity of demand and total and marginal revenue?

HOW DOES THE DEMAND CURVE FOR A MONOPOLIST DIFFER FROM THAT OF A PERFECTLY COMPETITIVE FIRM?

In monopoly, the market demand curve may be regarded as the demand curve for the firm's product because the monopoly firm *is* the market for that particular product. The demand curve indicates the quantities that the firm can sell at various possible prices. In monopoly, the price for the firm's product declines as additional units are placed on the market—the demand curve is downward sloping. That is, a monopolist can set the price at a desired level and allow consumers to decide how much they will purchase at that price, or alternatively, set production at a desired quantity and allow the market to determine the maximum price it will sell for. Even a monopolist, with its powerful presence in the market, cannot sell a larger quantity at a higher price—the market simply won't allow it. If the monopolist reduces output, the price will rise; if the monopolist expands output, the price will fall.

Recall that in perfect competition, because there are many buyers and sellers of homogeneous goods (resulting in a perfectly elastic demand curve for the firm), competitive firms can sell all they want at the market price. They face a horizontal

section 9.2 Exhibit 1	Comparing Demand Curves: Perfect Competition vs. Monopoly

a. Perfectly Competitive Firm's Demand Curve

b. Monopolist's Demand Curve

The demand curve for a perfectly competitive firm is perfectly elastic; competitive firms can sell all they want at the market price. The firm is a price taker. The demand curve for a monopolist is downward sloping; if the monopolist wants to expand output, it must accept a lower price. The monopolist is a price maker. Because a monopoly has no close competitors, it can change the product price by adjusting its output.

demand curve. The firm takes the price of its output as determined by the market forces of supply and demand. Monopolists, on the other hand, face a downward-sloping demand curve and if the monopolist wants to expand output, it must accept a lower price. The two demand curves are displayed side by side in Exhibit 1.

WHY IS MARGINAL REVENUE LESS THAN PRICE IN A MONOPOLY?

In Exhibit 2, we see the price of the good, the quantity of the good, the *total revenue* ($TR = P \times Q$), and the *average revenue,* the amount of revenue the firm receives per unit sold ($AR = TR/Q$). The average revenue is just the price per unit sold. We are also given the *marginal revenue*—the amount of revenue the firm receives from selling an additional unit ($MR = \Delta TR/\Delta Q$).

Taking the information from Exhibit 2, we can create the demand and marginal revenue curves as seen in Exhibit 3. We see that the marginal revenue curve for a monopolist lies below the demand curve. Why is this the case? Suppose the firm initially sets its price at $5. It sells only one unit per day and its total revenue is $5. To increase sales it decides to drop the price to $4. Sales increase to two units per day and total revenue increases to $8 (moving from point A to point B in Exhibit 3). The firm's marginal revenue is only $3. Why? When the firm cuts the price in order to induce the second customer to buy, it now receives only $4 from the first customer even though she is willing to pay $5. That is, because both customers are now paying $4, the company is receiving $4 more from customer two but it is now earning $1 less from customer one. Remember, the first customer was willing to pay $5. So, in order to get revenue from marginal customers, the firm has to lower the price. In Exhibit 3, the marginal revenue of selling a second unit per day is illustrated by point C on the marginal revenue curve.

In order to induce a third daily customer to purchase the good, the firm must cut its price to $3. In doing so, it gains $3 in revenue from the third customer, but it loses $2 in revenue because each of the first two customers is now paying $1 less than previously. The marginal revenue is $1 ($3 − $2), less than the price of the good ($3).

Finally, in order to get a fourth customer, the firm has to cut the price to $2. The firm finds that in doing so, it actually loses revenue, because the new revenue received from the fourth customer ($2) is more than offset by losses in revenues from the first three customers, $3, because each customer pays $1 less than before.

Hence, *the marginal revenue is always less than the price*—that is, the marginal revenue curve will always lie below the demand curve, as shown in Exhibit 3. Recall from Chapter 8 (Perfect Competition) that the firm could sell all it wanted at the market price and the price was equal to marginal revenue. However, in monopoly, if the seller

section 9.2 Exhibit 2	Total, Marginal, and Average Revenue			
Price	**Quantity**	**Total Revenue (TR = P × Q)**	**Marginal Revenue (MR = ΔTR/ΔQ)**	**Average Revenue (AR = TR/Q)**
$6	0	$0	—	—
5	1	5	$5	$5
4	2	8	3	4
3	3	9	1	3
2	4	8	−1	2
1	5	5	−3	1
0	6	0	−5	0

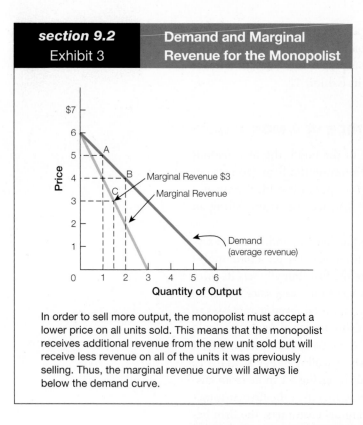

section 9.2
Exhibit 3

Demand and Marginal Revenue for the Monopolist

In order to sell more output, the monopolist must accept a lower price on all units sold. This means that the monopolist receives additional revenue from the new unit sold but will receive less revenue on all of the units it was previously selling. Thus, the marginal revenue curve will always lie below the demand curve.

wants to expand output, it will have to lower its price on *all* units. This means that the monopolist receives additional revenue from the new unit sold but it will receive less revenue on all of the units it was previously selling. So when the monopolist cuts price to attract new customers, the old customers benefit.

In Exhibit 4, we can compare marginal revenue for the perfectly competitive firm with marginal revenue for the monopolist. The firm in perfect competition can sell another unit of output without lowering its price; hence, the marginal revenue from selling its last unit of output is the market price. However, the monopolist has a downward-sloping demand curve. This means that to sell an extra unit of output, it must lower the price from P_0 to P_1, and the monopolist loses area c in Exhibit 4(b).

It is important to note that although a monopolist can set its price anywhere it wants, it will not set its price as high as possible—be careful not to confuse ability with incentive. As we will see in the next section, some prices along the demand curve will not be profitable for a firm. In other words, profits may be enhanced by either lowering the price or raising it.

WHAT IS THE RELATIONSHIP BETWEEN THE ELASTICITY OF DEMAND AND TOTAL AND MARGINAL REVENUE?

The relationship between the elasticity of demand and total and marginal revenue are shown in Exhibit 5. In Exhibit 5(a), elasticity varies along a linear demand curve. Recall from Chapter 5 that above the midpoint, the demand curve is elastic ($E_D > 1$); below the midpoint, it is inelastic ($E_D < 1$); and at the midpoint, it is unit elastic ($E_D = 1$). How does elasticity relate to total and marginal revenue? In the elastic portion of the curve, when the

section 9.2
Exhibit 4

Marginal Revenue—Competitive Firm vs. Monopolist

a. Perfectly Competitive Firm's Demand Curve

b. Monopolist's Demand Curve

Area b in Exhibit 4(a) represents the marginal revenue from an extra unit of output ($q + 1$) for the firm in perfect competition. The competitive firm's marginal revenue (area b) is equal to the market price. In Exhibit 4(b), we see that the monopolist's marginal revenue from an extra unit ($Q + 1$) is less than the price by area c, because the monopolist must lower its price on all units to sell another unit of output.

The Relationship between the Elasticity of Demand and Total and Marginal Revenue

a. Demand and Marginal Revenue

b. Total Revenue

In Exhibit 5(a) we see that along a linear demand curve, the elastic segment lies above the midpoint, the inelastic segment lies below the midpoint, and at the midpoint the demand is unit elastic. When demand is elastic, a decline in price will increase total revenue; when demand is inelastic, a decline in price will lead to a decrease in total revenue. In Exhibit 5(b), we see that over the range from 0 to 5 units, total revenue is rising, so that marginal revenue is positive. Over the range from 5 to 10 units, total revenue is falling, so that marginal revenue is negative. At 5 units of output, total revenue is maximized at $250 ($50 $\times$ 5), so that marginal revenue is zero.

price falls, total revenue rises in Exhibit 5(b), so that marginal revenue is positive. In the inelastic region of the demand curve, when the price falls, total revenue falls in Exhibit 5(b), so that marginal revenue is negative. At the midpoint of the linear demand curve, the total revenue curve reaches its highest point, as seen in Exhibit 5(b), so that $MR = 0$.

For example, suppose the price falls on the top half of the demand curve in Exhibit 5(a) from $90 to $80; total revenue increases from $90 ($90 $\times$ 1) to $160 ($80 $\times$ 2); the marginal revenue is positive at $70. Because a reduction in price leads to an increase in total revenue, the demand curve is elastic in this region. Now, suppose the price falls from $20 to $10 on the lower portion of the demand curve; total revenue falls from $160 ($20 $\times$ 8) to $90 ($10 $\times$ 9); the marginal revenue is negative at $-$70. Because a reduction in price leads to a decrease in total revenue, the demand curve is inelastic in this region.

A monopolist will never knowingly operate in the inelastic portion of its demand curve because increased output will lead to lower total revenue in this region. Not only are total revenues falling, but total costs will rise as you produce more output. Similarly, if a monopolist lowered its output, it could increase its total revenue and lower its total costs (because it costs less to produce fewer units), leading to greater economic profits.

section 9.3

The Monopolist's Equilibrium

- How does the monopolist determine the profit-maximizing output?
- How do we know whether the monopolist is making a profit or a loss?

HOW DOES THE MONOPOLIST DETERMINE THE PROFIT-MAXIMIZING OUTPUT?

In the last section we saw how a monopolist could choose any point along a demand curve. But the monopolist's decision on what level of output to produce depends on more than the marginal revenue derived at various outputs. The firm faces production costs, and the monopolist, like the perfect competitor, will maximize profits at that output where $MR = MC$. This point is demonstrated graphically in Exhibit 1.

As you can see in Exhibit 1, at output level Q_1, the marginal revenue exceeds the marginal cost of that production, so it is profitable for the monopolist to expand output. Profits continue to grow until output Q^* is reached. Beyond that output, say Q_2, the marginal cost of production exceeds the marginal revenue from production, so profits decline. The monopolist should cut production back to Q^*. Therefore, the equilibrium output is Q^*. At this output, marginal costs and marginal revenues are equal.

Four-Step Method for Monopolists

Let's return to the four-step method we introduced in Chapter 8. Determining whether a firm is generating economic profits, economic losses, or zero economic profits at the profit-maximizing level of output, Q^*, can be done in four easy steps.

1. The first step is to find the profit-maximizing level of output (Q^*). To do this, find where marginal revenues equal marginal costs and proceed straight down to the horizontal quantity axis to find the profit-maximizing output level.

2. The second step is to determine the total revenue (TR) being generated at Q^*. To do this, go straight up from Q^* to the demand curve and then to the left to find the market price, P^*. Once you have identified P^* and Q^*, you can find total revenue at the profit-maximizing output level, because $TR = P \times Q$.

3. The third step is to find total costs (TC) at Q^*. Again, go straight up from Q^* to the average total cost (ATC) curve and then left to the vertical axis to compute the average total cost *per unit*. If we multiply average total costs by the output level, we can find the total costs ($TC = ATC \times Q$).

4. The final step is to determine the amount of either profit or loss at Q^*. If total revenue (from step 2) is greater than total costs (from step 3) at Q^*, the firm is generating economic profits. If total revenue is less than total costs at Q^*, the firm is generating economic losses. If total revenue is equal to total cost at Q^*, there are zero economic profits (or a normal rate of return). Alternatively, to find total economic profits, we can take the product price at P^* and subtract the average total cost at Q^*. This will give us per-unit profit. If we multiply this by output, we will arrive at total economic profit: $(P^* - ATC) \times Q^* = $ Total economic profit.

HOW DO WE KNOW WHETHER THE MONOPOLIST IS MAKING A PROFIT OR A LOSS?

Exhibit 1 does not show what profits, if any, the monopolist is actually making. This is rectified in Exhibit 2, which shows the equilibrium position of a monopolist, this time adding an average total cost (ATC) curve. As we just discussed, the firm produces where $MC = MR$, or 100 units of output. At 100 units of output, the demand curve gives us a price of $6 per unit. The firm's total revenue is $P^* \times Q^*$ (6×100), or $600. The firm's total cost is $ATC \times Q^*$ (4×100), or $400. Thus, the firm has a total profit of $200. Or we can calculate total economic profit by using the following equation: $(P^* - ATC) \times Q^* = ($6 - $4) \times 100 = $200.$

In perfect competition, profits in an economic sense will persist only in the short run, because in the long run, new firms will enter the industry, increasing industry supply and thus driving down the price of the good. With this, profits are eliminated. In monopoly, however, profits are not eliminated because one of the conditions for monopoly is that barriers to entry exist. Other firms cannot enter, so economic profits persist in the long run.

Losses for a Monopolist

It is easy to imagine a monopolist ripping off consumers by charging prices resulting in long-run economic profits. However, there are also many companies with monopoly power that have gone out of business. Imagine that you received a patent on a bad idea like a roof ejection seat for a helicopter, or that you had the sole rights to turn an economics textbook into a screenplay for a motion picture. Although you may be the sole supplier of a product, that does not guarantee that consumers will demand

**section 9.3
Exhibit 1**

Equilibrium Output and Price for a Pure Monopolist

The monopolist maximizes profits at that quantity where $MR = MC$, at Q^*. At Q^* the monopolist finds P^* by extending a vertical line up to the demand curve and over to the vertical axis to find the price. Rather than charging a price equal to marginal cost or marginal revenue at their intersection, however, the monopolist charges the price that customers are willing to pay for that quantity as indicated on the demand curve at P^*. At Q_1, $MR > MC$ and the firm should expand output. At Q_2, $MC > MR$ and the firm should cut back its production.

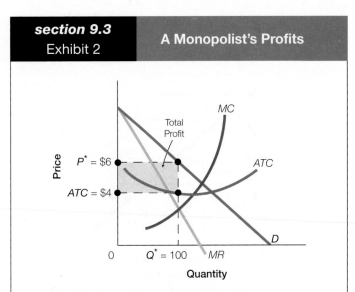

**section 9.3
Exhibit 2**

A Monopolist's Profits

The intersection of MR and MC determines the profit-maximizing level of output. The demand curve shows the price that can be charged. Total profit is total revenue minus total cost ($600 - 400$), or $200.

section 9.3
Exhibit 3

A Monopolist's Losses

Total losses equal $100—the difference between total costs ($700) and total revenues ($600).

your product. There may be no close substitute for your product, but there is always competition for the consumer dollar—other goods may provide greater satisfaction.

Exhibit 3 illustrates loss in a monopoly situation. In this graph, notice that the demand curve is well below the average total cost curve. In this case, the monopolist will incur a loss because there is insufficient demand to cover average total costs at any price and output combination along the demand curve. Total revenue is $600 ($P^* \times Q^* = \$6 \times 100$) and total cost is $700 ($ATC \times Q^* = \$7 \times 100$), for an economic loss of $100. Or we can calculate total economic profit by using the following equation: $(P^* - ATC) \times Q^* = (\$6 - \$7) \times 100 = -\$100$.

Notice that the total revenue is great enough to cover the total variable costs of $400 ($TVC = \$4 \times 100$). Thus, the firm can reduce its losses by operating rather than shutting down in the short run. However, in monopoly as in perfect competition, a firm will go out of business in the long run if it cannot generate enough revenue to cover its total costs.

In summary, if total revenue is greater than total costs at Q^*, the firm is generating total economic profits. And if total revenue is less than total costs at Q^*, the firm is generating total economic losses. If total revenue is equal to total costs at Q^*, the firm is earning zero economic profits. Remember, the cost curves include implicit and explicit costs—so in this case, we are covering the total opportunity costs of our resources and are earning a normal profit or rate of return.

Patents

One form of monopoly power conferred by governments is provided by patents and copyrights. A patent puts the government's police power behind the patent holder's exclusive right to make a product for a period of time (in Canada, the period of time is up to 20 years) without anyone else being able to make an identical product. As Exhibit 4 suggests, this gives the supplier at least temporary monopoly power over that good or service. This allows the firm with the patent to price its product well above marginal costs, at P_M. Notice the marginal cost curve is flat. The reason for this is that once the necessary research and development phase is completed and the drug is available for the market, the product can be produced at a relatively constant price—therefore generating a constant or flat MC curve.

When patents expire, the price of the patented good or service usually falls substantially with the entry of competing firms. The price will fall toward the perfectly competitive price P_{PC} and the output will increase toward $Q_{NO\ PATENT}$.

Why does the government give inventors this limited monopoly power, raising the prices of pharmaceutical drugs and other vital goods? The rationale is simple. Without patents, inventors would have little incentive to incur millions of dollars in research and development expenses to create new products

section 9.3
Exhibit 4

Impact of Patent Protection on Equilibrium Price and Quality

Patent power allows the firm to charge the higher monopoly price, P_M, which is well above the marginal cost of producing that good. However, when the patent expires, the price falls to a position closer to the perfectly competitive price, P_{PC}.

Without patents, would some life-saving drugs have been invented? Some drugs cost millions of dollars in research. Without the protection of a patent, the firm may not have been able to make profits from its inventive activity for very long, which is why the government issues patents that last up to 20 years. However, after the patent expires, many popular drugs soon lose their protection. In most cases, less costly generic drugs hit the market soon after the patent expiration and prices then move closer to the competitive price, although perhaps not all the way to the competitive level, as some companies are able to keep customers through brand loyalty. Pfizer lost its Canadian patent on Viagra in November 2012.

© C. SHERBURNE/PHOTOLINK/GETTY IMAGES

(e.g., life-saving drugs) if others could immediately copy the idea and manufacture the products without incurring the research expenses. Similarly, copyrights stimulate creative activity of other kinds, giving writers the incentive to write books that earn royalties and are not merely copied freely. Just as the enormous number of computer programs written for home computers reflects the fact that program writers receive royalties from the sale of each copy sold, that is why they and the firms they work for vehemently oppose unauthorized copying of their work.

SECTION CHECK

- The monopolist, like the perfect competitor, maximizes profits at that output where marginal revenue equals marginal cost. Price is set according to the demand for the product at the profit-maximizing output.
- Monopoly profits can be found by comparing price per unit and average total cost at Q^*. If $P > ATC$, there are economic profits. If $P < ATC$, there are economic losses. If $P = ATC$, there are zero economic profits (a normal rate of return).

Monopoly and Welfare Loss

**section
9.4**

- Does monopoly promote inefficiency?
- Does monopoly hinder innovation?

DOES MONOPOLY PROMOTE INEFFICIENCY?

Monopoly is often considered to be bad. But what is the basis in economic theory for concerns about the establishment of monopoly power? There are two main objections to monopoly. First, on equity grounds, many people feel that it is not "fair" for monopoly owners to have persistent economic profits when they do not work harder than other firms. However, to most economists, the more serious objection is that monopolies result in market inefficiencies. That is, monopoly leads to a lower output and to higher prices than would exist under perfect competition. To demonstrate why this is so, see Exhibit 1. In monopoly, the firm produces output Q_M and charges a price of P_M. Suppose, however, that we had perfect competition and that the industry was characterized by many small

Perfect Competition vs. Monopoly

Compared with perfect competition, the monopolist's equilibrium price is higher, P_M, and its equilibrium output is lower, Q_M. Also notice that P_M is greater than MC_M, which means the value of the last unit produced by the monopolist (P_M) is greater than the cost of the last unit (MC_M), so from society's point of view, the monopolist is producing too little output.

firms that could produce output with the same efficiency (at the same cost) as one large firm. Then the marginal cost curve shown in Exhibit 1 could be the sum of the individual marginal cost curves of the individual firms, and the upward portion of that curve might be considered the industry supply curve.

Equilibrium price and quantity with perfect competition would be determined where the marginal cost (or supply) curve intersects with the demand curve, at output Q_{PC} and price P_{PC}. Thus, the competitive equilibrium solution provides for more output and lower prices than the solution prevailing in monopoly. This provides the major efficiency objection to monopoly: Monopolists charge higher prices and produce less output. This may also be viewed as "unfair," in that consumers are burdened more than under the alternative competitive arrangement.

Welfare Loss in Monopoly

In addition to the monopolist producing lower levels of output at higher prices, notice that the monopolist produces at an output where the price (P_M) is greater than the marginal cost (MC_M). Because $P > MC$, it means that the value to society from the last unit produced is greater than the cost of the last unit (MC_M). That is, the monopoly is *not* producing enough of the good from society's perspective. We call the shaded area in Exhibit 1 the *welfare loss,* or *deadweight loss, due to monopoly.*

The actual amount of the deadweight loss in monopoly is of considerable debate among economists. Estimates across nations vary between one-tenth of 1 percent and 6 percent of national income. The variation depends on the researchers' estimates of elasticity of demand, whether firm or industry data were used, whether adjustments for profits were made (for the inclusion of royalties and intangibles), and last, whether the researcher included some proxy for scarce resources used in attempting to create a monopoly.

DOES MONOPOLY HINDER INNOVATION?

Another argument against monopoly is that a lack of competition tends to hinder technological advancement. Monopolists become comfortable, reaping their monopolistic profits, so they do not work hard at product improvement, technical advances designed to promote efficiency, and so forth. The railroad industry is sometimes cited as an example of this situation. Early in the last century, railroads had a strong amount of monopoly power, but they did not spend much on research or development; they did not aggressively try to improve rail transport. As a consequence, technical advances in other transport modes—like cars, trucks, and airplanes—led to a loss of monopoly power, as transportation substitutes came into existence.

However, the notion that monopoly hinders all innovation can be disputed. Many near-monopolists are, in fact, important innovators. Companies like Microsoft, IBM, Google, and Apple have all, at one time or another, had very strong market positions, in some instances approaching monopoly secured by patent protection, but they were also important innovators. Indeed, innovation helps firms initially obtain a degree of monopoly status, because patents can give a monopoly to new products and/or cost-saving technology. Also, the monopolist wants more profits, and any innovation that lowers costs or expands revenues creates profits for the monopolist. In addition, because patents expire, a monopolist may be expected to innovate in order to obtain additional patents and preserve its monopoly power. Therefore, the incentive to innovate may well exist in monopolistic market structures.

Business *CONNECTION*

DEREGULATION + PRIVATIZATION = A BETTER ECONOMY

Few businesses operate as monopolies, but it's helpful to understand the motivation and behaviour of companies operating in this extreme market structure.

All businesses, including monopolies, face two major decisions: (1) what price to charge and (2) how many units of goods or services to produce in order to maximize profits. Firms operating in perfect competition decide the level of production, but monopolies can choose both price and production levels. Monopolies always produce less than the market desires, which creates their own market shortage, so they can charge higher prices at all production levels. There is, in fact, a casual disregard for the needs of society or the community unless, of course, regulations demand otherwise.

Demand begins with those who are willing and able to buy, which determines the shape of the industry demand curve. So changes in buyers' tastes, expectations, or income influence shifts of the demand curve. If the monopolist is in the business of providing a good or service that is considered to be a necessity or a near-necessity, the effect of a shift in the demand curve is quite muted. Even though consumers have limited power in a monopoly market, they still hold the ultimate power: whether or not to buy. While having the ability to charge more than the market wants to pay helps to make monopolists profitable, they must also deal with higher costs—because they have to convince buyers of the value of paying the higher price. In essence, they are competing on anything but price—product, place, or promotion—in convincing buyers.

Like any other business, the monopoly has a cost curve that reflects the aggregate and average of the costs of its inputs. But, unlike a business operating in a competitive market structure, monopolists pay less attention to costs and more to getting the highest price they can charge. This lack of motivation to keep costs down leads to serious inefficiencies in the operation of most monopolies and eventually to inefficiencies in the economy. The net effect results in fewer prospective customers getting products or services at reasonable rates, which reflects monopolies' less-than-efficient production methods and processes.

Those who would like to compete with monopolies will argue about monopolies' inefficient cost structure, poor use of available resources, and general disservice to society. The fewer products sold (even at higher prices) has an impact on the numbers of people employed, which affects unemployment rates and tax revenues for governments. When monopolists benefit in excess and to a point that harms society and governments, deregulation and/or privatization can be used to adjust the market balance. Such adjustments do away with or pull apart special privileges that the monopolists have enjoyed, and other businesses are encouraged to compete in the market by offering the same or similar services.

Successful deregulation and privatization of industries leads to more competition, greater industry output, and lower prices. This is good for consumers, for other producers, and for governments in meeting society's needs. Increased innovation is another important result—it leads to new suppliers and subcontractors hoping to compete in providing better products and processes in revitalized industries. Control of aggressive monopolies can lead to measured growth for all sectors of the economy.

1. Satellite, cable, and telecommunications providers are monopolies regulated by the CRTC. Consumers have limited choice and pay high costs, often paying for channels they never watch. Discuss how new technology is changing how consumers engage with and consume media content.

2. Customers are not watching television, movies, and sports in traditional ways, but through the Internet and streaming services. How might the satellite, cable, and telecommunications companies respond?

3. The CRTC demands that traditional broadcasters (and cablecasters) support Canadian culture by running a certain percentage of Canadian-produced content. With new content provision models, will Canadian content disappear?

SECTION CHECK

- Monopoly results in smaller output and a higher price than would be the case under perfect competition. Since the monopolist produces at an output where $P > MC$, the value to society of the last unit produced is greater than its cost. In other words, the monopoly is not producing enough output from society's standpoint.
- Monopoly may lead to greater concentration of economic power and could hinder innovation.

Monopoly Policy

- What is the objective of anti-combine laws?
- What is government regulation?
- What is marginal cost pricing?
- What is average cost pricing?

Because monopolies pose certain problems with respect to efficiency, equity, and power, the public, through its governments, must decide how to deal with the monopoly phenomenon. Two major approaches to dealing with the monopoly problem are commonly used: anti-combine laws and government regulation. It should be pointed out that in these discussions, the word "monopoly" is sometimes used in a loose, general sense to refer to imperfectly competitive markets, not just to "pure" monopoly.

WHAT IS THE OBJECTIVE OF ANTI-COMBINE LAWS?

The rationale for anti-combine laws is to prevent monopoly, to promote competition, and to enhance economic efficiency. Canada's first anti-combine statute was passed in 1889. Around that time, monopolistic behaviour arose in a number of industries such as twine, sugar, and flour.

Canada's anti-combine laws are covered by the Competition Act of 1986. The act covers business practices that unduly prevent or lessen competition, and it differentiates between criminal and civil offences. Criminal offences are handled by the courts and the standard of evidence is "beyond a reasonable doubt." Penalties range from fines to possible imprisonment of guilty parties.

Criminal offences include conspiracy to fix prices, bid-rigging, and predatory pricing. Bid-rigging occurs when firms that bid on contracts arrange among themselves who will win each contract and at what price. Predatory pricing occurs when a firm temporarily reduces the price of its product below the product's average cost in order to drive the firm's competition out of business.

The federal Competition Bureau is responsible for the administration and enforcement of the Competition Act and other acts. The Bureau investigates complaints and decides whether to proceed with the filing of an application to the Competition Tribunal to hear a complaint. The Tribunal is a strictly adjudicative body that operates independently of any government department. The cases it hears are complex and deal with matters such as mergers (the combining of two organizations into one), misleading advertising, and restrictive trade practices.

If a merger would significantly reduce competition in an industry, the Competition Bureau has the power to stop the merger. On the other hand, if a merger would increase efficiency in an industry and consumers would benefit from the resulting lower prices, it could allow the merger. Abuse of a dominant market position occurs when a firm that controls most of the sales in a market uses its dominant position to engage in anticompetitive behaviour.

A number of high-profile cases have come under the Competition Act. For example, in September 2010, the Competition Bureau reached an agreement with The Coca-Cola Company regarding the acquisition of the North American business of its primary bottler, Coca-Cola Enterprises Inc. The Bureau concluded that the proposed acquisition likely would have lessened and/or prevented competition substantially in the supply of soft drinks in Canada. To satisfy the Competition Bureau's concerns, The Coca-Cola Company agreed to certain restrictions regarding commercially sensitive information and access to relevant personnel, with the Bureau appointing an independent monitor to ensure compliance.

In March 2013, the Competition Bureau reached an agreement with BCE Inc. (Bell) regarding Bell's proposed acquisition of Astral Media Inc. The Bureau concluded that Bell's acquisition of Astral's pay and specialty television channels would have likely resulted in higher prices, less innovation, and reduced choice in television programming. Bell was required to divest itself of Astral's ownership interests in a number of areas.

In December 2016, the Competition Bureau reached an agreement with pharmaceutical wholesaler McKesson Corporation related to its acquisition of pharmaceutical retailer Rexall Health. According to the Bureau, the proposed merger would likely result in a substantial lessening or prevention of competition in the wholesale and retail sale of certain pharmacy products and services, including prescription and over-the-counter pharmaceuticals. McKesson was required to sell Rexall retail pharmacies in 26 markets in British Columbia, Alberta, Saskatchewan, the Northwest Territories, and Ontario.

In February 2017, the Competition Bureau reached an agreement with BCE Inc. (Bell) and Xplornet Communications Inc. (Xplornet) related to Bell's acquisition of Manitoba Telecom Services (MTS). The Bureau determined that Bell's proposed merger with MTS would result in the removal of a strong regional competitor that was effective in constraining the pricing of Bell, Rogers, and TELUS products, and would likely result in a substantial lessening or prevention of competition for retail wireless services in Manitoba. This would likely lead to higher prices and fewer options for Manitobans. Bell was required to divest itself of certain retail assets and subscribers, thus creating a new wireless service provider, Xplornet. In addition to this, Bell has committed to selling a significant number of its MTS subscribers' contracts and approximately one-third of its MTS dealer locations to TELUS.*

WHAT IS GOVERNMENT REGULATION?

Government regulation is an alternative approach to dealing with monopolies. Under regulation, a company would not be allowed to charge any price it wants. Suppose the government does not want to break up a natural monopoly in the water or the power industry. Remember that natural monopolies occur when one large firm can produce as much output as many smaller firms but at a lower average cost per unit. The government may decide to regulate the monopoly price, but what price does it let the firm charge? The goal is to achieve the efficiency of large-scale production without permitting the high monopoly prices and low output that can promote allocative *inefficiency*.

The basic policy dilemma that regulators often face in attempting to fix maximum prices can be rather easily illustrated. Consider Exhibit 1. Without regulation, say the profit-maximizing monopolist operates at point A, at output Q_M, and price P_M. At that output, the price exceeds the average total cost, so economic profits exist. However, the monopolist is producing relatively little output and is charging a relatively high price, and it is producing at a point where price is above marginal cost. This is not the best point from society's perspective.

---

*Competition Bureau Rulings (Consent Agreements), http://www.competitionbureau.gc.ca/eic/site/cb-bc.nsf/eng/04337. html.

section 9.5
Exhibit 1   **Marginal Cost Pricing vs. Average Cost Pricing**

The marginal cost (*MC*) curve is less than the average total cost curve (*ATC*) for a natural monopolist as the average cost falls. If the monopolist is unregulated, it could produce a relatively small level of output, Q_M, at a relatively high price, P_M. If regulators require the natural monopolist to use marginal cost pricing, the monopoly will lose money, because P_{MC} is less than average total costs. Average cost pricing (at point B) would permit firms to make a normal rate of return, where $P_{AC} = ATC$. The monopolist's unregulated output at point A is not optimal from society's standpoint, and the optimal output at point C is not feasible.

WHAT IS MARGINAL COST PRICING?

From society's point of view, what would be the best price and output position? As we discussed in Chapter 8, the best position is at the competitive equilibrium output where $P = MC$, because the equilibrium price represents the marginal value of output. The marginal cost represents society's opportunity costs in making the good as opposed to something else. Where price equals marginal cost, *allocative efficiency* is achieved; that is, society matches marginal value and marginal cost. This is seen at point C in Exhibit 1. The decision to set production where the price of a good equals marginal cost is referred to as **marginal cost pricing**.

marginal cost pricing
the decision to set production where the price of a good equals marginal cost

Operation of the Regulated Monopolist

Unfortunately, the natural monopoly cannot operate profitably at the allocative efficient point, where $P = MC$, indicated at point C in Exhibit 1. At point C, the intersection of the demand and marginal cost curves, average total costs are greater than price. The optimal output, then, is an output that produces losses for the producer. Any regulated business that produced for long at this "optimal" output would go bankrupt; it would be impossible to attract new capital to the industry.

Therefore, the "optimal" output from a welfare perspective really is not viable because losses are incurred. The regulators cannot force firms to price their product at P_{MC} and to sell Q_{MC} output because the firm would go out of business. Indeed, in the long run, the industry's capital would deteriorate as investors failed to replace old capital when it became worn out or obsolete. If the monopolist's unregulated output at point A is not optimal from society's standpoint, and the short-run optimal output at point C is not feasible from the monopolist's standpoint, where should the regulated monopolist be allowed to operate?

One option to solving the problem is that the government could subsidize the losses associated with marginal cost pricing. However, the burden will ultimately fall on the taxpayers, as the government will have to raise the money to pay for the losses.

WHAT IS AVERAGE COST PRICING?

A compromise between monopoly pricing and marginal cost pricing is found at point B in Exhibit 1, output Q_{AC}, which is somewhere between the excessively low output and high prices of an unregulated monopoly and the excessively large output and low prices achieved when prices are equated with marginal cost pricing. At point B, price equals average total costs, a compromise called **average cost pricing**. The monopolist is permitted to price the product where economic profits are zero, meaning that there is a normal economic profit or rate of return, like firms experience in perfect competition in the long run.

average cost pricing
production where the price of a good equals average total cost

In the real world, regulators often permit utilities to receive a "fair and reasonable" return that is a rough approximation to that suggested by average cost pricing, at point B. Point B would seem "fair" in that the monopolist is receiving rewards equal to those that a perfect competitor would ordinarily receive—no more and no less. Point B permits more output at a significantly lower price than would occur if the monopolist was unregulated, point A, even though output is still somewhat less and price somewhat more than that suggested by point C, the social optimum or best position.

Difficulties in Average Cost Pricing

Accurate Calculations of Costs   The actual implementation of a rate (price) that permits a "fair and reasonable" return is more difficult than the analysis suggests. The calculations of costs and values are difficult. In reality, the firm may not know exactly what its demand and cost curves look like. This forces regulatory agencies to use profits, another somewhat ambiguous target, as a guide. If profits are "too high," lower the price, and if profits are "too low," raise the price.

No Incentives to Keep Costs Down   Another problem is that average cost pricing gives the monopolists no incentive to reduce costs. That is, if the firm's costs rise from ATC_0 to ATC_1 in Exhibit 2, the price will rise from P_0 to P_1. And if costs fall, the firm's price will fall. In either scenario, the firm will still be earning a normal rate of return. This is equivalent to saying that if the regulatory agency sets the price at any point where the ATC curve intersects the demand curve, the firm will earn a normal rate of return. So if the agency is going to set the price wherever ATC intersects the demand curve, why not let your average costs rise? Let your employees fly first class and dine in the finest restaurants. While you are at it, why not buy concert tickets and season tickets to sporting events? And if the regulated monopolist knows that the regulators will reduce prices if costs fall, the regulated monopolist does not benefit from lower costs. Regulators have tackled this problem by allowing the regulated firm to keep some of the profits that come from lower costs; that is, they do not adhere strictly to average cost pricing.

Special Interest Groups   In the real world, consumer groups are constantly battling for lower rates, while the utilities themselves are lobbying for higher rates so that they can approach the monopoly profits indicated by point A in Exhibit 1. Decisions are not always made in a calm, objective, dispassionate atmosphere, free of outside involvement. It is precisely the political economy of rate setting that disturbs some critics of this approach to dealing with the monopoly problem. For example, it is possible that a rate-making commissioner could become friendly with a utility company, believing that he can obtain a nice job after his tenure as a regulator is over. The temptation is great for the commissioner to be generous to the utilities. On the other hand, there may be a tendency for regulators to bow to pressure from consumer groups.

section 9.5
Exhibit 2

Changes in Average Costs

An increase in average total costs leads to a higher price and lower output (P_1, Q_1); lower average total costs lead to a lower price and greater output (P_0, Q_0). However, both situations lead to a normal rate of return. Because the regulated firm has little incentive to minimize costs, average total costs would have a tendency to rise.

A politician who wants to win votes can almost always succeed by attacking utility rates and promising rate "reform" (lower rates). If zealous rate regulators listen too closely to the consumer groups and push rates down to a level indicated by point C in Exhibit 1, the industry might be too unstable to attract capital for expansion.

A review of government behaviour in this case would reveal a trend away from regulation toward competition; for example, between 1980 and 1997, the federal government fully deregulated the telecommunications industry, ending Bell Canada's monopoly. Similar instances of deregulation have also occurred in the transportation industry and natural gas market. Technological advances now allow us to separate the production of electric power and natural gas from the distributor, which will ultimately lead to greater competition in these markets.

SECTION CHECK

- Anti-combine laws are designed to reduce the abuses of monopoly power and push production closer to the social optimum.
- Privately owned monopolies may be allowed to operate but under regulation of a government agency.
- Marginal cost pricing sets price equal to marginal cost, where demand intersects marginal cost. This regulation achieves allocative efficiency.
- Average cost pricing sets price equal to average total cost, where the demand curve intersects average total costs.

section 9.6

Price Discrimination

- What is price discrimination?
- Why does price discrimination exist?
- Does price discrimination lead to higher profits?

WHAT IS PRICE DISCRIMINATION?

price discrimination
the practice of charging different consumers different prices for the same good or service when the cost of providing that good or service is not different for different consumers

Price discrimination is the practice of charging different customers different prices for the same good or service when the cost of providing that good or service does not differ among the customers. For example, kids pay less for the movies than adults; senior citizens get discounts on hotels, restaurants, museums, and zoos; and most vacation travellers fly between places for less than business travellers. Under certain conditions, the monopolist finds it profitable to discriminate among various buyers, charging higher prices to those who are more willing to pay and lower prices to those who are less willing to pay.

Conditions for Price Discrimination

The ability to practise price discrimination is not available to all sellers. In order to practise price discrimination, the following three conditions must hold:

Monopoly Power. Price discrimination is possible only with monopoly or where members of a small group of firms (firms that are not price takers) follow identical pricing policies. When there is a large number of competing firms, discrimination is less likely because competitors tend to undercut the high prices charged by the firms that are engaging in price discrimination.

Market Segregation. Price discrimination can occur only if the demand curves for markets, groups, or individuals are different. If the demand curves are not different, a profit-maximizing monopolist would charge the same price in both markets. In short, price discrimination requires the ability to separate customers according to their willingness to pay.

No Resale. For price discrimination to work, the person buying at a discount must have difficulty in reselling the product to customers being charged more. Otherwise, those getting the items cheaply would want to buy extra amounts of the product at the discounted price and sell it at a profit to others. Price differentials between groups erode if reselling is easy.

WHY DOES PRICE DISCRIMINATION EXIST?

Price discrimination results from the profit-maximization motive. In our graphical analysis of monopoly, we suggested that there was a demand curve for the product and a corresponding marginal revenue curve. Sometimes, however, different groups of people have different demand curves and therefore react differently to price changes. A seller can make more money by charging those different buyers different prices. For example, if the price of a movie is increased from $7 to $10, many kids who would attend at $7 may have to stay home at $10, as they (and perhaps their parents) balk at paying the higher price. The impact on attendance of raising prices may be less, however, for adults, for whom the ticket price may represent a smaller part of the expenses of an evening out.

Thus, there is a different demand curve for those, say, under 16, as opposed to those who are older. Specifically, the elasticity of demand with respect to price is greater for children than for adults. This means that there is a different marginal revenue curve for children than for adults. Assume, for simplicity, that the marginal cost is constant. The profit-maximizing movie-theatre owner will price where the constant marginal costs equal marginal revenue for each group. As you can see in Exhibit 1(a), the demand curve for kids is rather elastic. The adult demand curve, shown in Exhibit 1(b), is more downward sloping at any given price and quantity (relatively inelastic), meaning the marginal revenue curve lies well below the demand curve at most output levels. Thus, the price charged adults is far above the point where marginal revenue equals marginal costs, whereas for kids, the price is not as much above the point where marginal revenue equals marginal costs.

Examples of Price Discrimination

There are other examples of price discrimination in Canada. The following are just a few.

Airline Tickets Seats on airplanes usually go for different prices. There are the high-prices, no-strings-attached fares and there are restricted fares—tickets that require Saturday-night layovers or must be purchased weeks in advance. This airline pricing strategy allows the airlines to discriminate against business travellers, who usually have little advance warning, travel on weekdays, and are not as willing to spend their weekends away from home and family. Because business travellers have a high willingness to pay (a relatively inelastic demand curve), airlines can charge them higher prices. If airlines were to cut prices for these clients, their revenues would fall. On the other hand, the personal traveller (perhaps a vacationer) can choose among many substitutes, such as other modes of transportation and different times. In short, the personal

---

traveller has a lower willingness to pay (a relatively elastic demand curve). Thus, the airlines can clearly make more money by charging a higher price to those who have a higher willingness to pay (less elastic demand) and a lower price to those who have a lower willingness to pay (more elastic demand)—those who are willing to book in advance and stay over on Saturday nights. If airlines charged a higher single price to everyone, those with a lower willingness to pay would not travel; if they charged a lower single price to everyone, they would lose profits by receiving less revenue from those who are willing to pay more.

High-Speed Internet   The key to price discrimination is observing the difference in demand curves for different customers. The business customer, who considers high-speed Internet an essential component of running a business, will probably have a relatively less elastic demand curve than, say, a personal customer who uses the Internet for social networking and entertainment. Consequently, telecommunication providers charge a higher price to business customers, who have a higher willingness to pay (less elastic demand)—and a lower price to those who access the Internet only for personal use (more elastic demand).

Quantity Discounts

Another form of price discrimination occurs when customers buy in large quantities. This is often the case with public utilities and wholesalers, but even stores will sell a six-pack of soft drinks for less than six single cans. Or the local bagel shop might sell you a baker's dozen, where you may get 13 bagels for the price of 12. This type of price discrimination allows the producer to charge a higher price for the first unit than for, say, the twentieth unit. This form of price discrimination is effective because a buyer's willingness to pay declines as additional units are purchased.

DOES PRICE DISCRIMINATION LEAD TO HIGHER PROFITS?

In our earlier discussion of monopoly behaviour (Section 9.3, Exhibit 2), the monopolist charged a single price of $6 and earned an economic profit of $200. In this section, let's examine the impact on economic profits of another monopolist that is able to price-discriminate.

The impact of price discrimination on economic profit for a single price monopolist and a perfect price-discriminating monopolist is provided in Exhibit 2 in this section. Looking at Exhibit 2(a), we see the demand (quantity and price per unit), total revenue, total cost, and total profit for a monopolist that is not price-discriminating. Recall that in order for this monopolist to sell additional units of output, it must first lower the price. The impact of this reality on total revenue (*TR*) (column 2, part [a]) is that, when the monopolist charges $4 per unit and sells two units, since $TR = P \times Q$, it earns $8 total revenue ($4 \times 2 = $8). A review of the total profit (column 5, part [a]) will reveal that our profit-maximizing monopolist will earn an economic profit of $3 by selling two units of output at $4 per unit.

In Exhibit 2(b) we see the demand (quantity and price per unit), total revenue, total cost, and total profit for a monopolist that is able to perfectly price-discriminate—that is, this monopolist is able to charge a different price for each unit of output. Being able to achieve perfect price discrimination means that this monopolist is able to sell the first unit for $5, the second unit for $4, the third unit for $3, and so on.

The impact of this reality on total revenue (column 3, part [b]) is that, should our price-discriminating monopolist sell three units, total revenue would be $12–the sum of all of the prices charged for the first three units sold ($5 + $4 + $3 = $12). With

section 9.6 Exhibit 2	Profit Maximization for Nonprice-Discriminating and Price-Discriminating Monopolists

a. Nonprice-Discriminating Monopolist

(1) Output (Q)	(2) Price (P)	(3) Total Revenue (TR)	(4) Total Cost (TC)	(5) Total Profit
0	$6	$0	$2	−$2
1	5	5	3	2
2	4	8	5	3
3	3	9	8	1
4	2	8	12	−4
5	1	5	17	−12
6	0	0	23	−23

b. Price-Discriminating Monopolist

(1) Output (Q)	(2) Price (P)	(3) Total Revenue (TR)	(4) Total Cost (TC)	(5) Total Profit
0	$6	$0	$2	−$2
1	5	5	3	2
2	4	9	5	4
3	3	12	8	4
4	2	14	12	2
5	1	15	17	−2
6	0	15	23	−8

total costs (column 4, part [b]) remaining the same, a review of total profit (column 5, part [b]) will reveal that our profit-maximizing (price-discriminating) monopolist will earn a greater amount of economic profit, $4, by selling a greater amount of output, three units.

SECTION CHECK

- When producers charge different prices for the same good or service when no cost differences exist, it is called *price discrimination*.
- Price discrimination is a result of the profit-maximization motive. If different groups have different demand curves for a good or service, a seller can make more money by charging these different buyers different prices.
- A monopolist that can perfectly price-discriminate will produce a greater amount of output and earn a greater amount of economic profit when compared to a monopolist that charges a single monopoly price.

For Your Review

Section 9.1

1. Which of the following could be considered a monopoly?
   a. Kate Hudson (an actress)
   b. BC Hydro
   c. the only doctor in a small town
   d. Ford Motor Company

2. Barriers to entry are important in the creation of monopolies because they keep competitors out of the industry. Although many types of barriers exist, historically, ownership of an essential resource, government patents and licences, and large entry costs have served as the primary barriers to entry. For each of the following cases, indicate which type of barrier created the monopoly.
   a. In the 1940s, the Aluminum Company of America owned all of the world's known bauxite deposits.
   b. A local cable TV company had the only government-issued licence to supply services in the area.
   c. The pharmaceutical company, MAXCO, invented and patented a new hair-growth drug.
   d. In the 1960s, Bell Canada provided long-distance telephone service by stringing millions of kilometres of copper wiring across Canada.

3. Evaluate the following statement regarding monopoly behaviour: "Since a monopoly firm is a *price maker*, it can charge whatever price it wants for whatever quantity it wants to sell."

4. Is it optimal for a monopolist to operate on the inelastic portion of the demand curve? Why or why not?

Section 9.2

5. Fill in the missing data for a monopolist in the following table.

Quantity	Price	Total Revenue	Marginal Revenue	Demand Elastic or Inelastic
1	$11			
2	10			
3	9			
4	8			
5	7			
6	6			
7	5			
8	4			
9	3			
10	2			
11	1			

6. Assume that the monopolist in problem 5 had fixed costs of $10 and a constant marginal cost of $4 per unit. In the following table, insert the relevant data in the columns for total cost, marginal cost, and profit.

Quantity	Price	Total Revenue	Marginal Revenue	Demand Elastic or Inelastic	Total Cost	Marginal Cost	Profit
1	$11						
2	10						
3	9						
4	8						
5	7						
6	6						
7	5						
8	4						
9	3						
10	2						
11	1						

7. Suppose Star Phone Company served remote northern Ontario as a government-authorized natural monopoly. The following table describes a portion of the demand curve for long-distance service facing Star Phone Company.

a. Complete the table.

Star Phone Company Demand for Phone Hours				
Quantity	Price	Total Revenue	Marginal Revenue	Elastic or Inelastic?
30	$3.65			
31	3.58			
32	3.51			
33	3.44			
34	3.37			
35	3.30			
36	3.22			
37	3.14			
38	3.06			
39	2.98			
40	2.90			
41	2.82			
42	2.74			
43	2.66			
44	2.58			
45	2.50			
46	2.42			
47	2.34			
48	2.25			
49	2.15			
50	2.04			

b. How does the company's marginal revenue change as the price changes? What is the relationship between marginal revenue and price?

c. At what price does demand become inelastic?

d. What will happen to the elasticity of demand when a new company, NorOnt Phones, starts a competing wireless phone company?

8. The following table shows the demand for water and cost conditions for the New South Springdale Water Utility, a pure monopoly.

   a. Complete the table.

Quantity (litres)	Price (per litre)	Total Revenue	Marginal Revenue	Marginal Costs	Average Total Costs	Profit
100	$1.28			$0.15	$1.252	
101	1.27			0.18	1.241	
102	1.26			0.21	1.231	
103	1.25			0.23	1.221	
104	1.24			0.26	1.212	

   b. What is true about the relationship between marginal revenue and marginal costs when profit is the greatest?

   c. Suppose the government imposed a tax of $103 on the firm that the firm had to pay even if it went out of business. What would be the profit-maximizing level of output? What would happen to profits? Would the firm stay in business?

9. Using the concepts of total revenue and marginal revenue, show why marginal revenue is less than price in a monopoly situation. Suppose a monopolist wants to expand output from one unit to two units. In order to sell two units rather than one, the monopolist must lower its price from $10 to $8—see the table below. Will the marginal revenue be less than the price?

Price	Quantity	Total Revenue	Marginal Revenue
$10	1	$10	
8	2	16	$6
6	3	18	2

Blueprint Problem

Suppose the following table describes revenue and cost of production figures for the monopoly firm Carl's Calculators.

Output	Price	TVC	TFC	TC	AVC	AFC	ATC	MC
0	45	$0.00	$40.00	$40.00	—	—	—	—
1	40	$10.00	$40.00	$50.00	$10.00	$40.00	$50.00	$10.00
2	35	$16.00	$40.00	$56.00	$8.00	$20.00	$28.00	$6.00
3	30	$20.00	$40.00	$60.00	$6.67	$13.33	$20.00	$4.00
4	25	$29.00	$40.00	$69.00	$7.25	$10.00	$17.25	$9.00
5	20	$44.00	$40.00	$84.00	$8.80	$8.00	$16.80	$15.00
6	15	$66.00	$40.00	$106.00	$11.00	$6.67	$17.67	$22.00
7	10	$104.00	$40.00	$144.00	$14.86	$5.71	$20.57	$38.00

   a. Determine Carl's profit-maximizing output using the total approach.

   b. Determine Carl's profit-maximizing output using the marginal approach. Use the four-step method and describe each step.

Blueprint Solution

a.

> Given that Carl must lower the price in order to sell more calculators, total revenue (*TR*) can be determined.
> $TR = P \times q$

Output	Price	TR	TC	Total Profit
0	$45.00	$0.00	$40.00	−$40.00
1	$40.00	$40.00	$50.00	−$10.00
2	$35.00	$70.00	$56.00	$14.00
3	$30.00	$90.00	$60.00	$30.00
4	$25.00	$100.00	$69.00	$31.00
5	$20.00	$100.00	$84.00	$16.00
6	$15.00	$90.00	$106.00	−$16.00
7	$10.00	$70.00	$144.00	−$74.00

> By determining total profit (*TR − TC*), the total approach reveals that *Q** is 4 calculators

b.

> $$MR = \frac{\Delta TR}{\Delta Q}$$

Output	Price	TR	MR	MC	Interpretation
0	$45.00	0	—	—	
1	$40.00	$40.00	$40.00	$10.00	Produce
2	$35.00	$70.00	$30.00	$6.00	Produce
3	$30.00	$90.00	$20.00	$4.00	Produce
4	$25.00	$100.00	$10.00	$9.00	Produce
5	$20.00	$100.00	$0.00	$15.00	Do not produce
6	$15.00	$90.00	-$10.00	$22.00	Do not produce
7	$10.00	$70.00	-$20.00	$38.00	Do not produce

> Being a rational decision maker, Carl will produce only the number of calculators that will give him positive net benefit (*MR > MC*). This rational decision rule will lead Carl to produce a total of 4 calculators.

Step 1: $MR = MC$ at 4 calculators (actually in this example, *MR* is as close to *MC* without exceeding it)

Step 2: $TR = P^* \times q^* = \$25 \times 4 = \$100$

Step 3: $TC = ATC_{q^*} \times q^* = \$17.25 \times 4 = \$69$

Step 4: Total profit $= TR - TC = \$100 - \$69 = \$31$

Section 9.3

10. Use the following diagram to answer questions (a) through (c).

   a. Assuming the monopolist indicated in the diagram produced at all, indicate its profit-maximizing quantity and price.

   b. Add an *ATC* curve that would show this monopolist earning an economic profit.

   c. Add an *ATC* curve that would show this monopolist experiencing an economic loss.

11. If economic profits were zero, would a monopolist ever stay in business? Why might it be possible for a monopolist to earn positive economic profits in the long run?

12. Consider the data in the following table.

Price	Quantity	Fixed Cost	Variable Cost
$100	0	$60	$ 0
90	1	60	25
80	2	60	40
70	3	60	50
60	4	60	70
50	5	60	100
40	6	60	140
30	7	60	190
20	8	60	250

   A simple monopolist with these fixed and variable cost schedules maximizes profits at what level of output?

13. Given the data in the following table, determine the short-run profit-maximizing (loss-minimizing) level of output and price for the monopolist. Fixed cost equals $10.

Quantity	Price	Total Cost
4	$35	$ 20
5	30	30
6	25	45
7	20	65
8	15	100

Section 9.4

14. What does the welfare cost of monopoly represent? How is it measured?

15. Consider the following graph for a monopolist.

a. At its profit-maximizing price and quantity, how much of a profit or loss is this monopolist realizing?

b. At its profit-maximizing level of output, is this monopolist productively efficient? Explain.

c. At its profit-maximizing level of output, is this monopolist allocatively efficient? Explain.

16. Governments around the world are allowing competition in the production of goods and services that have historically been considered natural monopolies, such as provision of local telephone service and electricity. Why might the introduction of competition increase the efficiency of these industries?

Section 9.5

17. Use the accompanying diagram to answer questions (a) through (c).

a. Indicate the efficient result on the graph.

b. Illustrate the profits or losses from the efficient result in (a).

c. Show the average cost-pricing solution. What profits are earned with that approach?

18. Suppose an industry experiences decreasing average costs of production over the relevant range of market demand. Discuss the merits of a regulation requiring the natural monopolist to set a price to service all willing customers where demand equals marginal cost. What about where demand equals average cost? Are any practical difficulties likely to be encountered with either regulatory program?

Section 9.6

19. Explain how each of the following is a form of price discrimination.
    a. a student discount at the movie theatre
    b. long-distance telephone service that costs 15 cents per minute for the first 10 minutes and 5 cents per minute after 10 minutes
    c. a senior citizen's dinner discount at a local restaurant
    d. coupon discounts on laundry detergent

20. In October of 1999, Coca-Cola announced that it was considering testing a new vending machine that was temperature-sensitive. The price of the soft drinks in the machines would be higher on hot days. The *Miami Herald* story read "Soda jerks." How is this practice a form of price discrimination? How can the placement of the vending machines create a monopoly? What if other vending machines are close by and are not owned by Coca-Cola?

21. Does the price schedule below reflect price discrimination? Why or why not?

Super Duper Cuts Hair Salon	
Permanent Price for Haircuts	
Long hair	$100
Short hair	75

22. Explain why a computer store offering significant student discounts may require student buyers to sign an agreement not to purchase another computer from the store for a period of six months.

23. Why do business travellers generally pay more for their flights than vacation travellers?

24. Tara loves to go through the Saturday paper and cut out supermarket coupons. How do you think Tara's coupon-clipping habits apply to the concept of price discrimination?

25. What is meant by the "welfare loss" of monopoly? Why does no welfare loss occur if a monopolist successfully practises perfect price discrimination?

chapter

10

Monopolistic Competition and Oligopoly

section 10.1

Monopolistic Competition

- What is monopolistic competition?
- What are the three basic characteristics of monopolistic competition?

WHAT IS MONOPOLISTIC COMPETITION?

monopolistic competition
a market structure with many firms selling differentiated products

Monopolistic competition is a market structure with many firms selling differentiated products. For example, a restaurant is a monopoly in the sense that it has a unique name, menu, quality of service, location, and so on, but it also has many competitors—others selling prepared meals. That is, monopolistic competition has features in common with both monopoly and perfect competition, even though this may sound like an oxymoron—like "jumbo shrimp" or "press release." As with monopoly, individual sellers in monopolistic competition believe that they have some market power. But monopolistic competition is probably closer to competition than monopoly. Entry into and exit out of the industry is unrestricted, and consequently, there are many independent sellers. In virtue of the relatively free entry of new firms, the long-run price and output behaviour, and zero long-run economic profits, monopolistic competition is similar to perfect competition. However, the monopolistically competitive firm produces a product that is different (i.e., *differentiated* rather than identical or homogeneous) from others, which leads to some degree of monopoly power. In a sense, sellers in a monopolistically competitive market may be regarded as "monopolists" of their own particular brands; however, unlike firms with a true monopoly, there is competition among many firms selling similar (but not identical) brands. Examples of monopolistically competitive markets include retail clothing, real estate, furniture, health and personal care, restaurant meals, running shoes, and music lessons.

WHAT ARE THE THREE BASIC CHARACTERISTICS OF MONOPOLISTIC COMPETITION?

The theory of monopolistic competition is based on three characteristics: (1) many sellers, (2) product differentiation, and (3) free entry.

Many Sellers

When many firms compete for the same customers, any particular firm has little control over or interest in what other firms do. That is, a restaurant may change prices or improve service without a retaliatory move on the part of other competing restaurants because the time and effort necessary to learn about such changes may have marginal costs that are greater than the marginal benefits.

Product Differentiation

Another characteristic of monopolistic competition is **product differentiation**—the accentuation of unique product qualities, real or perceived, to develop a specific product identity.

The significant feature of differentiation is the buyer's belief that various sellers' products are not the same, whether the products are actually different or not. Headache remedies and some brands of over-the-counter cold medicines are examples of products that are very similar or identical but have different brand names. Product differentiation leads to preferences among buyers dealing with or purchasing the products of particular sellers.

Physical Differences   Physical differences constitute a primary source of product differentiation. For example, brands of ice cream (such as Chapmans and Breyers) or fast-food restaurants (such as Wendy's and Burger King) differ significantly in taste to many buyers.

Prestige   Prestige considerations also differentiate products to a significant degree. Many people prefer to be seen using the currently popular brand, whereas others prefer the "off" brand. Prestige considerations are particularly important with gifts—Godiva chocolates, Rolex watches, and so on.

Location   Location is a major differentiating factor in retailing. Shoppers are not willing to travel long distances to purchase similar items, which is one reason for the large number of convenience stores and service station mini-marts. Because most buyers realize there are no significant differences among brands of gasoline, the location of a gas station might influence their choice of gasoline.

Service   Service considerations are also significant for product differentiation. Speedy and friendly service and lenient return policies are important to many people.

Restaurants can be very different. A restaurant that sells pizza competes with other Italian restaurants, but it also competes with restaurants that sell burgers and fries. Monopolistic competition has some elements of competition (many sellers) and some elements of monopoly power (differentiated products).

product differentiation
the accentuation of unique product qualities, real or perceived, to develop a specific product identity

Fast, warranty-approved automotive maintenance, all without an appointment, might differentiate one vehicle service depot from others.

Likewise, speed and quality of service may significantly influence a person's choice of where to take their car for scheduled maintenance.

Free Entry

Entry in monopolistic competition is relatively unrestricted in the sense that new firms may easily start the production of close substitutes for existing products; this is the case for restaurants, lawn care services, barbershops, and many forms of retail activity. Because of relatively free entry, economic profits tend to be eliminated in the long run, as is the case with perfect competition.

SECTION CHECK

- *Monopolistic competition* describes a market structure where many producers of somewhat different products compete with one another.
- The theory of monopolistic competition is based on three primary characteristics: many sellers, product differentiation, and free entry.

---

section 10.2

Price and Output Determination in Monopolistic Competition

- How is short-run equilibrium determined?
- How is long-run equilibrium determined?

HOW IS SHORT-RUN EQUILIBRIUM DETERMINED?

Because monopolistically competitive sellers are price makers rather than price takers, they do not regard price as given by market conditions as do perfectly competitive firms.

Because each firm sells a slightly different product for which there are many close substitutes, the firm's demand curve is downward sloping but quite flat (elastic). In perfect competition, the demand curve is horizontal because each firm, one of a great many sellers, sells the same homogeneous product. Given the position of an individual firm's demand curve, we can determine short-run equilibrium output and price by using a method similar to that used to determine monopoly output and price.

The cost and revenue curves of a typical seller are shown in Exhibit 1; the intersection of the marginal revenue and marginal cost curves indicates that the short-run profit-maximizing output will be q^*. By observing how much will be demanded at that output level, we find the profit-maximizing price, P^*. That is, at the equilibrium quantity, q^*, we go vertically to the demand curve and read the corresponding price on the vertical axis, P^*, just as we did for monopoly.

section 10.2
Exhibit 1

Short-Run Equilibrium in Monopolistic Competition

a. Determining Profits

b. Determining Losses

In Exhibit 1(a), the firm is making short-run economic profits because the firm's total revenue ($P^* \times q^* = \$800$) at output q^* is greater than the firm's total cost ($ATC \times q^* = \$700$). Because the firm's total revenue is greater than total cost, the firm has a total profit of \$100: $TR - TC = \$800 - \$700$. In Exhibit 1(b), the firm is incurring a short-run economic loss because at q^*, price is below average total cost. At q^*, total cost ($ATC \times q^* = \$800$) is greater than total ($P^* \times q^* = \$700$) revenue, so the firm incurs a total loss ($TR - TC = \$700 - \$800 = -\$100$).

Four-Step Method for Monopolistic Competition

Let us return to the same four-step method we used in Chapters 8 and 9. Determining whether a firm is generating economic profits, economic losses, or zero economic profits at the profit-maximizing level of output, q^*, can be done in four easy steps:

1. The first step is to find the profit-maximizing level of output (q^*). To do this, find where marginal revenues equal marginal costs and proceed straight down to the horizontal "Quantity" axis to find the profit-maximizing output level.

2. The second step is to determine the total revenue (TR) being generated at q^*. To do this, go straight up from q^* to the demand curve and then to the left to find the market price, P^*. Once you have identified P^* and q^*, you can find total revenue at the profit-maximizing output level, because $TR = P \times q$.

3. The third step is to find total costs (TC) at q^*. Again, go straight up from q^* to the average total cost (ATC) curve and then left to the vertical axis to compute the average total cost *per unit*. If we multiply average total costs by the output level, we can find the total costs ($TC = ATC \times q$).

4. The final step is to determine the amount of either profit or loss at q^*. If total revenue (from step 2) is greater than total costs (from step 3) at q^*, the firm is generating economic profits. If total revenue is less than total costs at q^*, the firm is generating economic losses. If total revenue is equal to total cost at q^*, there are zero economic profits (or a normal rate of return). Alternatively, to find total economic profits, we can take the product price at P^* and subtract the average total cost at q^*. This will give us per-unit profit. If we multiply this by output, we will arrive at total economic profit: $(P^* - ATC) \times q^* =$ Total economic profit.

Remember, the cost curves include implicit and explicit costs—that is, even at zero economic profits, the firm is covering the total opportunity costs of its resources and earning a normal profit or rate of return.

Short-Run Profits and Losses in Monopolistic Competition

Exhibit 1(a) shows the equilibrium position of a monopolistically competitive firm. As we just discussed, the firm produces where $MC = MR$, or output q^*. At output q^* and price P^*, the firm's total revenue is equal to $P^* \times q^*$, or \$800. At output q^*, the firm's total cost is $ATC \times q^*$, or \$700. In Exhibit 1(a), we see that total revenue is greater than total cost so the firm has a total economic profit. That is, TR (\$800) $- TC$ (\$700) $=$ Total economic profit (\$100) or P^*(\$8) $- ATC$ (\$7) $\times q^*$(100) $=$ \$100.

In Exhibit 1(b), at q^*, price is below average total cost, so the firm is minimizing its economic loss. At q^*, total cost (\$800) is greater than total revenue (\$700). So the firm incurs a total loss (\$100) or P^*(\$7) $- ATC$ (\$8) $\times q^*$(100) $=$ Total economic loss ($-$\$100).

HOW IS LONG-RUN EQUILIBRIUM DETERMINED?

The short-run equilibrium situation depicted in Exhibit 1, whether involving profits or losses, will probably not last long, because there is entry and exit in the long run. If market entry and exit are sufficiently free, new firms will enter when there are economic profits, and some firms will exit when there are economic losses.

Economic Profits when Firms Enter the Industry

In Exhibit 2(a), we see the market impact as new firms enter to take advantage of the economic profits. The result of this influx is more sellers of similar products, which means that each new firm will cut into the demand of existing firms. That is, the demand curve for each existing firm will fall. With entry, not only will the firm's demand curve move inward but it also will become relatively more elastic due to each firm's product having more substitutes (more choices for consumers). We see this situation in Exhibit 2(a) when demand shifts leftward from D_{SR} to D_{LR}. This decline in demand continues to occur until the average total cost (ATC) curve becomes tangent with the demand curve, and economic profits are reduced to zero.

section 10.2	
Exhibit 2	**Achieving Long-Run Equilibrium**

a. Firms Enter the Market

Price

MC
ATC
$P_{LR} = ATC$
MR_{LR}
D_{SR}
D_{LR}
0
q^*
Quantity

b. Firms Exit the Market

Price

MC
ATC
$P_{LR} = ATC$
D_{LR}
D_{SR}
MR_{LR}
0
q^*
Quantity

In Exhibit 2(a), excess profits attract new firms into the industry. As a result, the firm's share of the market declines and demand shifts down. Profits are eliminated when $P_{LR} = ATC$, that is, when the ATC curve is tangent to D_{LR}. In Exhibit 2(b), some firms exit because of economic losses. Their exit increases the demand for existing firms, shifting D_{SR} to D_{LR}, where all losses have been eliminated.

Economic Losses when Firms Exit the Industry

When firms are making economic losses, some firms will exit the industry. As some firms exit, it means fewer firms in the market, which increases the demand for the remaining firms' product, shifting their demand curves to the right, from D_{SR} to D_{LR} as seen in Exhibit 2(b). When firms exit, not only will the firm's demand curve move outward but it also will become relatively more inelastic due to each firm's products having fewer substitutes (fewer choices for consumers). The higher demand results in smaller losses for the existing firms until all losses finally disappear where the *ATC* curve is tangent to the demand curve.

Achieving Long-Run Equilibrium

The process of entry and exit will continue until all firms in the industry are making zero economic profits. When the market reaches this long-run equilibrium, no firms have an incentive to enter or exit.

section 10.2
Exhibit 3

Long-Run Equilibrium for a Monopolistically Competitive Firm

Long-run equilibrium occurs at q^*, where $D = ATC$ and $MR = MC$.

Once entry and exit have driven profits to zero, the demand curve and average total cost curve will be tangent to each other, as seen in Exhibit 3. At the profit-maximizing output level, the firm earns zero economic profits.

In short, the monopolistically competitive producers are a lot like monopolists; they face a downward-sloping demand curve and set marginal revenue to marginal cost to determine the profit-maximizing output level. However, the difference is that at this profit-maximizing level of output, the monopolistically competitive firm cannot make economic profits in the long run because the barriers to entry and exit in this market are assumed to be zero.

As a final note, complete adjustment toward equality of price with average cost may be checked by the strength of reputation built up by established firms. Those firms that are particularly successful in their selling efforts may create such strong consumer preferences that newcomers—even though they are able to enter the industry freely and cover their costs—will not take sufficient business away from the well-established firms to eliminate their excess profits. Thus, a restaurant that has been particularly successful in promoting customer goodwill may continue to earn excess profits long after the entry of new firms has brought about the equality of price and average costs. Adjustments toward a final equilibrium situation involving equality of price and average cost do not proceed with the certainty that is supposed to be characteristic of perfect competition.

SECTION CHECK

- In the short run, a monopolistically competitive firm achieves profit maximization at the intersection of the marginal revenue and marginal cost curves. A monopolistically competitive firm is making short-run economic profits when the equilibrium price is greater than average total costs at the equilibrium output; when equilibrium price is below average total cost at the equilibrium output, the firm is minimizing its economic losses.
- In the long run, equilibrium price equals average total costs. With that, economic profits are zero, so there are no incentives for firms to either enter or exit the industry.

Monopolistic Competition versus Perfect Competition

- What are the differences and similarities between monopolistic competition and perfect competition?
- What are the real costs of monopolistic competition?
- Are the differences between monopolistic competition and perfect competition exaggerated?

WHAT ARE THE DIFFERENCES AND SIMILARITIES BETWEEN MONOPOLISTIC COMPETITION AND PERFECT COMPETITION?

We have seen that both monopolistic competition and perfect competition have many buyers and sellers and relatively free entry. However, product differentiation enables a monopolistic competitor to have some influence over price. Consequently, a monopolistically competitive firm has a downward-sloping demand curve, but because of the large number of good substitutes for its product, the curve tends to be much more elastic than the demand curve for a monopolist.

Failing to Achieve Productive Efficiency

excess capacity
occurs when the firm produces below the level where average total cost is minimized

Because in monopolistic competition the demand curve is downward sloping, its point of tangency with the *ATC* curve will not and cannot be at the lowest level of average cost. What does this mean? It means that even when long-run adjustments are complete, firms are not operating at a level that permits the lowest average cost of production—the efficient scale of the firm. The existing plant, even though optimal for the equilibrium volume of output, is not used to capacity; that is, **excess capacity** exists at that level of output. Excess capacity occurs when the firm produces below the level where average total cost is minimized.

How much do you value variety in clothing? Imagine a world where everyone wore the same clothes, drove the same cars, and lived in identical houses. Most individuals are willing to pay for a little variety, even if it costs somewhat more.

Unlike a perfectly competitive firm, a monopolistically competitive firm could increase output and lower its average total cost, as shown in Exhibit 1(a). However, any attempt to increase output to attain lower average cost would be unprofitable because the price reduction necessary to sell the greater output would cause marginal revenue to fall below the marginal cost of the increased output. As we can see in Exhibit 1(a), to the right of q^*, marginal cost is greater than marginal revenue. Consequently, in monopolistic competition, there is a tendency toward too many firms in the industry, each producing a volume of output less than what would allow lowest cost. Economists call this tendency *a failure to reach productive efficiency*. For example, there may be too many grocery stores or too many service stations, in the sense that if the total volume of business was concentrated in a smaller number of sellers, average cost, and thus price, could in principle be less.

© iStockphoto.com/Judy Barranco

section 10.3 Exhibit 1	**Comparing Long-Run Perfect Competition and Monopolistic Competition**

Comparing the differences between perfect competition and monopolistic competition, we see that the monopolistically competitive firm fails to meet both productive efficiency, minimizing costs in the long run, and allocative efficiency, producing output where $P = MC$.

Also Failing to Meet Allocative Efficiency

Productive inefficiency is not the only problem with a monopolistically competitive firm. Exhibit 1(a) shows a firm that is not operating where price is equal to marginal costs. In the monopolistically competitive model, at the intersection of the MC and MR curves (q^*), we can clearly see that price is greater than marginal cost. This means that society is willing to pay more for the product (the price, P^*) than it costs society to produce it. In this case, the firm is failing to reach allocative efficiency, where price equals marginal cost. In short, this means that the firm is underallocating resources—too many firms are producing, each at output levels that are less than full capacity. Note that in Exhibit 1(b), the perfectly competitive firm has reached both productive efficiency ($P = ATC$ at the minimum point on the ATC curve) and allocative efficiency ($P = MC$). However, it is clear that these drawbacks in the monopolistically competitive market would be far greater in monopoly, where the demand curve is more inelastic (steeper).

Further, in defence of monopolistic competition, the higher average cost and the slightly higher price and lower output may simply be the price that firms pay for differentiated products—variety. That is, just because monopolistically competitive firms have not met the conditions for productive and allocative efficiency, it is not obvious that society is not better off.

WHAT ARE THE REAL COSTS OF MONOPOLISTIC COMPETITION?

We have just argued that perfect competition meets the tests of allocative and productive efficiency and that monopolistic competition does not. Can we "fix" a monopolistically competitive firm to look more like an efficient, perfectly competitive firm? One remedy might entail using government regulation, as in the case of a natural monopoly. However, this process would be costly because a monopolistically competitive firm makes no economic profits in the long run. Therefore, asking monopolistically competitive firms to equate price and marginal cost would lead to economic losses because long-run average total cost would be greater than price at $P = MC$. Consequently, the government would have to subsidize the firm. Living with the inefficiencies in monopolistically competitive markets might be easier than coping with the difficulties entailed by regulations and the cost of the necessary subsidies.

We argued that the monopolistically competitive firm does not operate at the minimum point of the *ATC* curve, whereas the perfectly competitive firm does. However, is this a fair comparison? In monopolistic competition, there are differentiated goods and services, whereas in perfect competition, there are not. In other words, the excess capacity that exists in monopolistic competition is the price we pay for product differentiation. Have you ever thought about the many restaurants, movie theatres, and gasoline stations that have "excess capacity"? Can you imagine a world where all firms were working at full capacity? After all, choice is a good, and most of us value some choice.

In short, the inefficiency of monopolistic competition is a result of product differentiation. Since consumers value variety—the ability to choose from competing products and brands—the loss in efficiency must be weighed against the gain in increased product variety. The gains from product diversity can be large and may easily outweigh the inefficiency associated with a downward-sloping demand curve.

ARE THE DIFFERENCES BETWEEN MONOPOLISTIC COMPETITION AND PERFECT COMPETITION EXAGGERATED?

The significance of the difference between the relationship of marginal cost to price in monopolistic competition and in perfect competition can easily be exaggerated. As long as preferences for various brands are not extremely strong, the demand for a firm's products will be highly elastic (very flat). Accordingly, the points of tangency with the *ATC* curves are not likely to be far above the point of lowest cost, and excess capacity will be small, as illustrated in Exhibit 2. Only if differentiation is strong will the difference between the long-run monopolistic competition price level and the price that would prevail under perfectly competitive conditions be significant.

section 10.3
Exhibit 2   **The Impact of Product Differentiation**

a. Strong Preferences

Price / Minimum Point of *ATC* / *ATC* / Excess Capacity / *D* / 0 / q^* / Efficient Scale / Quantity of Output

b. Weak Preferences

Price / Minimum Point of *ATC* / *ATC* / Excess Capacity / *D* / 0 / q^* Efficient Scale / Quantity of Output

If the preferences for various brands are strong, there will be more excess capacity than when the preferences are weak.

Remember this little caveat: The theory of the firm is like a road map that does not detail every gully, creek, and hill but does give directions to get from one geographic point to another. Any particular theory of the firm may not tell precisely how an individual firm will operate, but it does provide valuable insight into the ways firms will tend to react to changing economic conditions such as entry, demand, and cost changes.

SECTION CHECK

- While both the competitive firm and the monopolistically competitive firm may earn short-run economic profits, these profits will be eliminated in the long run. Because monopolistically competitive firms face a downward-sloping demand curve, average total cost is not minimized in the long run after entry and exit have eliminated profits. Monopolistically competitive firms fail to reach productive efficiency, producing at output levels less than the efficient output. The monopolistically competitive firm does not achieve allocative efficiency because it does not operate where the price is equal to marginal costs.
- The inefficiencies of monopolistic competition are a by-product of product differentiation and must be weighed against the social benefits of increased product variety.
- The difference between the long-run monopolistically competitive price level and the price that would prevail under perfect competition varies directly with the strength of product differentiation.

section
10.4

Advertising

- Why do firms advertise?
- Is advertising good or bad from society's perspective?

WHY DO FIRMS ADVERTISE?

Advertising is an important nonprice method of competition that is commonly used in monopolistic competition. Why do firms advertise? The reason is simple: By advertising, firms hope to increase demand and create a less elastic demand curve for their products, thus enhancing revenues and profits. Advertising is part of our life, whether we are watching television, listening to the radio, reading a newspaper or magazine, or simply driving down the highway. Firms that sell differentiated products can spend between 10 and 20 percent of their revenue on advertising.

Advertising Can Change the Shape and Position of the Demand Curve

Consider Exhibit 1, which shows how a successful advertising campaign can increase demand and change elasticity. If an ad campaign convinces buyers that a firm's product is truly different, the demand curve for that good will become less elastic. Consequently, price changes (up or down) will have a relatively smaller impact on the quantity demanded of the product. The firm hopes that this change in elasticity, ideally coupled with an increase in demand, will increase profits.

The Impact of a Successful Advertising Campaign

A successful advertising campaign can increase demand and lead to a less elastic demand curve, such as $D_{\text{AFTER ADVERTISING}}$.

The degree to which advertising affects demand will vary from market to market. For example, in the laundry detergent market, empirical evidence shows that it is very important to advertise because the demand for any one detergent critically depends on the amount of money spent on advertising. That is, if you don't advertise your detergent, you don't sell much of it.

IS ADVERTISING GOOD OR BAD FROM SOCIETY'S PERSPECTIVE?

The Impact of Advertising on Society

Questions about whether advertising's impact on society is good or bad elicit sharply different responses. Some have argued that advertising manipulates consumer tastes and wastes billions of dollars annually creating "needs" for trivial products. Advertising helps create a demonstration effect, whereby people have new urges to buy products that were previously unknown to them. In creating additional demands for private goods, the ability to provide needed public goods (for which there is little advertising to create demand) is potentially reduced. Moreover, sometimes advertising is based on misleading claims, so people find themselves buying products that do not provide the satisfaction or results promised in the ads. Finally, advertising itself requires resources that raise average costs.

On the other hand, who is to say that the purchase of any product is frivolous or unnecessary? If one believes that people are rational and should be permitted freedom of expression, the argument against advertising loses some of its force.

Furthermore, defenders of advertising argue that firms use advertising to provide important information about the price and availability of a product, the location and hours of store operation, and so on. This allows for customers to make better choices and allows markets to function more efficiently.

Advertising and Costs

Although it is true that advertising may raise the average total cost, it is possible that when substantial economies of scale exist, the average production cost will decline more than the amount of the per-unit cost of advertising. In other words, average total cost, in some situations, actually declines after extensive advertising. This can happen because advertising may allow the firm to operate closer to the point of minimum cost on its *ATC* curve. Specifically, notice in Exhibit 2 that the average total cost curve before advertising is $ATC_{\text{BEFORE ADVERTISING}}$. After advertising, the curve shifts upward to $ATC_{\text{AFTER ADVERTISING}}$. If the increase in demand resulting from advertising is significant, economies of scale from higher output levels may offset the advertising costs. Average total cost may fall from C_0 to C_1, a movement from point A to point B, and allow the firm to sell its product at a lower price. Canadian Tire versus a smaller owner-operated retailer provides an example.

However, it also is possible that an advertising war between two firms, say Burger King and McDonald's, will result in higher advertising costs for both and no gain in market share (increased output) for either. This is shown as a movement from point A to point C in Exhibit 2. Output remains at q_0, but average total cost rises from C_0 to C_2.

Firms in monopolistic competition are not likely to experience substantial cost reductions as output increases. Therefore, they probably will not be able to offset advertising costs with lower production costs, particularly if advertising costs are high. Even if advertising does add to total cost, however, it is true that advertising conveys information. Through advertising, customers become aware of the options available to them in terms of product choice. Advertising helps customers choose products that best meet their needs, and it informs price-conscious customers about the costs of products. In this way, advertising lowers information costs, which is one reason that the Competition Bureau opposes bans on advertising.

Advertising and Competition

If advertising reduces information costs, this leads to some interesting economic implications. For example, say that as a result of advertising, we know about more products that may be substitutes for the products we have been buying for years. That is, the more goods that are advertised, the more consumers are aware of "substitute" products, which leads to increasingly competitive markets. Studies in the eyeglass, toy, and drug industries have shown that advertising has increased competition and led to lower prices in these markets.

section 10.4
Exhibit 2

Advertising and Economies of Scale

The average total cost before advertising is shown as $ATC_{\text{BEFORE ADVERTISING}}$. After advertising, the curve shifts to $ATC_{\text{AFTER ADVERTISING}}$. If the increase in demand resulting from advertising is significant, economies of scale from higher output levels may offset the advertising costs, lowering average total cost. The movement from point A to point B allows the firm to sell its product at a lower price. However, when two firms engage in an advertising war, it is possible that neither will gain market share (increased output) but each will incur higher advertising costs. This is shown as a movement from point A to point C in Exhibit 2—output remains at q_0, but average total cost rises from C_0 to C_2.

SECTION CHECK

- With advertising, a firm hopes it can alter the elasticity of the demand for its product, making it more inelastic and causing an increase in demand that will enhance profits.
- To some, advertising manipulates consumer tastes and creates "needs" for trivial products. Where substantial economies of scale exist, it is possible that average production costs will decline more than the amount of per-unit costs of advertising in the long run. By making consumers aware of different "substitute" products, advertising may lead to more competitive markets and lower consumer prices.

section 10.5

Oligopoly

- What is oligopoly?
- Why do oligopolies exist?
- Why is it so difficult for the oligopolist to determine its profit-maximizing price and output?

WHAT IS OLIGOPOLY?

oligopoly
a market structure with only a few sellers offering similar or identical products

As we first stated in Chapter 8, an **oligopoly** is a market structure with only a few sellers offering similar or identical products. While the goods and services produced by oligopolists can be either homogeneous or differentiated, the barriers to entry are often high, which makes it difficult for firms to enter the industry. Consequently, long-run economic profits may be earned by firms in the industry. Examples of oligopolistic markets include commercial airlines, oil, automobiles, steel, breakfast cereals, computers, and tobacco. For all these products, the market is dominated by anywhere from a few to several big companies, although they may have many different brands.

In Canada specifically, a number of industries could be considered to be oligopolistic. The Canadian banking sector is dominated by six large financial institutions: Bank of Nova Scotia, Royal Bank, TD Canada Trust, the Canadian Imperial Bank of

Business *CONNECTION*

TESLA AND ELECTRIC VEHICLES—A NEW PLAYER IN THE AUTO SECTOR

Tesla, Inc., which was established in 2003 and was formerly known as Tesla Motors, Inc., designs, develops, manufactures, and sells fully electric vehicles (EVs), battery technologies, and charging systems. The company strongly emphasizes solar energy and energy storage technologies.

Initially, Tesla has targeted the luxury vehicle market, and early adopters of high-tech vehicles, including vehicles that automate the driving process. More recently, it added a less costly EV to its line of automobiles: the Model 3. The company will have to increase production to meet volume sales targets, if it is going to be successful in the wider automobile sector. At the same time, it is trying to utilize solar energy in its "Gigafactories" and is encouraging potential purchasers to pay a deposit to be added to a waiting list for its cars—eliminating the car dealership.

Tesla has certainly captured a lot of interest. It is currently a publicly traded company with a captivating, dynamic, and sometimes eccentric leader in the form of Elon Musk. Musk is known for having big ideas that often involve considerable risk. Because he is widely followed on social media by millions of people, Musk's use of Twitter is not always appreciated by his boards of directors and investors. It also attracts the attention of the Securities and Exchange Commission, which is the U.S. regulatory body that ensures that federal securities rules are followed and that businesses do not try to influence the

equities markets for personal gain. While Musk is innovative and dynamic in his business strategies, he can also place his companies at risk, especially his publicly traded firms.

The automotive and energy sectors are competitive, but the market structure is oligopolistic. It is difficult and risky to enter the auto sector. In the early part of the 2010s, governments' ongoing concerns about the role fossil fuels play in global warming prompted many governments to start to offset the high cost of purchasing an electric vehicle and to develop the charging infrastructures that need to be built, using consumer incentives and infrastructure development grants. However, these are all subject to taxpayer and political support. In the middle of 2018, for instance, changes in government direction in the province of Ontario meant that cash incentives to purchasers of EVs were cancelled.

1. Discuss what the future might be for EVs and high-tech cars and production facilities like Tesla.

2. What might the traditional players, such as General Motors, Volkswagen, and Toyota, do in response? Skip ahead in this chapter and read about game theory. Use it in your analysis.

3. What are some of the challenges a company like Tesla faces in the longer term? How might the company address these concerns?

Commerce, the Bank of Montreal, and National Bank, controlling over 90 percent of total banking assets in Canada. As of 2016, three telecommunication service providers (Rogers, Bell, and Telus) shared over 90 percent of the Canadian wireless industry. Finally, five major Internet service providers (ISPs) account for over 85 percent of market share (based on revenue). The five major ISPs are Rogers, Telus, Bell, Shaw, and Quebecor.

Mutual Interdependence

Oligopoly is characterized by **mutual interdependence** among firms; that is, each firm shapes its policy with an eye to the policies of competing firms. Oligopolists must strategize, much like good chess or bridge players, who are constantly observing and anticipating the moves of their rivals. Oligopoly is likely to occur whenever the number of firms in an industry is so small that any change in output or price on the part of one firm appreciably impacts the sales of competing firms. In this situation, it is almost inevitable that competitors will respond directly to each other's actions in determining their own policies.

WHY DO OLIGOPOLIES EXIST?

Primarily, oligopoly is a result of the relationship between the technological conditions of production and potential sales volume. For many products, a firm cannot obtain a reasonably low cost of production unless it is producing a large fraction of the market output. In other words, substantial economies of scale are present in oligopoly markets. Automobile and steel production are classic examples of this. Because of legal concerns such as patents, large start-up costs, and the presence of pronounced economies of scale, the barriers to entry are quite high in oligopoly.

Economies of Scale as a Barrier to Entry

Economies of large-scale production make operation on a small scale extremely unprofitable during a new firm's early years. A firm cannot build up a large market overnight; in the interim, average total cost is so high that losses are heavy. Recognition of this fact discourages new firms from entering the market, as illustrated in Exhibit 1.

We can see that if an automobile company produces quantity Q_{LARGE} rather than Q_{SMALL}, it will be able to produce cars at a significantly lower cost. If the average total cost to a potential entrant is equivalent to point A on the *ATC* curve and the price of automobiles is less than P_0, a new firm would be deterred from entering the industry.

WHY IS IT SO DIFFICULT FOR THE OLIGOPOLIST TO DETERMINE ITS PROFIT-MAXIMIZING PRICE AND OUTPUT?

It is difficult to predict how firms will react when there is mutual interdependence. No firm knows what its demand curve looks like with any degree of certainty, and therefore it has a very limited knowledge of its marginal revenue curve.

section 10.5
Exhibit 1

Economies of Scale as a Barrier to Entry

Economies of large-scale production make operation on a small scale more costly, *ceteris paribus.*

mutual interdependence
when a firm shapes its policy with an eye to the policies of competing firms

Do you think economies of scale are important in this industry? Unlike home-cooked meals, few cars are "homemade." The barriers to entry in the auto industry are formidable. A new entrant would have to start out as a large producer (investing billions of dollars in plant, equipment, and advertising) to compete with existing firms, which have lower average total costs per unit because of economies of large-scale production.

To know anything about its demand curve, the firm must know how other firms will react to its prices and other policies. In the absence of additional assumptions, then, equating marginal revenue and marginal cost is relegated to guesswork. Thus, it is difficult for an oligopolist to determine its profit-maximizing price and output.

SECTION CHECK

■ Oligopolies exist where relatively few firms control all or most of the production and sale of a product. The products may be homogeneous or differentiated, but the barriers to entry are often very high and, consequently, there may be long-run economic profits.

■ In oligopoly markets, economies of large-scale production make operation on a small scale extremely unprofitable. Recognition of this fact discourages new firms from entering the market and is the primary reason why oligopolies exist.

■ Because in oligopoly the pricing decision of one firm influences the demand curve of competing firms, the oligopolist faces considerable uncertainty as to the location and shape of its demand and marginal revenue curves. Thus, it is difficult for an oligopolist to determine its profit-maximizing price and output.

---

section

10.6

Collusion and Cartels

● Why do firms collude?
● What is joint profit maximization?
● Why are most collusive oligopolies short-lived?

Because each firm is interdependent, the behaviour of an individual firm is difficult to predict. The firm is aware that if it changes price, quality, or output, its rival is likely to react. In oligopoly, each firm can influence the market price and its rival's behaviour. Hence, the oligopolist's profit-maximizing decision is much more difficult than it is for those in perfect competition or monopoly. The oligopolist who fails to accurately predict the behaviour of market rivals will lose profits.

WHY DO FIRMS COLLUDE?

collude

when firms act together to restrict competition

Because the actions and profits of oligopolists are so dominated by mutual interdependence, the temptation is great for firms to **collude**—act together to restrict competition. If firms believe they can increase their profits by coordinating their actions, they will be tempted to collude. Collusion reduces uncertainty and increases the potential for monopoly profits. From society's point of view, however, collusion has the same disadvantages monopoly does; namely, it creates a situation in which goods very likely become overpriced and underproduced, with consumers losing out as the result of a misallocation of resources.

Collusion Is Like a Monopoly

From the standpoint of pricing and output decisions, a truly collusive oligopoly that involves all the firms in an industry could act as the equivalent of one large firm with several plants. Acting in this manner, the economic effect of the collusive oligopoly would be exactly the same as that of a monopoly: a single demand curve would exist for the group of companies. Once the profit-maximization price was determined, they could agree on how much output each firm in the group would provide.

WHAT IS JOINT PROFIT MAXIMIZATION?

Agreements between or among firms on sales, pricing, and other decisions are usually referred to as *cartel agreements*. A **cartel** is a collection of firms that agree on sales, pricing, and other decisions.

Cartels may lead to what economists call **joint profit maximization**: the determination of price based on the marginal revenue function (derived from the market demand schedule) and the marginal cost schedule of the firms in the industry. Exhibit 1 illustrates this. With outright agreements—necessarily secret because of anti-combine laws (in Canada, at least)—firms that make up the market will attempt to estimate demand and cost schedules and then set optimum price and output levels accordingly.

Equilibrium price and quantity for a collusive oligopoly, like those for a monopoly, are determined according to the intersection of the marginal revenue curve (derived from the market demand curve) and the horizontal sum of the short-run marginal cost curves for the oligopolists. As shown in Exhibit 1, the resulting equilibrium quantity is Q^* and the equilibrium price is P^*. Collusion facilitates joint profit maximization for the oligopoly. Like monopoly, if the oligopoly is maintained in the long run, it charges a higher price, produces less output, and fails to maximize social welfare, relative to perfect competition, because $P^* > MC$ at Q^*.

The manner in which total profits are shared among firms in the industry depends in part on the relative costs and sales of the various firms. Firms with low costs and large supply capabilities will obtain the largest profits because they have greater bargaining power. Sales, in turn, may depend in large measure on consumer preferences for various brands if there is product differentiation. With outright collusion, firms may agree on market shares and the division of profits. The division of total profits will depend on the relative bargaining strength of each firm, influenced by its relative financial strength, ability to inflict damage (through price wars) on other firms if an agreement is not reached, ability to withstand similar actions on the part of other firms, relative costs, consumer preferences, and bargaining skills.

Organization of the Petroleum Exporting Countries

The most spectacularly successful example of a collusive oligopoly able to earn monopoly-type profits is the Organization of the Petroleum Exporting Countries (OPEC) cartel. Although organized in 1960, it didn't become successful as a collusive oligopoly until 1973.

For 20 years before 1973, the price of crude oil had hovered around US$2 per barrel. Then, in 1973, OPEC members agreed to quadruple oil prices in nine months; later price increases pushed the cost of a barrel of oil to more than US$20.

cartel
a collection of firms that agree on sales, pricing, and other decisions

joint profit maximization
determination of price based on the marginal revenue (derived from the market demand schedule) and marginal cost schedule of the firms in the industry

section 10.6
Exhibit 1

Collusion in Oligopoly

In collusive oligopoly, the producers would restrict joint output to Q^*, setting their price at P^*. The price and output situation is identical to that for monopoly. The members of the collusive oligopoly would share the profits in the shaded area.

The share of the world's proven oil reserves produced by companies that are OPEC members has steadily increased, from around 20 percent in the early 1940s to more than 80 percent by 2012. While ongoing world events have seen the price of a barrel of oil fluctuate, OPEC has had remarkable success at managing world price for the benefit of its member states. In May of 2018, a barrel of oil was selling for just over US$72.

WHY ARE MOST COLLUSIVE OLIGOPOLIES SHORT-LIVED?

Collusive oligopolies are potentially highly profitable for participants but detrimental to society. Fortunately, most strong collusive oligopolies are rather short-lived, for two reasons. First, in Canada and in some other nations, collusive oligopolies are strictly illegal under anti-combine laws. For example, according to court documents released in January 2018, retailers Loblaw, Walmart, Sobeys, Metro, and Giant Tiger, along with suppliers Canada Bread Company Ltd. and George Weston Ltd., were involved in a 14-year bread price-fixing scheme, spanning 2001 to 2015. Senior officers at Canada Bread and Weston Bakeries agreed to fix wholesale prices of bread and then met individually with their retail customers to get them to agree to the fixed price. The agreed-on

DEBATE

RIDE-SHARING—SHOULD IT BE BANNED?

For:

The advent of ride-sharing services looks set to continue to disrupt the livelihoods of taxi drivers and other professional driving services that have paid considerable sums of money to obtain and maintain their professional licences. The owners of professional driving services usually have to meet strict regulations, pay drivers at least the minimum wage, offer pensions and benefits (in many cases), and manage and maintain fleets of cars to service thousands of riders every day.

When Uber and Lyft arrived in Toronto, protests by taxi companies and professional taxi drivers were quick to follow. They see the ride-sharing services as taking away their business by getting around the regulations that they are forced to adhere to. Cities are also affected since they earn revenues through taxation and licence fees (circumvented by ride-sharing services). Moreover, there are insurance and safety concerns about ride-sharing services that have some policy analysts uncomfortable with the possible risks. Concerns include no video cameras, no driver images, no posted fares and rates, and no obligation to serve any and all customers.

The services are banned or highly regulated in some places, such as Denmark and London, England. In Toronto, they should be banned, or strongly regulated, just like the taxi companies.

Against:

Using an app to help you find a driver to take you somewhere in a clean, late-model car is just the modern way of doing business. Ride-sharing apps have reduced the economic transaction costs associated with matching customers and drivers.

Uber or Lyft drivers utilize a commission-based approach to compensation. As well, there is a ratings system in place, with customer experiences with the service posted for all to see. Transactions are all negotiated ahead of time, and there is no need for in-the-car payments. The drivers work as much or as little as they like. A 2017 study revealed that ride-sharing drivers gain considerably from the opportunity to drive without leasing and without having to meet the requirements involved in acquiring a formal taxi licence.

Granted the services did have some issues in the early days, when they seemed to be avoiding regulations and suffered some image issues. But these are being addressed. Taxi owners are also responding by adding apps of their own and cleaning up their images. A wake-up call to the taxi industry is long overdue. The competition is benefitting everybody.

Questions:

1. Discuss how technology change can disrupt an industry and introduce new competition.
2. Do you prefer using a taxi or a ride-sharing service? Why? What would make you change your mind?
3. What could government do to support taxi drivers who are losing their livelihoods because of ride-sharing?

price increases were, on average, about ten cents per product per year, with seven cents going to the suppliers and three cents to the retailers.*

Second, for collusion to work, firms must agree to restrict output to a level that will support the profit-maximizing price. At that price, firms can earn positive economic profits. However, there is great temptation for firms to cheat on the agreement of the collusive oligopoly, and because collusive agreements are illegal, the other parties have no way to punish the offender. Why do they have a strong incentive to cheat? Because any individual firm could lower its price slightly and thereby increase sales and profits, as long as it goes undetected. Undetected price cuts could bring in new customers, including rivals' customers. In addition, there are nonprice methods of defection— better credit terms, rebates, prompt delivery service, and so on.

SECTION CHECK

- The mutual interdependence of oligopolists tempts them to collude in order to reduce uncertainty and, therefore, increases the potential for monopoly profits.
- Joint profit maximization requires the determination of price based on the market demand for the product and the marginal costs of the various firms.
- Most strong collusive oligopolies are rather short-lived for two reasons: (1) Collusive oligopolies are strictly illegal under Canadian anti-combine laws, and (2) there is great temptation for firms to cheat on the agreement of the collusive oligopoly.

Game Theory and Strategic Behaviour

section 10.7

- What is game theory?
- What are cooperative and noncooperative games?
- What about repeated games?
- What are network externalities?

In some respects, noncollusive oligopoly resembles a military campaign or a poker game. Firms take certain actions not because these actions are necessarily advantageous in themselves but because they improve the position of the oligopolist relative to its competitors and may ultimately improve its financial position. For example, a firm may deliberately cut prices, sacrificing profits either to drive competitors out of business or to discourage them from undertaking actions contrary to the interests of other firms.

---

*Source: *Toronto Star*, "Loblaw, Walmart, Sobeys, Metro, Giant Tiger allegedly involved in alleged bread price-fixing scheme: Court documents," https://www.thestar.com/business/2018/01/31/at-least-7-companies-committed-indictable-offences-in-bread-price-fixing-scandal-competition-bureau.html.

WHAT IS GAME THEORY?

game theory
Firms attempt to maximize profits by acting in ways that minimize damage from competitors.

Some economists have suggested that the entire approach to oligopoly equilibrium and output should be recast. They replace the analysis that assumes that firms attempt to maximize profits with one that examines firm behaviour in terms of a strategic game. This point of view, called **game theory**, stresses how firms attempt to maximize profits by acting in ways that minimize damage from competitors. This approach involves a set of alternative actions (e.g., with respect to price and output levels); the action that would be taken in a particular case depends on the specific policies followed by each firm. The firm may try to figure out its competitors' most likely countermoves to its own policies and then formulate alternative defensive measures.

Each firm will react to the price, quantity, and quality of rival firms. Because each firm is interdependent, each must observe the moves of its rivals.

WHAT ARE COOPERATIVE AND NONCOOPERATIVE GAMES?

cooperative game
collusion by firms in order to improve their profit maximizations

noncooperative game
Each firm sets its own price without consulting other firms.

Games, in interactions between oligopolists, can be either cooperative or noncooperative. A **cooperative game** involves collusion by firms in order to improve their profit maximizations. However, as discussed earlier, enforcement costs are usually too high to keep all firms from cheating on collusive agreements. Consequently, most games are **noncooperative games**, in which each firm sets its own price without consulting other firms. The primary difference between cooperative and noncooperative games is the contract. For example, players in a cooperative game can talk and set binding contracts, while those in noncooperative games are assumed to act independently, with no communication and no binding contracts. Because Canadian competition laws forbid firms to collude, we will assume that most strategic behaviour in the marketplace is noncooperative.

The Prisoners' Dilemma

dominant strategy
will be optimal regardless of the opponents' actions

A firm's decision makers must map out a pricing strategy based on a wide range of information. They must also decide whether their strategy will be effective and whether it will be affected by competitors' actions. A strategy that will be optimal regardless of the opponents' actions is called a **dominant strategy**. The classic game that has a dominant strategy and demonstrates the basic problem confronting noncolluding oligopolists is known as the *prisoners' dilemma.*

payoff matrix
a summary of the possible outcomes from the various strategies

Imagine that a bank robbery occurs and two suspects are caught. The suspects are placed in separate jail cells and are not allowed to talk to each other. Four results are possible in this situation: both prisoners confess, neither confesses, Prisoner A confesses but Prisoner B doesn't, or Prisoner B confesses but Prisoner A doesn't. In Exhibit 1, we see the **payoff matrix**, a summary of the possible outcomes from the various strategies. Looking at the payoff matrix, we can see that if each prisoner confesses to the crime, each will serve two years in jail. However, if neither confesses, each prisoner may only get one year because of insufficient evidence. Now, if Prisoner A confesses and Prisoner B does not, Prisoner A will get six months (because of his cooperation with the authorities and his evidence) and Prisoner B will get six years. Alternatively, if Prisoner B confesses and Prisoner A does not, Prisoner B will get six months and Prisoner A will get six years. As you can see, then, the prisoners have a dilemma. What should each prisoner do?

Looking at the payoff matrix, we can see that if Prisoner A confesses, it is in the best interest for Prisoner B to confess. If Prisoner A confesses, he will get either two years or six months, depending on what Prisoner B does. However, Prisoner B knows the temptation to

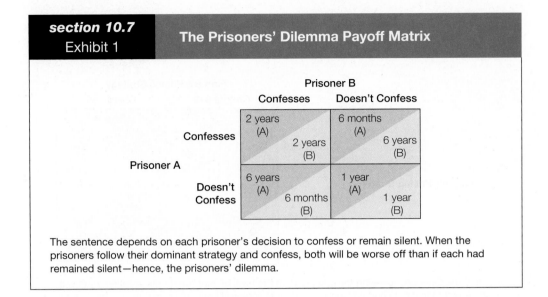

The Prisoners' Dilemma Payoff Matrix

The sentence depends on each prisoner's decision to confess or remain silent. When the prisoners follow their dominant strategy and confess, both will be worse off than if each had remained silent—hence, the prisoners' dilemma.

confess facing Prisoner A, so confessing is also the best strategy for Prisoner B. A confession would mean a lighter sentence for Prisoner B—two years rather than six years.

It is clear that both would be better off confessing *if* they knew for sure that the other was going to remain silent, because that would lead to a six-month sentence for each. However, in each case, can the prisoner take the chance that the co-conspirator will not talk? The dominant strategy, although it may not lead to the best joint outcome, is to confess. That is, the prisoners know that confessing is the way to make the best of a bad situation. No matter what their counterpart does, the maximum sentence will be two years for each, and each understands the possibility of being out in six months. In summary, when the prisoners follow their dominant strategy and confess, both will be worse off than if each had remained silent—hence, the "prisoners' dilemma."

Firms in an oligopoly often behave like the prisoners in the prisoners' dilemma, carefully anticipating the moves of their rivals in an uncertain environment. For example, should a firm cut its prices and try to gain more sales by luring customers away from its competitors? What if the firm keeps its price stable and competitors all lower their prices? What if all of the firms decide to raise their prices? Each of these situations will have vastly different implications for an oligopolist, so it must carefully watch and anticipate the moves of its competitors.

Profits under Different Pricing Strategies

To demonstrate how the prisoners' dilemma can shed light on oligopoly theory, let us consider the pricing strategy of two firms. In Exhibit 2, we present the payoff matrix—the possible profits that each firm would earn under the different pricing strategies. Assume that each firm has total production costs of $1 per unit. When both firms set their price at $10 and each sells 1000 units per week, then each earns a profit of $9000 a week. If each firm sets its price at $9, each sells 1100 units per week for a profit of $8800 [($9 − $1) × 1100]. However, what if one firm charges $10 and the other firm charges $9? The low-price firm increases its profits through additional sales. It now sells, say, 1500 units for a profit of $12 000, while the high-price firm sells only 600 units per week for a profit of $5400.

When the two firms each charge $9 per unit, they are said to have reached a Nash equilibrium (named after the Nobel prize-winning economist and mathematician John Nash, who was the subject of the movie *A Beautiful Mind*). At a **Nash equilibrium,**

Nash equilibrium
When firms interact with one another, each chooses its best strategy given the strategies of the other firms.

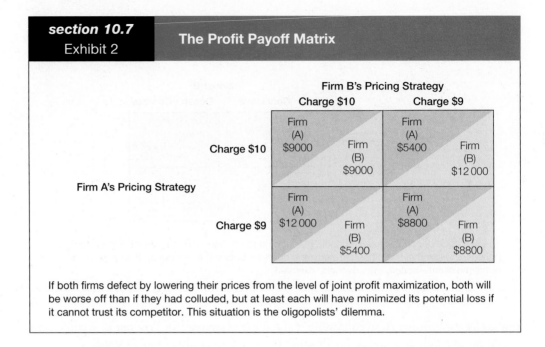

The Profit Payoff Matrix

If both firms defect by lowering their prices from the level of joint profit maximization, both will be worse off than if they had colluded, but at least each will have minimized its potential loss if it cannot trust its competitor. This situation is the oligopolists' dilemma.

each firm that is interacting with others chooses its best strategy given the strategies of the other firms. For example, if each firm believes the other is going to charge $9, then the best strategy for both firms is to charge $9. In this scenario, if Firm A charges $9, the worst possible outcome is a profit of $8800. However, if Firm A prices at $10 and Firm B prices at $9, Firm A will have a profit of only $5400. Hence, the choice that minimizes the risk of the worst scenario is $9. The same is true for Firm B; it too minimizes risk of the worst scenario by choosing to price at the Nash equilibrium, $9. In this case, the Nash equilibrium is also the dominant strategy. The Nash equilibrium takes on particular importance because it is a self-enforcing equilibrium. That is, neither firm has an incentive to move.

In sum, we see that if the two firms were to collude and set the price at $10, it would be in their best interest. However, each firm has a strong incentive to lower its price to $9 if this pricing strategy goes undetected by its competitor. However, if both firms defect by lowering their prices from the level of joint profit maximization, both will be worse off than if they had colluded, but at least each will have minimized its potential loss if it cannot trust its competitor. This situation is the oligopolists' dilemma.

Advertising

Advertising can lead to a situation like the prisoners' dilemma. For example, perhaps the decision makers of a large firm are deciding whether to launch an advertising campaign against a rival firm. According to the payoff matrix in Exhibit 3, if neither company advertises, the two companies split the market, each making $100 million in profits. They also split the market if they both advertise, but their net profits are smaller, $75 million, because they would both incur advertising costs that are greater than any gains in additional revenues from advertising. However, if one advertises and the other does not, the company that advertises takes customers away from the rival. Profits for the company that advertises would be $125 million, and profits for the company that does not advertise would be $50 million.

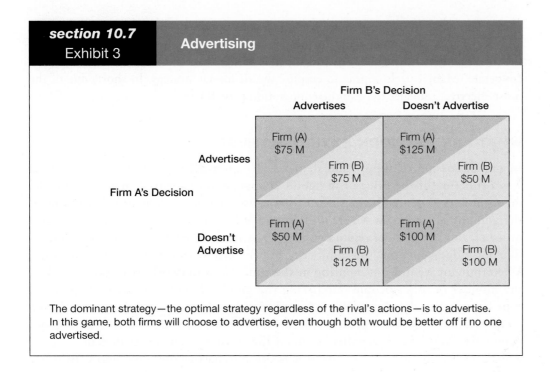

section 10.7
Exhibit 3

Advertising

Firm B's Decision

	Advertises	Doesn't Advertise
Advertises	Firm (A) $75 M / Firm (B) $75 M	Firm (A) $125 M / Firm (B) $50 M
Doesn't Advertise	Firm (A) $50 M / Firm (B) $125 M	Firm (A) $100 M / Firm (B) $100 M

Firm A's Decision

The dominant strategy—the optimal strategy regardless of the rival's actions—is to advertise. In this game, both firms will choose to advertise, even though both would be better off if no one advertised.

The dominant strategy—the optimal strategy regardless of the rival's actions—is to advertise. In this game, both firms will choose to advertise, even though both would be better off if no one advertised. But one company can't take a chance and not advertise, because if its competitor then elects to advertise, the competitor could have a big year, primarily at the expense of the firm that doesn't advertise.

WHAT ABOUT REPEATED GAMES?

In the one-shot prisoners' dilemma game in Exhibit 1, we saw that the best strategy was to confess regardless of what your opponent does—your behaviour does not influence the other player's behaviour. In one-shot prisoners' dilemma games, self-interest prevents cooperative behaviour and leads to an inferior joint outcome for the participants. However, cooperation is not impossible, because most oligopolistic interactions are not one-shot games. Instead they are repeated games. Most firms assume that they will have repeat customers. For example, if a grocery store fails to provide fresh produce, customers can punish the store by shopping elsewhere in the future. These future consequences change the incentives from those in a one-shot game. All stores might have gained short-run profits from low-quality (and low-cost) produce, but all may offer high-quality produce because of the adverse future effects of offering lower quality produce. In a repeated game, cooperation occurs as long as others continue to cooperate.

Suppose two firms are both going to be in business for many years. Several studies have shown that, in this type of situation, the best strategy is to do what your opponent did to you earlier. This form of strategic behaviour is called **tit-for-tat strategy**—a strategy used in repeated games, where one player follows the other player's move in the previous round, often leading to greater cooperation.

A repeated game allows the firm to establish a reputation of cooperation. Cooperation may mean maintaining a high price or a certain advertising budget, providing that the other firm did the same in the previous round. In short, a firm has an incentive to cooperate now, so there is greater cooperation in the future. However, if your opponent

tit-for-tat strategy
used in repeated games, where one player follows the other player's move in the previous round; leads to greater cooperation

cheats, you cheat in the next round to punish your opponent for a lack of cooperation. You do what your opponent did in the previous round. In the tit-for-tat game, both firms will be better off if they stick to the plan rather than cheating—that is, failing to cooperate. Many cartels appear to employ the tit-for-tat strategy. In short, one of the most effective strategies to promote cooperation is tit-for-tat.

WHAT ARE NETWORK EXTERNALITIES?

In our discussion of supply and demand (Chapter 3), we assumed that demand was a function of the price of the good (a change in quantity demanded) and the determinants of demand (the shifters that cause changes in demand). For example, the amount of ice cream we are willing and able to buy is a function of the price of ice cream, the price of related goods—substitutes like yogurt and complements like hot fudge—income, the number of buyers, tastes, and expectations. However, a determinant we did not mention at the time was a **network externality**—when the number of other people purchasing the good influences quantity demanded. A **positive network externality** occurs when a consumer's quantity demanded for a good increases because a greater number of consumers purchase the same good. A **negative network externality** occurs if the consumer's quantity demanded for a good increases because fewer consumers are purchasing the same good. In other words, sometimes an individual's demand curve is influenced by the other people purchasing the good.

Positive Network Externalities

Many examples of network externalities can be found in the communications area, such as with fax machines, telephones, and the Internet. Imagine you had a telephone, but nobody else did; it would be relatively worthless without others with whom to talk. It is also true that if you were the only one to own a Blu-ray player, it would make little sense for manufacturers to make Blu-ray discs and your Blu-ray player would be of little value.

The software industry has many examples of positive network externalities. For example, it is a lot easier to coordinate work if people are using the same software on their computers. It is also a lot easier (less costly) to get help if you need it because many people are familiar with the product, which may result in more available options (less costly) than calling the software supplier for help. Another example is Apple's FaceTime application—others have to have this video calling software (not to mention an Apple product to run it on). In short, our demand increases as the number of users increases.

Another type of positive network externality is called the **bandwagon effect**, where a consumer's demand for a product increases because other consumers own it. In recent years, we watched people get on the bandwagon in the toy industry with Beyblades, Silly Bandz, Bratz, Tickle Me Elmo, and Furbies, among others. It can happen in the clothing industry, too (e.g., lululemon athletic clothes or UGG boots).

Negative Network Externalities

Other goods and services are subject to negative network externalities, which may be a result of the snob effect. The *snob effect* is a negative network externality, where a consumer wants to own a unique good. For example, a rare junior hockey card of Wayne

network externality
when the number of other people purchasing the good influences quantity demanded

positive network externality
when a consumer's quantity demanded for a good increases because a greater number of consumers purchase the same good

negative network externality
when a consumer's quantity demanded for a good increases because fewer consumers are purchasing the same good

bandwagon effect
a positive network externality where a consumer's demand for a product increases because other consumers own it

Gretzky, a Model T car, a Vincent Van Gogh painting, a Rolex watch, or an expensive sports car may qualify as snob goods, where the quantity that a particular individual demands of a good increases when fewer other people own it. Firms seek to achieve a snob effect though marketing and advertising, knowing that if they can create a less elastic demand curve for their product they can raise the price.

Negative network externalities can arise from congestion too. If you are a member of a health club, a negative network externality may occur because too many people are in the gym working out at the same time. However, even though most people may prefer a ski resort with shorter lift lines, for example, others may view this as a positive externality and would increase their quantity demanded when more people are on the ski slopes—or in the gym or on the beach. Perhaps they do not want to ride up on the chair lift by themselves, work out alone, or hang out on a lonely beach. That is, whether it is a positive or negative externality may depend on the consumer's tastes and preferences.

Switching Costs

Along with the possible advantages of joining a larger network from capturing positive network externalities, you may also encounter costs if you leave. **Switching costs** are the costs involved in changing from one product to another or in changing suppliers. For example, costs are associated with switching to a new social networking site. If you were very familiar with Facebook and had established an extensive network of "friends," it would be costly to switch to Google+ and start over again. Network externalities and switching costs are two of the reasons that eBay and Amazon.com have done so well. The first firm in a market, where everybody in its large customer base is familiar with the operation, gains huge advantages. Other potential competitors recognize this advantage and, as a result, are leery of entering into the business.

switching costs
the costs involved in changing from one product to another or in changing suppliers

In short, in industries that see significant positive network effects, oligopoly is likely to be present. That is, a small number of firms may be able to secure most of the market. Consumers tend to choose the products that everyone else is using. Thus, behaviour may allow these firms to increase their output and achieve economies of scale that smaller firms cannot obtain. Hence, the smaller firms will go out of business or be bought out by larger firms.

SECTION CHECK

- Game theory stresses the tendency of various parties to minimize damage from opponents. A firm may try to figure out its competitors' most likely countermoves to its own policies and then formulate alternative defensive measures.
- Players in cooperative games can communicate and set binding contracts, while those in noncooperative games are assumed to act independently with no communications and no binding contracts. The prisoners' dilemma is an example of a noncooperative game.
- In one-shot games, the participants' self-interest tends to prevent cooperative behaviour, but in repeated games, cooperation occurs as long as others continue to cooperate (a tit-for-tat strategy).
- Positive network externality occurs when a consumer's quantity demanded increases because a greater number of consumers purchase the same good. Negative network externality occurs when a consumer's quantity demanded increases because a smaller number of consumers purchase the same good.

For Your Review

Section 10.1

1. Which of the following would be considered perfectly competitive or monopolistically competitive? Why?
   a. soy market
   b. retail clothing stores
   c. CUT Steakhouse in Halifax

2. List three ways in which a grocery store might differentiate itself from its competitors.

3. How is monopolistic competition a mixture of monopoly and perfect competition?

4. If Frank's hot dog stand was profitable when he first opened, why should he expect those profits to fall over time?

5. Can you explain why some restaurants are highly profitable while other restaurants in the same general area are going out of business?

6. Suppose that half of the restaurants in a city are closed so that the remaining eateries can operate at full capacity. What "cost" might restaurant patrons incur as a result?

7. How does Starbucks differentiate its product? Why does Starbucks stay open until late at night but a doughnut or bagel shop might close at noon?

8. Product differentiation is a hallmark of monopolistic competition, and the text lists four sources of such differentiation: physical differences, prestige, location, and service. How do firms in the industries listed below differentiate their products? Give the most important source of differentiation in each case.
   a. fast-food restaurants
   b. espresso shops/carts
   c. hair stylists
   d. soft drink company
   e. wine merchant

Section 10.2

9. Draw a graph showing a monopolistically competitive firm in a short-run equilibrium where it is earning positive economic profits. What must be true of price versus average total cost for such a firm? What will happen to the firm's demand curve as a result of the short-run profits? How would this analysis change if the monopolistically competitive firm was earning economic losses?

10. How is the long-run equilibrium of monopolistic competition different from that of perfect competition?

11. How is price related to marginal cost and average total cost for monopolistically competitive firms in the following situations?
    a. a short-run equilibrium where it is earning positive economic profits
    b. a short-run equilibrium where it is earning economic losses
    c. a short-run equilibrium where it is earning zero economic profits
    d. a long-run equilibrium

12. The following graph shows the long-run equilibrium for a monopolistically competitive firm.

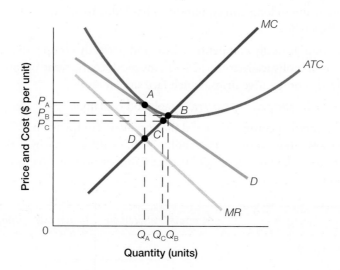

a. For this monopolistically competitive firm, what is the profit-maximizing output level and at what price will it sell this output?

b. At profit maximization, explain why this firm is considered to be in long-run equilibrium.

13. The following table displays the daily quantity sold, prices, and costs for an automotive oil-change business. While competing with several other companies that offer similar services, this operation differentiates itself by offering warranty-approved service without having to make an appointment.

Quantity (number of oil changes)	Price ($)	MC ($)	ATC ($)
0	50.00		
1	45.00	13.00	30.50
2	40.00	18.00	26.75
3	35.00	23.00	24.75
4	30.00	28.00	26.25
5	25.00	33.00	28.75
6	20.00	38.00	32.50

a. Why would this automotive oil-change business be considered monopolistically competitive?

b. In the short run, what would be the profit-maximizing number of oil changes? What price would this monopolistically competitive firm charge in the short run?

c. Determine whether our monopolistically competitive firm is generating economic profits in the short run. If so, how much?

Section 10.3

14. Refer to the diagram in question 12. Explain why this monopolistically competitive firm, despite being in long-run equilibrium, has failed to achieve either productive or allocative efficiency.

15. How are monopolistically competitive firms and perfectly competitive firms similar? Why don't monopolistically competitive firms produce the same output in the long run as perfectly competitive firms, which face similar costs?

16. What is meant by the *price of variety*? Graph and explain.

17. As you know, perfect competition and monopolistic competition differ in important ways. Show your understanding of these differences by listing the following terms below under either "Perfect Competition" or "Monopolistic Competition."

	Perfect Competition	Monopolistic Competition
Standardized product		
Differentiated product		
Allocative efficiency		
Excess capacity		
Productive efficiency		
Horizontal demand curve		
Downward-sloping demand curve		
No control over price		

Section 10.4

18. Why is advertising more important for the success of chains such as Canadian Tire and Office Depot than for the corner barbershop?

19. Think of your favourite ads on television. Do you think that these ads have an effect on your spending? These ads are expensive; do you think they are a waste from society's standpoint?

20. In what way is the use of advertising another example of Adam Smith's "invisible hand," according to which entrepreneurs pursuing their own best interest make consumers better off?

21. How does advertising shift demand? How does it change the elasticity of demand?

22. Why is it so important for monopolistically competitive firms to advertise?

Section 10.5

23. Which of the following markets are oligopolistic?

    a. corn

    b. funeral services

    c. airline travel

    d. hamburgers

    e. oil

    f. breakfast cereals

24. Which of the following are characteristic of oligopolistic industries?
    a. a large number of firms
    b. few firms
    c. a high degree of product differentiation
    d. high barriers to entry
    e. free entry and exit
    f. mutual interdependence

25. Explain how the long-run equilibrium under oligopoly differs from that of perfect competition.

26. Important differences exist between perfect competition and oligopoly. Show your understanding of these differences by listing the following terms under either "Perfect Competition" or "Oligopoly" in the table below.

allocative efficiency	high barriers to entry	downward sloping demand curve
large economies of scale	horizontal demand curve	
many small firms	few large firms	no control over price
productive efficiency	mutual interdependence	

Perfect Competition	Oligopoly

Section 10.6

27. Suppose Farmer Smith from Saskatchewan and Farmer Jones from Alberta agree to restrict their combined output of wheat in an attempt to increase the price and profits. How likely do you think the Smith–Jones cartel is to succeed? Explain.

28. Explain how the joint profit-maximizing price of colluding firms under oligopoly is determined? How about output?

29. One of the world's most successful cartels has been the De Beers Central Selling Organization (CSO), which controls about three-quarters of the world's diamonds. This collusive oligopoly has kept diamond prices high by restricting supply. The CSO has also promoted the general consumption of diamonds through advertising and marketing. New supplies of diamonds have been found in Canada and Russia. These new mines, which are outside the direct control of the CSO, want to sell their diamonds on the open market.
    a. How might the CSO cartel be in jeopardy if these new mines in Canada and Russia do not cooperate with the cartel and instead supply their diamonds to the market outside the collusive agreement established by the CSO?
    b. Given the situation described in part (a), what do you think would happen to CSO diamond advertising?

30. Why are collusive agreements typically unstable and short-lived?

Section 10.7

31. Two firms compete in the breakfast cereal industry producing Wheat Krinkles and Rice Krinkles cereal, respectively. Each manufacturer must decide whether to promote its product with a large or small advertising budget. The potential profits for these firms are as shown below (in millions of dollars).

Firm A
Wheat Krinkles Cereal

		Small Advertising Budget	Large Advertising Budget
Firm B Rice Krinkles Cereal	**Small Advertising Budget**	Firm (A) $50 M / Firm (B) $50 M	Firm (A) $30 M / Firm (B) $100 M
	Large Advertising Budget	Firm (A) $140 M / Firm (B) $20 M	Firm (A) $150 M / Firm (B) $150 M

Describe the nature of the mutual interdependence of the two firms. Is a Nash equilibrium evident?

32. Suppose Pepsi is considering an ad campaign aimed at rival Coca-Cola. What is the dominant strategy if the payoff matrix is similar to the one shown in Exhibit 3 in Section 10.7?

33. The following payoff matrix shows the possible sentences that two suspects, arrested on suspicion of car theft, could receive. The suspects are interrogated separately and are unable to communicate with one another. Use the payoff matrix to answer the questions that follow it.

Suspect 2

		Confess	Don't Confess
Suspect 1	**Confess**	1 6 years / 2 6 years	1 1 year / 2 10 years
	Don't Confess	1 10 years / 2 1 year	1 2 years / 2 2 years

For the information given in the payoff matrix above:

a. Is there a dominant strategy? If so, what is it?

b. Is there a Nash equilibrium? How do you know?

34. Why are repeated games more likely to be more cooperative than one-shot games?

35. Why might shirking on a team project in school be a dominant strategy, but not shirking on a team project at work?

chapter
11
Labour Markets and the Distribution of Income

Labour Markets

section
11.1

- What determines the price paid to workers?
- What is derived demand?

WHAT DETERMINES THE PRICE PAID TO WORKERS?

Approximately 70 percent of net national income goes to wages and salaries for labour services. After labourers take their share, the remaining 30 percent of net national income is compensation received by the owners of land and capital and the entrepreneurs who use those resources to produce valued goods and services. In this chapter, we will see how supply and demand in the labour market determines the salary levels among different workers.

Actor Keanu Reeves was paid $262 million to make the *Matrix Trilogy*. Singer Celine Dion's income is many times larger than that of the average college professor or medical doctor. Female models make more than male models, yet male basketball players make more than female basketball players. Why is this the case? To understand why some workers receive such vastly different compensation for their labour than others, we must focus on the workings of supply and demand in the labour market.

WHAT IS DERIVED DEMAND?

Input markets are the markets for the factors of production used to produce output. Output (goods and services) markets and input markets have one major difference. In input or factor markets, the demand for an input is called a **derived demand**. That is, the demand for an input like labour is derived from the consumer demand for the good or service. So consumers do *not* demand the labour directly—it is the goods and services that labour produces that consumers demand. For example, the chef at a

derived demand
The demand for an input is derived from the consumer's demands for a good or service.

restaurant is paid for her skills, which are in demand because she produces what the customer wants—a meal. The "price" of any productive factor is directly related to consumer demand for the final good or service.

SECTION CHECK

- Supply and demand determine the prices paid to workers.
- In factor or input markets, demand is derived from consumers' demand for the final good or service that the input produces.

---

section 11.2

Supply and Demand in the Labour Market

- Will hiring that extra worker add more to revenue than to costs?
- Why is the labour demand curve downward sloping?
- How many workers will an employer hire?
- What is the shape of the labour supply curve?

WILL HIRING THAT EXTRA WORKER ADD MORE TO REVENUE THAN TO COSTS?

marginal revenue product (MRP)

the additional revenue that a firm obtains from one more unit of input

marginal resource cost (MRC)

the amount that an extra input adds to the firm's total costs

Because firms are trying to maximize their profits, they try to make the *difference* between total revenue and total cost as large as possible. An input's attractiveness, then, varies with what the input can add to the firm's revenues relative to what the input adds to costs. The demand for labour is determined by its **marginal revenue product (MRP)**—the additional revenue that a firm obtains from one more unit of input. Why? Suppose a worker adds $500 per week to a firm's sales by his productivity; he produces 100 units that add $5 each to firm revenue. In order to determine if the worker adds to the firm's profits, we would need to calculate the marginal resource cost associated with the worker. The **marginal resource cost (MRC)** is the amount that an extra input adds to the firm's total costs. In this case, the marginal resource cost is the wage the employer has to pay to entice an extra worker. Assume that the marginal resource cost of the worker, the market wage, is $350 per worker a week. In our example, the firm would find its profits growing by adding one more worker, because the marginal

Restaurant owners are willing to pay a wage to workers because the owners expect to be able to sell the food and services produced at a price high enough to cover workers' wages and all other costs of production.

Sean Gallup/Getty Images News/Thinkstock

benefit (*MRP*) associated with the worker, $500, would exceed the marginal cost (*MRC*) of the worker, $350. So we can see that just by adding another worker to its labour force, the firm would increase its weekly profits by $150 ($500 – $350). Even if the market wage was $490 per week, the firm could slightly increase its profits by hiring the employee because the marginal revenue product, $500, is greater than the added labour cost, $490. At wage payments above $500, however, the firm would not be interested in adding the worker because the marginal resource cost would exceed the marginal revenue product, making additional hiring unprofitable.

WHY IS THE LABOUR DEMAND CURVE DOWNWARD SLOPING?

The downward-sloping demand curve for labour indicates a negative relationship between the wage and the quantity of labour demanded. Higher wages will decrease the quantity of labour demanded, whereas lower wages will increase the quantity of labour demanded. But why does this relationship exist?

The major reason for the downward-sloping demand curve for labour (illustrated in Exhibit 1) is the law of diminishing marginal product. Remember that the law of diminishing marginal product states that as increasing quantities of some variable input (say, labour) are added to fixed quantities of another input (say, land or capital), output will rise, but at some point it will increase by diminishing amounts.

Consider a farmer who owns a given amount of land. Suppose he is producing wheat, and the relationship between his output and his labour force requirements is that indicated in Exhibit 2. Output expands as more workers are hired to cultivate the land, but the growth in output steadily slows, meaning the added output associated with one more worker declines as more workers are added. For example, in Exhibit 2 when a third worker is hired, total wheat output increases from 5500 tonnes to 7000 tonnes, an increase of 1500 tonnes in terms of marginal product. However, when a fourth worker is added, total wheat output increases from 7000 tonnes to only 8000 tonnes, or a marginal increase of 1000 tonnes.

Note that the reason for this is *not* that the workers being added are steadily inferior in terms of ability or quality relative to the first workers. Indeed, for simplicity, we assume that each worker has exactly the same skills and productive capacity. But as more workers are added, each additional worker has fewer of the fixed resources with which to work, and marginal product falls. For example, the fifth worker might just cultivate the same land more intensively. The work of the fifth worker, then, might only slightly improve output. That is, the marginal product (*MP*)—the number of physical units of added output from the addition of one additional unit of input—falls.

As we discussed earlier, the marginal revenue product (*MRP*) is the change in total revenue associated with an additional unit of input. The marginal revenue product

section 11.2 Exhibit 1	**The Marginal Revenue Product of Labour**

The marginal revenue product of labour curve shows how the marginal revenue product depends on the number of workers employed. The curve is downward sloping because of the diminishing marginal product of labour.

section 11.2 Exhibit 2	**Diminishing Marginal Productivity on a Hypothetical Farm**

Units of Labour Input (workers)	Total Wheat Output (tonnes per year)	Marginal Product of Labour (tonnes per year)
0	—	—
1	3000	3000
2	5500	2500
3	7000	1500
4	8000	1000
5	8500	500
6	8800	300
7	9000	200

| | | **section 11.2** Exhibit 3 | **Marginal Revenue Product, Output, and Labour Inputs** | | |

Quantity of Labour	Total Output (tonnes per week)	Marginal Product of Labour (tonnes per week)	Product Price (dollars per tonne)	Marginal Revenue Product of Labour	Wage Rate (MRC) (dollars per week)
0	0				
1	100	100	$10	$1000	$500
2	190	90	10	900	500
3	270	80	10	800	500
4	340	70	10	700	500
5	400	60	10	600	500
6	450	50	10	500	500
7	490	40	10	400	500
8	520	30	10	300	500

is equal to the marginal product, the units of output added by a worker, multiplied by marginal revenue, in this case the price of the output (e.g., $10 per tonne of wheat).

$$MRP = MP \times P$$

(Note that in this case the price of the output, wheat, is the same at all levels of output because the farmer is a price taker in a competitive wheat market.)

The marginal revenue product of labour declines because of the diminishing marginal product of labour when additional workers are added. This is illustrated in Exhibit 3, which shows various output and revenue levels for a wheat farmer using different quantities of labour. We see in Exhibit 3 that the marginal product, or the added physical volume of output, declines as the number of workers grows because of diminishing marginal product. Thus, the fifth worker adds only 60 tonnes of wheat per week, compared with 100 tonnes for the first worker.

HOW MANY WORKERS WILL AN EMPLOYER HIRE?

Profits are maximized if the firm hires only to the point where the wage equals the expected marginal revenue product. Because the demand curve for labour and the value of the marginal revenue product show the quantity of labour that a firm demands at a given wage in a competitive labour market, we say that the marginal revenue product (*MRP*) is the same as the demand curve for labour for a competitive firm.

Using the data in Exhibit 3, if the market wage is $500 per week, it would pay for the grower to employ six workers. The sixth worker's marginal revenue product ($500) equals the wage, so profits are maximized. Adding a seventh worker would be unprofitable, though, as that worker's marginal revenue product of $400 is less than the wage of $500. Hiring the seventh worker would reduce profits by $100.

But what if the market wage increases from $500 to $700? In this case, the firm would employ only four workers, since the fourth worker's marginal revenue product

The Competitive Firm's Hiring Decision

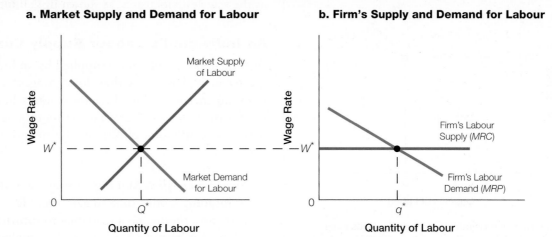

a. Market Supply and Demand for Labour

b. Firm's Supply and Demand for Labour

A competitive firm can hire any number of potential workers at the market-determined wage; it is a wage taker. At employment levels less than q^*, additional workers add profits. At employment levels beyond q^*, additional workers are unprofitable; at q^*, profits are maximized.

($700) equals the wage ($700), so profits are maximized. That is, a higher wage rate, *ceteris paribus,* lowers the employment levels of individual firms.

In a competitive labour market, many firms are competing for workers and no single firm is big enough by itself to have any significant effect on the level of wages. The intersection of the market supply of labour and the market demand for labour determines the competitive market wage, as shown in Exhibit 4(a). The firm's ability to hire all the workers it wants at the prevailing wage is similar to perfect competition in output markets, where a firm could sell all it wanted at the going price.

In Exhibit 4, when the firm hires fewer than q^* workers, the marginal revenue product exceeds the market wage, so adding workers expands profits. With more than q^* workers, though, the "going wage" exceeds marginal revenue product, and hiring additional workers lowers profits. With q^* workers, profits are maximized.

In this chapter, we assume that labour markets are competitive—there are many buyers and sellers of labour, with no individual firm or no individual worker having an impact on wages. This is generally a realistic assumption because in most labour markets, firms compete with each other to attract workers and workers can choose from many possible employers.

WHAT IS THE SHAPE OF THE LABOUR SUPPLY CURVE?

How much work effort are individuals collectively willing and able to supply in the marketplace? This is the essence of the market supply curve. Just as was the case in our earlier discussion of the law of supply, a positive relationship exists between the wage rate and the quantity of labour supplied. As the wage rate rises, the quantity of labour supplied increases, *ceteris paribus*; as the wage rate falls, the quantity of labour

section 11.2
Exhibit 5

The Market Supply Curve of Labour

An increase in the wage rate, from W_0 to W_1, leads to an increase in the quantity of labour supplied, *ceteris paribus*. A decrease in the wage rate, from W_1 to W_0, leads to a decrease in the quantity of labour supplied, *ceteris paribus*.

section 11.2
Exhibit 6

An Individual's Backward-Bending Labour Supply Curve

The movement of A → B results from the substitution effect being stronger than the income effect. The movement of B → C results from the income effect being stronger than the substitution effect.

backward-bending labour supply curve

Above a certain wage rate, a worker might prefer to work less and enjoy more leisure (the income effect dominates the substitution effect).

supplied falls, *ceteris paribus*. This positive relationship is consistent with the actual empirical evidence that the total quantity of labour supplied by *all* workers increases as the wage rate increases, as shown in Exhibit 5.

An Individual's Labour Supply Curve

Will the quantity of labour supplied by an individual be greater at higher wages than lower wages? The answer is by no means obvious because workers have another use for their time—leisure. Furthermore, wage increases have two conflicting effects on the quantity of labour supplied:

1. *Substitution effect:* At a higher wage rate, the cost of forgoing labour time to gain more leisure time increases, producing a tendency to substitute labour for leisure. In other words, a higher wage rate makes leisure more expensive—its opportunity cost rises.
2. *Income effect:* At a higher wage rate, the quantity of labour supplied tends to decrease because many individuals consider leisure a normal good. So when income increases, people demand more leisure. That is, at some wage rate, some workers feel that they can afford more leisure.

Thus, the individual's labour supply curve might be backward-bending. At a lower wage rate, as wages increase, the worker might supply more hours of work to obtain as much money income as possible (the substitution effect dominates the income effect), resulting in an upward-sloping labour supply curve. However, above a certain wage rate, a worker might prefer to work less and enjoy more leisure (the income effect dominates the substitution effect), resulting in a **backward-bending labour supply curve**. That is, if the substitution effect is stronger than the income effect, the individual's labour supply curve is upward sloping. If the income effect is stronger than the substitution effect, the individual's labour supply curve is backward-bending.

For example, a student working during the summer to earn money for the school year might quit her job once she has reached a certain level of earnings; she then concentrates on leisure for the rest of the summer. In this case, the student's labour supply curve might appear as shown in Exhibit 6. Actually, the market supply curve might also bend backward, too, but at a much higher wage rate than currently exists. In the rest of this chapter, therefore, we will assume that the market supply curve is upward sloping, at least in the relevant range.

section

11.3

Labour Market Equilibrium

- How is equilibrium determined in a competitive labour market?
- What shifts the labour demand curve?
- What shifts the labour supply curve?
- What is a monopsony?

HOW IS EQUILIBRIUM DETERMINED IN A COMPETITIVE LABOUR MARKET?

The equilibrium wage and quantity in the labour market is determined by the intersection of labour demand and labour supply. Referring to Exhibit 1, the equilibrium wage, W^*, and equilibrium employment level, Q^*, are found at that point where the quantity of labour demanded equals the quantity of labour supplied. At any wage higher than W^*, like at W_1, the quantity of labour supplied exceeds the quantity of labour demanded, resulting in a surplus of labour. In this situation, unemployed workers would be willing to undercut the established wage in order to get jobs, pushing the wage down and returning the market to equilibrium. Likewise, at a wage below the equilibrium level, like at W_2, quantity demanded would exceed quantity supplied, resulting in a labour shortage. In this situation, employers would be forced to offer higher wages in order to hire as many workers as they would like. Note that only at the equilibrium wage are both suppliers and demanders able to exchange the quantity of labour they desire.

section 11.3 Exhibit 1	Supply and Demand in the Labour Market

Equilibrium prices and quantities in the labour market are determined in the same way that prices and quantities of goods and services are determined: by the intersection of demand and supply. At wages above the equilibrium wage, like W_1, quantity supplied exceeds quantity demanded, and potential workers will be willing to supply their labour services for an amount lower than the prevailing wage. At a wage lower than W^*, like W_2, potential demanders will overcome the resulting shortage of labour by offering workers a wage greater than the prevailing wage. In both cases, wages are pushed toward the equilibrium value.

WHAT SHIFTS THE LABOUR DEMAND CURVE?

In Chapter 3, we demonstrated that changes in the determinants of demand can shift the demand curve for a good or service. In the case of an input such as labour, two important factors can shift the demand curve: increases in labour productivity, such as those due to technological advances, or changes in the output price of the good, such as those due to increased demand for the firm's product. Exhibit 2 highlights the impact of these changes.

Changes in Labour Productivity

Workers can increase productivity if they have more capital or land with which to work, if technological improvements occur, or if they acquire additional skills or experience. This increase in productivity will increase the marginal product of the labour and shift the demand curve for labour to the right from D_0 to D_1 in Exhibit 2(a). However, if labour productivity falls, then marginal product will fall and the demand curve for labour will shift to the left, as shown in Exhibit 2(b).

Changes in the Demand for the Firm's Product

The greater the demand for the firm's product, the greater the firm's demand for labour or any other variable input (the "derived demand" discussed earlier). This is because the higher demand for the firm's product increases the firm's marginal revenue, which increases marginal revenue product. That is, the greater demand for the product will cause prices to rise, and the price of the product is part of the value of the labour to the firm ($MRP = MP \times P$)—so the rising product price shifts the labour demand curve to the right. Of course, if demand for the firm's product falls, the labour demand curve will shift to the left as marginal revenue product falls.

section 11.3
Exhibit 2

Shifts in the Labour Demand Curve

a. Increase in Labour Demand

Wage Rate

D_0 D_1

Quantity of Labour

b. Decrease in Labour Demand

Wage Rate

D_1 D_0

Quantity of Labour

An increase in labour demand will shift the demand curve for labour to the right. A decrease in labour demand will shift the demand curve for labour to the left.

WHAT SHIFTS THE LABOUR SUPPLY CURVE?

In Chapter 3, we learned that changes in the determinants of supply can shift the supply curve for goods and services to the right or left. Likewise, several factors can cause the labour supply curve to shift. These factors include immigration and population growth, the number of hours workers are willing to work at a given wage (worker tastes or preferences), nonwage income, and amenities. Exhibit 3 illustrates the impact of these factors on the labour supply curve.

Immigration and Population Growth

If new workers enter the labour force, it will shift the labour supply curve to the right, as from S_0 to S_1 in Exhibit 3(a). Of course, if workers leave the country or the labour force population declines, it will cause the supply curve to shift to the left, as shown in Exhibit 3(b).

Number of Hours People Are Willing to Work (Worker Preferences)

If people become willing to work more hours at a given wage (due to changes in worker tastes or preferences), the labour supply curve will shift to the right, shown in the movement from S_0 to S_1 in Exhibit 3(a). If they become willing to work fewer hours at a given wage (e.g., as they approach retirement age), then the labour supply curve will shift to the left, as shown in Exhibit 3(b).

Nonwage Income

Increases in income from sources other than employment can cause the labour supply curve to shift to the left. For example, if you just won $20 million in the lottery, you might decide to take yourself out of the labour force. Likewise, a decrease in nonwage

section 11.3
Exhibit 3   **Shifts in the Labour Supply Curve**

a. Increase in Labour Supply

Wage Rate

S_0 S_1

0   Quantity of Labour

b. Decrease in Labour Supply

Wage Rate

S_1 S_0

0   Quantity of Labour

An increase in labour supply shifts the supply curve to the right, whereas a decrease in labour supply shifts the curve to the left.

income (say, if pension benefits were reduced) might push a person back into the labour force, thus shifting the labour supply curve to the right.

Amenities

Amenities associated with a job or a location—like good fringe benefits, safe and friendly working conditions, a child-care centre, and so on—will make for a more desirable work atmosphere, *ceteris paribus.* These amenities would cause an increase in the supply of labour, resulting in a rightward shift, such as from S_0 to S_1 in Exhibit 3(a). If job conditions deteriorated, it would lead to a reduction in the labour supply, shifting the labour supply curve to the left, as shown in Exhibit 3(b).

WHAT IS A MONOPSONY?

monopsony
a market with a single buyer

So far our discussion has assumed that the labour market is competitive—many buyers of labour and many sellers of labour, with no one having a marked impact on wages. Recall that, in the case of a single seller of a product or input, we say that a monopoly exists. When the market involves a single buyer, however, we say that a **monopsony** exists. While monopsony could exist in any single-buyer situation, the situation considered most relevant in the real world is the labour market. Monopsony usually refers, then, to circumstances where only one employer is bidding for the services of many labourers. Where monopsony is present, the buyer of labour may have market power and may be able to affect wages. However, pure monopsony, like pure monopoly, is rare. For example, monopsony may arise because a person within a given locality has only a relatively few choices of where to work. However, if the individual was willing to move or if the number of buyers increased, then the role of a monopsony would be diminished. So, monopsony power is more likely to be present where movement and search costs impede workers from seeking employment in different locales.

In the nineteenth century, one or two lumber mills often dominated northern Ontario towns; in other areas, a single mining or manufacturing firm dominated the community to the point that it might be called a *company town.* Monopsony power existed in such situations and increased the opportunities for monopsonistic exploitation. Even though no fences around the town kept workers from leaving, high transportation costs and the expense involved in investigating job opportunities elsewhere made it expensive, sometimes prohibitively so, for workers to move to another locale. Economic theory suggests that where monopsony exists, fewer workers will be hired at lower wages than if perfect competition prevailed in the labour market. That is, the monopsony firm moves down along the positively sloped labour supply curve it faces, lowering the wages it pays and increasing profits. In short, workers will work for less than their marginal revenue product—they are in this sense exploited.

An example of monopsony power is the situation in some professional sports, where drafted players are assigned to teams until they are eligible to be free agents (after six years in baseball). Because other teams cannot compete for these players, the outcome is lower salaries, as team owners exercise their monopsony power. However, for the most part, in most occupations, many potential employers in many different locations compete for workers.

Business *CONNECTION*

IS A RETAIL GIANT HEALTHY FOR THE ECONOMY?

Historically, there has been much debate in economic circles about market inefficiencies resulting from monopolies. Governments too have considered the costs and benefits of monopolies, but there has been little serious concern about monopsonies—markets with a single buyer. Why? To date, markets just haven't experienced situations where there is a single buyer that has any significant impact on the market. As markets mature, though, we see ever-increasing economic concentration through international mergers and acquisitions. Walmart has come to have a dominant position in the retail sector, and even though it doesn't technically have monopsony power, it's acting as if it does because of the concentration and power it exerts on its suppliers. Should governments review Walmart's market dominance with thoughts of bringing in new regulations?

While Walmart does experience competition from a number of other large retailers, in the United States, Walmart bigger than Home Depot, Sears, Costco, Target, Kmart, and Kroger combined. At Walmart in the United States, the average family of four spends over $4000 a year, and one out of every four grocery dollars; the company does $474.88 billion a year in sales.* With these numbers, Walmart controls both access to the retail customer and what suppliers can charge to get access to that market.

At what cost does the economy accept this control? For one, suppliers' margins are squeezed, not to be competitive, but to get access to the market. Fewer dollars are available to suppliers for innovation and product development. Suppliers also have to squeeze their workforce in order to reduce costs, which means fewer jobs and those that remain are likely part-time positions with fewer hours and benefits. These supply companies used to be able to provide reasonable benefits, but now they can't, which means employees are forced to seek publicly funded, low-quality benefits—in essence, governments are funding Walmart's employee costs.

*Barry Ritholtz, "Always Low Wages? Wal-Mart's Other Choices," *Bloomberg View*, December 18, 2013, www.bloombergview.com/articles/2013-12-18/always-low-wages-wal-mart-s-other-choices.

With fewer suppliers, Walmart is contributing to the destruction of small and medium-sized enterprises (SMEs), which are the backbone of the North American manufacturing base and the backbone of a healthy economy. It's not only the SMEs that are under siege from Walmart, but even large multinationals that have relied on so much concentrated revenue coming from Walmart that they have no leverage to increase prices for fear of losing the Walmart account. (Walmart, with its market power, could easily contract third-party suppliers to manufacture house-brand products at higher margins than name brands have traditionally held.)

The long-term health of the retail sector depends on fair and open competition. Governments took aim at firms that amassed market power by being the sole producer. They now need to rewrite their anti-trust laws to reflect market conditions where one firm amasses power by being the controlling buyer and restricting access to the consumer market.

In its defence, Walmart has so far successfully argued that it has reduced prices for consumers and been one of North America's largest and most consistent employers. It's been able to provide many jobs and offer the chance of corporate advancement while other companies were cutting back on opportunities. Where Walmart stores act as anchor retailers, other retailers benefit from the traffic that Walmart generates. Walmart says it's not taking market share, but rather is growing the overall retail market. In the end, Walmart has continually argued that it is a net benefit to society.

1. You are the owner of a small hardware store in a town close to where a big box store is located. How would you compete with the big box store?

2. Do you think big box stores have more impact on the supply-side or on the demand-side of the economy? Is your opinion the same when you think about the problem over the different economic terms (short versus long term)?

3. You are living in a town that has a big box retailer. You want to open a business and you don't want to leave town. What type of business would you open and how would you compete?

SECTION CHECK

- The intersection of the labour demand curve and the labour supply curve determines the equilibrium wage and employment in competitive labour markets.
- The labour demand curve can shift if there is a change in productivity or a change in the demand for the final product.
- The labour supply curve can shift if there are changes in immigration or population growth, workers' preferences, nonwage income, or amenities.
- Any market with a single buyer is a monopsony; the labour market represents the most relevant situation.

Labour Unions

- Why do labour unions exist?
- What is the impact of unions on wages?
- Can unions increase worker productivity?

WHY DO LABOUR UNIONS EXIST?

The supply and demand curves for labour can help us better understand the impact of labour unions. Labour unions like the Canadian Auto Workers (CAW) and the United Food and Commercial Workers (UFCW) were formed to increase their members' wages and to improve working conditions. Negotiations between representatives of employers and unions (on behalf of union members) is a process called **collective bargaining**. Why is this necessary? The argument is that when economies begin to industrialize and urbanize, firms become larger and often the "boss" becomes more distant from the workers. In small shops or on farms, workers usually have a close relationship with an owner–employer, but in larger enterprises, the workers may know only a supervisor and have no direct contact with either the owner or upper management. Workers realize that acting together, as a union of workers, gives them more collective bargaining power than acting individually.

collective bargaining
negotiations between representatives of employers and unions

Labour Unions in Canada

On average, just over 4.8 million employees were members of a union and/or covered by a collective agreement in Canada in 2017, up from 4.6 million in 2016. In terms of the overall working population, that means that about 30 percent of total employees were either members of a union or covered by a collective agreement in 2017. Employees in the public sector (governments, Crown corporations, schools, and hospitals) were over four times as likely to have union coverage than employees in the private sector (76 percent versus 16 percent). Low union coverage rates were found for 15- to 24-year-olds (16 percent) compared to 55- to 64-year-olds (36 percent). Geographically, the highest union coverage rate was in Newfoundland and Labrador (39 percent), whereas the lowest union coverage rate was in Alberta (25 percent).*

Wide variation in union coverage rates is observed across different industries. Industries with high rates of union coverage include health care (63 percent), and education, law, and social, community, and government services (59 percent). Low rates of union coverage are found in sales and service occupations (17 percent); natural resources, agriculture, and related production occupations (15 percent); and management occupations (10 percent). Another interesting observation is that sex did not prove to be a significant determinant when it came to union coverage. In 2017, 47.5 percent of total male employees and 52.5 percent of total female employees were members of a union and/or covered by a collective agreement.**

---

*Statistics Canada, https://www150.statcan.gc.ca/n1/daily-quotidien/180309/dq180309a-eng.htm; https://www150.statcan.gc.ca/n1/daily-quotidien/180105/dq180105a-cansim-eng.htm.

**Employment and Social Development Canada, https://www.canada.ca/en/employment-social-development/services/collective-bargaining-data/reports/union-coverage.html.

WHAT IS THE IMPACT OF UNIONS ON WAGES?

Labour unions influence the quantity of union labour hired and the wages at which they are hired primarily through their ability to alter the supply of labour services from what would exist if workers acted independently. One way to do this, of course, is by raising barriers to entry into a given occupation. For example, by restricting membership, unions can reduce the quantity of labour supplied to industry employers from what it otherwise would be, and as a result, wages in that occupation would increase from W_0 to W_1, as shown in Exhibit 1(a). As you can see in the shift from Q_0 to Q_1 in Exhibit 1(a), although some union workers will now receive higher wages, others will become unemployed. Many economists believe that this is why wages are approximately 10–25 percent higher in union jobs, even when nonunion workers have comparable skills. Of course, some of these gains will be appropriated by the unions in the form of union dues, initiation fees, and the like, so the workers themselves will not receive the full benefit.

Wage Differences for Similarly Skilled Workers

Suppose you had two labour sectors: the union sector and the nonunion sector. If unions are successful in obtaining higher wages through bargaining, threatening to strike, or by restricting membership, wages will rise and employment will fall in the union sector, as seen in Exhibit 1(a). With a downward-sloping demand curve for labour, higher wages mean that less labour is demanded in the union sector. Those workers that are equally skilled but are unable to find union work will seek nonunion work, thus increasing supply in that sector and, in turn, lowering wages in the nonunion sector. This effect is shown in Exhibit 1(b). As a result, comparably skilled workers will experience higher wages in the union sector (W_1) than in the nonunion sector (W_2).

section 11.4
Exhibit 1   **The Effect of Unions on Wages**

a. Union Sector

b. Nonunion Sector

Through restrictive membership practices and other means, a union can reduce the labour supply in its industry, thereby increasing the wage rate workers can earn (from W_0 to W_1) but reducing employment (from Q_0 to Q_1), as shown in Exhibit 1(a). However, as workers unable to get jobs in the union sector join the nonunion sector, the supply of labour in the nonunion sector increases (from Q_0 to Q_2), lowering wages in those industries (from W_0 to W_2), as shown in Exhibit 1(b).

CAN UNIONS INCREASE WORKER PRODUCTIVITY?

Harvard University economists Richard Freeman and James Medoff* argue that unions might actually increase worker productivity. Their argument is that unions provide a collective voice that workers can use to communicate their discontents more effectively. This might lower the number of union workers that quit their jobs. Resignations can be particularly costly for firms, because they have often invested in training and job-specific skills for their employees. In addition, by handling workers' grievances, unions may increase worker motivation and morale. The combined impact of fewer resignations and improved morale could boost productivity.

However, this improvement in worker productivity in the union sector should show up on the bottom line—the profit statement of the firm. Although the empirical evidence is mixed, it appears that unions may lower the profitability of firms, not raise it.

---

*Richard B. Freeman and James L. Medoff, *What Do Unions Do?* New York: Basic Books, 1984.

DEBATE

AS LABOUR MARKETS EVOLVE, SHOULD COLLEGE ATHLETES GET UNION RIGHTS?

For:

North American college athletes have begun seeking power through union representation—at a time when governments around the world have been moving to limit the powers of unions. Scholarship student athletes at Northwestern University in Illinois have been spearheading this new drive to seek compensation for the work and risks that the athletes take on.*

Central to the college athletes' argument for union representation is the idea that they are employees of their colleges. As employees, the law would give them the right to form a union if the majority votes for union representation.

While history has proved that unions have protected workers' rights and ensured safe work places, these safeguards have never been in place to protect college athletes, who may be injured during their college careers to the point where they are unable to realize a potential pro career. Further, while the colleges have negotiated multi-billion dollar sponsorships and media contracts, none of those dollars are reaching the relatively few athletes themselves.

What's worse is that athletes are actually barred from receiving any form of compensation for their participation in the sport and for their images that are being used by video game developers. The only benefits they receive are their scholarships and exposure to pro teams.

Against:

Some argue that unions provide the foundations for fair working wages that benefit workers, employers, and society as a whole. But athletes in college are not employees in the eyes of the law—or at least that is the argument that college administrators have been making to defend against unions organizing their players. Administrators believe that they have offered scholarships to attract students to attend their institutions, not as compensation for playing sports.

The players have argued that playing on a team has rules and policies that are in essence similar to those of other employees within the colleges, but the administrators say that team rules can't be compared with terms of employment—they are there to build team unity, not to serve as rules for employment.

A key argument against unionization of athletes is that if it went ahead, only a small group of high-profile athletes would benefit and unionization would actually act as a hindrance to lower-level athletes or athletes of lower-profile sports. Many of these students enter college by using sport scholarships as their main way of getting an affordable education. Many of these athletes could lose out if colleges were forced to offer equal or equitable terms for all athletes.

In recent times, the courts in some parts of the world have heard appeals aimed at trying to save collective bargaining rights, but there have been few instances where people have sought union membership. The college athletes seem to be going against labour market trends. Surely they are clearly not employees.

Questions:
1. Should college athletes be recognized as college employees?
2. Can you think of other reasons why college athletes should be represented by a union?
3. What reasons can you think of that would support those who are against such unionization?

---

*Ben Strauss and Steve Eder, "College Players Granted Right to Form Union," *The New York Times*, March 26, 2014, www.nytimes.com/2014/03/27/sports/ncaafootball/national-labor-relations-board-rules-northwestern-players-are-employees-and-can-unionize.html.

Income Distribution

section

11.5

- What has happened to income distribution since 1976?
- How much income inequality exists in other countries?
- Are we overstating the disparity in the distribution of income?
- Why do some earn more than others?
- How can we remedy discrimination?

The ultimate purpose of producing goods and services is to satisfy the material wants of people. Up to this point, we have examined the process by which society decides which wants to satisfy in a world characterized by scarcity; we have examined the question of how goods are produced; and we have examined the question of how society can fully utilize its productive resources. We have not, however, looked carefully into the question of for whom society produces consumer goods and services. Why are some people able to consume much more than others?

WHAT HAS HAPPENED TO INCOME DISTRIBUTION SINCE 1976?

Exhibit 1 shows a breakdown of 2016 mean (average) household income before tax. Economists rank Canadian households by income and then divide them into five groups (quintiles) based on their income levels. The average income of the richest fifth of Canadian households, at $195 250 was over eleven times greater than that of the poorest fifth of Canadian households, at $16 600.

The Record since 1976

Exhibit 2 illustrates the distribution of income in Canada from 1976 to 2016. The series in Exhibit 2 represents the shares of the total before-tax income in Canada going to each fifth (quintile) of Canadian households. For example, in 2016 the fifth of Canadian households with the lowest incomes received only about 4 percent of the total before-tax income in Canada. The highest fifth (20 percent) of Canadian households received more than

section 11.5 Exhibit 1	Mean Household Income by Quintile, 2016
Quintile	**Income (constant 2016 dollars)**
Lowest quintile	$ 16 600
Second quintile	34 350
Third quintile	64 450
Fourth quintile	100 300
Highest quintile	195 250

SOURCE: Statistics Canada, Table 206-003—Upper income limit, income share and average of market, total and after-tax income by economic family type and income decile, Canada and provinces, annual (accessed May 23, 2018). Reproduced and distributed on an "as is" basis with the permission of Statistics Canada.

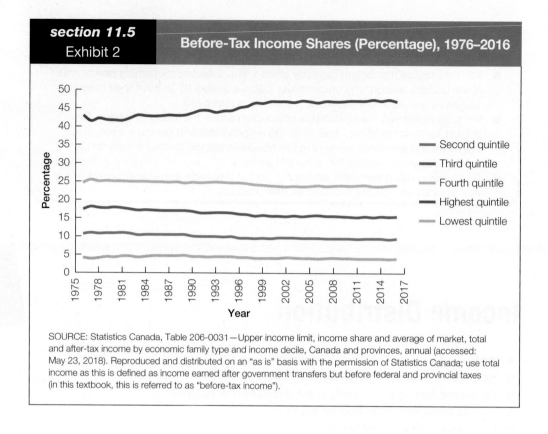

section 11.5
Exhibit 2

Before-Tax Income Shares (Percentage), 1976–2016

SOURCE: Statistics Canada, Table 206-0031—Upper income limit, income share and average of market, total and after-tax income by economic family type and income decile, Canada and provinces, annual (accessed: May 23, 2018). Reproduced and distributed on an "as is" basis with the permission of Statistics Canada; use total income as this is defined as income earned after government transfers but before federal and provincial taxes (in this textbook, this is referred to as "before-tax income").

47 percent of the total before-tax income. In other words, the income share of the highest fifth of Canadian households was over eleven times greater than the income share of the lowest fifth of households.

Looking at the distribution of income in Canada from 1976 to 2016, it is interesting to note that the income shares remained relatively stable over that period. The share of income going to the lowest fifth of households was about 4 percent over the whole period, whereas the share of income going to the middle fifth of households was roughly 15–18 percent over the same period. It is noticeable, however, that the share of income going to the highest fifth of Canadian households had risen from about 43 percent to over 47 percent, suggesting that the rich were getting richer.

HOW MUCH INCOME INEQUALITY EXISTS IN OTHER COUNTRIES?

Is Canada typical of advanced, industrialized nations with respect to the distribution of income among its population? This is a difficult question to answer with absolute certainty, given international differences in defining income, difficulties in measuring the impact of taxes, the problem of nonmonetary payments, and so on. Despite these obstacles, international comparisons of income distribution have been made.

Exhibit 3, constructed with data from the World Bank, shows that income inequality is greater in Canada and the United States than in Iceland and Denmark. Denmark's ratio of 5.5 means that the richest 10 percent of the population makes 5.5 times as much income as the bottom 10 percent. In Zambia, the richest 10 percent of the population makes a staggering 44.4 times as much income as the bottom 10 percent. However, Exhibit 3 also shows that some of the greatest disparities in income are found in developing countries such as Bolivia, Columbia, and Brazil.

		Gap between Rich and Poor (ratio)
Income Inequality	**Country**	
Most Equal	Iceland	5.5
	Denmark	6.4
	Hungary	7.9
	Germany	8
	Ireland	8
	France	8.6
	United Kingdom	8.8
	Canada	10.5
	Russian Federation	10.6
	Italy	12.8
	Greece	13.8
	Mexico	15.8
	Argentina	17.2
	United States	19.1
	Chile	22.4
	Bolivia	29.2
	Colombia	30.8
	Brazil	33.7
Least Equal	Zambia	44.4

section 11.5 Exhibit 3 — **Global Income Inequalities**

The ratio of the richest 10 percent to the poorest 10 percent gives us the gap between rich and poor. A smaller ratio indicates a greater degree of income equality in that country.

SOURCE: The World Bank, *World Development Report*, and author calculations, https://data.worldbank.org/indicator/SI.DST.10TH.10?end=2016&name_desc=false&start=2005&view=chart.

Although income inequality within nations is often substantial, it is far less than income inequality among nations. The majority of global income inequality comprises differences in living standards among countries rather than disparities within nations.

ARE WE OVERSTATING THE DISPARITY IN THE DISTRIBUTION OF INCOME?

Failing to take into consideration differences in age, certain demographic factors, and government taxation and transfer programs, which have all been identified as elements that influence income distribution data, suggests that we might be overstating inequality.

Differences in Age

At any moment in time, middle-aged people tend to have higher incomes than both younger and older people. At middle age, most people are at their peak in terms of productivity, and participate in the labour force to a greater extent than the very old or very young. Put differently, if every individual earned exactly the same total income over his or her lifetime, there would still be some observed inequality at any given moment in time, simply because people earn more in middle age.

Camilla Watson/AWL Images/Getty Images

The contrasts between rich and poor are more extreme in Brazil than in almost any other country in the world. According to the UN Development Program, nearly half of Brazil's population lives in absolute poverty. Those who are unable to make a living as vendors of newspapers or lottery tickets, shoeshine boys, guards for parked cars, or the like are often forced to earn a living illegally. The number of children who work on the streets, or even live there permanently, is estimated to be in the millions.

Other Demographic Trends

Other demographic trends, like the increased number of divorced couples and the rise of two-income families, have also caused the measured distribution of income (which is measured in terms of household income) to appear more unequal. For example, in the 1950s, the majority of families had single incomes. Many modern households have two breadwinners instead of one. Suppose their incomes rise from $50 000 a year to roughly $100 000; these households thus move into a higher-income quintile and create greater apparent income inequality. At the same time, divorces create two households instead of one, lowering income per household for divorced couples; thus, they move into lower-income quintiles, also creating greater apparent income inequality.

Government Activities

The impact of government activity should be considered in evaluating the measured income distribution. Government-imposed taxes burden different income groups in different ways. Most importantly, Canada has a progressive income tax system, which means that higher-income individuals pay a larger proportion of their income in tax than lower-income individuals. The progressivity of the tax system results in the after-tax income distribution being more equal than the before-tax income distribution. In 2016, for example, the shares of after-tax income going to each of the five quintiles were 4 percent, 9.5 percent, 15.5 percent, 24.1 percent, and 46.9 percent, respectively. As you can see when compared to the before-tax shares in Exhibit 2, the share of after-tax income going to each of the lower two quintiles is slightly greater, whereas the after-tax share of the highest quintiles is lower.

Also, government programs benefit some groups of income recipients more than others. For example, it has been argued that government-subsidized higher education has benefited the high- and middle-income groups more than the poor (because far more students from these income groups go to university or college), as have such things as government subsidies to airports, operas, and art museums. Some programs, though, clearly aid the poor more than the rich. Food banks, school lunch programs, housing subsidies, day-care subsidies, and several other programs provide recipients with **in-kind transfers**—that is, transfers of goods and services (nonmonetary) rather than cash (monetary). Many economists conclude that these in-kind transfers have served to reduce levels of inequality from the levels suggested by aggregate income statistics.

in-kind transfers
transfers of goods and services rather than cash

WHY DO SOME EARN MORE THAN OTHERS?

There are many reasons why some people make more income than others. Some reasons for the differences in income include differences in age, skill, education, training, preferences with respect to risk and leisure, and discrimination.

Age

The amount of income people earn varies over their lifetimes. Younger people with few skills tend to make little income when they begin their working careers. Income rises as workers gain experience and on-the-job training. As productivity increases, workers can command higher wages. These wage earnings generally increase up to the age of 50 and fall dramatically at retirement age, around 65.

Skills and Human Capital

Some workers are just more productive than others and therefore earn higher wages. The greater productivity may be a result of innate skills or of improvements in human capital, such as training and education. Still others, like star athletes and rock stars, have specialized talents that are in huge demand, so they make more money than those with fewer skills or with skills that are in less demand.

Worker Preferences

Aside from skills, education, and training, people have different attitudes about and preferences regarding their work. Workaholics work longer hours and so they earn more than others with comparable skills. Some earn more because they work more intensely than others. Still others may choose jobs that pay less but have more amenities—flexible hours, favourable job location, generous benefit programs, child care, and so on. And some may choose to work less and spend more time pursuing leisure activities, like travelling, hobbies, or spending time with family and friends. It is not for us to say that one preference is better than another but simply to recognize that these choices lead to differences in earnings.

Job Preferences

Some of the differences in income are the result of the risks or undesirable features of some occupations. Police officers and firefighters are paid higher wages because of the dangers associated with their jobs. Nickel miners and garbage collectors are paid more than other workers with comparable skill levels because of the unpleasantness of the jobs. In short, some workers have higher earnings because they are compensated for the difficult, risky, or unappealing nature of their jobs.

Discrimination

Finally, some of the differences in income result from employment and wage discrimination. Employment discrimination occurs when a worker is denied employment or promotion on the basis of some feature, such as gender, age, religion, or race, without any regard to his or her productivity. Wage discrimination occurs when a worker is given employment at a wage lower than that of other workers based on an attribute other than productivity. These types of discrimination are illegal but, because they can be difficult to detect, still sometimes occur.

Discrimination is one factor in explaining why men, on average, earn more than women. Studies have shown that even after accounting for a wide range of factors that determine incomes, such as education, training, experience, seniority, and hours worked, a male–female wage gap remains that can be attributed to discrimination in the labour market. Moreover, it is important to note that discrimination outside of the labour market may also contribute to male–female wage inequality. Because women, on average, perform a greater share of household responsibilities, especially child-rearing, this impacts the labour market choices women make in areas such as occupational choice, mobility, training, absenteeism, and hours worked.

HOW CAN WE REMEDY DISCRIMINATION?

In Canada, the problem of employment discrimination is addressed primarily through the Employment Equity Act (1995). This federal legislation requires or encourages Canadian employers to give preferential treatment in employment practices to a list of designated groups—specifically women, persons with disabilities, Indigenous peoples, and visible minorities.

Applying only to companies in federally regulated industries (such as banking, telecommunications, and the airline industry, to name a few) and those corporations that are controlled by two or more provincial/territorial governments, the Act ultimately provides limited coverage. Although some provincial/territorial governments have chosen to incorporate employment equity standards into their provincial/territorial-level human rights legislation, no province/territory has preferential employment practices equivalent to those in the Employment Equity Act.

Policies designed around the concepts of *pay equity* and *pay equality* are intended to address the existence of wage discrimination in Canada. Pay equality, or equal pay for equal work, is required by law in Canada. The principle of pay equality works as follows: Suppose an organization employs both male and female truck drivers, with reasonable allowances for differences in skill or seniority, the female truck drivers would have to be paid the same as the male truck drivers.

Alternatively, pay equity legislation, or equal pay for work of equal value, exists only in certain jurisdictions in Canada (e.g., in Ontario, pay equity is guaranteed through the Ontario Pay Equity Act, 1987). The principle of pay equity works as follows: Suppose an organization's nurses are seen as doing a job that is equal in importance to its plumbers; they must all then be paid the same.

Employment equity programs are controversial. Employment equity may increase the probability that someone will be hired on some basis other than productivity. Although this may be desirable from the standpoint of equalizing opportunities among demographic groups, it also can serve to lower society's output and firms' profits. Furthermore, some critics have raised the "reverse discrimination" equity argument. For example, with respect to productivity, a firm may be forced to hire a worker from one of the designated groups with a marginal revenue product of $80 instead of a nondesignated worker whose marginal revenue product may be $100. Society ultimately loses $20 of output (the difference in the value of marginal output). Moreover, if the firm that hires the worker from one of the designated groups has to pay the prevailing wage (say, $90) to avoid wage discrimination charges, hiring that worker will lower profits. With that, the firm might decide not to hire anyone, knowing that employment equity will prevent it from hiring the profitable nondesignated worker (whose marginal revenue product exceeds the prevailing wage by $10) instead of the worker from one of the designated groups (whose hiring will reduce profits by $10).

Employers' actions to protect profits, then, might negate some or all of the expected gains from employment equity. One alternative to using implicit quotas would be to subsidize employers for hiring members from one of the designated groups. Opponents to this approach regard it as a gift or bailout for business enterprise more than a help to underrepresented workplace groups. The subsidy approach would, however, provide employers with greater incentives to increase job opportunities for designated group members.

SECTION CHECK

- Since 1976, the distribution of income in Canada has been relatively stable.
- Income inequality among nations is substantial.
- Demographics and government programs affect the disparity in income inequality. Not taking these issues into consideration when evaluating income distribution could result in the inequality being overstated.
- Differences in ages, skill, education, training, preferences related to risk and leisure, and discrimination are all possible reasons why some people make more money than others.
- In Canada, the problem of employment discrimination is addressed primarily through the Employment Equity Act (1995).

Poverty

- How do we define *poverty*?
- How many people live in poverty?
- What government programs help to reduce poverty?

At several points in this chapter, the words "rich" and "poor" have been used without being defined. Of particular interest is the question of poverty. Our concern over income distribution largely arises because most people believe that those with low incomes have lower satisfaction than those with higher incomes. Thus, the "poor" people are those who, in a material sense, suffer relative to other people. It is desirable, therefore, to define and measure the extent of poverty in Canada.

HOW DO WE DEFINE *POVERTY*?

Poverty is the condition of a person who is deprived of the resources, means, choices, and power necessary to acquire and maintain a basic level of living standards and to facilitate integration into and participation in society. In Canada, poverty is now measured on an absolute income basis: If someone's income is not enough to afford a fixed basket of goods and services, that person is considered to be living in poverty. This basket of goods and services includes such items as clothing and footwear, transportation, nutritious food, and shelter (including electricity, heat, and clean water) as well as other necessary goods and services, such as personal care items, household supplies, basic telephone service, and entertainment. Previously, poverty in Canada was measured on a relative basis. If someone's income was lower than is socially acceptable when compared to the income of other Canadians, that person would have been considered poor.

Based on the absolute definition, Employment and Social Development Canada has introduced a measure called *Canada's Official Poverty Line* (formerly known as the Market Basket Measure) that now represents Canada's official measure of poverty. **Canada's Official Poverty Line** measures the level of income necessary to allow a household to buy a specific basket of goods and services that allows them to meet their basic needs and achieve a modest standard of living in their community. The reference family for calculating Canada's Official Poverty Line is two adults between 25 and 49 years, and two children, a 9-year-old girl and a 13-year-old boy. These expenditures are then adjusted for family size and extrapolated to all other Canadians.

The cost of this basket of goods and services is adjusted to reflect poverty thresholds for 50 different regions across the country, including 19 specific communities. In 2016, the official poverty line for a family of two adults and two children averaged $37 650 across the 50 regions for which it was calculated, varying from $32 970 in parts of the province of Quebec to $41 287 in the city of Toronto.

HOW MANY PEOPLE LIVE IN POVERTY?

Based on Canada's Official Poverty Line, we can measure the incidence of poverty as the percentage of households whose income falls below the income cut-off. Exhibit 2 provides a summary of poverty rates among households based on selected characteristics of the household.

poverty
the condition of a person who is deprived of the resources, means, choices, and power necessary to acquire and maintain a basic level of living standard and to facilitate integration into and participation in society

Canada's Official Poverty Line
level of income necessary to allow a household to buy a specific basket of goods and services that allows them to meet their basic needs and achieve a modest standard of living in their community

Canada's Official Poverty Line, by Region, 2016

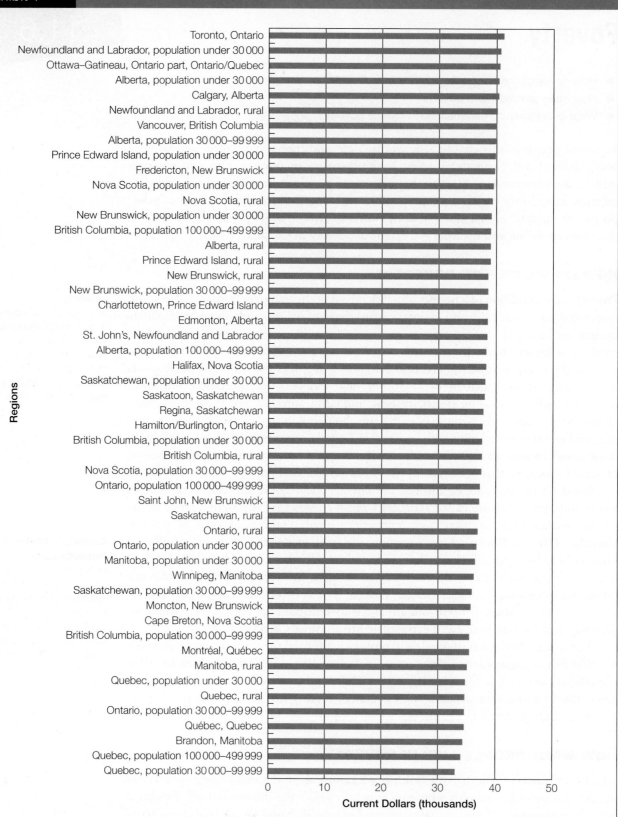

SOURCE: Statistics Canada, Table 11-10-0230-01—Market Basket Measure (MBM) thresholds (2011 base) for reference family, by Market Basket Measure region and component, in current dollars and 2016 constant dollars. Reproduced and distributed on an "as is" basis with the permission of Statistics Canada.

section 11.6 Exhibit 2	The Incidence of Low Income, by Selected Household Characteristics, 2016

Characteristic	Percentage of Persons in Poverty
Persons in economic families	7.4
Persons not in an economic family	27.6
Persons in lone-parent families	29.2
Persons in female lone-parent families	33.5
Non-elderly males not in an economic family	32.0
Non-elderly females not in an economic family	36.4

SOURCES: Statistics Canada, Income in Canada, 75-202-XIE2009000, June 2011; http://www.statcan.gc.ca/bsolc/olc-cel/olc-cel?catno=75-202-XIE&lang=eng#formatdisp; Statistics Canada, Table 206-0041—Low income statistics by age, sex and economic family type, Canada, provinces and selected census metropolitan areas (CMAs), annual; and Statistics Canada, Table 206-0042—Low income statistics by economic family type, Canada, provinces and selected census metropolitan areas (CMAs), annual.

Attached individuals—those belonging to a group of two or more persons who live in the same dwelling and are related to each other by a blood, marriage, common-law, adoption, or foster relationship—have a 7.4 percent incidence of poverty, whereas unattached individuals have a 27.6 percent incidence of poverty. Being a single parent also appears to contribute to poverty. Persons in lone-parent families are four times more likely to experience poverty when compared to persons in couple families (29.2 percent compared to 7.4 percent, respectively). This rate increases to 33.5 percent when the lone parent is a female.

Some of the highest instances of poverty result from the combined effect of sex, family circumstances, and age. For example, for single males under 65 years of age, the

section 11.6 Exhibit 3	The Poverty Rate in Canada, 2002—16

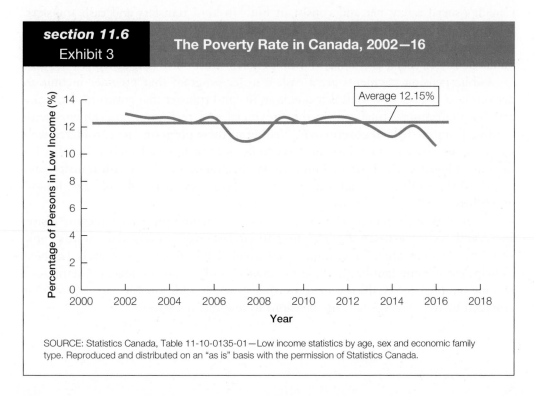

SOURCE: Statistics Canada, Table 11-10-0135-01—Low income statistics by age, sex and economic family type. Reproduced and distributed on an "as is" basis with the permission of Statistics Canada.

incidence of poverty is 32.0 percent. For single females under 65, the poverty incidence rate is 36.4 percent.

Overall then, how many Canadian families are considered poor, and is the problem getting better or worse? The incidence of poverty in Canada, as defined by the percentage of households that cannot afford a fixed basket of goods and services, is illustrated in Exhibit 3. Commonly referred to as the *poverty rate*, the measure has most recently ranged between a high of just over 13 percent in 2002 to a low of just over 10.5 percent in 2016. While the current poverty rate is below the average rate of 12 percent, there appears to be no defined trend in poverty.

WHAT GOVERNMENT PROGRAMS HELP TO REDUCE POVERTY?

A variety of government programs are designed to reduce poverty and redistribute income. We examine several of them here.

Taxes

progressive tax system

As a person's income rises, the amount of his or her tax as a proportion of income rises.

One way to redistribute income to reduce disparities among individuals is through federal and provincial income taxes. The federal income tax (and the majority of provincial income tax) is designed to be a **progressive tax system**—as a person's income rises, the amount of tax as a proportion of income rises. For example in 2018, an individual would pay 15 percent federal tax on the first $46 605 of taxable income, 20.5 percent on the next $46 603 of taxable income, 26 percent on the next $51 281 of taxable income, 29 percent on the next $61 353 of taxable income, and 33 percent on taxable income over $205 842.

Social Insurance Programs

cash transfer

direct cash payment such as public pensions, social assistance, and Employment Insurance benefits

A second means by which income redistribution can be carried out by the government is through social insurance programs operated by the federal government, the provinces and territories, and municipalities. These programs are often referred to as Canada's social safety net and consist of both in-kind transfers and cash transfers. In-kind transfers are direct transfers of goods and services such as education vouchers and school lunch programs, whereas **cash transfers** are direct cash payments such as public pensions, social assistance, and Employment Insurance (EI) benefits.

Public pension payments are a cash transfer program that provides income to persons over the age of 65. Health care is an in-kind transfer that covers medical care and hospitalization—financed by the provincial and territorial governments with funding from the federal government. Neither of these programs are considered welfare programs because one does not have to be poor to receive benefits. Benefits for the unemployed in the form of Employment Insurance are also a cash transfer payment. All three of these social insurance programs are event-based—old age, illness, or job loss.

Known by such names as "social assistance," "income support," "income assistance," and "welfare assistance," these programs of last resort are targeted toward people with little or no income. For example, the Canada Child Benefit program is designed to help low-income families provide for their children, and the federal Guaranteed Income Supplement (GIS) is a program that provides additional money (above that provided by the Old Age Security pension) to low-income seniors.

Government Subsidies

A third way that governments can help the less affluent is by using government revenues to provide low-cost public services. Inexpensive public housing, subsidized public transportation, and even public parks are services that probably serve the poor to a greater extent than the rich. "Free" public education is viewed by many as an equalizing force in that it opens up opportunities for children of less prosperous members of society to obtain employment that could improve their economic status. Of course, not all government programs benefit the relatively poor at the expense of the rich. For example, provincial government subsidies to universities may help middle-income and upper-income groups more than the poor. In addition, there are agricultural subsidies that often provide large benefits to farmers who may already have sufficient incomes.

Minimum Wage

Can a higher minimum wage ease the burden on the poor? We discussed the minimum wage in Chapter 4. You may recall that the minimum-wage law forbids employers to pay a wage less than the minimum wage. In Canada, provinces and territories administer their own minimum-wage legislation—for example, the minimum-wage in the Northwest Territories is $13.46 (effective April 1, 2018).

Almost all economists would agree that a large increase in the minimum wage—say, to $20—would have a devastating effect on the unskilled labour market: Many small businesses would have to shut their doors, leaving many unskilled workers without jobs. There is some debate among economists over the elasticity of the demand curve for labour. If the demand curve for labour is relatively inelastic, an increase in the minimum wage leads to only a small reduction in employment. However, if the demand curve for labour is relatively elastic, the reduction in employment is larger.

Critics of a higher minimum wage argue that it is poorly targeted if its object is to reduce poverty, because many of the recipients of the minimum wage are teenagers living in households that are not facing poverty. Some argue that a policy focusing on subsidizing the wages of the poor would go much further in reducing poverty. That is, society needs to find more effective policies for low-wage workers—perhaps job-training programs.

SECTION CHECK

- In Canada, poverty is defined on an absolute income basis. If a household's income is too low to afford the fixed basket of goods and services, it is classified as being poor.
- The incidence of low income varies depending on the characteristics of the household, such as family type, age, sex, and education.
- A variety of government programs are designed to reduce poverty: progressive income tax, cash transfers, in-kind transfers, social assistance, and minimum wages.

For Your Review

Section 11.1

1. What would happen to the demand for unskilled labour if there was an increase in the demand for hamburgers and fries?

2. The following figure illustrates the market for apple pickers.

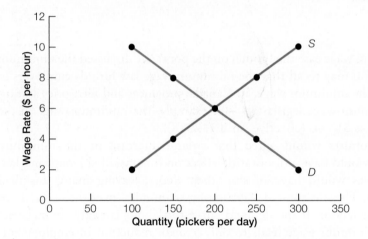

   a. What is the wage rate paid to apple pickers?

   b. How many apple pickers have been hired?

   c. If the demand for apples increases, resulting in 100 more apple pickers per day being hired, what would be the new wage rate paid to pickers?

Section 11.2

Blueprint Question

Consider a company operating in a perfectly competitive market. It sells its output for $26 a unit and pays its workers $250 a day. The following table shows the marginal productivity of each worker.

Number of Workers	Marginal Productivity (number of units/day)
0	
1	16
2	13
3	9
4	6
5	2

What is the profit-maximizing number of workers that this company should hire at this market wage rate?

Blueprint Solution

Notice that in this question you are given the marginal productivity (*MP*) of each worker. Had you been given total productivity (*TP*), you would have needed to compute *MP* (to see how to do this, consult the Blueprint Problem in Chapter 1).

Profit-maximizing decision rule for firm:
Hire workers until
$MRP = MRC$

A	B	C	D	E
Number of Workers	Marginal Productivity (number of units/day)	Marginal Revenue of Product (*MRP*) of Labour ($ per day)	Marginal Resource Cost (*MRC*) (wage per day)	Profit-Maximizing Decision, Firm
0				
1	16	$416	$250	Hire
2	13	$338	$250	Hire
3	9	$234	$250	Do not hire
4	6	$156	$250	Do not hire
5	2	$52	$250	Do not hire

The *MRP* of labour (per day) $= MP \times P$

The company's demand curve for labour is given by the downward-sloping portion of the marginal revenue of product (*MRP*) curve. A profit-maximizing firm will add labour as long as *MRP* > wage. By referring to column E, you can see that the firm will choose to hire two workers.

Use the following table to answer questions 3 and 4.

Quantity of Labour	Total Output/Week	Marginal Product of Labour	Marginal Revenue Product of Labour
0	–		
1	250		
2	600		
3	900		
4	1125		
5	1300		
6	1450		
7	1560		

3. The table above shows the total output each week of workers in a perfectly competitive apple orchard. The equilibrium price of a kilogram of apples is $4. Complete the Marginal Product of Labour and the Marginal Revenue Product of Labour columns in the table.

4. Using the same table, how many workers will the owner hire if the equilibrium wage rate is $550 per week? $650 per week?

5. Fill in the missing data in the following table.

Workers	Total Corn Output	Marginal Product of Labour
1	4000	
2	10 000	
3	15 000	
4		3000
5		1000
6		−1000

6. What is responsible for a backward-bending individual supply curve for labour?

7. Fill in the missing data for a perfectly competitive firm in the following table.

Workers	Total Output	Marginal Product	Price	Marginal Revenue Product
1	200		$20	
2	380		20	
3	540		20	
4	680		20	
5	800		20	
6	900		20	
7	980		20	
8	1040		20	

8. Would the owner of University Pizza Parlour hire another worker for $60 per day if that worker added 40 pizzas a day and each pizza added $2 to University Pizza Parlour's revenues? Why or why not?

Section 11.3

9. If a competitive firm is paying $8 per hour (without fringe benefits) to its employees, what would tend to happen to its equilibrium wage if the company began to give on-the-job training or free dental insurance to its workers? What would happen to its on-the-job training or dental insurance for its workers if the government mandated a minimum wage of $12 an hour?

10. Professional athletes command and receive higher salaries than teachers. Yet teachers, not athletes, are considered essential to economic growth and development. If this is in fact the case, why do athletes receive higher salaries than teachers?

11. The availability of jobs at higher real wages motivates many people to migrate to Canada. Other things equal, what impact would a large influx of immigrants have on Canadian real wages?

12. The dean of Anara University knows that poets generally earn less than engineers in the private market; that is, the equilibrium wage for engineers is higher than that for poets—in the same way that professional athletes command and receive higher salaries than teachers do. The administration at Anara University believes that salaries should be equal across all disciplines because its professors work equally hard and because all of the professors have similar qualifications. As a result, Anara University opts to pay all of its professors a mid-range wage. Suppose that all colleges and universities, except Anara University, paid their professors according to their potential private market wage. What do you think is likely to happen to the engineering and poetry programs at Anara University?

13. Use the following diagram to answer questions (a) through (i).

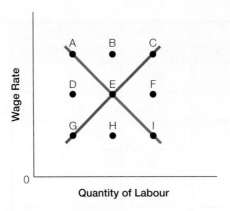

Indicate which point could correspond to the equilibrium wage and quantity hired

a. at the initial equilibrium.

b. if the price of the output produced by the labour increased.

c. if the price of the output produced by the labour decreased.

d. with an increase in immigration.

e. with a reduction in the quality of workplace amenities.

f. if worker productivity increased and workers' nonwage incomes increased.

g. if worker productivity decreased and population decreased.

h. if the price of output produced by the labour increased and the number of hours that workers were willing to work increased.

i. if the price of output produced by the labour decreased and workers' nonwage incomes decreased.

14. How would each of the following affect the demand or supply of workers? In each case, determine the impact on equilibrium wage and quantity.

a. Immigration increases dramatically.

b. Demand for Canadian manufactured goods declines.

c. New computerized technology increases the productivity of Canadian workers.

d. Canadian firms increase job amenities for workers.

e. Canadian workers choose more leisure.

Section 11.4

15. Use the following diagrams to answer questions (a) through (c).

a. If unions are unable to have any effect on wages, draw the supply curve for the nonunion market.

b. If unions become able to restrict the supply of labour in the union sector, indicate what would happen in both the union and nonunion sectors.

c. What happens to the union wage and the number of union workers hired in (b)? What happens to the nonunion wage and the number of nonunion workers hired in (b)?

16. Explain why some economists believe that labour unions are responsible for increasing workplace productivity.

Section 11.5

17. Explain at least three reasons why the official data on the distribution of income may overstate the actual degree of income inequality.

18. In 2016, the average employment income (2016 constant dollars) for Canadian males was $51900, but it was only $36000 for Canadian women.* Provide some possible explanations for this difference in annual earnings.

19. How might each of the following affect the distribution of income in the near term?

   a. a massive influx of low-skilled immigrants

   b. a new baby boom occurs

   c. the babies in (b) enter their twenties

   d. the babies in (b) reach age 65 or older

20. The following table contains income distributions from five nations—divided into quintiles (20 percent segments of the population).

Income Distribution Data by Country, 2008					
	Switzerland	Peru	Sweden	Mexico	Honduras
Highest quintile	38.7	54.8	33.4	54.9	58.4
Fourth quintile	22.4	20.8	22.7	19.8	20.4
Third quintile	17.3	13.0	18.7	12.8	12.1
Second quintile	13.2	7.8	15.2	8.3	6.7
Lowest quintile	8.4	3.6	10	4.2	2.5

a. Based on the evidence presented in the table, which country displayed the greatest degree of income inequality (the greatest difference between the top quintile and the bottom quintile)?

b. Based on the evidence presented in the table, which country displayed the lowest degree of income inequality (the least difference between the top quintile and the bottom quintile)?

21. If every individual earned the same total income over his or her lifetime, why would we still see inequality at a given point in time?

---

*Statistics Canada, Table 11-10-0240-01 (formerly CANSIM Table 206-0053)—Distribution of employment income of individuals by sex and work activity, Canada, provinces and selected census metropolitan areas.

22. How might a significant reduction in the divorce rate affect the distribution of income?

Section 11.6

23. Can economic growth reduce poverty? How does the answer depend on whether we are using an absolute or relative measure of poverty?

24. Refer to Section 11.6, Exhibit 1, to answer this question. Ryan and Trisha live in Medicine Hat, Alberta (population 63 500) with their two children, who are both under the age of 18. Ryan works as a factory labourer and earns $37 000 a year. Trisha is a stay-at-home mother.

    a. According to the Canada's Official Poverty Line (2016), are Ryan, Trisha, and their two children "poor"? Explain.

    b. Suppose Ryan and Trisha decide to move their family to rural New Brunswick and become potato farmers. If their projected income is $45 000, according to Canada's Official Poverty Line, are Ryan, Trisha, and their two children still "poor"? Explain.

25. What are some of the Canadian programs designed to reduce poverty and redistribute income?

chapter

12

Market Failure and the Environment

Externalities

- What are externalities?
- What are negative externalities?
- What are positive externalities?
- What can the government do to correct for positive externalities?
- Are there nongovernmental solutions to externalities?

WHAT ARE EXTERNALITIES?

Even if the economy is competitive, it is still possible that the market system fails to produce the efficient level of output because of side effects that economists call *externalities*. An **externality** is a benefit or cost from consumption or production that spills over onto those that are not consuming or producing the good. Externalities are caused by economic agents—producers and consumers—receiving the wrong signals. That is, the free market works well in providing most goods but does less well without regulations, taxes, and subsidies in providing others.

externality
a benefit or cost from consumption or production that spills over onto those that are not consuming or producing the good

WHAT ARE NEGATIVE EXTERNALITIES?

A **negative externality** occurs when costs spill over to an outside party that is not involved in producing or consuming the good. The classic example of a negative externality, which we will be investigating in the next section, is pollution from an air-polluting factory, such as a steel mill. If the firm uses clean air in production and returns dirty air to the atmosphere, it has created a negative externality. The polluted air has "spilled over" to outside parties. Now people in the neighbouring communities may experience higher incidences of disease, dirtier houses, and other property damage. Such damages are real costs, but because no one owns the air, the firm does

negative externality
when costs spill over to an outside party that is not involved in producing or consuming the good

not have to pay for its use, unlike the other resources the firm uses in production. A steel mill has to pay for labour, capital, energy, and raw materials because it must compensate the owners of those inputs for their use. If a firm can avoid paying the cost it imposes on others—the external costs—it has lowered its own costs of production, but not the true cost to society.

Examples of negative externalities are numerous: the roommate who plays his stereo too loud at 2:00 A.M.; the neighbour's dog that barks all night long or leaves "messages" on your front lawn; the commuter who talks loudly on her cellphone while riding on a crowded bus. Driving our cars may be another area in which people don't bear the full costs of their choices. We pay the price to purchase cars, as well as to maintain, insure, and fuel them—those are the private costs. But do we pay for all of our external costs such as emissions, congestion, wear and tear on our highways, and the possible harm to those driving in cars smaller than ours?

WHAT ARE POSITIVE EXTERNALITIES?

positive externality
when benefits spill over to an outside party that is not involved in producing or consuming the good

A **positive externality** occurs when benefits spill over to an outside party that is not involved in producing or consuming the good. So, unlike negative externalities, positive externalities benefit others. For some goods, the individual consumer receives all of the benefits. If you buy a hamburger, for example, you get all of its benefits. But take, for example, a company that landscapes its property with beautiful flowers and sculptures. The landscaping may create a positive externality for those who walk or drive by the company grounds. Or, consider education. Certainly, when you "buy" an education, you receive many of its benefits: greater future income, more choice of future occupations, and the consumption value of knowing more about life as a result of classroom (and extracurricular) learning. These benefits, however, great as they may be, are not all of the benefits associated with your education. You may be less likely to be unemployed or commit crimes, and you may end up curing cancer or solving some other social problem. These nontrivial benefits are the positive external benefits of education.

The government frequently subsidizes education. Why? Presumably because the private market does not provide enough. It is argued that the education of a person benefits not only that person, but all of society, because a more informed citizenry can make more intelligent collective decisions that benefit everyone. Another example: Why do public-health departments sometimes offer free inoculations against certain communicable diseases, such as influenza? Partly because by protecting one group of citizens, everyone gets some protection; if the first citizen does not get the disease, it prevents that person from passing it on to others. Many governmental efforts in the field of health and education are justified on the basis of perceived positive externalities. Of course, because positive externalities are often difficult to measure, it is hard to empirically demonstrate whether many governmental educational and health programs achieve their intended purpose.

In short, the presence of positive externalities interferes with reaching economic efficiency because of the tendency for the market to underallocate (produce too little) of this good.

Graphing Positive External Benefits

Let's take the case of a new vaccine against the common cold. The market for the vaccine is shown in Exhibit 1. The demand curve $D_{PRIVATE}$ represents the prices and quantities that buyers would be willing to pay in the private market to reduce their

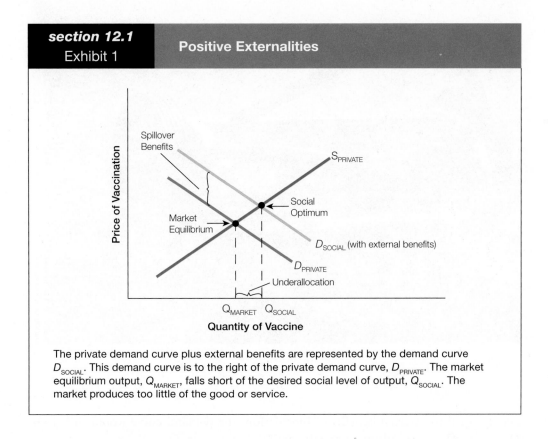

section 12.1
Exhibit 1

Positive Externalities

The private demand curve plus external benefits are represented by the demand curve D_{SOCIAL}. This demand curve is to the right of the private demand curve, $D_{PRIVATE}$. The market equilibrium output, Q_{MARKET}, falls short of the desired social level of output, Q_{SOCIAL}. The market produces too little of the good or service.

probability of catching the common cold. The supply curve shows the amounts that suppliers would offer for sale at different prices. However, at the equilibrium market output, Q_{MARKET}, we are far short of the socially optimum level of output for vaccinations, Q_{SOCIAL}. Why? Many people benefit from the vaccines, including those who do not have to pay for them; they are now less likely to be infected because others took the vaccine. If we could add the benefits derived by nonpaying consumers, the demand curve would shift to the right, from $D_{PRIVATE}$ to D_{SOCIAL}. The greater level of output, Q_{SOCIAL}, which would result if D_{SOCIAL} was the observed demand, reflects the socially optimal output level. However, because producers are unable to collect payments from all of those who are benefiting from the good or service, the market has a tendency to underproduce. In this case, the market is not producing enough vaccinations from society's standpoint, so there is an *underallocation* of resources because from society's standpoint we are producing too little of this good or service, producing Q_{MARKET} rather than Q_{SOCIAL}.

WHAT CAN THE GOVERNMENT DO TO CORRECT FOR POSITIVE EXTERNALITIES?

How could society correct for this market failure? Two particular methods of achieving the higher preferred output are subsidies and regulation.

Subsidies

Government could provide a subsidy to achieve the higher preferred output—either give refunds to individuals who receive an inoculation or provide an incentive for businesses to give their employees "free" inoculations at the office. If the subsidy was

People might take steps on their own to minimize negative externalities. For example, to lower pollution, some people might use battery-powered mowers, or even old-fashion push mowers, rather than gasoline mowers.

exactly equal to external benefits of inoculation, the demand curve would shift from D_{PRIVATE} to D_{SOCIAL}, resulting in an efficient level of output, Q_{SOCIAL}.

Regulation

The government could also pass a regulation requiring each person to get an inoculation. This would also shift the demand curve to the right toward the efficient level of output.

In summary, when there are positive externalities, the private market supplies too little of the good in question (such as education or inoculations for communicable diseases). When there are negative externalities, the market supplies too much. In either case, buyers and sellers are receiving the wrong signals. The free market works fine in providing most goods because most goods do not have externalities. When there are externalities, the market fails to allocate resources efficiently.

ARE THERE NONGOVERNMENTAL SOLUTIONS TO EXTERNALITIES?

Sometimes the externality problems can be handled by individuals without the intervention of government, and people may decide to take steps on their own to minimize negative externalities. Moral and social codes may prevent some people from littering, driving gas-guzzling cars, or using gas-powered mowers. The same self-regulation also applies to positive externalities. Philanthropists, for example, frequently donate money to universities and colleges. In part, this must be because they view the positive externalities from education as a good buy for their charitable dollars.

> **SECTION CHECK**
>
> ■ Externalities are the costs or benefits from either production or consumption that spill over onto those that are not producing or consuming the good.
> ■ If a market activity has a negative impact on an outside party, that side effect is called a *negative externality.*
> ■ If a market activity has a positive impact on an outside party, that side effect is called a *positive externality.*
> ■ The government can provide subsidies or regulations to correct the underallocation problem associated with positive externalities.
> ■ Nongovernment solutions to externalities are possible if people self-regulate personal behaviour either to prevent negative externalities or to promote positive externalities.

Negative Externalities and Pollution

section
12.2

● What are social costs?
● Can externalities be accurately measured?

WHAT ARE SOCIAL COSTS?

As we learned in the previous section, whenever an economic activity has benefits or costs that are shared by individuals other than the demanders or suppliers of a good or service, an externality is involved. If the activity imposes costs on individuals other than the demanders or suppliers of a good or service, it is said to have negative externalities. Put another way, negative externalities exist any time the social costs of producing a good or service exceed the private costs. *Social costs* refer to costs that spill over to other members of society. *Private costs* refer to costs incurred by the producers or consumers of the good or service.

Negative Externalities and Pollution

The classic example of a negative externality is pollution. When a steel mill puts soot into the air as a by-product of making steel, it imposes costs on others not connected with the steel mill or with buying or selling steel. The soot requires nearby homeowners to paint their houses more often, entailing costs. Studies show that respiratory diseases are more prevalent in areas with high air pollution, imposing substantial costs and often shortening lives. In addition, the steel mill might discharge chemicals or overheated water into a stream, killing wildlife, ruining business for those who make a living fishing, spoiling recreational activities for the local population, and so on.

In deciding how much to produce, the steelmakers are governed by demand and supply. They do not worry (unless forced to) about the external costs imposed on members of society, and in all likelihood, the steelmakers would not even know the full extent of those costs.

section 12.2
Exhibit 1

The Effect of a Negative Externality

MSC (MPC + External costs)

S = MPC

Price of Steel

P_{SOCIAL}

$P_{PRIVATE}$

Marginal External Cost

0

Q_{SOCIAL} $Q_{PRIVATE}$

D

Quantity of Steel

The industry would normally produce where demand equals supply (where supply is equal to the marginal private costs), at output $Q_{PRIVATE}$ and charging price $P_{PRIVATE}$. If, however, the industry was forced to also pay those external costs imposed on others, the industry would produce where demand equals marginal social costs, at output Q_{SOCIAL} and price P_{SOCIAL}. When firms are not forced to pay for negative externalities, output tends to be larger and prices lower than at the optimal output, where the marginal benefits to society (as measured by demand) equal the marginal costs to society.

internalized externalities
when an industry is forced to compensate those enduring some negative externality caused by its production

Consider the hypothetical steel industry in Exhibit 1. It produces where demand and supply intersect, at output $Q_{PRIVATE}$ and $P_{PRIVATE}$. Let us assume that the marginal social cost of producing the product is indicated by the marginal social cost (*MSC*) curve, lying above the supply curve, which represents the industry's marginal private costs (*MPC*). The marginal social costs of production are higher at all output levels, as those costs include all of the industry's private costs plus the costs that spill over to other members of society from the pollution produced by the industry—that is, the external costs.

At output Q_{SOCIAL}, the marginal social costs to society equal the marginal social benefits (as indicated by the demand curve) from the sale of the last unit of steel. At that output, the price of steel is P_{SOCIAL}. If the firm was somehow forced to compensate people who endure the costs of its pollution, the firm would produce at output Q_{SOCIAL} and price steel at P_{SOCIAL}. When an industry is forced to compensate those enduring some negative externality caused by its production, the industry is said to have **internalized externalities**. When negative externalities are internalized, steel firms produce less output (Q_{SOCIAL} instead of $Q_{PRIVATE}$) and charge higher prices (P_{SOCIAL} instead of $P_{PRIVATE}$). Optimal output occurs where the marginal social costs are equal to the marginal social benefits. When firms do not pay all of the social costs they incur, and therefore produce too much output, the result is too much pollution. The output of pollution is directly related to the output of the primary goods produced by the firm.

CAN EXTERNALITIES BE ACCURATELY MEASURED?

It is generally accepted that in the absence of intervention, the market mechanism will underproduce goods and services with positive externalities, such as education,

Besides polluting the air, this factory is polluting water downstream from it, creating a negative externality for those who fish downstream. It is possible that the people who fish could try to bargain with the factory, perhaps even pay it to pollute less. However, sometimes private bargaining does not work and the government can provide a solution through regulation or pollution taxes.

and overproduce those with negative externalities, such as pollution. But the exact extent of these market misallocations is quite difficult to establish in the real world because the divergence between social and private costs and benefits is often difficult to measure. For example, exactly how much damage at the margin does a steel mill's air pollution do to nonconsumers of the steel? No one really knows because no market fully measures those costs. Indeed, the costs are partly nonpecuniary, meaning that no outlay of money occurs. Even though we pay dollars to get medicine for respiratory ailments and pay dollars for paint to repair pollution-caused paint peeling of homes in the vicinity of plants, we do not make explicit money payments for the visual pollution and undesirable odours that the mill might produce as a by-product of making steel. Nonpecuniary costs

Business *CONNECTION*

CAPITALISM IN TRANSITION

One challenge of the capitalistic model of economics is that growth is necessary for it to continue over the long run. Over the past millennia, attaining growth has never been a real problem, but doing so at the right levels has—and it's been left to economists and politicians to debate what those levels are.

Also at the forefront of decision making is how to distribute the fruits of growth: in an efficient manner or in an equitable manner? Choosing efficiency means extracting the greatest amount of growth for the least amount of cost. In this model, profits are of the greatest importance, and economists argue that once we achieve the highest profits or the greatest growth, there is more to distribute to the wider economy. In essence, this is the building of a bigger pie. But building a bigger pie has its limits, and now both business and society are having to rethink the profit-maximizing model.

Many businesses (and countries) are recognizing that there is a limit to the resources that the earth has to offer, as well as a limit to the demand for products that consumers want and are able to buy. There are now concerns that the capitalism model can't hold up, given current conventional thought. This doesn't necessarily mean the end of capitalism, but perhaps a revised edition is coming! How would businesses respond or what would they need to do to survive in this new form of capitalism?

We already see some evidence of progressive companies changing their goals and missions. Instead of operating their businesses to make the most profit, they're operating in a socially responsible and sustainable manner. This might mean they will limit profits and redirect funds back into the business for hiring employees (who in turn buy the products they make) or invest in the environment so that the resources that the company uses will be there for millennia. It may also change the way that they view waste: At one time, waste was seen as a cost, but now corporations are looking at waste as a beneficial resource.

Other companies are looking at changes to their manufacturing systems with a view to conserving resources. For an example of this new approach to manufacturing, we have

to look no further than BMW's C$600 million assembly facility for its "i" series of electric and hybrid vehicles. Requiring 50 percent less power and 70 percent less water per car (as compared to its traditional production), BMW claims this new facility is the most sustainable automobile plant in the world.

Manufacturing decisions such as those undertaken by BMW have higher short-term costs but lower long-term costs, especially when the company considers internalizing the externality costs of waste. In the near future, these companies will opt for longer-term solutions and benefits over the shorter-term answers. They will also be considering the benefits and costs to all stakeholders (which is society at large), not just the shareholders. So we will be looking at what is good for the masses and finding ways to make it good for individuals as well. This is not socialism—it's sustainable capitalism—but it will require an acceptance of looking at our problems from a different perspective. Few things are more effective at forcing markets to function differently than when they are confronted with scarcity. Perhaps corporations of the future will act in a socially responsible manner, not because they are forced politically to do so, but because it just makes good business sense.

1. To encourage companies to be more sustainable, what do you think consumers can do that would have an impact on the companies' decisions?

2. What are some ideas you have that companies could undertake on the supply-side to promote sustainable capitalism? What could they do on the demand-side?

3. What do you think are the biggest challenges businesses face in attempting to change into more socially responsible organizations?

4. Remember that demand is based on want and ability to purchase. Do you think consumers would pay more to ensure the survival of socially responsible firms? Do you think prices are the primary motivator on the demand-side? Are prices the primary inhibitor on the supply-side? Explain your comments.

are real costs and potentially have a monetary value that can be associated with them, but assessing that value in practical terms is immensely difficult. You might be able to decide how much you would be willing to pay to live in a pollution-free world, but no current mechanism allows anyone to express the perceived monetary value of having clear air to breathe and smell. Even some pecuniary, or monetary, costs are difficult to truly measure: How much respiratory disease is caused by pollution and how much by other factors such as secondhand cigarette smoke? Environmental economists continue to make progress in valuing these difficult damages.

Can skyscrapers be good for the environment? People who live in the city usually drive less, use more public transportation, and also use less electricity and home heating because they tend to live in smaller living spaces compared to suburbanites. As a result, central city residents may emit less carbon into the atmosphere than suburbanites.

Crocodile Images/Thinkstock

DEBATE

ARE THE OIL SANDS WORTH THE ENVIRONMENTAL COSTS FOR CANADA?

For:

The strongest argument for the ongoing development of the Alberta oil sands centres on the revenues they create for the Canadian economy—revenues that are shared among a wide range of stakeholders. This industry creates hundreds of thousands of jobs, mainly in western Canada but also across the nation and across borders. Think about how much Alberta, British Columbia, and Saskatchewan have grown over the past 40 years.

The oil sands mean jobs not only in the oil industry, but also in virtually every facet of a modern economy— housing, manufacturing, and transportation. So vast is this employment need that workers literally fly across Canada to meet the demand. Think also of the R&D that has been done in relation to the oil sands, the results of which have been used in faraway regions.

The need for low-cost fuel justifies the development of key transportation links, such as Keystone and Northern Gateway developments; once completed, they will provide an almost endless supply of secure oil to refineries around North America and the world. While it's recognized that the oil sands development does some harm, that actually occurs in a remote area, with limited impact. What has to be considered is the greatest good for the greatest number of people, and the remoteness of this development provides a strong argument for its continued growth.

The Alberta oil sands have replaced the manufacturing engine of central Canada. If environmentalists slow down the oil sands development, the impact on the Canadian GDP and federal and provincial coffers will be great, with higher unemployment rates, higher tax rates to offset the declining royalties, and lower levels of public service across the nation.

Against:

The fact that the oil sands have been developed in a remote area of the country is tragic—most people have experienced only the benefits. But this development is not a clean technology and there has been little regard so far for the costs to our environment. It's not just the land that's affected, but the health and vitality of the whole ecosystem, including human welfare.

The land where the oil sands are located is boreal forest and muskeg and it acts as a key ecological area in water and forestation. Recovering the bitumen from the sands requires vast amounts of water and natural gas, because water is heated into steam and injected into the ground to unlock the viscous oil. Three to five cubic metres of water are needed to recover a single cubic metre of oil.

The key watershed is the Athabasca River, from which this water is drawn. Once the water has been drawn and used, it is polluted and has to be either treated and released or stored as tailing pond water. Vast ponds have been created, but they fill to capacity in short order and cannot be truly contained, which means thousands of cubic metres of toxic tailings entering back into the watershed. These tailing contain highly toxic components that even in trace concentrations have dire consequences to human and animal health in the areas.

The oil sands also release some of the world's largest concentrations of CO_2 deposits into the atmosphere, which will grow with increased U.S. and Asian demand for a secured oil source.

In 1990, Canada agreed to the Kyoto target of reducing its greenhouse emissions by 6 percent by 2012, but in fact Canada increased its emissions by 24 percent, of which the oil sands accounted for about 7 percent of the Canadian total. That doesn't seem like much, but in 1990, the oil sands contributed just over 1 percent of the Canadian total. Over the medium and longer term, these increases in greenhouse emissions will have a dramatic effect on global warming and on our climate.

Questions:
1. Taking into consideration both private and social benefits, can you think of other arguments in favour of continuing development of the oil sands?
2. On the other hand, is this development worth the environmental costs for Canada?
3. Using a demand-supply diagram, how would you illustrate the "Against" argument presented in this debate? That is, how would consideration of the negative externalities (the environmental impact associated with the operation of the oil sands) affect the determination of how much oil should be extracted from the oil sands?

SECTION CHECK

- Social costs are those costs that accrue to the total population; private costs are incurred by the producers or consumers of the good or service.
- Given the difficulties in establishing real-world social and private costs and benefits, externalities are often difficult to measure.

Public Policy and the Environment

section 12.3

- Why is a clean environment not free?
- What can be done to reduce pollution?
- What is an ideal pollution-control policy?

WHY IS A CLEAN ENVIRONMENT NOT FREE?

In many respects, a clean environment is no different from any other desirable good. In a world of scarcity, we can improve our environment only by giving up something else. The problem that we face is choosing the combination of goods that does the most to enhance human well-being. Few people would enjoy a perfectly clean environment if they were cold, hungry, and generally destitute. On the other hand, it is unlikely that an individual hospitalized due to smog will be envied, no matter how great his or her material wealth.

Only by considering the additional cost as well as the additional benefit of increased consumption of all goods, including clean air and water, can decisions on the desirable combination of goods to consume be made properly.

The Costs and Benefits of Pollution Control

It is possible, even probable, that pollution elimination, like nearly everything else, is subject to diminishing returns. Initially, a large amount of pollution can be eliminated fairly inexpensively, but getting rid of still more pollution may prove more

section 12.3
Exhibit 1

Costs and Benefits of Pollution Controls

With the principles of diminishing marginal utility and increasing marginal cost at work, the marginal benefits of further expenditures on pollution control will, at some point, fall below the marginal costs to society of imposing stricter controls. At output Q_1, pollution control is inadequate; on the other hand, elimination of Q_2 pollution will entail costs that exceed the benefits. Only at Q^* is pollution-control expenditure at an optimum level. Of course, in practice, it is difficult to know exactly the position and slope of these curves.

costly. Likewise, it is also possible that the benefits from eliminating soot from the air might decline as more and more pollution is eliminated. For example, perhaps some pollution elimination initially would have a profound impact on health costs, home repair expenses, and so on, but as pollution levels fall, further elimination of pollutants brings fewer marginal benefits.

The cost–benefit trade-off just discussed is illustrated in Exhibit 1, which examines the marginal social benefits and marginal social costs associated with the elimination of air pollution. In the early 1960s, we had few regulations as a nation on pollution control, and as a result, private firms had little incentive to eliminate the problem. In the context of Exhibit 1, we may have spent Q_1 on controls, meaning that the marginal social benefits of greater pollution-control expenditures exceeded the marginal costs associated with having the controls. Investing more capital and labour to reduce pollution is efficient in such a situation.

Optimum pollution control occurs when Q^* of pollution is eliminated. As indicated in Exhibit 1, Q^* is achieved where the marginal social benefits of greater pollution-control expenditures are equal to the marginal social costs of having them; that is, $MSB = MSC$. Overly stringent regulations force companies to control pollution to the level indicated by Q_2 in Exhibit 1, where the additional costs from the controls far outweigh the additional environmental benefits. It should be noted, however, that increased concerns about pollution have probably caused the marginal social benefit curve to shift to the right over time, increasing the optimal amount of pollution control. Because of measurement problems, however, it is difficult to state whether we are generally below, at, or above the optimal pollution level.

WHAT CAN BE DONE TO REDUCE POLLUTION?

Even though measuring externalities, both negative and positive, is often nearly impossible, it does not necessarily mean that it is better to ignore the externality and allow the market solution to continue. As already explained in the previous section, the market-determined solution for a negative externality will almost certainly result in excessive output by polluters unless some intervention occurs. What form should the intervention take?

Environmental Regulation

One approach to dealing with externalities is to regulate behaviour in response to the externality. The range of environmental regulations is significant, as the government can choose to prohibit certain activities that cause pollution, dictate maximum permissible levels of pollution, or require producers to adopt certain pollution-control technologies. In Canada, environmental policy is the joint responsibility of all three levels of government (federal, provincial/territorial, and municipal), with Environment Canada as the central department responsible for developing and enforcing regulations designed to protect the environment.

Evidence suggests that pollution levels have declined in recent years, although these statistics do not measure exactly what Environment Canada's impact has been, as other things were also changing. However, it does appear that the regulatory approach adopted by Environment Canada to limit key pollutants has led to a reduction in pollution levels. For example, the phasing-out of leaded gasoline, which started in the 1980s, has dramatically reduced the levels of lead in the atmosphere.

Pollution Taxes

Another means of solving the misallocation problem posed by the existence of externalities is for the government to create incentives for firms to internalize the external costs resulting from their activities. For example, returning to the case of pollution, suppose that the marginal private cost of making steel was $150 a tonne. Suppose further that at the margin, each tonne of steel caused $40 in environmental damages per tonne. If the government was then to levy a **pollution tax**—a tax levied by government on a firm for environmental pollution—on the steelmaker equal to $40 per tonne, the manufacturer's marginal private cost would rise from $150 to $190; the $190 figure would then be equal to the true marginal social cost of making steel. The firm would accordingly alter its output and pricing decisions to take into account its higher marginal cost, leading ultimately to reduced output (and pollution) and higher prices. The firm also has an incentive to seek new, less pollution-intensive methods of making steel.

pollution tax
tax levied by government on a firm for environmental pollution

In July of 2007, the Alberta government became the first jurisdiction in North America to put a price on CO_2 emissions—$15 for each tonne of carbon released in the province. The actual implementation of the program, however, was considerably more complex. Only firms that emitted more than 100 000 tonnes of greenhouse gas annually were subject to the policy and even then, companies were subject to the $15-per-tonne policy only if they failed to reduce their "carbon intensity" by the required 12 percent. Quebec introduced a carbon tax in October 2007, the first North American province or state to do so. The tax required oil companies to pay 0.8 cents per litre of gasoline distributed in the province and 0.938 cents for each litre of diesel fuel.

In 2008, the province of British Columbia implemented a carbon tax of $10 per tonne on carbon dioxide equivalent (CO_2e) emissions (2.41 cents per litre on gasoline)—the most significant carbon tax in the western hemisphere. This *carbon tax* is based on greenhouse gas (GHG) emissions generated from the burning of fossil fuels, particularly on the amount of carbon in the fuel. It puts a price on each tonne of GHG emitted, effectively sending a price signal to the economy that the government intends to reduce emissions. In July of 2012, the British Columbia government implemented the final scheduled increase in its carbon tax program. As of April 1, 2018, British Columbia's carbon tax rate is $35 per tonne of carbon dioxide equivalent (CO_2e)—an equivalent measure of greenhouse gas emissions. This tax rate will increase each year by $5 per tonne until it reaches $50 per tonne in 2021.

At the beginning of 2017, Alberta implemented a $20 a tonne tax on carbon dioxide emissions for burning fossil fuels used for transportation and heating. On January 1, 2018, this tax was increased to $30 a tonne.

The Government of Canada, along with the majority of the provinces and territories and in consultation with Indigenous peoples, agreed to the Pan-Canadian Framework on Clean Growth and Climate Change in December of 2016. At the centre of this framework is a carbon pricing system designed to help Canada meet its greenhouse gas emission reduction targets. This federal option applies to those provinces/territories without a provincial/territorial carbon pricing system in place by 2018. According to this federal system, carbon pricing would apply to a common and broad set of sources, starting at a minimum of $10 a tonne in 2018, rising to a maximum of $50 a tonne by 2022.

Using taxes to internalize external costs is appealing because it allows the relatively efficient private sector to operate according to market forces in a manner that takes socially important spillover costs into account. A major objection to the use of such taxes is that, in most cases, it is difficult to measure externalities with any precision. Choosing a tax rate involves some guesswork, and poor guessing might lead to a solution that is far from optimal. But it is likely to be better than ignoring the problem. In spite of the severe difficulties in measurement, however, many economists would like to see greater effort made to force internalization of externalities through taxes rather than using regulation. Why? We know that firms will seek out the least expensive (in terms of using society's scarce resources) approaches to compliance because they want more profits. This plan is good for them and good for society because we can have more of everything that way, including environmental quality.

Transferable Pollution Rights: Cap and Trade

transferable pollution rights

a right given to a firm to discharge a specified amount of pollution; its transferable nature creates an incentive to lower pollution levels

Economists see an opportunity to control pollution through a government-enforced system of property rights. **Transferable pollution rights** are rights given to a firm to discharge a specified amount (smaller than the uncontrolled amount) of pollution. In this plan, firms have an incentive to lower their levels of pollution because they can sell their permits if they go unused. Specifically, firms that can lower their emissions at the lowest costs will do so and trade their pollution rights to firms that cannot reduce their pollution levels as easily. That is, each polluter—required either to reduce pollution to the level allowed by the number of rights it holds or to buy more rights—will be motivated to eliminate all pollution that is cheaper than the price of pollution rights. The crucial advantage to the pollution rights approach comes from the fact that the rights are private property and can be sold.

It is worth emphasizing that this least-cost pattern of abatement does not require any information about the techniques of pollution abatement on the part of the government—more specifically, Environment Canada. Environment Canada does not need to know the cheapest abatement strategy for each and every polluter. Faced with a positive price for pollution rights, each polluter has a motivation to discover and use the cheapest way to reduce pollution. Nor does Environment Canada need to know anything about the differences in abatement costs among polluters. Each polluter is motivated to reduce pollution as long as the cost of reducing one more unit is less than the price of pollution rights. The information and incentives generated by private ownership and market exchange of these pollution rights automatically leads to the desirable pattern of pollution abatement—namely, having those best at cleaning up doing all the cleanup.

The pollution rights approach also creates an incentive for polluters to develop improved pollution abatement technologies.

The prospect of buying and selling pollution permits would allow firms to move into an area that is already as polluted as allowed by Environment Canada standards. Under the tradable permits policy, the firm can set up operation by purchasing pollution permits from an existing polluter in the area. This type of exchange allows the greatest value to be generated with a given amount of pollution. It also encourages polluters to come up with cheaper ways of reducing pollution, because the firm that reduces pollution is able to sell its pollution credits to others, making pollution reduction profitable. An example of transferrable pollution rights in action is the Western Climate Initiative (WCI), a nonprofit corporation involved in the administration and implementation of state and provincial/territorial greenhouse gas emission trading programs.

Currently, WCI includes officials from the provinces of Quebec and Ontario, and the state of California.

In January of 2013, Quebec's cap-and-trade program took effect. Intended for the province's industrial and electricity sectors as well as fossil fuel distributors, the primary purpose of the system was to reduce GHG emissions in the province's highest-emitting sectors. Under the cap-and-trade program, GHG emission allowances would permit capped emitters to release a specified quantity of CO2e. One emission allowance would be equal to one tonne of CO2e. The program caps would decline each year, allowing the province to achieve its GHG emission reduction targets.

In July of 2016, Ontario introduced its cap-and-trade system, mirroring the program introduced in Quebec. The initial distribution of emission allowances was free of charge to help facilitate the transition to greener technology; however, the government announced that this rate of free allowances would decrease over time. Ultimately, as the program matured, companies would either need to take action to reduce their emissions or purchase emission allowances or credits at auction.

The pulp and paper industry is one of the largest and most polluting industries in North America. One of the primary environmental concerns is the use of chlorine-based bleaches and resultant toxic emissions to air, water, and soil.

WHAT IS AN IDEAL POLLUTION-CONTROL POLICY?

What would be the objectives of an ideal pollution-control policy? First, and most obviously, we want pollution reduced to the efficient level—the level that maximizes the value of all of our resources. This goal would involve continuing to reduce pollution by one more unit only as long as the value of the improved environmental quality is greater than the value of ordinary goods that are sacrificed.

A second related objective is to reduce pollution as cheaply as possible. Two separate considerations are important here. If pollution is to be reduced as cost-effectively as possible, it is obvious that each pollution source has to abate at minimum cost. Of the many ways to cut back on pollution, not all are equally costly. But even if all polluters are abating as cheaply as possible, it does not necessarily mean that pollution overall is being reduced at least cost.

The pattern of pollution abatement over all sources is of great importance here. Because some polluters will be more efficient at pollution reduction than others, the least-cost abatement pattern will require some polluters to clean up more than others.

A third objective of a pollution-control policy is to establish incentives that will motivate advances in pollution abatement technology. Over the long run, this objective may be even more important than the first two. For example, the cost of controlling pollution can be significantly reduced over time, even if the second objective is not fully realized, if consistent advances are made in the technology of pollution control.

It should be clear that these three objectives—(1) achieving the efficient level of pollution, (2) achieving pollution reduction at least cost, and (3) motivating advances in abatement technology—may never be fully realized, especially the first objective.

Because we cannot own and control identifiable and separate portions of the atmosphere, we are not in a position to require that a price be paid in exchange for fouling clean air that we each consider ours alone. Without such exchanges and prices, we have no way of knowing the value people place on clean air. Without this information, it is not possible to determine the efficient level of air pollution. Likewise, private ownership of identifiable and separate portions of water in our lakes, rivers, and oceans is not possible, leaving no precise ways of determining the efficient level of water pollution. In the absence of market exchange, we rely on the political process to determine the efficient level of pollution.

In a democratic political order, the presumption is that the information provided by voting and lobbying will keep the political process at least somewhat responsive to the preferences of the citizens. To the extent that this presumption is justified, the hope is that political decision makers will arrive at a level of pollution near the efficient level.

SECTION CHECK

- In a world of scarcity, we can improve our environment only by giving up something else—the opportunity cost of environmental policy.
- Environmental regulations force companies to find less pollution-intensive ways of producing goods and services. Pollution taxes can be used to force firms to internalize externalities and allow the relatively efficient private sector to operate according to market forces in a manner that takes socially important spillover costs into account. The transferable pollution rights policies encourages polluters to come up with cheaper ways of reducing pollution because the firm that reduces pollution is able to sell its remaining pollution credits to others.
- The objectives of pollution-control policies are to achieve the efficient level of pollution, achieve pollution reduction at least cost, and motivate advances in abatement technology.

---

section 12.4 Property Rights

- What is the relationship between externalities and property rights?
- What is the Coase theorem?

WHAT IS THE RELATIONSHIP BETWEEN EXTERNALITIES AND PROPERTY RIGHTS?

The existence of externalities and the efforts to deal with them in a manner that will enhance the social good can be considered a question of the nature of property rights. If Environment Canada limits the soot that a steel company emits from its smokestack, then the property rights of the steel company with respect to its smokestack have been altered or restricted. Similarly, zoning laws restrict how property owners can use their property. Sometimes, to deal with externalities, governments radically alter arrangements of property rights.

Indeed, the entire matter of dealing with externalities ultimately evolves into a question of how property rights should be altered. If no externalities existed in the world, reasons for prohibiting property owners from using their property in any manner they voluntarily chose would be few. Ultimately, then, externalities involve an evaluation of the legal arrangements under which we operate our economy and thus illustrate one area where law and economics merge.

WHAT IS THE COASE THEOREM?

In a classic paper, Nobel laureate Ronald Coase observed that when the benefits are greater than the costs for some course of action (say, environmental cleanup), potential transactions can make some people better off without making anyone worse off. Formally known as the **Coase theorem**, it states that where property rights are defined in a clear-cut fashion, externalities are internalized. To appreciate this important insight, consider the following problem: A cattle rancher lives downstream from a paper mill. The paper mill dumps waste into the stream, which injures the rancher's cattle. If the rancher is not compensated, an externality exists. The question is, why does the externality persist? Suppose the courts have established (perhaps because the paper mill was there first) that the property rights to use (or abuse) the stream reside with the mill. If the benefits of cleanup are greater than the costs, the rancher should be willing to pay the mill owner to stop polluting. Let's assume that the rancher's benefits (say $10 000) from the cleanup undertaken by the mill are greater than the cost (say $5000). If the rancher was to offer $7500 to the mill owner to clean up the stream, both the rancher and the mill owner would be better off than with continued pollution. If, on the other hand, the rancher had the property rights to the stream and the mill owner received a sufficiently high benefit from polluting the river, then it would be rational for the mill owner to pay the rancher up to the point where the marginal benefit to the mill owner of polluting equalled the marginal damage to the rancher from pollution.

If a rancher lives downstream from a polluting factory and the courts have given the rights to the factory to pollute, economists say that the property rights to pollute are well defined. However, the rancher may be able to negotiate privately and pay the polluting firm to reduce the amount of pollution—and make both parties better off.

Coase theorem
states that where property rights are defined in a clear-cut fashion, externalities are internalized

Transaction Costs and the Coase Theorem

The mill owner and rancher example hinges critically on low transaction costs. Transaction costs are the costs of negotiating and executing an exchange, excluding the cost of the good or service bought. For example, when buying a car, it is usually rational for the buyer to spend some time searching for the "right" car and negotiating a mutually agreeable price.

Suppose instead that the situation involved 1000 ranchers and 10 mill owners. Trying to coordinate the activity between the ranch owners and mill owners would be almost impossible. Now imagine the complexities of more realistic cases: Nearly 6.5 million people live in the Greater Toronto Area (GTA). Each of them is damaged a little by a large number of firms and other consumers (e.g., automobile drivers) in the GTA.

It thus becomes apparent why the inefficiencies resulting from pollution control are not eliminated by private negotiations. First is the issue of ambiguity regarding property rights in air, water, and other environmental media. Firms that have historically polluted resent controls, giving up their rights to pollute only if compensated, yet consumers feel they have the right to breathe clean air and use clean bodies of water. These conflicting positions can be resolved in court, with the winner being, of course, made wealthier. Second, transaction costs increase greatly with the number of transactors, making it next to impossible for individual firms and citizens to negotiate private agreements. Finally, the properties of air or water quality (and similar public goods) are such that additional people can enjoy the benefits at no additional cost and cannot be excluded from doing so. Hence, in practice, private agreements are unlikely to solve many problems of market failure.

It is, however, too easy to jump to the conclusion that governments should solve any problems that cannot be solved by private actions. No solution may be possible, or all solutions may involve costs that exceed benefits. In any event, the ideas developed in this chapter should enable you to think critically about such problems and the difficulties in formulating appropriate policies.

SECTION CHECK

- In a world with no externalities, property owners with only a few exceptions, could use their property in any manner they desired. Ultimately, then, externalities involve an evaluation of the legal arrangements in which we operate our economy.
- The Coase theorem states that when property rights are defined in a clear-cut fashion, externalities are internalized. This condition holds when information and transaction costs are close to zero.

section 12.5

Public Goods

- What are private goods vs. public goods?
- What is the free-rider problem with public goods?
- Why does the government provide public goods?
- What is a common resource?

WHAT ARE PRIVATE GOODS VERSUS PUBLIC GOODS?

Externalities are not the only cause of market failure. A public good is another source of market failure. As used by economists, this term refers not to how particular goods are purchased—by a government agency rather than some private economic agent—but to the properties that characterize them. Specifically, the term **public good** refers to a good that is nonrivalrous in consumption and nonexcludable. In this section, we learn the difference between private goods, public goods, and common resources.

public good
a good that is nonrivalrous in consumption and nonexcludable

Private Goods

A **private good** is a good with rivalrous consumption and excludability (such as a cheeseburger). First, a cheeseburger is rival in consumption because if one person eats a particular cheeseburger, nobody else can eat the same cheeseburger. Second, a cheeseburger is excludable. It is easy to keep someone from eating your cheeseburger by not giving it to them. Most goods in the economy like food, clothing, cars, and houses are private goods that are rival and excludable.

private good
a good with rivalrous consumption and excludability

Public Goods

The consumption of public goods, unlike private goods, is neither excludable nor rival. A public good is not rival because everyone can consume the good simultaneously; that is, one person's use of it does not diminish another's ability to use it. A public good is likewise *not excludable* because once the good is produced, it is prohibitively costly to exclude anyone from consuming the good. Consider national defence. Once the military has its defence in place, everyone enjoys the benefits of national defence (not rival) and it would be prohibitively costly to exclude anyone from consuming national defence (not excludable).

Another example of a public good is the environment (fresh air, clean water). An environmental protection program would allow all of the people who live in the jurisdiction governed by the program to enjoy the protection of the new program simultaneously. It would be very difficult to exclude someone who lived in the middle of the jurisdiction who said they did not want to pay. Like national defence, the good is neither rival nor excludable in consumption. Other examples of public goods include outdoor fireworks displays and flood-plain projects.

WHAT IS THE FREE-RIDER PROBLEM WITH PUBLIC GOODS?

The fact that a public good is not rival and not excludable makes the good difficult to produce privately. Some people would know they could derive the benefits from the good without paying for it because once it is produced, it is too difficult to exclude anyone. That is, some people try to be a **free rider**—derive benefits from something without paying for it.

free rider
a party that derives benefits from something without paying for it

Let's return to our public good example of national defence. Suppose national defence is actually worth $100 to you. Assume that 10 million households in Canada are each willing to make a $100 contribution for national defence. This would add up to $1 billion. You might write a cheque for $100. Or you might reason as follows: "If I don't give $100 and everybody else does, I will be equally well protected plus derive the benefits of the $100 in my pocket." Taking the latter course represents a rational attempt to be a free rider. The rub is that if everyone attempts to take a free ride, the ride will not exist.

The free-rider problem prevents the private market from supplying the efficient quantity of public goods. That is, little incentive exists for individuals in the private sector to provide public goods because it is too difficult to make a profit. Therefore, the government provides important public goods such as national defence.

Government provides important public goods, such as national defence. Voters may disagree on whether we have too much or too little national defence, but most agree that we must have it. If national defence was provided privately and people were asked to pay for the use of national defence, many would free-ride, knowing they could derive the benefits of the good without paying for it.

WHY DOES THE GOVERNMENT PROVIDE PUBLIC GOODS?

Everything the government provides has an opportunity cost. What is the efficient level of national defence? More national defence means less of something else that society may value more, like health care or education. To be efficient, public goods must also follow the rule of rational choice—pursue additional government activities only if the expected marginal benefits exceed the expected marginal costs. It all comes back to the saying "There are no free lunches."

In addition, there is also the problem of assessing the value of these goods. Consider the case of a new highway. Before it builds the highway, the appropriate government agency will undertake a benefit–cost analysis of the situation. In this case, it must evaluate consumers' willingness to pay for the highway against the costs that will be incurred for construction and maintenance. However, those individuals who want the highway have an incentive to exaggerate their desire for it. At the same time, individuals who will be displaced or otherwise harmed by the highway have an incentive to exaggerate the harm that will be done to them. Together, these elements make it difficult for the government to assess benefits and costs accurately. Ultimately, government evaluations are reduced to educated guesses about the net impact of the highway on all parties concerned.

WHAT IS A COMMON RESOURCE?

In many cases we do not have exclusive private-property rights to things such as the fish in the sea. They are common resources—goods that are owned by everyone and therefore not owned by anyone. When a good is not owned by anyone, individuals feel little incentive to conserve or use the resource efficiently.

common resource
a rival good that is not excludable

A **common resource** is a rival good that is not excludable; that is, nonpayers cannot be easily excluded from consuming the good, and when one unit is consumed by one person, it means that it cannot be consumed by another. Fish in the vast ocean waters are a good example of a common resource. They are rival because fish are limited—a fish taken by one person is not available for others. They are not excludable because it is prohibitively costly to keep anyone from catching them—almost anyone with a boat and a fishing rod could catch one.

The failure of private incentives to provide adequate maintenance of common resources can lead to their degeneration and ultimate extinction; that is, common resources can lead to a tragedy of the commons. While there is no shortage of examples of such tragedies in modern society, one situation that could potentially have a significant impact on human society is ocean garbage. Since no single nation has the authority to pass laws or regulations to protect the entire ocean, this exposes a vast common resource to abuse and degradation. As a result, throughout the world's oceans, enormous patches of garbage have accumulated. This destruction of ocean ecosystems will most certainly have a detrimental effect on human society.

SECTION CHECK

- A public good is both nonrivalrous in consumption (one person's usage of it does not diminish another's ability to use it) and nonexclusive (no one can be excluded from using it), whereas a private good is both rivalrous and excludable.
- The free-rider problem prevents the private market from supplying the efficient quantity of public goods, whereas a private good is both rivalrous and excludable.
- Despite their demand, because public goods are not rival and not excludable, there is little incentive for private individuals to produce them.
- A common resource good is rival in consumption but not excludable.

For Your Review

Section 12.1

1. Indicate which of the following activities create a positive externality, a negative externality, or no externality at all:
   a. During a live-theatre performance, an audience member's cellphone rings loudly.
   b. You are given a flu shot.
   c. You purchase and drink a soft drink during a break from class.
   d. A local youth group cleans up trash along a two-kilometre stretch of highway.
   e. A firm dumps chemical waste into a local stream.
   f. Someone down the hall in your residence plays a hip-hop playlist loudly while you are trying to sleep.

2. Draw a standard supply and demand diagram for widgets, and indicate the equilibrium price and output. Assuming that the production of widgets generates external benefits, illustrate the effect of a producer subsidy equal to the external benefits generated, and indicate the equilibrium output.

Section 12.2

3. Say that the last tonne of steel produced by a steel company imposes three types of costs: labour costs of $25, additional equipment costs of $10, and the cost of additional "crud" dumped into the air of $15. What costs will the steel company consider in deciding whether to produce another tonne of steel?

4. Why can a homeowner make a better argument for compensation for noise pollution if a local airport was built after he moved in than if it was already there when he moved in? Would it matter whether he knew it was going to be built?

5. A newly released study demonstrates that populated areas with significant air pollution caused by diesel engines experience a much higher incidence of cancer. If diesel engines were then banned, what sorts of results would you expect?

6. Draw a standard supply and demand diagram for widgets, and indicate the equilibrium price and output. Assuming that the production of widgets generates external costs, illustrate the effect of the producers being forced to pay a tax equal to the external costs generated, and indicate the equilibrium output.

7. a. Why does internalizing externalities with taxes or subsidies sometimes increase the prices of goods and sometimes decrease them?
   b. When would workers in an industry benefit from internalizing its externalities?

8. Many communities have launched programs to collect recyclable materials but have been unable to find buyers for the salvaged materials. If the government was to offer a subsidy to firms using recycled materials, how might this affect the market for recycled materials? Illustrate using a demand and supply diagram.

Section 12.3

9. Discuss the incentive effects of each of these policies to reduce air pollution:
   a. a higher tax on gasoline
   b. an annual tax on automobiles based on average emissions
   c. an annual tax on total emissions from a particular model of car

10. If a firm can reduce its sulphur dioxide emissions for $30 per tonne but it owns tradable emissions permits that are selling for $40 per tonne, what will the firm want to do if it is trying to maximize profits?

11. Compare a pollution-reduction program that permits a certain level of pollution using emissions standards with one that permits the same level of pollution using tradable emissions permits.

12. Evaluate the following statement: "Public health is at stake when drinking water is contaminated by pollution. Local governments should take all measures necessary to ensure that zero pollutants contaminate the water supply."

13. How could transferable pollution rights lead to pollution being reduced at the lowest possible opportunity cost?

14. If an industry created both external benefits and external losses, would a tax or subsidy be appropriate? Why would someone be hurt by either one?

Section 12.4

15. A chemical factory dumps pollutants into a nearby river (permissible under the existing laws). In lieu of dumping into the river, the factory could pay for the pollution to be hauled to a toxic waste dump site at a cost of $125 000 per year. A vacation resort located downstream from the factory suffers damages estimated at $200 000 per year. Evaluate whether a change in law is necessary to achieve an efficient outcome in this situation.

16. A factory releases air pollutants that have a negative impact on the adjacent neighbourhood (populated by 2000 households). If the government could assign property rights to the air either to the factory or to the residents of the neighbourhood, would this make a difference in the quantity of pollution generated? Explain.

Section 12.5

17. For each of the goods below, indicate whether they are nonrival and/or nonexclusive. Also indicate whether they are private or public goods.
    a. hot dogs
    b. cable TV
    c. broadcast TV
    d. automobiles
    e. national defence
    f. pollution-control policy
    g. parking spot in a parking structure
    h. a sunset
    i. admission to a theme park

18. Is a lighthouse a public good if it benefits many ship owners? What if it primarily benefits ships going to a port nearby?

19. Why do you think buffalo became almost completely extinct on the Great Plains but cattle did not? Why is it possible to buy buffalo burgers in a store or restaurant today?

20. How does a TV broadcast have characteristics of a public good? What about specialty cable services such as the Discovery Channel?

21. Why does the free-rider problem arise in the case of public goods, and in what way can government provision of public goods solve this free-rider problem?

Answers to Odd-Numbered Problems

CHAPTER 1: THE ROLE AND METHOD OF ECONOMICS

1. The definition of *economics* must recognize the central parts of the economist's point of view: Resources are scarce, scarcity forces us to make choices, and the cost of any choice is the cost of the lost opportunity with the highest value.

3. **a.** The first is positive and the other is normative. The first statement (a positive statement) expresses a fact or a testable theory that a higher income tax rate would generate increased tax revenues. The second statement (a normative statement) expresses an opinion regarding how any additional tax revenues should be used.

   b. Both are normative statements that express opinions. The first regards the relative value of studying physics as opposed to studying sociology, and the second regards the value of studying either physics or sociology.

   c. Both statements are positive. They are expressions of facts or testable theories regarding the relationship between the price of wheat and how much wheat will be purchased and produced.

   d. The first is positive and the other is normative. The first statement (positive) expresses a fact or testable theory regarding the relationship between the price of butter and how much will be purchased. The second statement (normative) is an expression of opinion about the social value of buying butter.

   e. Both statements are positive. They are expressions of fact or testable theory regarding demographic change.

5. **a.** This involves confusing correlation with causation.

   b. This involves confusing correlation with causation.

   c. This involves the fallacy of composition.

   d. This is a violation of the *ceteris paribus* conditions.

   e. There is no fallacy in this statement.

7. Economics is concerned with reaching generalizations about human behaviour. If you generalize on the basis of observed individual behavior, you risk committing the fallacy of composition. Generalizations based on observed group behaviour are likely to be both more realistic and useful (reliable).

9. The automobile freed Canadians to travel and helped to create the tourism business. New wants included motels, resorts, and theme parks. The increased importance of automobile and truck transportation also created the desire for more and better roads and highways. The automobile also allowed people to live farther from where they worked, so that people wanted more land and newer houses.

11. Since Sarah's time is probably worth more during the school year (it would cost part of her salary), the opportunity cost of the trip is higher in February than in July.

13. **a.** The opportunity cost of going to college or university includes the income you could have earned by working instead; it also includes the money spent on school-specific expenses like tuition and textbooks. Room and board and transportation would not necessarily be included, since you would need those services even if you were not going to school.

   b. The opportunity cost of missing a lecture includes the potential damage to one's grade in a course from not being present while important subject material is covered, as well as the knowledge's forgone value in the "real world." The magnitude of the opportunity cost depends partly on how much essential information the instructor provides during the missed class session or if any activities were conducted.

   c. The opportunity cost of spending $100 today is the $105 you could have spent next year. If you are withdrawing the money just to have cash in your pocket, the opportunity cost of holding money is the 5 percent interest you could have been earning.

   d. The opportunity cost of snowboarding the weekend before final examinations is the expected reduction in grades that will result, in addition to the cost of a lift ticket.

15. One of the most important resources used raising children has historically been the mother's time. As opportunities for women to hold jobs, start businesses, and participate in political life increase, the cost of using women's time for raising children increases. As the cost of the mother's time rises, fewer children are born.

17. **a.** $57; $88

   b. 43; 44; he would produce widgets as long as the price (marginal benefit) exceeded the marginal cost.

19. Marginal thinking involves incremental changes to a plan of action. All of the activities listed involve marginal thinking. When studying, one chooses whether or not to study for one more hour; when eating, one chooses whether or not to consume one more portion; when driving, one chooses whether or not to travel one more kilometre (or one more kilometre per hour); when shopping, one chooses whether or not to buy one more item or visit one more store; when getting ready for a night out, one chooses whether or not to spend another minute styling one's hair.

21. Positive incentives are those that either increase benefits or reduce costs and thus tend to increase the level of an activity. Both of the following are examples of positive incentives: (b) a trip to Hawaii paid for by your parents or significant other for earning an A in your economics course; (d) a subsidy for installing solar panels on your house. Negative incentives either reduce benefits or increase costs, and thus tend to decrease the level of the related activity or behaviour. Both of the following are examples of negative incentives: (a) a fine for not cleaning up after your dog defecates in the park; (c) a higher tax on cigarettes and alcohol.

23. The Chinese government was attempting to promote population control. As the world's most populated country, China has historically struggled with controlling population growth in its attempts to manage economic growth and national standards of living. The sanctions and penalties associated with not following the one-child policy would be considered negative incentives designed to discourage couples from having more than one child. The rewards and honours associated with following the policy would be considered positive incentives designed to promote adherence to the policy.

25. The opportunity cost to Fran of growing soybeans is the lost value because she can't grow corn. This opportunity cost is equal to $1800 (3000 kg × $0.60/kg). The opportunity cost of growing corn is the lost opportunity to grow and sell soybeans, which is equal to $2250 (1500 kg × $1.50/kg). Fran should specialize in soybeans, which is the crop with the lower opportunity cost. For each hectare of corn that Fran converts to soybeans, she will gain $450.

27. **a.** If the country or region with the lower opportunity cost produces the good, the opportunity cost of consuming that good is minimized.

   b. Trade allows people, regions, and countries to specialize in producing those goods in which they have the lowest opportunity cost, so reducing trade restrictions will encourage specialization, thereby increasing efficiency.

29. No, Karl is wrong. Markets provide important signals, and the signal being sent in this situation is that Adam should look for some other way to support his ambitions, something that society values. Remember the function of consumer sovereignty in the marketplace. Clearly, consumers were not voting for Adam's art.

CHAPTER 1 APPENDIX: WORKING WITH GRAPHS

1. **A.** (−2, 2)

   B. (2, 1)

   C. (3, 2)

    D. (−1, −2)
    E. (2, −1)
    F. (−2, −1)
3. a. Semester 1
    b. Semesters 3 and 4
    c. Semester 2
    d. Total number of boys: 372; total number of girls: 366
5. a. 2
    b. −3
    c. −0.5
    d. Undefined
    e. 0

CHAPTER 2: SCARCITY, TRADE-OFFS, AND PRODUCTION POSSIBILITIES

1. a.

    b. 1 side of beef; 6 kegs of beer; 9 kegs of beer
    c. 35 kegs of beer
    d. No; that combination is inside the production possibilities curve, which means more of one good could be produced without giving up any production of the other good.
    e. No; that combination is beyond the production possibilities curve and therefore unattainable.

3. This is the law of increasing opportunity cost in action. As you planted more and more of your land in wheat, you would move into some of the less fertile land and, consequently, wheat yields on this additional land would fall. If you were to go so far as to plant the entire island with wheat, you would find that some of the less fertile land would yield virtually no extra wheat. It would, however, have been great for cattle grazing—a large loss. So the opportunity cost of using that marginal land for wheat rather than cattle grazing would be very high.

5. a.

b.

	A	B	C	D	E	F
	−3	−6	−9	−12	−15	
Cheese	45	42	36	27	15	0
Tractors	0	10	20	30	40	50
	+10	+10	+10	+10	+10	

As indicated in the table above, if the province of Quebec is to continually increase tractor production by 10 tractors it must give up increasing amounts of cheese—thus illustrating the law of increasing opportunity cost.

c.

    d. The alteration in production from production alternative B to alternative E represents an increase in capital goods and a decrease in consumption goods. As a result, the prediction would be that the province of Quebec would experience greater economic growth in the future.

7. Investment in capital goods increases the future productive potential of an economy. Economy A will grow more rapidly, shifting the production possibilities curve outward to a greater extent over time, if it invests in a higher proportion of capital goods than does Economy B.

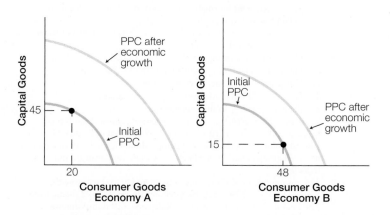

9. a. A country will fail to grow if its sacrificed consumption is spent in other countries.
    b. A country will fail to grow if it chooses not to sacrifice because it cares so much about current consumption.
    c. Growth will be limited if a country does not invest in human capital.
    d. A country will fail to grow if its sacrificed consumption is spent on goods other than capital goods.

11. The definition of a market focuses on the process of exchange not on the physical location where the exchange takes place. Therefore, even though online buyers and sellers are never actually in the same place, their behaviour still constitutes a market transaction due to the fact that goods and services are being exchanged.

13. Options (a), (b), and (c) would cause increases in the relative value and price of potatoes. In option (d), the reduction in the prices of potato substitutes would make alternatives more attractive and reduce the relative value and price of potatoes.

15. The market is global. Manufacturers sell to dealers throughout the world. Transportation costs are low relative to the costs of a laptop computer. Middlepersons make information about prices and quality easily available.

17. **a.** Product market
   b. Factor market
   c. Product market
   d. Factor market

   Furniture is a good purchased in the product market from firms. Labour is a resource that households sell to firms in the factor market. Restaurant food is a good purchased by consumers in the product market. Finally, Billy's entrepreneurial resource is paid a profit, which is the amount left over after all his other costs have been paid. This takes place in the factor market.

CHAPTER 3: SUPPLY AND DEMAND

1. **a.**

P	Q_D
$5	4
4	8
3	12
2	16
1	20

b.

P	Q_D
$5	6
4	12
3	18
2	24
1	30

c.

P	Q_D
$5	5
4	10
3	15
2	20
1	25

3.

5. **a.** Demand decreases (Determinant: Price of substitute falls)
   b. Demand decreases (Determinant: Price of complement rises)
   c. Demand increases (Determinant variable: Taste and preference increase)
   d. Demand increases (Determinant: Number of consumers increases)

7. **a.** Point B represents an increase in quantity demanded.
   b. Point E represents an increase in demand.
   c. Point F represents a decrease in demand.
   d. Point C represents a decrease in quantity demanded.

9. **a.** Hamburgers and ketchup are complements. An increase in the price of hamburger will decrease the demand for ketchup.

b. Coca-Cola and Pepsi are substitutes. An increase in the price of Coca-Cola will increase the demand for Pepsi.

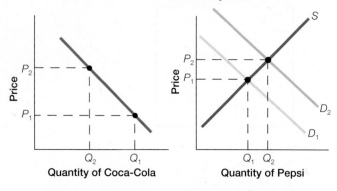

c. iPhones and iPhone cases are complements. An increase in the price of iPhones will decrease the demand for iPhone cases.

d. Golf clubs and golf balls are complements. An increase in the price of golf clubs will decrease the demand for golf balls, *ceteris paribus*.

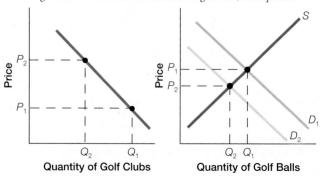

e. Assuming that skateboards and razor scooters are substitutes, an increase in the price of skateboards will increase the demand for razor scooters.

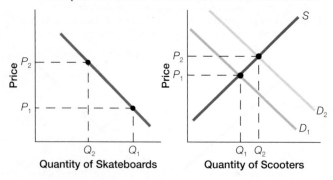

11. a. The shift from D_0 to D_1 is called an *increase in demand*.
   b. The movement from B to A is called a *decrease in the quantity demanded*.
   c. The movement from A to B is called an *increase in the quantity demanded*.
   d. The shift from D_1 to D_0 is called a *decrease in demand*.

13. The market price of wheat would have to rise for Felix to have the incentive to produce from the second field. Because costs are higher in the second field, Felix must receive a higher price to compensate him for his higher costs.

15.

Quantity Supplied (barrels per month)				
Price ($ per barrel)	Rolling Rock	Armadillo Oil	Pecos Petroleum	Market
$5	10 000	8 000	2 000	20 000
10	15 000	10 000	5 000	30 000
15	20 000	12 000	8 000	40 000
20	25 000	14 000	11 000	50 000
25	30 000	16 000	14 000	60 000

17. a. The shift from S_0 to S_1 is called an *increase in supply*.
   b. The movement from A to B is called an *increase in the quantity supplied*.
   c. The movement from B to A is called a *decrease in the quantity supplied*.
   d. The shift from S_1 to S_0 is called a *decrease in supply*.

19. a. An increase in the price of corn would increase the quantity of corn supplied, but not the supply of corn. This is because a change in the price of corn causes the market for corn to experience a movement in supply (as opposed to a shift in supply).
   b. An increase in the price of corn would decrease the supply of wheat, which is a substitute in production to corn. This is because a change in the price of corn—a substitute in production with wheat—causes the market for wheat to experience a shift in supply (as opposed to a movement).

21. a. Supply decreases (Determinant: Bad weather)
   b. Supply decreases (Determinant: Input prices rise)
   c. Supply increases (Determinant: Subsidies)
   d. Supply increases (Determinant: Technology advance)
   e. Supply decreases today (Determinant: Expected future price increases)

23. a. Point B represents an increase in quantity supplied
   b. Point C represents an increase in supply
   c. Point D represents a decrease in quantity supplied
   d. Point E represents a decrease in supply

25. An increase in wages, or any other input price, would decrease the supply of guitars (the supply curve would shift to the left), making fewer guitars available for sale at any given price, by raising the opportunity cost of producing guitars.

CHAPTER 4: BRINGING SUPPLY AND DEMAND TOGETHER

1. When a price is above the equilibrium price, the quantity of a good or service willingly supplied by sellers exceeds the quantity willingly demanded by buyers. If sellers want to sell a greater quantity of goods or services, it is necessary to reduce the price (or otherwise improve the terms of sale, such as with free delivery or lower interest rate financing) in order to induce buyers to make additional purchases. Market forces thus exert a downward pressure on price in the direction of equilibrium price. A surplus is eliminated once price falls to the equilibrium price.

   If a price is below the equilibrium price, then the quantity of a good or service willingly demanded by buyers exceeds the quantity willingly supplied by sellers. In order to induce sellers to provide a greater quantity to the marketplace, it is necessary for buyers to offer a higher price for the good or service. Market forces exert upward pressure on price in the direction of the equilibrium. A shortage is eliminated once price increases to the equilibrium price.

3. **a.** Equilibrium price = $400; Equilibrium quantity = 6.3 million units
   b. A shortage exists at any price below $400; market forces would raise the price of a tablet computer up to $400 to self-regulate a solution to this shortage situation.
   c. A surplus exists at any price above $400; market forces would lower the price of a tablet computer down to $400 to self-regulate a solution to this surplus situation.

5. **a.**

   b. $7; 40 units traded.
   c. Surplus. At $9, above the equilibrium price, there will be a surplus of 30 units of Z [the quantity supplied at $9 (50) minus the quantity demanded at $9 (20)].
   d. Shortage. At $3, below the equilibrium price, there will be a shortage of 60 units of Z [the quantity demanded at $3 (80) minus the quantity supplied at $3 (20)].
   e. $8, with 45 units traded (at the new supply and demand intersection).
   f. $6, with 50 units traded (at the new supply and demand intersection).

7. An increase in supply increases the quantity supplied at the original equilibrium price, but it does not change the quantity demanded at that price, meaning that it would create a surplus at the original equilibrium price.

9. **a.** Effect on the hamburger market of an increase in the price of hot dogs:

b. Effect on cab trips of a decrease in the number of taxi companies:

c. Effect of El Niño rainstorm destruction of strawberry crops:

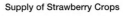

11. Even though the tuition "price" is the same in both cases, student demand for 10 a.m. classes is typically greater than for 8 a.m. classes. Students often prefer to sleep in later than punctual attendance at an 8 a.m. class would allow. A shortage of 10 a.m. class spaces relative to demand is the likely result. There may be a surplus of class spaces in 8 a.m. courses if the demand for early-morning classes is sufficiently low.

13. Fresh fruit is less expensive in the summer because the supply curve for fresh fruit shifts rightward in the summer, thus lowering equilibrium price and increasing equilibrium quantity.
   • This event is supply-side, since it deals with how growers are making product available for sale.
   • The event is a shift since the price of fresh fruit is not independently changing in the question.
   • The event is expansionary, since Canadian producers are seen as being able to make more fresh fruit available in the summer, when it is in season, as opposed to in the winter.

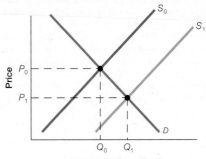

15. a. To get to point A would require a decrease in supply; to get to point B would require a decrease in supply and an increase in demand; to get to point C would require an increase in demand; to get to point D would require a decrease in supply and a decrease in demand; point E is the current equilibrium; to get to point F would require an increase in supply and an increase in demand; to get to point G would require a decrease in demand; to get to point H would require an increase in supply and a decrease in demand; and to get to point I would require an increase in supply.

b. The new equilibrium would be point F, because it is an increase in supply and an increase in demand. Equilibrium quantity would increase and if the magnitude of the demand and supply changes were equal, equilibrium price would remain constant.

c. Indeterminate; because one of the changes decreases supply and the other increases supply, we don't know what the net effect is on supply. If the effects were of the exact same magnitude, the result would be E; if the increase in supply was greater than the decrease in supply, the answer would be I; if the decrease in supply was greater than the increase in supply, the answer would be A.

d. C; A; A.

e. G; I; G.

17.

a. If the price ceiling is raised, the quantity supplied increases, the quantity demanded decreases, and the shortage is reduced; if the price ceiling is lowered, the quantity supplied decreases, the quantity demanded increases, and the shortage is increased.

b. The quantity supplied does not change, the quantity demanded increases, and the shortage is increased.

c. The quantity supplied increases, the quantity demanded does not change, and the shortage is decreased.

19. A price floor set above the equilibrium price for dairy products would result in a surplus. A price floor set below the equilibrium price would have no impact on the price or quantity of dairy products traded. (A price floor is a minimum allowed price, not a mandated market price.)

CHAPTER 5: ELASTICITY

1. a. Chevrolets (more substitutes). Chevrolets have more substitutes than cars in general since any other brand is a good substitute.

b. Housing (greater share of budget). The price elasticity of demand for housing will be greater than for salt because of the large role housing plays in the household budget.

c. Natural gas over the course of several years (more time to adjust). Natural gas has a more price-elastic demand in the long run since this gives consumers time to adjust their habits and complementary capital to any change. Also, the price elasticity of demand for a product will increase as more and better substitutes are available—the availability of more and better energy substitutes possibly increasing with time.

3. a. Demand for Paul Mitchell Shampoo is likely more elastic than the demand for shampoo in general. There are more substitutes available for a particular brand of shampoo than there are substitutes for shampoo generally.

b. The urgent need to travel quickly and on short notice to visit an ill family member makes demand relatively more inelastic than that for vacation air travel.

c. Elasticity of demand is likely much greater for apartment rentals. The rent on an apartment comprises a much larger portion of one's annual budget than do paper clips.

d. More substitutes are generally available for a generic headache remedy than for prescription heart medication. Therefore, the elasticity of demand for a generic headache remedy will be greater than that for heart medicine.

5. The average of prices and quantities demanded does not change when the direction of movement is reversed, so the percentage changes in price and quantity demanded do not change. However, when the initial price and quantity demanded are used for calculating the percentage changes, a *movement* down along a demand curve starts with a higher initial price and lower initial quantity demanded than the same movement up along it, changing the percentage changes.

7. If the price increases by 10 percent, quantity demanded will fall by 15 percent when the elasticity of demand for hamburgers equals −1.5. Hamburger sales will decline by approximately 6000 (15 percent of 40 000). If the price of hamburgers decreases by 5 percent, quantity demanded will increase by approximately 3000 hamburgers (7.5 percent of 40 000).

9. If the price rises from $3 to $5, the change in price is $2. Using the midpoint technique, the midpoint price ($4) is used to calculate the percentage change in price. It will be (2/4 × 100 percent) = 50 percent. Similarly, the percentage change in quantity is based on the change in quantity (−600) divided by the midpoint (1200) or −50 percent. The elasticity of demand is 1.

11. If the elasticity of demand is estimated to equal −1.6, then demand is relatively elastic. A decrease in ticket prices would increase the quantity of tickets demanded sufficiently to increase the overall revenue from ticket sales. If the elasticity of demand is estimated to equal −0.4, then demand is relatively inelastic. In this case, an increase in ticket prices would boost the revenue from ticket sales.

13. The demand is relatively elastic at prices above the midpoint of a straight-line demand curve and relatively inelastic below the midpoint, so it is relatively elastic for a price change from $12 to $10 but relatively inelastic for a price change from $6 to $4.

15. a. Total revenue increases from $200 ($4 × 50) to $300 ($3 × 100).

b. Since total revenue increased with a decrease in price, demand must be relatively elastic.

c. Since total revenue goes down from $300 ($2 × 150) to $200 ($1 × 200) as price falls from $2 to $1, demand must be relatively inelastic in that range of the demand curve.

17. 20 percent ÷ −10 percent = −2.

19. a. If the income elasticity of demand for a good is positive, it is a normal good.

b. If the income elasticity of demand for a good is negative, it is an inferior good.

21. a. The income elasticity of demand equals (Percentage change in the quantity demanded)/(Percentage change in incomes). The percentage change in quantity demanded over the period equals (19.5 − 20)/ ([20 + 19.5]/2) = −0.025. The income elasticity of demand for rail travel equals (−0.025)/(0.13) = −0.19.

b. The cross-price elasticity equals (Percentage change in quantity demanded)/(Percentage change in the price of air travel). The percentage change in quantity demanded equals (19 − 17.5)/ ([19 + 17.5]/2) = 0.082. The cross-price elasticity of demand for rail travel equals (0.082)/(0.075) = 1.09.

c. The positive cross-price elasticity shows us that air travel and rail travel are substitute goods. The negative income elasticity shows us that rail travel is an inferior good.

23. a. The elasticity of supply would equal 1.

b. The elasticity of supply would equal 0.5.

c. The elasticity of supply would equal 2.

25. If the price of tablet computers increases by 5 percent, quantity supplied will increase by 3 percent when price elasticity of supply is 0.6. Production volumes will increase by 1.5 million units (3 percent of 50 million). If the price of tablet computers decreases by 8 percent, then quantity supplied will decrease by 4.8 percent, or 2.4 million units (4.8 percent of 50 million).

27. Relative elasticities of supply and demand determine the incidence of a tax. If the difference between the short-run and long-run elasticity was greater on one side of the market than the other, the long-run incidence could be dramatically different from the short-run incidence. For example, if supply was very inelastic in the short run but very elastic in the long run, suppliers could bear most of the short-run burden of a tax, but very little of the burden in the long run. As both demand and supply become more elastic in the long-run, this will lead to larger reductions in the quantity exchanged; the revenue from a given tax would tend to decrease over time, other things being equal.

CHAPTER 6: CONSUMER CHOICE AND MARKET EFFICIENCY

1. We know that the person's marginal utility for the next bite is negative—that the person's total utility will be reduced if she or he eats one more bite.

3. The ski resort knows that the utility you derive from an additional 4 hours of skiing will be less than the first 4 hours of skiing (law of diminishing marginal utility). As a result, in order to make the second 4 hours of skiing economically justifiable, the resort must sell the second 4 hours of skiing at a lower price ($10 instead of $23).

5. The red numbers in the table below are the ones that were missing.

Number of Smartphone Apps.	Total Utility	Marginal Utility
0	0	—
1	12	12
2	22	10
3	29	7
4	33	4
5	33	0
6	31	−2

7. The marginal utility per dollar derived from soft drinks equals 6 utils/$1, while the marginal utility derived from pizza consumption equals 2 utils per dollar (4 utils/$2). Since the satisfaction per dollar derived from the last soft drink consumed exceeds the satisfaction per dollar derived from the last slice of pizza, Brandy should purchase more soft drinks and less pizza. As Brandy consumes more soft drinks, the marginal utility per dollar spent on soft drinks will fall (since marginal utility will diminish). As less pizza is consumed, the marginal utility per dollar spent on pizza will increase (since the marginal utility derived from pizza will increase).

9. In consumer equilibrium, the typical student will purchase 4 cups of coffee (49 utils) and 1 muffin (6 utils), for a total of 55 utils of satisfaction.

Cups of Coffee					Muffins			
Number of Cups	TU	MU	MU/P		Number of Muffins	TU	MU	MU/P
0	0	—	—		0	0	—	—
1	16	16	8		1	6	6	6
2	29	13	6.5		2	10	4	4
3	40	11	5.5		3	11	1	1
4	49	9	4.5		4	11	0	0
5	54	5	2.5		5	9	−2	−2

11. The red numbers in the table below are the ones that were missing. The sports fan will attend 2 football games (30 utils) and 4 hockey games (58 utils), generating a total of 88 utils of satisfaction.

Hockey Games					Football Games			
Number	TU	MU	MU/P		Number	TU	MU	MU/P
0	0	—	—		0	0	—	—
1	20	20	1.25		1	18	18	1.5
2	36	16	1		2	30	12	1
3	48	12	0.75		3	36	6	0.5
4	58	10	0.625		4	42	6	0.5
5	66	8	0.5		5	45	3	0.25
6	72	6	0.375		6	45	0	0

13. a. Steve is willing to pay $4.50 for one bag of potato chips.
    b. Steve is willing to pay $4.00 for a second bag of potato chips.
    c. Steve's consumer surplus is $5.00 when he buys five bags. He gets a $2.00 surplus on the first bag, $1.50 on the second, $1.00 on the third, and $0.50 on the fourth. At $2.50 per bag, he gets no consumer surplus on the fifth bag.
    d. Steve's total willingness to pay for 5 bags is $17.50. He is willing to pay $4.50 for the first bag, $4.00 for the second, $3.50 for the third, $3.00 for the fourth, and $2.50 for the fifth bag.

15. If the demand for apples increased from D_0 to D_1 in the diagram below as a result of a news story that highlighted the health benefits of two apples a day, producer surplus would increase as indicated.

17. a. $30
    b. Producer surplus will increase from $30 to $60, an increase of $30

CHAPTER 7: PRODUCTION AND COSTS

1. As urban development continues, placing increasing pressures on key scarce resources such as the Greenbelt, the opportunity cost (forgone alternative) of using the Greenbelt for farming and environmental protection will continue to increase. As the opportunity cost increases, so will the economic cost of using this land for farming and environmental protection.

3. Anglers may not have to pay their relatives to work as crew but that does not mean this strategy has no cost. Employing relatives reduces the anglers' explicit cost because crew salaries are reduced. However, there are still opportunity costs. Implicit costs will increase as long as the relatives have alternative uses of their time. Employing relatives might increase accounting profits but it can decrease economic profits at the same time.

5. a.

Labour (workers)	Total Product (visits per hour)	Marginal Product
0	0	—
1	10	10
2	22	12
3	31	9
4	39	8
5	43	4
6	41	−2

    b. Beginning with the third worker.
    c. Beginning with the sixth worker.

7.

Labour (workers)	Total Product (kilograms)	Marginal Product (kilograms)
0	0	—
1	20	20
2	44	24
3	62	18
4	74	12
5	80	6
6	78	−2

    a. Candy's Candies begins to experience diminishing marginal product with the third worker, the first one for which marginal product begins to fall.
    b. Candy's Candies experiences a negative marginal product beginning with the sixth worker.

9. a. The marginal product of the seventh worker equals 6 units of output.
    b. The law of diminishing product begins with the fifth worker hired.
    c. A firm would never choose to hire nine workers under these conditions, since the marginal product of the ninth worker is negative.

11.

Output	Total Fixed Costs	Total Variable Costs	Total Costs	Average Fixed Costs	Average Variable Costs	Average Total Costs	Marginal Costs
1	$100	$30	$130	$100	$30	$130	$30
2	100	50	150	50	25	75	20
3	100	60	160	33.33	20	53.33	10
4	100	64	164	25	16	41	4
5	100	90	190	20	18	38	26
6	100	126	226	16.67	21	37.67	36
7	100	168	268	14.29	24	38.29	42
8	100	218	318	12.50	27.25	39.75	50

13. Your choice will affect your fixed and variable costs. If you choose to pay the flat fee, your fixed costs for the film will equal $5000 for the week. Your variable costs associated with the leasing of the film would then equal zero. If you choose to pay $2 per customer, then the costs associated with leasing the film will all be variable.

15. Not necessarily. It is marginal cost that is critical. The next barrel of oil might cost $30 to produce because the well might be drying up or the company might have to drill deeper to get additional oil, making it even more costly to retrieve. It is possible that the *marginal cost* of the additional barrels of oil might be greater than the market price; therefore, the situation is no longer profitable.

17. The note-taker's wage is a fixed cost, which does not vary with the number of subscriptions sold.

19. **a.** Average fixed cost (*AFC*)
    b. Average variable cost (*AVC*)
    c. Average total cost (*ATC*)
    d. Marginal cost (*MC*)
    e. Where *MC* is less than *AVC*, *AVC* is falling; when *MC* equals *AVC*, *AVC* does not change; and when *MC* exceeds *AVC*, *AVC* is rising, so the intersection of *MC* and *AVC* is at the minimum point of *AVC*. When *MC* is less than *ATC*, *ATC* is falling, when MC equals *ATC*, *ATC* does not change, and when *MC* exceeds *ATC*, *ATC* is rising, so the intersection of *MC* and *ATC* is at the minimum point of *ATC*.
    f. The point where *MC* equals *AFC* has no economic significance.

21. **a.** *AVC* is at its minimum at the q_1 level of output, where the *AVC* and *MC* curves intersect. This point marks the minimum of *AVC* because at levels of output below this (such as q_0) *MC* is less than *AVC*, forcing *AVC* downward. For levels of output above this (such as q_2) *MC* is greater than *AVC*, pulling *AVC* upward.
    b. *ATC* is at its minimum at the q_2 level of output, where the *ATC* and *MC* curves intersect. This point marks the minimum of *ATC* because at levels of output below this (such as q_1), *MC* is less than *ATC*, forcing *ATC* downward. For levels of output above this (such as q_3), *MC* is greater than *ATC*, pulling *ATC* upward.
    c. *MC* is at its minimum at the q_0 level of output. This level of output marks the minimum of *MC* since it coincides with the point where diminishing marginal productivity sets in.

23. **a.** C
    b. B
    c. Diseconomies of scale

25.

Change	AVC	MC	ATC
a. The government imposes a tax that is applied to every unit produced.	↑	↑	↑
b. The price of rent increases.*	R/u	R/u	↑
c. New technology that improves productivity is introduced.	↓	↓	↓
d. The cost of labour increases.	↑	↑	↑
e. The cost of materials used in manufacturing decreases.	↓	↓	↓
f. Property taxes increase.*	R/u	R/u	↑

*These changes impact only *ATC* (and have no effect on *AVC* and *MC*) because they cause only *FC* to change.
Note: "R/u" stands for "Remains unchanged."

CHAPTER 8: PERFECT COMPETITION

1. If a perfectly competitive firm sells only a small amount relative to the total market supply, even sharply reducing its output will make virtually no difference in the market quantity supplied; therefore, it will make virtually no difference in the market price. In this case, a firm is able to sell all it wants at the market equilibrium price but is unable to appreciably affect that price; therefore, it takes the market equilibrium price as given—that is, it is a price taker.

3. Farms can be thought of as perfectly competitive businesses, which produce products that are very close to perfect substitutes. For example, one farmer's eggs are very good substitutes for any other farmer's eggs. Any advertising for eggs—such as that by an industry council—will increase the market demand for all farmers' eggs. All farms will benefit since the market price will rise. In this situation, no single farm has an incentive to invest in advertising since it will benefit from the advertising of others and the price it can charge will increase.

5. A perfectly competitive firm is able to sell all it wants at the market equilibrium price. Therefore, it has no incentive to lower prices (sacrificing revenues and therefore profits) in an attempt to increase sales. Because other firms are willing to sell perfect substitutes for each other's product (because goods are homogeneous) at the market equilibrium price, trying to raise the price would lead to the firm losing all of its sales. Therefore, it has no incentive to try to raise its price, either.

7. Average revenue equals total revenue divided by output, or $25 at all output levels. Marginal revenue is the addition to total revenue from selling one more unit of output, also equal to $25 at all levels of output. If marginal revenue is constant and equal to $25 at all levels of output, $25 must be the market price. The short-run profit-maximizing (loss-minimizing) level of output is found where marginal revenue equals marginal cost (provided that price exceeds average variable cost). Marginal revenue equals marginal cost for the third unit.

9. When average total cost is $3, profit will be total revenue (1000 × $5 = $5000) minus total costs (1000 × $3 = $3000) or $2000. When average total cost is $6, profit will be total revenue (1000 × $5 = $5000) minus total costs (1000 × $6 = $6000) or −$1000. A firm will make a profit if price exceeds average total cost for the quantity produced and sold, and a loss if price is less than average total cost for the quantity produced and sold.

11. **a.**

Quantity	Price	Total Revenue	Marginal Revenue	Marginal Cost	Total Profit
10	$12	$120	$12	$8	$25
11	12	132	12	9	28
12	12	144	12	11	29
13	12	156	12	12	29
14	12	168	12	14	27

The profit-maximizing level of output is 13 units.
b. Marginal revenue equals marginal costs at 13 units of output, so 13 units is the profit-maximizing output level (to be precise, the entrepreneur could produce either 12 or 13 and earn the same profit, since *MR* and *MC* are equal on the 13th unit). Even though the firm does not increase profits on the 13th unit, it will still produce this quantity since it is covering its costs, so the entrepreneur is earning an amount equal to his opportunity costs.
c. At a price of $9, the profit-maximizing output would be 11 units, where price equals marginal cost. If the firm produced 12 units, profits would fall by $2 (marginal cost minus marginal revenue).

13. **a.** $35 per unit, 85 units
    b. *TR* = $35 × 85 = $2975, *TC* = $31 × 85 = $2635, Economic profits = $2975 − $2635 = $340
    c. *TR* = $25 × 65 = $1625, *TC* = $31 × 65 = $2015, Economic profits = $1625 − $2015 = −$390 (loss)
    The firm should continue to produce in the short run, since price (*MR*) is greater than its *AVC*.
    d. The firm should choose to shut down in the short run, since price (*MR*) is now less than its *AVC*.

15. **a.** False. When economic profits are zero, firms are earning normal profits. Total revenue is sufficient to cover all costs of production, including a normal rate of return for business owners.
    b. False. In the long run, a perfectly competitive firm maximizes profit at a level of output where average total cost is minimized. In the short run, however, if a profit-maximizing firm is earning economic profits, it will not produce at an output level where average total cost (or any other cost) is minimized. Rather, the firm chooses output where marginal revenue equals marginal cost.

c. False. The statement is ambiguous. For example, a firm could minimize overall costs by not producing any output at all. Such a strategy would certainly not result in positive economic profits. In the long run, if a firm is producing at the output level where average total cost is minimized, it is also maximizing its profits. However, in the short run, choosing an output level at which average total cost is minimized is unlikely to yield maximum profits for the firm. Instead, to maximize profits, the firm should choose to produce a quantity of output where marginal revenue equals marginal cost.

17. If firms are currently earning economic profits, that will attract entry into the industry, shifting the industry supply to the right. That will lower the price and reduce economic profits. If firms are currently earning economic losses, firms will exit the industry, shifting the industry supply curve to the left. That will raise the price and reduce economic losses.

19.

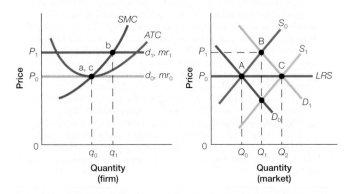

a. The short-run effect of an increase in demand on the perfectly competitive firm is illustrated by the movement from point a to point b in the firm diagram and from point A to point B in the market diagram. As a result of this increase in demand, the firm is now earning positive economic profits in the short run.

b. The long-run effect of an increase in demand for a constant-cost industry is illustrated by the movement from point b to point c (same as point a) in the firm diagram and from point B to point C in the market diagram. The entry triggered by the short-run profits will lower market price; this lower market price will result in lower economic profits for the individual perfectly competitive firm. Entry into the industry will continue and market price will continue to fall until economic profits are eliminated and all firms are once again earning a normal amount of economic profit.

21. a. Increasing-cost, since more teams will bid up the price of good pitchers and reduce the quality of the average pitcher.

b. Constant-cost, since expansion of output will not significantly increase the price of these unspecialized inputs.

c. Increasing-cost, since industry expansion will put upward pressure on the wages offered to these trained workers.

CHAPTER 9: MONOPOLY

1. a. Although many actresses compete for acting roles, in some sense, an actress like Kate Hudson has a monopoly over her own special talents.

b. While not the only means, electricity is the predominant way in which we power the various items we use on a daily basis. Electricity is therefore largely a product without alternative. Since BC Hydro is the sole provider of electricity for most if not all of the province of British Columbia, we could consider BC Hydro to be a monopoly.

c. The only doctor in a small town has a local monopoly over physician services. Such a doctor's monopoly power is likely to be limited, however, if physicians are available in nearby towns.

d. Ford Motor Company would not be considered to be a monopoly.

3. Being a price maker does give the monopolist the ability to set price at a desired level. However, in doing so, the monopolist must accept whatever quantity consumers are willing to buy at that price. A monopolist can determine either price or quantity sold, but not both.

5.

Quantity	Price	Total Revenue	Marginal Revenue	Demand Elastic or Inelastic
1	$11	$11	$11	Elastic
2	10	20	9	Elastic
3	9	27	7	Elastic
4	8	32	5	Elastic
5	7	35	3	Elastic
6	6	36	1	Elastic
7	5	35	−1	Inelastic
8	4	32	−3	Inelastic
9	3	27	−5	Inelastic
10	2	20	−7	Inelastic
11	1	11	−9	Inelastic

7. a.

Quantity	Price	Total Revenue	Marginal Revenue	Elastic or Inelastic
30	$3.65	$109.50		
31	3.58	110.98	$1.48	Elastic
32	3.51	112.32	1.34	Elastic
33	3.44	113.52	1.20	Elastic
34	3.37	114.58	1.06	Elastic
35	3.30	115.50	0.92	Elastic
36	3.22	115.92	0.42	Elastic
37	3.14	116.18	0.26	Elastic
38	3.06	116.28	0.10	Elastic
39	2.98	116.22	(0.06)	Inelastic
40	2.90	116.00	(0.22)	Inelastic
41	2.82	115.62	(0.38)	Inelastic
42	2.74	115.08	(0.54)	Inelastic
43	2.66	114.38	(0.70)	Inelastic
44	2.58	113.52	(0.86)	Inelastic
45	2.50	112.50	(1.02)	Inelastic
46	2.42	111.32	(1.18)	Inelastic
47	2.34	109.98	(1.34)	Inelastic
48	2.25	108.00	(1.98)	Inelastic
49	2.15	105.35	(2.65)	Inelastic
50	2.04	102.00	(3.35)	Inelastic

b. At first, marginal revenue is positive as the price declines. After the price falls below $3.06, marginal revenue becomes negative as the price declines. Marginal revenue is always less than price beyond the first unit of output.

c. Marginal revenue is negative as the price declines when the demand curve is inelastic, so the demand becomes inelastic below a price of $3.06.

d. NorOnt Phones will increase the number of substitutes for northern Ontario long-distance phone service. An increase in the number of substitutes will increase the elasticity of the demand facing Star Phone.

9. To sell two units, the monopolist would have to lower the price on both units to $8. That is, the seller would not receive $10 from unit one and $8 for unit two, but rather, would receive $8 for each of the units. So what happens to marginal revenue? There are two parts to this answer. One, there is a loss in revenue, $2, from selling the first unit at $8 instead of $10. Two, there is a gain in revenue from selling the additional output—the second unit—at $8. So the marginal revenue is $6 ($8 – $2), which is less than the price of the good, $8.

11. If economic profits are zero, the firm is earning a normal profit, so there is no incentive to leave the industry. It is possible for a monopolist earning positive economic profits to maintain them in the long run, because barriers prevent new firms from entering and reducing economic profits through competition.

13. The short-run profit-maximizing level of output is found where marginal revenue equals marginal cost at five units of output ($MR = \$10 = MC$). Price equals $30 at that level of output and the firm earns an economic profit (positive profit), because total revenue exceeds total cost.

15. a. At profit maximization: $P^* = \$18$, $Q^* = 60$ units, $ATC_{Q^*} = \$13$. $TR = \$18 \times 60 = \$1080$, $TC = \$13 \times 60 = \$780$; therefore, Total profit = $300.

b. No, the monopolist is not achieving productive efficiency at Q^*. This is because the monopolist is not producing at the minimum of ATC when operating at Q^* (minimum of ATC is $12).

c. No, the monopolist is not achieving allocative efficiency at Q^*. This is because, at Q^*, the monopolist experiences $P > MC$ (allocative efficiency is achieved where $P = MC$).

17. a. The efficient result is determined by the marginal cost pricing alternative—point C.

b. Since price is below average total cost at point C, the monopolist is incurring a loss (indicated by the shaded area).

c. The average cost-pricing alternative is detailed in the graph at point B. A normal rate of return is earned.

19. a. Students' demand for movie tickets tends to be more elastic than for the average individual. To entice students to the movie theatre more frequently, theatres offer discounts to students who can show a student ID.

b. The long-distance service is practising price discrimination by offering lower rates to those who make longer calls than to those who make very short calls. This type of quantity discount is a form of price discrimination.

c. Seniors, who often live on fixed incomes and perhaps have more time to search for good deals, tend to have more elastic demands for many goods and services. Local restaurants offer discounts to seniors to attract them to their restaurants (but often restrict them to "early bird" times, so seniors don't crowd out regular-price dinner customers at the peak demand period).

d. Coupon discounts are offered only to those individuals who are willing to take the time and effort to locate, clip, and bring the laundry detergent coupon to the store. People whose demand for laundry detergent is relatively elastic are more likely to clip and organize coupons than are those with relatively inelastic demand. The use of coupons separates customers into groups with different elasticities of demand, charging different groups different effective prices.

21. If the differences in prices of haircuts for people with different hair lengths reflect differences in the costs of providing a haircut, then it is not price discrimination.

23. The airline industry has found that business travellers have a more inelastic demand for air travel than vacationers do. The airlines know that business travellers are generally unwilling to stay over for the weekend (away from home, family, or their favourite golf course), spend only a day or two at their destination, and often do not make their reservations far in advance. All of which means the business traveller has a more inelastic demand curve for flights (fewer substitutes). If the airlines cut prices for business travellers, airline revenues would fall. Personal travellers (perhaps vacationers) are operating on a much more elastic demand curve—they are much more flexible. For these travellers, many substitutes are available, such as other modes of transportation and different travel times (non-peak times). Clearly the airlines can make more money by separating the market according to each group's elasticity of demand rather than by charging all users the same price.

25. A welfare loss is associated with monopoly because the monopolist produces at a level of output such that price is greater than marginal cost. The marginal value to society of the last unit produced is greater than its marginal cost. The monopolist is not producing enough of the good from society's perspective. There would be no welfare loss if a price-discriminating monopolist was able to perfectly price-discriminate, because the monopolist would sell units until price just equalled the marginal cost, charging each customer the maximum price that customer would be willing to pay.

CHAPTER 10: MONOPOLISTIC COMPETITION AND OLIGOPOLY

1. The market for soybeans is perfectly competitive, as large numbers of buyers and sellers trade standardized products on a world market. Retail clothing stores and restaurants offer differentiated products and services and are therefore monopolistically competitive.

3. Monopolistic competition is like monopoly in that sellers' actions can change the price. It is like competition in that it is characterized by competition from substitute products, many sellers, and relatively free entry.

5. Some restaurants are more successful at differentiating their establishments and appealing to customers than are others. Restaurants that are particularly successful in promoting customer goodwill may continue to earn economic profits even while other restaurants in the area fail.

7. Starbucks differentiates its product by location, hours of operation, service, and product choice and quality. Starbucks operates thousands of stores worldwide, offering its patrons a large variety of sandwiches, salads, speciality deserts, and speciality beverages, as opposed to just doughnuts, bagels, and coffee. Starbucks is also open very early, when many people want to drink coffee because of its caffeine stimulant. Another differentiating feature found at Starbucks is its cup sizes. In place of the standard small, medium, and large sizes, Starbucks sells its beverages in trenta, short, tall, grande, and venti cup sizes

9.

In the above diagram, the firm is making economic profits because the price the firm is able to charge (P^*) at output q^* is greater than the firm's average total costs at output q^*. These positive economic profits will attract the entry of new firms into the industry, cutting into the market demand of existing firms. The demand curves for each of these existing firms will therefore shift downward. This decline will continue until the average total cost (ATC) curve becomes tangent to the demand curve and economic profits are reduced to zero.

In the above diagram, the firm is suffering economic losses because the price the firm is able to charge (P^*) at output q^* is less than the firm's average total costs at output q^*. These economic losses will result in the exit of firms from the industry, increasing the market demand of existing firms. The demand curves for each of these existing firms will therefore shift upward. This increase will continue until the average total cost (ATC) curve becomes tangent to the demand curve and economic losses are reduced to zero.

11. **a.** When price is greater than average total cost at q^* (the intersection of marginal revenue and marginal cost), the firm will earn positive economic profits.

b. When price is less than average total cost at q^* (the intersection of marginal revenue and marginal cost), the firm will earn economic losses.

c. and d. When price is equal to average total cost at q^* (the intersection of marginal revenue and marginal cost), the firm will earn zero economic profits. This is also the long-run condition as a result of entry and exit.

13. **a.** In reading the brief opening description of this firm, we would consider it to be monopolistically competitive because (1) it is one of several firms in the industry, (2) it has differentiated its service from its competition, and (3) firms have been able to enter the industry with relative ease.

b.

Quantity (number of oil changes)	Price ($)	TR ($)	MR ($)	MC ($)	ATC ($)
0	50.00	0.00			
1	45.00	45.00	45.00	13.00	30.50
2	40.00	80.00	35.00	18.00	26.75
3	35.00	105.00	25.00	23.00	24.75
4	30.00	120.00	15.00	28.00	26.25
5	25.00	125.00	5.00	33.00	28.75
6	20.00	120.00	−5.00	38.00	32.50

According to the above table, $MR = MC$ at a quantity of 3 oil changes ($q^* = 3$). If we assume that the firm cannot provide a partial

oil change, the profit-maximizing number of oil changes is 3, since the 4th oil change delivers more marginal cost than marginal revenue. Our monopolistically competitive business will charge a price of $35 per oil change as a result.

c. At the q^* of 3 oil changes, P^* is greater than ATC_{q^*}; as a result, this firm is generating positive economic profits at profit maximization. TR (at q^*) = $105; TC (at q^*) = $74.25 ($24.75 × 3). Therefore, total profits = $30.75.

15. Both types of firms operate in industries with many other sellers and with no real barriers to entry or exit. They follow similar rules when choosing the level of output. Both types of firms also will experience zero economic profits in the long run. In the short run, monopolistic competitors and perfectly competitive firms follow similar rules for choosing the profit-maximizing output. They produce where marginal revenue equals marginal cost. Monopolistic competitors will produce less than perfectly competitive firms because the relationship between price and marginal revenue differs between those types of firms. Since firms that are monopolistic competitors face a negatively sloped demand curve, they produce less output than the output where price equals marginal cost for perfectly competitive firms. In the long run, entry will force both types of firms to the output where economic profits are equal to zero, which occurs where the demand curves are tangent to the average total cost curve. Because the monopolistic competitor faces a negatively sloped demand curve, this point will be at a level of output less than that of the perfect competitor.

17.

Perfect Competition	Monopolistic Competition
Standardized product	Differentiated product
Allocative efficiency	Downward-sloping demand curve
Productive efficiency	Excess capacity
Horizontal demand curve	
No control over price	

19. Answers will vary. Certainly not all individuals will respond to each and every advertisement. By advertising, a firm hopes it can both increase demand and make it more inelastic, thereby enhancing profits. Critics of advertising argue that advertisers attempt to manipulate preferences and engender brand loyalty to reduce competition. Defenders of advertising argue that production costs can be reduced if substantial economies of scale exist. Also, by raising consumer awareness of substitute products, advertising can help increase the competitiveness within markets and lead to lower prices. Advertising may be considered a waste by someone who always knows which good he or she wants, but advertising would not be used by sellers who do not think it would increase demand sufficiently to make it profitable.

21. By advertising, firms hope to increase demand and create a less elastic demand curve for their products, thus enhancing revenues and profits.

23. The following markets are oligopolistic: (b) funeral services, (c) airline travel, (e) oil, and (f) breakfast cereals.

25. Unlike perfectly competitive firms, oligopolists can earn economic profits in the long run if barriers to entry are sufficiently high to deter new firms from entering the market.

27. Since the market for wheat is highly competitive, it is unlikely that the Smith–Jones cartel will be at all successful or have any impact on the price of wheat. There are too many good substitutes available for the wheat produced by Farmers Smith and Jones. If Smith and Jones choose to restrict their combined output, their profits will in all likelihood fall, with virtually no effect on the market price.

29. **a.** If the Canadian and Russian mines provide a significant share of the world's supply, increasing the supply will result in the price of diamonds falling. This could result in the breakdown of the cartel.

b. CSO will no longer be willing to advertise to increase the demand for all diamonds in general. This type of advertising might instead sell more Canadian or Russian diamonds and generate no profit for CSO. If CSO continues to advertise diamonds, it will try to distinguish the diamonds it is selling. CSO might try to establish a brand to differentiate its product from the others.

31. If both firms employ small advertising budgets, then they both earn modest profits of $50 million. If one firm opts for a large ad budget, but the other does not, then the firm with the large ad budget enjoys significantly greater profits than the firm that does not. If both firms spend large sums of money on advertising, then each earns the greatest amount of profit possible, equal to $150 million. This is a Nash equilibrium.

33. a. There is a dominant strategy, which is for both prisoners to confess. Whichever strategy the other prisoner adopts, the prisoner in question gets less time by confessing.

b. Since each does as well as possible given the actions of the other, this same strategy (both prisoners confessing) is a Nash equilibrium.

35. Shirking at school may be a one-shot game with no future consequences. At work, however, it is a repeated game with adverse future consequences.

CHAPTER 11: LABOUR MARKETS AND THE DISTRIBUTION OF INCOME

1. The demand for unskilled labour used to produce hamburgers and fries would increase as well.

3.

Quantity of Labour	Total Output/Week	Marginal Product of Labour	Marginal Revenue Product of Labour
0	—		
1	250	250	$1000
2	600	350	1400
3	900	300	1200
4	1125	225	900
5	1300	175	700
6	1450	150	600
7	1560	110	440

5.

Workers	Total Corn Output	Marginal Product of Labour
1	4 000	4000
2	10 000	6000
3	15 000	5000
4	18 000	3000
5	19 000	1000
6	18 000	−1000

7.

Workers	Total Output	Marginal Product	Price	Marginal Revenue Product
1	200	200	20	4000
2	380	180	20	3600
3	540	160	20	3200
4	680	140	20	2800
5	800	120	20	2400
6	900	100	20	2000
7	980	80	20	1600
8	1040	60	20	1200

9. The equilibrium wage would tend to decrease if a competitive firm provided on-the-job training and dental benefits to its workers (since part of the compensation to employees would come in the form of these benefits). If the government mandated a minimum wage of $12 per hour, employers would likely respond by reducing benefits such as dental insurance and on-the-job training.

11. An influx of immigrants into a country will increase the supply of labour and decrease real wages. On the other hand, the home countries of the departing immigrants will experience a decrease in the supply of available labour, which puts upward pressure on real wages.

13. a. E; b. C; c. G; d. I; e. A; f. B; g. D; h. F; i. H.

15. a. and **b.**

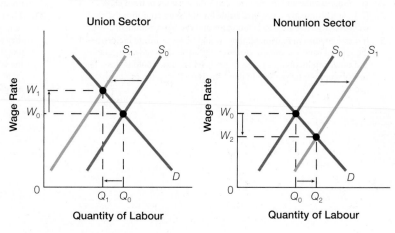

c. Union wages go up and the number of union workers hired goes down; nonunion wages go down, and the number of nonunion workers hired goes up.

17. The official data may overstate the actual degree of income inequality because it fails to take into consideration differences in age, demographic factors such as the increasing number of both divorced couples and double-income families, and government redistributive activities (by ignoring the effects of taxes and in-kind subsidies).

19. **a.** A massive influx of low-skilled immigrants would increase the proportion of the overall population earning low incomes.

b. In the event of a baby boom, some individuals would opt to become full-time parents, transforming two-income families into single-income families. This would tend to reduce the proportion of the population in high-income quintiles and increase the proportion in the low-income quintiles.

c. When the babies in (b) enter their twenties and begin working, the proportion of the population in low-income quintiles will likely increase (since young workers earn lower incomes on average then middle-aged workers).

d. When the babies in (b) reach age 65 or older, again the proportion of the population in low-income quintiles will increase (as retirees earn lower incomes on average than middle-aged workers do).

21. Even with the same lifetime incomes, some would be in their peak earning years and others would be in low earning years (e.g., young or retired people) at a given point in time, resulting in current income inequality.

23. Economic growth could potentially reduce absolute measures of poverty by increasing real incomes. However, economic growth by itself cannot eliminate relative measures of poverty because there will always be some with lower real incomes than others.

25. These programs include progressive income taxes; cash transfers such as Employment Insurance and in-kind transfers such as educational vouchers; social assistance programs such as the Guaranteed Income Supplement; government subsidies in the form of public housing; and minimum-wage laws.

CHAPTER 12: MARKET FAILURE AND THE ENVIRONMENT

1. **Positive externalities:**
   b. You are given a flu shot.
   d. A local youth group cleans up trash along a two-kilometre stretch of highway.

   Negative externalities:
   a. During a live-theatre performance, an audience member's cellphone rings loudly.
   e. A firm dumps chemical waste into a local stream.
   f. The person down the hall in your residence plays a hip-hop playlist loudly while you are trying to sleep.

   No externalities:
   c. You purchase and drink a soft drink during a break from class.

3. If the steel company is not held liable for dumping crud into the air, it will consider only the $25 labour costs and the $10 equipment costs.

5. If diesel engines were banned, there would be fewer future incidences of the sorts of cancer it causes. However, the advantages of transportation and other production processes using diesel engines would be lost. The cost of shipping freight would likely increase, raising the prices of many goods.

7. **a.** When taxes are imposed to address external costs, the costs of production to producers will rise, shifting supply curves up (left). The market result of such decreases in supply is higher prices for the goods whose production imposes external costs. When subsidies are given to address external benefits, the net of subsidy costs of production to producers will fall, shifting supply curves down (right). The market result of such increases in supply is lower prices for the goods whose production creates external benefits.

   b. Workers would benefit from subsidies to an industry that address external benefits—more output will increase the demand for workers and other inputs—but they would be hurt by taxes that address external costs.

9. **a.** A higher tax on gasoline encourages people to drive less and therefore reduces air pollution.

   b. An annual tax on automobiles based on average emissions might discourage some people from buying a car, but is unlikely to alter the driving habits of individual car owners in any significant way.

   c. An annual tax on total emissions from a particular model of car would encourage both less driving and more switching to more environmentally friendly cars.

11. A pollution reduction program that relies on emissions standards would force firms to limit pollution levels, regardless of the cost of doing so. With an emissions permit program, firms that can reduce pollution levels at relatively low marginal cost can sell their permits to firms that can reduce pollution levels only at higher marginal costs. The same level of pollution reduction can be achieved with either program. However, the latter program would achieve the reduction in pollution at lower cost to society.

13. Transferable pollution rights would create a market for pollution reduction. Every polluter would then find it profitable to reduce pollution as long as they could do it more cheaply than the price of a pollution right. Therefore, producers would employ the lowest-cost pollution control methods for a given amount of pollution reduction.

15. A change in the law is not necessary to achieve an efficient outcome in this situation. If the resort owner and chemical factory could reach an agreement whereby the resort owner compensates the chemical factory for hauling the pollution to the toxic waste dump, the socially efficient outcome could be achieved. Since the damage to the resort owner exceeds the cost of hauling the pollution to the toxic waste dump site, this is a possibility, as long as the property rights are clearly defined and the cost of negotiating and transacting is low enough.

17. **a.** Hot dogs: Private good
    b. Cable TV: Nonrival; private good
    c. Broadcast TV: Nonrival; nonexclusive; public good
    d. Automobiles: Private good
    e. National defence: Nonrival; nonexclusive; public good
    f. Pollution-control policy: Public good
    g. Parking spot in a parking structure: Private good
    h. A sunset: Nonrival; nonexclusive; public good
    i. Admission to a theme park: Private good

19. Buffalo almost became extinct because people did not have clear property rights for buffalo, unlike cattle. You can buy a buffalo burger today because people now have clear property rights to buffalo.

21. The free-rider problem arises in the case of public goods because people cannot be prevented from enjoying the benefits of public goods once they are provided. Therefore, people have an incentive not to voluntarily pay for those benefits, making it difficult or even impossible to finance the efficient quantity of public goods through voluntary market arrangements. The government can overcome the free-rider problem by forcing people to pay for the provision of a public good through taxes.

Glossary

accounting profits total revenues minus total explicit costs p. 161

aggregate the total amount—such as the aggregate level of output p. 3

allocative efficiency where $P = MC$ and production is allocated to reflect consumer preferences p. 208

average cost pricing production where the price of a good equals average total cost p. 235

average fixed cost (*AFC*) a per-unit measure of fixed costs; fixed costs divided by output p. 169

average product (*AP*) the total product divided by the number of units of the variable input used to produce it p. 166

average revenue (*AR*) total revenue divided by the number of units sold p. 193

average total cost (*ATC*) a per-unit cost of operation; total cost divided by output p. 169

average variable cost (*AVC*) a per-unit measure of variable costs; variable costs divided by output p. 169

backward-bending labour supply curve Above a certain wage rate, a worker might prefer to work less and enjoy more leisure (the income effect dominates the substitution effect). p. 282

bads items that we do not desire or want p. 11

bandwagon effect a positive network externality where a consumer's demand for a product increases because other consumers own it p. 270

bar graph represents data using vertical bars rising from the horizontal axis between price and quantity demanded p. 32

Canada's Official Poverty Line level of income necessary to allow a household to buy a specific basket of goods and services that allows them to meet their basic needs and achieve a modest standard of living in their community p. 297

capital the equipment and structures used to produce goods and services p. 10

capital-intensive production that uses a large amount of capital p. 24

cartel a collection of firms that agree on sales, pricing, and other decisions p. 263

cash transfer direct cash payment such as public pensions, social assistance, and Employment Insurance benefits p. 300

causation when one event causes another event to occur p. 7

ceteris paribus holding everything else constant p. 5

change in demand a change in a determinant of demand leads to a change in demand, a shift of the entire demand curve p. 70

change in quantity demanded a change in a good's price leads to a change in quantity demanded, a move along a given demand curve p. 70

circular flow model of income and output an illustration of the continuous flow of goods, services, inputs, and payments between firms and households p. 58

Coase theorem states that where property rights are defined in a clear-cut fashion, externalities are internalized p. 323

collective bargaining negotiations between representatives of employers and unions p. 288

collude when firms act together to restrict competition p. 262

command economy The government uses central planning to coordinate most economic activities. p. 23

common resource a rival good that is not excludable p. 326

comparative advantage occurs when a person or a country can produce a good or service at a lower opportunity cost than others can p. 21

complement An increase (a decrease) in the price of one good causes a decrease (an increase) in the demand of another good. p. 71

constant-cost industry an industry where input prices (and cost curves) do not change as industry output changes p. 204

constant returns to scale occur in an output range where *LRATC* does not change as output varies p. 177

consumer equilibrium allocation of consumer income that balances the ratio of marginal utility to the price of the goods purchased p. 145

consumer sovereignty consumers vote on economic affairs with their dollars in a market economy p. 23

consumer surplus the monetary difference between the price a consumer is willing and able to pay for an additional unit of a good and the price the consumer actually pays; for the entire market, it is the sum of all of the individual consumer surpluses for those consumers who have purchased the good p. 147

cooperative game collusion by firms in order to improve their profit maximizations p. 266

correlation two events that usually occur together p. 7

cross-price elasticity of demand a measure of the impact that a price change of one good will have on the quantity demanded of another good at a given price p. 127

deadweight loss net loss of total surplus that results from the misallocation of resources p. 152

decreasing-cost industry an industry where input prices fall (and cost curves fall) as industry output rises p. 207

demand the quantity of a good or service that consumers are both willing and able to purchase over a period of time at various prices p. 66

derived demand The demand for an input is derived from the consumer's demands for a good or service. p. 277

diminishing marginal product as a variable input increases, with other inputs fixed, a point will be reached where the additions to output will eventually decline p. 167

diminishing marginal utility the concept that as an individual consumes more and more of a good, each successive unit generates less and less utility (or satisfaction) p. 143

diseconomies of scale occur in an output range where *LRATC* rises as output expands p. 177

dominant strategy will be optimal regardless of the opponents' actions p. 266

economic profits total revenues minus explicit and implicit costs p. 161

economics the study of the allocation of our limited resources to satisfy our unlimited wants p. 1

economies of scale occur in an output range where *LRATC* falls as output increases p. 176

efficiency getting the most from society's scarce resources p. 54

elastic demand segment a portion of the demand curve where the percentage change of quantity demanded is greater than the percentage change in price ($E_D > 1$) p. 117

empirical analysis the examination of data to see if the hypothesis fits well with the facts p. 5

entrepreneurship the process of combining labour, land, and capital together to produce goods and services p. 10

equilibrium price the price at the intersection of the market supply and demand curves; at this price, the quantity demanded equals the quantity supplied p. 94

equilibrium quantity the quantity at the intersection of the market supply and demand curves; at this quantity, the quantity demanded equals the quantity supplied p. 94

excess capacity occurs when the firm produces below the level where average total cost is minimized p. 254

explicit costs the opportunity costs of production that require a monetary payment p. 160

externality a benefit or cost from consumption or production that spills over onto those that are not consuming or producing the good p. 309

factor (input) markets the market where households sell the use of their inputs (capital, land, labour, and entrepreneurship) to firms p. 58

fallacy of composition Even if something is true for an individual, it is not necessarily true for a group. p. 7

fixed costs costs that do not vary with the level of output in the short run p. 169

free rider a party that derives benefits from something without paying for it p. 325

game theory Firms attempt to maximize profits by acting in ways that minimize damage from competitors. p. 266

goods items we value or desire p. 11

goods and services flow the continuous flow of inputs and outputs in an economy p. 58

human capital the productive knowledge and skill people receive from education and on-the-job training p. 10

hypothesis a testable proposition p. 5

implicit costs the opportunity costs of production that do not require a monetary payment p. 161

income effect At higher prices, buyers feel poorer, causing a lowering of quantity demanded. p. 67

income elasticity of demand a measure of the responsiveness of the quantity demanded of a good to a change in income p. 128

income flow the continuous flow of income and expenditure in an economy p. 58

increasing-cost industry an industry where input prices rise (and cost curves rise) as industry output rises p. 206

individual demand curve a graphical representation that shows the inverse relationship p. 67

individual demand schedule a table that shows the relationship between price and quantity demanded p. 67

individual supply curve a graphical representation that shows the positive relationship between the price and the quantity supplied p. 78

inelastic demand segment a portion of the demand curve where the percentage change in quantity demanded is less than the percentage change in price ($E_D < 1$) p. 117

inferior good If income increases, the demand for a good decreases; if income decreases, the demand for a good increases. p. 72

in-kind transfers transfers of goods and services rather than cash p. 294

internalized externalities when an industry is forced to compensate those enduring some negative externality caused by its production p. 314

joint profit maximization determination of price based on the marginal revenue (derived from the market demand schedule) and marginal cost schedule of the firms in the industry p. 263

labour the physical and mental effort used by people in the production of goods and services p. 10

labour-intensive production that uses a large amount of labour p. 24

land the natural resources used in the production of goods and services p. 10

law of demand the quantity of a good or service demanded varies inversely (negatively) with its price, *ceteris paribus* p. 66

law of increasing opportunity cost As more of one item is produced by an economy, the opportunity cost of additional units of that product rises. p. 46

law of supply The higher (lower) the price of the good, the greater (smaller) the quantity supplied, *ceteris paribus*. p. 77

long run a period over which all production inputs are variable p. 165

macroeconomics the study of the aggregate economy, including the topics of inflation, unemployment, and economic growth p. 3

marginal cost (*MC*) the change in total costs resulting from a one-unit change in output p. 169

marginal cost pricing the decision to set production where the price of a good equals marginal cost p. 234

marginal product (*MP*) the change in total product resulting from a unit change in input p. 166

marginal resource cost (*MRC*) the amount that an extra input adds to the firm's total costs p. 278

marginal revenue (*MR*) the increase in total revenue that results from the sale of one more unit p. 193

marginal revenue product (*MRP*) the additional revenue that a firm obtains from one more unit of input p. 278

marginal thinking focusing on the additional, or incremental, choices p. 15

marginal utility (*MU*) extra satisfaction generated by an additional unit of a good that is consumed in a particular time period p. 141

market the process of buyers and sellers exchanging goods and services p. 53

market demand curve the horizontal summation of individual demand curves p. 68

market economy Goods and services are allocated based on the private decisions of consumers, input suppliers, and firms. p. 24

market equilibrium the point at which the market supply and the market demand curves intersect p. 94

market failure when the economy fails to allocate resources efficiently on its own p. 56

market supply curve the horizontal summation of individual supply curves p. 78

microeconomics the study of the smaller units within the economy, including the topics of household and firm behaviour and how they interact in the marketplace p. 3

minimum efficient scale the output level where economies of scale are exhausted and constant returns to scale begin p. 177

mixed economy Government and the private sector together determine the allocation of resources. p. 24

monopolistic competition a market structure with many firms selling differentiated products p. 248

monopoly a market with only one seller of a product that has no close substitute and there are natural and legal barriers to entry that prevent competition p. 218

monopsony a market with a single buyer p. 286

mutual interdependence when a firm shapes its policy with an eye to the policies of competing firms p. 260

Nash equilibrium When firms interact with one another, each chooses its best strategy given the strategies of the other firms. p. 267

natural monopoly a firm that can produce at a lower cost than a number of smaller firms could p. 221

negative externality when costs spill over to an outside party that is not involved in producing or consuming the good p. 309

negative incentives incentives that either increase costs or reduce benefits, resulting in a decrease in the activity or behaviour p. 19

negative network externality when a consumer's quantity demanded for a good increases because fewer consumers are purchasing the same good p. 270

negative relationship when two variables change in opposite directions p. 34

net benefits the difference between the expected marginal benefits and expected marginal costs p. 16

network externality when the number of other people purchasing the good influences quantity demanded p. 270

noncooperative game Each firm sets its own price without consulting other firms. p. 266

normal good If income increases, the demand for a good increases; if income decreases, the demand for a good decreases. p. 72

normative analysis a subjective, biased approach p. 8

oligopoly a market structure with only a few sellers offering similar or identical products p. 259

opportunity cost the highest or best forgone opportunity resulting from a decision p. 13

payoff matrix a summary of the possible outcomes from the various strategies p. 266

perfect competition a market with many buyers and sellers, all selling a homogeneous product; market entry and exit is easy, and no firm can affect the market price p. 188

pie chart a circle divided into proportionate slices that represent various quantities that add up to 100 percent p. 32

pollution tax tax levied by government on a firm for environmental pollution p. 319

positive analysis an objective, value-free approach, utilizing the scientific method p. 8

positive externality when benefits spill over to an outside party that is not involved in producing or consuming the good p. 310

positive incentives incentives that either reduce costs or increase benefits, resulting in an increase in the activity or behaviour p. 19

positive network externality when a consumer's quantity demanded for a good increases because a greater number of consumers purchase the same good p. 270

positive relationship when two variables change in the same direction p. 34

poverty the condition of a person who is deprived of the resources, means, choices, and power necessary to acquire and maintain a basic level of living standard and to facilitate integration into and participation in society p. 297

price ceiling a legally established maximum price p. 104

price controls government-mandated minimum and maximum prices p. 104

price discrimination the practice of charging different consumers different prices for the same good or service when the cost of providing that good or service is not different for different consumers p. 236

price elasticity of demand a measure of the responsiveness of quantity demanded to a change in price p. 116

price elasticity of supply the measure of the sensitivity of the quantity supplied to changes in the price of a good p. 129

price floor a legally established minimum price p. 104

price maker a monopolistic firm that sets the price of its product so as to maximize its profits p. 218

price taker A perfectly competitive firm takes the price that it is given by the intersection of the market demand and market supply curves. p. 188

private good a good with rivalrous consumption and excludability p. 324

producer surplus the difference between what a producer is paid for a good and the cost of producing that unit of the good; for the market, it is the sum of all the individual sellers' producer surpluses—the area above the market supply curve and below the market price p. 149

product differentiation the accentuation of unique product qualities, real or perceived, to develop a specific product identity p. 249

product markets the markets for consumer goods and services p. 58

production function the relationship between the quantity of inputs and the quantity of outputs produced p. 165

production possibilities curve the potential total output combinations of any two goods p. 43

productive efficiency where a good or service is produced at the lowest possible cost p. 208

profit-maximizing output rule A firm should always produce at the level of output where MR = MC. p. 194

profits the difference between total revenue and total cost p. 161

progressive tax system As a person's income rises, the amount of his or her tax as a proportion of income rises. p. 300

public good a good that is nonrivalrous in consumption and nonexcludable p. 324

resources inputs used to produce goods and services p. 1

rule of rational choice Individuals will pursue an activity if the expected marginal benefits are greater than the expected marginal costs. p. 15

scarcity the situation that exists when human wants exceed available resources p. 10

services intangible acts that people want p. 11

shortage where quantity demanded exceeds quantity supplied p. 95

short run a period too brief for some production inputs to be varied p. 164

short-run market supply curve the horizontal summation of the individual firms' supply curves in the market p. 199

short-run supply curve As a cost relationship, this curve shows the marginal cost of producing any given output; as a supply curve, it shows the equilibrium output that the firm will supply at various prices in the short run. p. 198

slope the ratio of rise (change in the *Y* variable) over the run (change in the *X* variable) p. 38

specializing concentrating on the production of one, or a few, goods or services p. 21

substitute An increase (a decrease) in the price of one good causes an increase (a decrease) in the demand for another good. p. 71

substitution effect At higher prices, buyers increasingly substitute other goods for the good that now has a higher relative price. p. 67

sunk costs costs that have been incurred and cannot be recovered p. 162

supply the quantity of a good or service that producers are both willing and able to make available for sale p. 77

surplus where quantity supplied exceeds quantity demanded p. 95

switching costs the costs involved in changing from one product to another or in changing suppliers p. 271

tax incidence the analysis of the effect of a particular tax on the distribution of economic welfare p. 132

the economic problem Scarcity forces us to choose, and choices are costly because we must give up other opportunities that we value. p. 1

theory an established explanation that accounts for known facts or phenomena p. 4

time-series graph shows changes in the value of a variable over time p. 32

tit-for-tat strategy used in repeated games, where one player follows the other player's move in the previous round; leads to greater cooperation p. 269

total cost (*TC*) the sum of the firm's total fixed costs and total variable costs p. 169

total fixed cost (*TFC*) the sum of the firm's fixed costs p. 169

total product (*TP*) the total output of a good produced by the firm p. 165

total revenue (*TR*) the product price times the quantity sold p. 192

total utility (*TU*) total amount of satisfaction derived from the consumption of a certain number of units of a good or service p. 141

total variable cost (*TVC*) the sum of the firm's variable costs p. 169

total welfare gains the sum of consumer and producer surplus p. 152

transferable pollution rights a right given to a firm to discharge a specified amount of pollution; its transferable nature creates an incentive to lower pollution levels p. 320

unintended consequences the secondary effects of an action that may occur after the initial effects p. 108

unit elastic demand demand with a price elasticity of 1; the percentage change in quantity demanded is equal to the percentage change in price p. 117

util one unit of satisfaction p. 141

utility a measure of the relative levels of satisfaction consumers get from the consumption of goods and services p. 141

variable something that is measured by a number, such as your height p. 33

variable costs costs that vary with the level of output p. 169

***X*-axis** the horizontal axis on a graph p. 32

***Y*-axis** the vertical axis on a graph p. 32

Index

The Role and Method of Economics

Section 1.1 Economics: A Brief Introduction

- *What is economics?*

  Economics is the study of the allocation of our limited resources to satisfy our unlimited wants.

- *Why study economics?*

  Economics is a problem-solving science that teaches you to ask intelligent questions.

- *What distinguishes macroeconomics from microeconomics?*

  Macroeconomics deals with the aggregate, or total, economy, while microeconomics focuses on smaller units within the economy.

Section 1.2 Economic Theory

- *What are economic theories?*

  Economic theories are statements used to explain and predict patterns of human behaviour.

- *Why do we need to abstract?*

  Economic theories, through abstractions, provide a broad view of human economic behaviour.

- *What is a hypothesis?*

  A hypothesis makes a prediction about human behaviour and is then tested.

- *What is the* ceteris paribus *assumption?*

  In order to isolate the effects of one variable on another, we use the *ceteris paribus* assumption.

- *Why are observations and predictions harder in the social sciences?*

  With its focus on human behaviour, which is more variable and less predictable, observation and prediction are more difficult in the social sciences.

- *What distinguishes between correlation and causation?*

  The fact that two events are related does not mean that one caused the other to occur.

- *What are positive analysis and normative analysis?*

  Positive analysis is objective and value-free, while normative analysis involves value judgments and opinions about the desirability of various actions.

Section 1.3 Scarcity

- *What is scarcity?*

  Scarcity exists when our wants exceed the available resources of land, labour, capital, and entrepreneurship.

- *What are goods and services?*

  Goods and services are things that we value.

Section 1.4 Opportunity Cost

- *Why do we have to make choices?*

  Scarcity means we all have to make choices.

- *What do we give up when we have to choose?*

  When we are forced to choose, we give up the next highest-valued alternative.

Key Terms

economics *the study of the allocation of our limited resources to satisfy our unlimited wants* p. 1

resources *inputs used to produce goods and services* p. 1

the economic problem *Scarcity forces us to choose, and choices are costly because we must give up other opportunities that we value.* p. 1

macroeconomics *the study of the aggregate economy, including the topics of inflation, unemployment, and economic growth* p. 3

aggregate *the total amount— such as the aggregate level of output* p. 3

microeconomics *the study of the smaller units within the economy, including the topics of household and firm behaviour and how they interact in the marketplace* p. 3

theory *an established explanation that accounts for known facts or phenomena* p. 4

hypothesis *a testable proposition* p. 5

empirical analysis *the examination of data to see if the hypothesis fits well with the facts* p. 5

ceteris paribus *holding everything else constant* p. 5

correlation *two events that usually occur together* p. 7

causation *when one event causes another event to occur* p. 7

fallacy of composition *Even if something is true for an individual, it is not necessarily true for a group.* p. 7

positive analysis *an objective, value-free approach, utilizing the scientific method* p. 8

normative analysis *a subjective, biased approach* p. 8

scarcity *the situation that exists when human wants exceed available resources* p. 10

- *Why are "free" lunches not free?*

Because the production of any good uses up some of society's resources, there is no such thing as a free lunch.

Section 1.5 Marginal Thinking

- *What do we mean by marginal thinking?*

Economists are usually interested in the effects of additional, or incremental, changes in a given situation.

- *What is the rule of rational choice?*

The rule of rational choice states that individuals will pursue an activity if they expect the marginal benefits to be greater than the marginal costs, or $E(MB) > E(MC)$.

Section 1.6 Incentives Matter

- *Can we predict how people will respond to changes in incentives?*

Incentives change the expected marginal benefits and expected marginal costs of certain behaviour. Therefore, when people are acting rationally, they respond to incentives in predictable ways.

- *What are positive and negative incentives?*

A negative incentive increases costs or reduces benefits, thus discouraging consumption or production, while a positive incentive decreases costs or increases benefits, thus encouraging consumption or production.

Section 1.7 Specialization and Trade

- *Why do people specialize?*

Specialization is important for individuals, businesses, regions, and nations. It allows them to make the best use of their limited resources.

- *How do specialization and trade lead to greater wealth and prosperity?*

Specialization and trade increase wealth by allowing a person, a region, or a nation to specialize in those products that it produces at a lower opportunity cost and to trade for those products that others produce at a lower opportunity cost.

Section 1.8 The Three Questions Every Society Faces

- *What is to be produced?*

Every economy has to decide what to produce. In a decentralized market economy, millions of buyers and sellers determine what and how much to produce. In a mixed economy, the government and the private sector determine the allocation of resources.

- *How are the goods and services to be produced?*

The best form of production is the one that conserves the relatively scarce (more costly) resources and uses more of the abundant (less costly) resources. When capital is relatively scarce and labour is plentiful, production tends to be labour-intensive. When capital is relatively abundant and labour is relatively scarce, production tends to be capital-intensive.

- *Who will get the goods and services?*

In a market economy, the amount of goods and services one is able to obtain depends on one's income. The amount of one's income depends on the quantity and the quality of the scarce resources that the individual controls.

Scarcity, Trade-Offs, and Production Possibilities

Section 2.1 The Production Possibilities Curve

- *What is a production possibilities curve?*

  A production possibilities curve represents the potential total output combinations of any two goods available to a society, given its resources and existing technology.

- *What is efficiency?*

  Efficiency requires society to use its resources to the fullest extent—no wasted resources. If the economy is operating within the production possibilities curve, the economy is operating inefficiently.

- *How is opportunity cost measured?*

  The cost of altering production within the production possibilities curve framework, at efficiency, is measured in forgone units of the sole alternative.

- *What is the law of increasing opportunity costs?*

  A bowed production possibilities curve means that the opportunity costs of producing additional units of a good rise as society produces more of that good (the law of increasing opportunity costs).

Section 2.2 Economic Growth and the Production Possibilities Curve

- *How do we show economic growth on the production possibilities curve?*

  Economic growth is represented by an outward shift of the production possibilities curve, indicating the possibility of producing more of all goods. Despite this, scarcity inevitably remains a fact of life.

- *How can we summarize the production possibilities curve?*

  The production possibilities model is an effective way of illustrating the economic concepts of scarcity, choice, opportunity costs, efficiency, and economic growth.

Section 2.3 Market Prices Coordinate Economic Activity

- *What is a market?*

  Markets consist of buyers and sellers exchanging goods and services with one another.

- *What are the roles of buyers and sellers in a market?*

  Buyers determine the demand side of the market and sellers determine the supply side of the market.

- *How does a market system allocate scarce resources?*

  Through voluntary exchange and the price system, the market system provides a way for producers and consumers to allocate scarce resources.

- *What is a market failure?*

  A market failure occurs when an economy fails to allocate resources efficiently on its own.

Key Terms

production possibilities curve *the potential total output combinations of any two goods for an economy, given the inputs and technology available* p. 43

law of increasing opportunity cost *As more of one item is produced by an economy, the opportunity cost of additional units of that product rises.* p. 46

market *the process of buyers and sellers exchanging goods and services* p. 53

efficiency *getting the most from society's scarce resources* p. 54

market failure *when the economy fails to allocate resources efficiently on its own* p. 56

product markets *the markets for consumer goods and services* p. 58

factor (input) markets *the market where households sell the use of their inputs (capital, land, labour, and entrepreneurship) to firms* p. 58

goods and services flow *the continuous flow of inputs and outputs in an economy* p. 58

income flow *the continuous flow of income and expenditure in an economy* p. 58

circular flow model of income and output *an illustration of the continuous flow of goods, services, inputs, and payments between firms and households* p. 58

Key Exhibits/ Graphs

Section 2.4 The Circular Flow Model

- *What are product markets?*

  In the product market, households are buyers and firms are sellers.

- *What are factor markets?*

  In the factor markets, households are the sellers and firms are the buyers.

- *What is the goods and services flow?*

  The goods and services flow represents the continuous flow of inputs and outputs in an economy.

- *What is the income flow?*

  The income flow represents the continuous flow of income and expenditure in an economy.

- *What is the circular flow model?*

  The circular flow model illustrates the flow of goods, services, and payments among firms and households.

Supply and Demand

Section 3.1 Demand

- *What is the law of demand?*

  The law of demand states that when the price of a good falls (rises), the quantity demanded rises (falls), *ceteris paribus*.

- *What is an individual demand schedule and curve?*

  An individual demand schedule is a table that shows the relationship between the price of a good and the quantity demanded.

- *What is a market demand curve?*

  A market demand curve shows the amount of a good that all the buyers in the market would be willing and able to buy at various prices.

Section 3.2 Shifts in the Demand Curve

- *What is the difference between a change in demand and a change in quantity demanded?*

  A change in the quantity demanded describes a movement along a given demand curve in response to a change in the price of the good. A change in demand shifts the entire demand curve in response to a change in some determinant of demand.

- *What are the determinants of demand?*

  Some possible determinants of demand (demand shifters) are the prices of related goods, income, number of buyers, tastes, and expectations.

- *Can we review the distinction between changes in demand and changes in quantity demanded?*

Change in Variable and Change in Demand

Variable	Change in Variable	Change in Demand
1. Price of a complement good	↑	↓
2. Price of a substitute good	↑	↑
3. Income (normal good)	↑	↑
4. Income (inferior good)	↑	↓
5. Number of buyers	↑	↑
6. Tastes and preferences	↑	↑
7. Expected future price	↑	↑

Key Terms

demand *the quantity of a good or service that consumers are both willing and able to purchase over a period of time at various prices* p. 66

law of demand *the quantity of a good or service demanded varies inversely (negatively) with its price, ceteris paribus* p. 66

substitution effect *At higher prices, buyers increasingly substitute other goods for the good that now has a higher relative price.* p. 67

income effect *At higher prices, buyers feel poorer, causing a lowering of quantity demanded.* p. 67

individual demand schedule *a table that shows the relationship between price and quantity demanded* p. 67

individual demand curve *a graphical representation that shows the inverse relationship between price and quantity demanded* p. 67

market demand curve *the horizontal summation of individual demand curves* p. 68

change in quantity demanded *a change in a good's price leads to a change in quantity demanded, a move along a given demand curve* p. 70

change in demand *a change in a determinant of demand leads to a change in demand, a shift of the entire demand curve* p. 70

substitute *An increase (a decrease) in the price of one good causes an increase (a decrease) in the demand for another good.* p. 71

complement *An increase (a decrease) in the price of one good causes a decrease (an increase) in the demand of another good.* p. 71

Key Exhibits/ Graphs

Section 3.3 Supply

- *What is the law of supply?*

  The law of supply states that the higher (lower) the price of the good, the greater (smaller) the quantity supplied.

- *What is an individual supply curve?*

  The individual supply curve shows the positive relationship between the price and quantity supplied of a given good or service.

- *What is a market supply curve?*

  The market supply curve is a graphical representation of the amount of goods and services that suppliers are willing and able to supply at various prices.

Section 3.4 Shifts in the Supply Curve

- *What is the difference between a change in supply and a change in quantity supplied?*

  A movement along a given supply curve is caused by a change in the price of the good in question. A shift of the entire supply curve is called a *change in supply*.

- *What are the determinants of supply?*

  Input prices, the prices of related products, expectations, the number of suppliers, technology, regulation, taxes and subsidies, and weather can all lead to changes in supply (shifts in supply).

- *Can we review the distinction between a change in supply and a change in quantity supplied?*

Change in Variable and Change in Supply

Variable	Change in Variable	Change in Supply
1. Input prices	↑	↓
2. Price of substitute in production	↑	↓
3. Price of complement in production	↑	↑
4. Expected future price	↑	↓
5. Number of suppliers	↑	↑
6. Government regulation	↑	↓
7. Taxes	↑	↓
8. Subsidies	↑	↑
9. Technology	↑	↑

Chapter in Review

Bringing Supply and Demand Together

Section 4.1 Market Equilibrium Price and Quantity

- *What are the equilibrium price and the equilibrium quantity?*

  The intersection of the supply and demand curve shows the equilibrium price and equilibrium quantity in a market.

- *What is a shortage and what is a surplus?*

  A surplus is where quantity supplied exceeds quantity demanded. A shortage is where quantity demanded exceeds quantity supplied.

Section 4.2 Changes in Equilibrium Price and Quantity

- *What happens to equilibrium price and equilibrium quantity when the demand curve shifts?*

  Changes in demand will cause a change in the equilibrium price and quantity, *ceteris paribus.* An increase (decrease) in demand will cause an increase (decrease) in both equilibrium price and equilibrium quantity.

- *What happens to equilibrium price and equilibrium quantity when the supply curve shifts?*

  Changes in supply will cause a change in the equilibrium price and quantity, *ceteris paribus.* An increase (decrease) in supply will cause a decrease (increase) in equilibrium price and an increase (decrease) in equilibrium quantity.

- *What happens when both supply and demand shift in the same time period?*

  When there are simultaneous shifts in both supply and demand curves, either the equilibrium price or the equilibrium quantity will be indeterminate without more information.

Section 4.3 Price Controls

- *What are price controls?*

  Price controls involve government mandates to keep prices above or below the market-determined equilibrium price.

- *What are price ceilings?*

  Price ceilings are government-imposed maximum prices. When price ceilings are set below the equilibrium price, shortages will result.

- *What are price floors?*

  Price floors are government-imposed minimum prices. When price floors are set above the equilibrium price, surpluses will result.

Key Terms

market equilibrium *the point at which the market supply and the market demand curves intersect* p. 94

equilibrium price *the price at the intersection of the market supply and demand curves; at this price the quantity demanded equals the quantity supplied* p. 94

equilibrium quantity *the quantity at the intersection of the market supply and demand curves; at this quantity, the quantity demanded equals the quantity supplied* p. 94

surplus *where quantity supplied exceeds quantity demanded* p. 95

shortage *where quantity demanded exceeds quantity supplied* p. 95

price controls *government-mandated minimum and maximum prices* p. 104

price ceiling *a legally established maximum price* p. 104

price floor *a legally established minimum price* p. 104

unintended consequences *the secondary effects of an action that may occur after the initial effects* p. 108

Key Exhibits/ Graphs

Notes

Elasticity

Section 5.1 Price Elasticity of Demand

- *What is price elasticity of demand?*

  Price elasticity of demand measures the percentage change in quantity demanded divided by the percentage change in price.

- *How do we measure consumers' responses to price changes?*

  If the demand for a good is price elastic in the relevant range, quantity demanded is very responsive to a price change. If the demand for a good is relatively price inelastic, quantity demanded is not very responsive to a price change.

- *How do we use the "midpoint method" in calculating price elasticities of demand?*

  The midpoint method for calculating percentage change involves using the average of the changing values, thereby eliminating the direction bias found in the traditional approach.

- *What determines the price elasticity of demand?*

  The price elasticity of demand depends on (1) the availability of close substitutes, (2) the proportion of income spent on the good, and (3) the amount of time that buyers have to respond to a price change.

Section 5.2 Total Revenue and Price Elasticity of Demand

- *How does the price elasticity of demand impact total revenue?*

  If demand is price elastic ($E_D > 1$), total revenue will vary inversely with a change in price. If demand is price inelastic ($E_D < 1$), total revenue will vary in the same direction as a change in price.

- *How does the price elasticity of demand change along a linear demand curve?*

  A linear demand curve is more price elastic at higher price ranges and more price inelastic at lower price ranges, and it is unit elastic at the midpoint: $E_D = 1$.

Section 5.3 Other Demand Elasticities

- *What is the cross-price elasticity of demand?*

  The cross-price elasticity of demand is the percentage change in the quantity demanded of one good divided by the percentage change in the price of another related good (complements and substitutes).

- *What is the income elasticity of demand?*

  The income elasticity of demand is the percentage change in quantity demanded divided by the percentage change in income (normal and inferior goods).

Section 5.4 Price Elasticity of Supply

- *What is the price elasticity of supply?*

  The price elasticity of supply measures the relative change in the quantity supplied that results from a change in price.

- *What determines the price elasticity of supply?*

  Supply tends to be more elastic in the long run than in the short run.

Key Terms

price elasticity of demand *a measure of the responsiveness of quantity demanded to a change in price   p. 116*

elastic demand segment *a portion of the demand curve where the percentage change of quantity demanded is greater than the percentage change in price ($E_D > 1$)   p. 117*

inelastic demand segment *a portion of the demand curve where the percentage change in quantity demanded is less than the percentage change in price ($E_D < 1$)   p. 117*

unit elastic demand *demand with a price elasticity of 1; the percentage change in quantity demanded is equal to the percentage change in price p. 117*

cross-price elasticity of demand *a measure of the impact that a price change of one good will have on the quantity demanded of another good at a given price   p. 127*

income elasticity of demand *a measure of the responsiveness of the quantity demanded of a good to a change in income p. 128*

price elasticity of supply *the measure of the sensitivity of the quantity supplied to changes in the price of a good   p. 129*

tax incidence *the analysis of the effect of a particular tax on the distribution of economic welfare   p. 132*

Key Exhibits/ Graphs

Section 5.1, Exhibit 1
Section 5.1, Exhibit 2
Section 5.1, Exhibit 3
Section 5.2, Exhibit 5
Section 5.4, Exhibit 1
Section 5.5, Exhibit 1

Section 5.5 Elasticity and Taxes

- *What is tax incidence?*

  Tax incidence refers to the analysis of the effect of particular taxes on the distribution of economic welfare.

- *How does the relative elasticity of supply and demand determine the tax burden?*

  If demand is more elastic than supply, producers bear the greater burden of the tax; however, if supply is more elastic than demand, consumers bear the greater burden of the tax.

Key Equations

$$E_D = \frac{\text{Percentage change in quantity demanded}}{\text{Percentage change in price}}$$

$$E_{AB} = \frac{\text{Percentage change in quantity demanded of A}}{\text{Percentage change in price of B}}$$

$$E_I = \frac{\text{Percentage change in quantity demanded}}{\text{Percentage change in income}}$$

$$E_s = \frac{\text{Percentage change in quantity supplied}}{\text{Percentage change in price}}$$

Midpoint Method

$$E_D = \frac{\left[\dfrac{Q_A - Q_B}{\left(\dfrac{Q_A + Q_B}{2}\right)}\right]}{\left[\dfrac{P_A - P_B}{\left(\dfrac{P_A + P_B}{2}\right)}\right]}$$

Chapter in Review

Consumer Choice and Market Efficiency

Section 6.1 Consumer Behaviour

* *What is utility?*

  Utility is the level of satisfaction an individual receives from consumption of a good or service. Total utility measures the amount of satisfaction derived from all units consumed, while marginal utility measures the change in utility from consuming one additional unit of a good or service.

* *What is diminishing marginal utility?*

  The less and less satisfaction an individual enjoys as he or she consumes more and more of a good or service describes the concept of diminishing marginal utility.

Section 6.2 Consumer Choice

* *What is the "best" decision for consumers?*

  To maximize consumer satisfaction, income must be allocated so that the ratio of the marginal utility to the price is the same for all goods purchased.

* *What is the connection between the law of demand and the law of diminishing marginal utility?*

  A fall in a good's price will raise its marginal utility–price (MU/P) ratio above that of other goods purchased. This relatively greater MU/P ratio will lead a rational consumer to purchase more of this good at the expense of other goods.

Section 6.3 Consumer and Producer Surplus

* *What is consumer surplus?*

  The difference between how much a consumer is willing and able to pay and how much a consumer has to pay for a unit of the good is called *consumer surplus*. An increase (decrease) in supply will lead to an increase (decrease) in consumer surplus.

* *What is producer surplus?*

  Producer surplus is the difference between what a producer is paid for a good and the cost of producing that good. An increase (decrease) in demand will lead to an increase (decrease) in producer surplus.

* *How do we measure the total gains from exchange?*

  The economy's total welfare gains from exchange can be measured by the sum of consumer and producer surplus.

Key Equations

$$MU = \frac{\Delta TU}{\Delta Q}$$

Key Terms

utility *a measure of the relative levels of satisfaction that consumers get from the consumption of goods and services* p. 141

util *one unit of satisfaction* p. 141

total utility *(TU)* *total amount of satisfaction derived from the consumption of a certain number of units of a good or service* p. 141

marginal utility *(MU)* *extra satisfaction generated by an additional unit of a good that is consumed in a particular time period* p. 141

diminishing marginal utility *the concept that as an individual consumes more and more of a good, each successive unit generates less and less utility (or satisfaction)* p. 143

consumer equilibrium *allocation of consumer income that balances the ratio of marginal utility to the price of the goods purchased* p. 145

consumer surplus *the monetary difference between the price a consumer is willing and able to pay for an additional unit of a good and the price the consumer actually pays; for the entire market, it is the sum of all the individual consumer surpluses for those consumers who have purchased the good* p. 147

producer surplus *the difference between what a producer is paid for a good and the cost of producing that unit of the good; for the market, it is the sum of all the individual sellers' producer surpluses—the area above the market supply curve and below the market price* p. 149

total welfare gains *the sum of consumer and producer surplus* p. 152

deadweight loss *net loss of total surplus that results from the misallocation of resources* p. 152

Key Exhibits/ Graphs

Production and Costs

Section 7.1 Profits: Total Revenues Minus Total Costs

- *What are explicit and implicit costs?*

  Total cost consists of both explicit costs and implicit costs. Explicit costs are the opportunity costs of production that require a monetary payment, while implicit costs are the opportunity costs that do not represent an outlay of money or a contractual obligation.

- *What are profits?*

  Profits are the difference between the total revenues of a firm and its total costs. Accounting profits are revenues minus explicit costs, while economic profits are revenues minus total opportunity costs—both explicit and implicit.

- *What are sunk costs?*

  Sunk costs are irretrievable and irrelevant to the firm.

Section 7.2 Production in the Short Run

- *What is the difference between the short run and the long run?*

  The short run is defined as a period too brief for some inputs to be varied, whereas the long run is a period of time long enough to allow the firm to adjust all inputs. Inputs like buildings and equipment that do not change with output are called *fixed inputs*.

- *How does production in the short run behave?*

  Total output increases as variable inputs are increased. Marginal product initially rises but eventually declines as variable inputs are added. Finally, negative marginal product can occur, indicating a fall in total output.

- *What is the relationship between marginal and average amounts?*

  Adding a marginal amount affects the value of the average amount—the average will rise (fall) when the marginal amount is larger (smaller) than the initial average.

Section 7.3 Costs in the Short Run

- *What are fixed costs, variable costs, and total costs?*

  Total fixed costs do not change with the level of output, total variable costs change as the level of output changes, and total costs are the sum of total variable costs and total fixed costs.

- *What are average costs?*

  Average total cost (ATC) is total cost divided by output; average fixed cost (AFC) is fixed cost divided by output; and average variable cost (AVC) is variable cost divided by output.

- *What is marginal cost?*

  Marginal cost (MC) is the added cost of producing one more unit of output; it is the change in total cost associated with one more unit of output. It is this cost that is relevant to decisions to produce more or less.

Section 7.4 The Shape of the Short-Run Cost Curves

- *What is the relationship between marginal costs and marginal product?*

  An inverse relationship exists between marginal product and marginal cost—when marginal product increases, marginal cost must fall, and when marginal product falls, marginal cost must rise.

Key Terms

explicit costs *the opportunity costs of production that require a monetary payment* p. 160

implicit costs *the opportunity costs of production that do not require a monetary payment* p. 161

profits *the difference between total revenue and total cost* p. 161

accounting profits *total revenues minus total explicit costs* p. 161

economic profits *total revenues minus explicit and implicit costs* p. 161

sunk costs *costs that have been incurred and cannot be recovered* p. 162

short run *a period too brief for some production inputs to be varied* p. 164

long run *a period over which all production inputs are variable* p. 165

production function *the relationship between the quantity of inputs and the quantity of outputs produced* p. 165

total product (*TP*) *the total output of a good produced by the firm* p. 165

average product (*AP*) *the total product divided by the number of units of the variable input used to produce it* p. 166

marginal product (*MP*) *the change in total product resulting from a unit change in input* p. 166

diminishing marginal product *as a variable input increases, with other inputs fixed, a point will be reached where the additions to output will eventually decline* p. 167

fixed costs *costs that do not vary with the level of output in the short run* p. 169

total fixed cost (*TFC*) *the sum of the firm's fixed costs* p. 169

Key Exhibits/ Graphs

- *Why is the average total cost curve U-shaped?*

  Average total cost declines with expanding output as average fixed costs decline, but then increases as output expands due to increasing marginal cost.

- *What is the relationship between marginal cost and average variable and average total cost?*

  When marginal cost is less than (greater than) an average cost, the average cost must be falling (rising); when marginal cost is greater than (less than) an average cost, the average cost must be rising (falling).

Section 7.5 Cost Curves: Short Run and Long Run

- *How is the long-run average total cost curve created?*

  In the long run, firms can vary inputs that are fixed in the short run, such as plant size and equipment, in some cases, lowering average costs per unit. The long-run average total cost curve shows the lowest average total cost for producing each output in the long run.

- *What are economies of scale?*

  At low output levels, when all inputs can be varied, some firms will experience economies of scale, where their per-unit costs are decreasing as output increases. In intermediate output ranges, firms may exhibit roughly constant returns to scale; in this range, their per-unit costs remain stable as output increases. Firms that expand all inputs beyond a certain point will encounter diseconomies of scale, incurring rising per-unit costs as output grows in the long run.

- *Why would cost curves shift?*

  Input prices, taxes, technology, and regulation can shift the cost curves.

Key Equations

$$MP = \frac{\Delta TP}{\Delta L}$$

Total cost (*TC*) = Total variable cost (*TVC*) + Total fixed cost (*TFC*)

$$\text{Average fixed cost } (AFC) = \frac{TFC}{Q}$$

$$\text{Average variable cost } (AVC) = \frac{TVC}{Q}$$

$$\text{Average total cost } (ATC) = \frac{TC}{Q} = AVC + AFC$$

$$\text{Marginal cost } (MC) = \frac{\Delta TC}{\Delta Q}$$

Perfect Competition

Section 8.1 The Four Major Market Structures

- *What are the four major market structures?*

  There are four major market structures: perfect competition, monopoly, monopolistic competition, and oligopoly.

- *What are the characteristics of a perfectly competitive market?*

  A perfectly competitive market has the following characteristics: many buyers and sellers, so that neither buyers nor sellers have control over price; a homogeneous product—consumers believe that all firms sell virtually identical products; no significant barriers to entry or exit.

- *Why is it useful to study the perfectly competitive market structure?*

  Studying the perfectly competitive market structure provides us with important information about how markets operate (entry, exit, costs) that can be applied to imperfect market structures. In addition, the perfectly competitive structure can give us a point of comparison to evaluate real-world markets.

Section 8.2 An Individual Price Taker's Demand Curve

- *What does the individual price taker's demand curve look like?*

  Individual sellers won't sell at a higher price than the going price because buyers can purchase the same good from someone else at the going price. Individual sellers won't sell for less than the going price, either, because they are so small relative to the market that they can sell all they want at the going price. Therefore, the individual price taker's demand curve is horizontal over its entire range of output.

- *What effect will a change in market price have on an individual price taker's demand curves?*

  The position of the individual firm's demand curve varies directly with the market price.

Section 8.3 Profit Maximization

- *What is total revenue?*

  Total revenue is price times the quantity sold ($TR = P \times q$).

- *What are average revenue and marginal revenue?*

  Average revenue is total revenue divided by the quantity sold ($AR = TR/q$). Marginal revenue is the change in total revenue from the sale of an additional unit of output ($MR = \Delta TR/\Delta q$). In a competitive industry, $P = AR = MR$.

- *How do firms maximize profits?*

  The profit-maximizing output rule says a firm should always produce where $MR = MC$. When $MR > MC$, the seller should expand production because producing and selling those units adds more to revenues than to costs, or increases profits. However, if $MR < MC$, the seller should decrease production.

Section 8.4 Short-Run Profits and Losses

- *How do we determine whether a firm is generating an economic profit or loss?*

  The profit-maximizing output level is found by equating $MR = MC$ at q^*. If at q^* the firm's price is greater than its ATC, it is making an economic profit. If at q^* the price is less than ATC, the firm is incurring an economic loss. If at q^* the price is equal to ATC, the firm is making zero economic profits; that is, it is making a normal rate of return.

Key Terms

perfect competition *a market with many buyers and sellers, all selling a homogeneous product; market entry and exit is easy, and no firm can affect the market price* p. 188

price taker *A perfectly competitive firm takes the price that it is given by the intersection of the market demand and market supply curves.* p. 188

total revenue (TR) *the product price times the quantity sold* p. 192

average revenue (AR) *total revenue divided by the number of units sold* p. 193

marginal revenue (MR) *the increase in total revenue that results from the sale of one more unit* p. 193

profit-maximizing output rule *A firm should always produce at the level of output where* MR = MC. p. 194

short-run supply curve *as a cost relationship, this curve shows the marginal cost of producing any given output; as a supply curve, it shows the equilibrium output that the firm will supply at various prices in the short run* p. 198

short-run market supply curve *the horizontal summation of the individual firms' supply curves in the market* p. 199

constant-cost industry *an industry where input prices (and cost curves) do not change as industry output changes* p. 204

increasing-cost industry *an industry where input prices rise (and cost curves rise) as industry output rises* p. 206

decreasing-cost industry *an industry where input prices fall (and cost curves fall) as industry output rises* p. 207

- *What is the individual firm's short-run supply curve?*

  The portion of the *MC* curve that lies above the minimum of the *AVC* curve is the short-run supply curve for the individual competitive seller.

- *Can we review the short-run production decisions of an individual competitive firm?*

  As market price rises, the output decisions of a competitive firm evolve from not producing at all (shutting down) to operating at an economic loss, to economically breaking even, to generating an economic profit.

Section 8.5 Long-Run Equilibrium

- *What happens to economic profits and losses in the long run?*

  Economic profits will encourage the entry of new firms, which will shift the market supply curve to the right, driving down the firm's prices and therefore its revenues. Any economic losses signal resources to leave the industry, leading to supply reduction, higher prices, and increased revenues.

- *What is the long-run equilibrium for the competitive firm?*

  Only at zero economic profits is there no tendency for firms to either enter or exit the industry. This is the long-run equilibrium for the competitive firm.

Section 8.6 Long-Run Supply

- *What are constant-cost industries?*

  In constant-cost industries, the cost curves of the firm are not affected by changes in the output of the entire industry. Such industries must be very small demanders of resources in the market.

- *What are increasing-cost and decreasing-cost industries?*

  In an increasing-cost industry, the cost curves of the individual firms rise as total output increases. In a decreasing-cost industry, the cost curves decline as total output increases. The increasing-cost case is the most typical.

- *How is perfect competition economically efficient?*

  Perfect competition long-run equilibrium achieves productive efficiency (production at least possible cost), allocative efficiency (*P* = *MC*), and production allocated to reflect consumers' wants, thereby making perfect competition economically efficient.

Key Equations

$$TR = P \times q$$

Total profit $= TR - TC$

$$AR = \frac{TR}{q} \text{ or } \frac{P \times q}{q} = P$$

$$MR = \frac{\Delta TR}{\Delta q}$$

Monopoly

Section 9.1 Monopoly: The Price Maker

- *What is a monopoly?*

  A pure monopoly exists where there is only one seller of a product for which no close substitute is available.

- *What are the sources of monopoly power?*

  Sources of monopoly power include legal barriers, economies of scale, and control over important inputs.

Section 9.2 Demand and Marginal Revenue in Monopoly

- *How does the demand curve for a monopolist differ from that of a perfectly competitive firm?*

  The monopolist's demand curve is downward sloping because it is the market demand curve. To produce and sell another unit of output, the firm must lower its price on all units. As a result, the marginal revenue curve lies below the demand curve.

- *Why is marginal revenue less than price in a monopoly?*

  The monopolist's marginal revenue will always be less than price because there is a downward-sloping demand curve. In order to sell more output, the monopolist must accept a lower price on all units sold. This means that the monopolist receives additional revenue from the new unit sold but receives less revenue on all of the units it was previously selling.

- *What is the relationship between the elasticity of demand and total and marginal revenue?*

  Along the elastic portion of the demand curve, a fall in price leads to an increase in total revenue, making marginal revenue positive. Along the inelastic portion of the demand curve, a fall in price leads to a fall in total revenue, making marginal revenue negative. Therefore, the monopolist will operate in the elastic portion of its demand curve.

Section 9.3 The Monopolist's Equilibrium

- *How does the monopolist determine the profit-maximizing output?*

  The monopolist, like the perfect competitor, maximizes profits at that output where marginal revenue equals marginal cost. Price is set according to the demand for the product at the profit-maximizing output.

- *How do we know whether the monopolist is making a profit or a loss?*

  Monopoly profits can be found by comparing price per unit and average total cost at Q^*. If $P > ATC$, there are economic profits. If $P < ATC$, there are economic losses.

Section 9.4 Monopoly and Welfare Loss

- *Does monopoly promote inefficiency?*

  Monopoly results in smaller output and a higher price than would be the case under perfect competition. Since the monopolist produces at an output where $P > MC$, this means the value to society of the last unit produced is greater than its cost. In other words, the monopoly is not producing enough output from society's standpoint.

- *Does monopoly hinder innovation?*

  Monopoly may lead to greater concentration of economic power and could hinder innovation.

Key Terms

monopoly *a market with only one seller of a product that has no close substitute and there are natural and legal barriers to entry that prevent competition* p. 218

price maker *a monopolistic firm that sets the price of its product so as to maximize its profits* p. 218

natural monopoly *a firm that can produce at a lower cost than a number of smaller firms could* p. 221

marginal cost pricing *the decision to set production where the price of a good equals marginal cost* p. 234

average cost pricing *production where the price of a good equals average total cost* p. 235

price discrimination *the practice of charging different consumers different prices for the same good or service when the cost of providing that good or service is not different for different consumers* p. 236

Key Exhibits/ Graphs

Section 9.5 Monopoly Policy

- *What is the objective of anti-combine laws?*

  Anti-combine laws are designed to reduce the abuses of monopoly power and push production closer to the social optimum.

- *What is government regulation?*

  Privately owned monopolies may be allowed to operate, but under the regulation of a government agency.

- *What is marginal cost pricing?*

  Marginal cost pricing sets price equal to marginal cost, where demand intersects marginal cost. This regulation achieves allocative efficiency.

- *What is average cost pricing?*

  Average cost pricing sets price equal to average total cost, where the demand curve intersects average total costs.

Section 9.6 Price Discrimination

- *What is price discrimination?*

  When producers charge different prices for the same good or service when no cost differences exist, it is called *price discrimination*.

- *Why does price discrimination exist?*

  Price discrimination is a result of the profit-maximization motive. If different groups have different demand curves for a good or service, a seller can make more money by charging these different buyers different prices.

- *Does price discrimination lead to higher profits?*

  A monopolist that can perfectly price-discriminate will produce a greater amount of output and earn a greater amount of economic profit when compared to a monopolist that charges a single monopoly price.

Monopolistic Competition and Oligopoly

Section 10.1 Monopolistic Competition

- *What is monopolistic competition?*

  Monopolistic competition describes a market structure where many producers of somewhat different products compete with one another.

- *What are the three basic characteristics of monopolistic competition?*

  The theory of monopolistic competition is based on three primary characteristics: many sellers, product differentiation, and free entry.

Section 10.2 Price and Output Determination in Monopolistic Competition

- *How is short-run equilibrium determined?*

  In the short run, a monopolistically competitive firm achieves profit maximization at the intersection of the marginal revenue and marginal cost curves. A monopolistically competitive firm is making short-run economic profits when the equilibrium price is greater than average total costs at the equilibrium output. When equilibrium price is below average total cost at the equilibrium output, the firm is minimizing its economic losses.

- *How is long-run equilibrium determined?*

  In the long run, equilibrium price equals average total costs. With that, economic profits are zero, so there are no incentives for firms to either enter or exit the industry.

Section 10.3 Monopolistic Competition vs. Perfect Competition

- *What are the differences and similarities between monopolistic competition and perfect competition?*

  While both the competitive firm and the monopolistically competitive firm may earn short-run economic profits, these profits will be eliminated in the long run. Because monopolistically competitive firms face a downward-sloping demand curve, average total cost is not minimized in the long run, after entry and exit have eliminated profits. Monopolistically competitive firms fail to reach productive efficiency, producing at output levels less than the efficient output. The monopolistically competitive firm does not achieve allocative efficiency because it does not operate where the price is equal to marginal costs.

- *What are the real costs of monopolistic competition?*

  The inefficiencies of monopolistic competition are a by-product of product differentiation and must be weighed against the social benefits of increased product variety.

- *Are the differences between monopolistic competition and perfect competition exaggerated?*

  The difference between the long-run price level and the price that would prevail under perfect competition varies directly with the strength of product differentiation.

Section 10.4 Advertising

- *Why do firms advertise?*

  With advertising, a firm hopes it can alter the elasticity of the demand for its product, making it more inelastic and causing an increase in demand that will enhance profits.

Key Terms

monopolistic competition *a market structure with many firms selling differentiated products* p. 248

product differentiation *the accentuation of unique product qualities, real or perceived, to develop a specific product identity* p. 249

excess capacity *occurs when the firm produces below the level where average total cost is minimized* p. 254

oligopoly *a market structure with only a few sellers offering similar or identical products* p. 259

mutual interdependence *when a firm shapes its policy with an eye to the policies of competing firms* p. 260

collude *when firms act together to restrict competition* p. 262

cartel *a collection of firms that agree on sales, pricing, and other decisions* p. 263

joint profit maximization *determination of price based on the marginal revenue (derived from the market demand schedule) and marginal cost schedule of the firms in the industry* p. 263

game theory *Firms attempt to maximize profits by acting in ways that minimize damage from competitors.* p. 266

cooperative game *collusion by firms in order to improve their profit maximizations* p. 266

noncooperative game *Each firm sets its own price without consulting other firms.* p. 266

dominant strategy *will be optimal regardless of the opponents' actions* p. 266

payoff matrix *a summary of the possible outcomes from the various strategies* p. 266

Key Exhibits/ Graphs

- *Is advertising good or bad from society's perspective?*

  To some, advertising manipulates consumer tastes and creates "needs" for trivial products. Where substantial economies of scale exist, it is possible that average production costs will decline more than the amount of per-unit costs of advertising in the long run. By making consumers aware of different "substitute" products, advertising may lead to more competitive markets and lower consumer prices.

Section 10.5 Oligopoly

- *What is oligopoly?*

  Oligopolies exist where relatively few firms control all or most of the production and sale of a product. The products may be homogeneous or differentiated, but the barriers to entry are often very high and, consequently, there may be long-run economic profits.

- *Why do oligopolies exist?*

  In oligopoly markets, economies of large-scale production make operation on a small scale extremely unprofitable. Recognition of this fact discourages new firms from entering the market and is the primary reason why oligopolies exist.

- *Why is it so difficult for the oligopolist to determine its profit-maximizing price and output?*

  Because in oligopoly the pricing decision of one firm influences the demand curve of competing firms, the oligopolist faces considerable uncertainty as to the location and shape of its demand and marginal revenue curves. Thus, it is difficult for an oligopolist to determine its profit-maximizing price and output.

Section 10.6 Collusion and Cartels

- *Why do firms collude?*

  The mutual interdependence of oligopolists tempts them to collude in order to reduce uncertainty and increase potential for monopoly profits.

- *What is joint profit maximization?*

  Joint profit maximization requires the determination of price based on the market demand for the product and the marginal costs of the various firms.

- *Why are most collusive oligopolies short-lived?*

  Most strong collusive oligopolies are rather short-lived for two reasons: (1) Collusive oligopolies are strictly illegal under Canadian anti-combine laws, and (2) there is a great temptation for firms to cheat on the agreement of the collusive oligopoly.

Section 10.7 Game Theory and Strategic Behaviour

- *What is game theory?*

  Game theory stresses the tendency of various parties to minimize damage from opponents. A firm may try to figure out its competitors' most likely countermoves to its own policies and then formulate alternative defence measures.

- *What are cooperative and noncooperative games?*

  Players in cooperative games can talk and set binding contracts, while those in noncooperative games are assumed to act independently, with no communication and no binding contracts. The prisoners' dilemma is an example of a noncooperative game.

- *What about repeated games?*

  In one-shot games, the participants' self-interest tends to prevent cooperative behaviour, but in repeated games, cooperation occurs as long as others continue to cooperate (a tit-for-tat strategy).

- *What are network externalities?*

  Positive (negative) network externality occurs when a consumer's quantity demanded increases (decreases) because a greater (smaller) number of consumers purchase the same good.

Labour Markets and the Distribution of Income

Section 11.1 Labour Markets

* *What determines the price paid to workers?*

  Supply and demand determine the prices paid to workers.

* *What is derived demand?*

  In factor or input markets, demand is derived from consumers' demand for the final good or service that the input produces.

Section 11.2 Supply and Demand in the Labour Market

* *Will hiring that extra worker add more to revenue than costs?*

  Whether an additional worker is hired depends on the worker's marginal revenue product (*MRP*) and marginal resource cost (*MRC*).

* *Why is the labour demand curve downward sloping?*

  The demand curve for labour is downward sloping because of diminishing marginal product. That is, if additional labour is added to a fixed quantity of land or capital equipment, output will increase, but at some point it will increase by diminishing amounts.

* *How many workers will an employer hire?*

  Profits are maximized if the firm hires only up to the point where the wage equals the expected marginal revenue product.

* *What is the shape of the labour supply curve?*

  Along a market supply curve, a higher wage rate will increase the quantity supplied of labour supplied and a lower wage rate will decrease the quantity of labour supplied.

Section 11.3 Labour Market Equilibrium

* *How is equilibrium determined in a competitive labour market?*

  The intersection of the labour demand curve and the labour supply curve determines the equilibrium wage and employment in competitive labour markets.

* *What shifts the labour demand curve?*

  The labour demand curve can shift if there is a change in productivity or a change in the demand for the final product.

* *What shifts the labour supply curve?*

  The labour supply curve can shift if there are changes in immigration or population growth, workers' preferences, nonwage income, or amenities.

* *What is a monopsony?*

  Any market with a single buyer is a monopsony; the labour market represents the most relevant situation.

Section 11.4 Labour Unions

* *Why do labour unions exist?*

  Workers realize that acting together gives them collective bargaining power; this is the primary reason why unions exist. Labour unions try to increase their members' wages and improve working conditions.

Key Terms

derived demand *The demand for an input is derived from the consumer's demands for a good or service.* p. 277

marginal revenue product (*MRP*) *the additional revenue that a firm obtains from one more unit of input* p. 278

marginal resource cost (*MRC*) *the amount that an extra input adds to the firm's total costs* p. 278

backward-bending labour supply curve *Above a certain wage rate, a worker might prefer to work less and enjoy more leisure (the income effect dominates the substitution effect).* p. 282

monopsony *a market with a single buyer* p. 286

collective bargaining *negotiations between representatives of employers and unions* p. 288

in-kind transfers *transfers of goods and services rather than cash* p. 294

poverty *the condition of a person who is deprived of the resources, means, choices, and power necessary to acquire and maintain a basic level of living standard and to facilitate integration into and participation in society* p. 297

Canada's Official Poverty Line *level of income necessary to allow a household to buy a specific basket of goods and services that allows them to meet their basic needs and achieve a modest standard of living in their community* p. 297

- *What is the impact of unions on wages?*

  Through restrictive membership, a union can reduce the labour supply in the market for union workers, thus reducing employment and raising wages. This increases the supply of workers in the nonunion sector, shifting supply to the right and lowering wages for nonunion workers.

- *Can unions increase worker productivity?*

  By reducing discontent and increasing worker retention, some economists argue that unions can actually increase worker productivity.

Section 11.5 Income Distribution

- *What has happened to income distribution since 1976?*

  Since 1976, the distribution of income in Canada has been relatively stable.

- *How much income inequality exists in other countries?*

  Income inequality among nations is substantial.

- *Are we overstating the disparity in the distribution of income?*

  Demographics and government programs affect the disparity in income inequality. Not taking these issues into consideration when evaluating income distribution could result in the inequality being overstated.

- *Why do some earn more than others?*

  Differences in ages, skill, education, training, preferences related to risk and leisure, and discrimination are all possible reasons why some people make more money than others.

- *How can we remedy discrimination?*

  In Canada, the problem of employment discrimination is addressed primarily through the Employment Equity Act (1995).

Section 11.6 Poverty

- *How do we define poverty?*

  In Canada, poverty is defined as the condition of a person who is deprived of the resources, means, choices, and power necessary to acquire and maintain a basic level of living standard and to facilitate integration into and participation in society.

- *How many people live in poverty?*

  The incidence of low income varies depending on the characteristics of the household, such as family type, age, and education.

- *What government programs help to reduce poverty?*

  A variety of programs are designed to reduce poverty: progressive income tax, cash transfer, in-kind transfers, social assistance, and minimum-wage regulation.

Key Equations

$$MRP = MP \times P$$

Market Failure and the Environment

Section 12.1 Externalities

- *What are externalities?*

  Externalities are the costs or benefits from either production or consumption that spill over onto those that are not producing or consuming the good.

- *What are negative externalities?*

  If a market activity has a negative physical impact on an outside party, that side effect is called a negative externality.

- *What are positive externalities?*

  If a market activity has a positive physical impact on an outside party, that side effect is called a positive externality.

- *What can the government do to correct for positive externalities?*

  The government can provide subsidies or other forms of regulation to correct the underallocation problem associated with positive externalities.

- *Are there nongovernmental solutions to externalities?*

  Nongovernment solutions to externalities are possible if people self-regulate personal behaviour to either prevent negative externalities or to promote positive externalities.

Section 12.2 Negative Externalities and Pollution

- *What are social costs?*

  Social costs are those costs that accrue to the total population; private costs are incurred only by the producer of a good or service.

- *Can externalities be accurately measured?*

  Given the difficulties in establishing real-world social and private costs and benefits, externalities are often difficult to measure.

Section 12.3 Public Policy and the Environment

- *Why is a clean environment not free?*

  In a world of scarcity, we can increase our consumption of a clean environment only by giving up something else—the opportunity cost of environmental policy.

- *What can be done to reduce pollution?*

  Environmental regulations force companies to find less pollution—intensive ways of producing goods and services. Pollution taxes can be used to force firms to internalize externalities and allow the relatively efficient private sector to operate according to market forces in a manner that takes socially important spillover costs into account. The transferable pollution rights policy encourages polluters to come up with cheaper ways of reducing pollution because the firm that reduces pollution is able to sell its remaining pollution credits to others.

- *What is an ideal pollution-control policy?*

  The objectives of pollution-control policies are to achieve the efficient level of pollution, achieve pollution reduction at the lowest cost, and motivate advances in abatement technology.

Key Terms

externality *a benefit or cost from consumption or production that spills over onto those that are not consuming or producing the good* p. 309

negative externality *when costs spill over to an outside party that is not involved in producing or consuming the good* p. 309

positive externality *when benefits spill over to an outside party that is not involved in producing or consuming the good* p. 310

internalized externalities *when an industry is forced to compensate those enduring some negative externality caused by its production* p. 314

pollution tax *tax levied by government on a firm for environmental pollution* p. 319

transferable pollution rights *a right given to a firm to discharge a specified amount of pollution; its transferable nature creates an incentive to lower pollution levels* p. 320

Coase theorem *states that where property rights are defined in a clear-cut fashion, externalities are internalized* p. 323

public good *a good that is nonrivalrous in consumption and nonexcludable* p. 324

private good *a good with rivalrous consumption and excludability* p. 324

free rider *a party that derives benefits from something without paying for it* p. 325

common resource *a rival good that is not excludable* p. 326

Key Exhibits/ Graphs

Section 12.4 Property Rights

- *What is the relationship between externalities and property rights?*

  In a world with no externalities, property owners (with only a few exceptions) could use their property in any manner they desired. Ultimately, then, externalities involve an evaluation of the legal arrangements in which we operate our economy.

- *What is the Coase theorem?*

  The Coase theorem states that where property rights are defined in a clear-cut fashion, externalities are internalized. This condition holds where information and transaction costs are close to zero.

Section 12.5 Public Goods

- *What are private goods vs. public goods?*

  A public good is both nonrivalrous in consumption (one person's usage of it does not diminish another's ability to use it) and nonexclusive (no one can be excluded from using it), whereas a private good is both rivalrous and excludable.

- *What is the free-rider problem with public goods?*

  Despite their demand, because public goods are not rival and not excludable, there is little incentive for private individuals to produce them.

- *Why does the government provide public goods?*

  The free-rider problem prevents the private market from supplying the efficient quantity of public goods, whereas a private good is both rivalrous and excludable.

- *What is a common resource?*

  A common resource is rival in consumption but is not excludable.

Key Equations

$MSC = MPC + $ External costs